Du Bois
and His Rivals

Du Bois
and His Rivals

Raymond Wolters

University of Missouri Press   Columbia and London

Library of Congress Cataloging-in-Publication Data

Wolters, Raymond, 1938–
   Du Bois and his rivals / Raymond Wolters.
     p.   cm.
   Includes bibliographical references and index.
   ISBN 0-8262-1385-5 (alk. paper)
   1. Du Bois, W. E. B. (William Edward Burghardt), 1868–1963.
2. Du Bois, W. E. B. (William Edward Burghardt), 1868–1963—
Friends and associates.   3. Du Bois, W. E. B. (William Edward
Burghardt), 1868–1963—Political and social views.   4. African
American civil rights workers—Biography.   5. Civil rights workers—
United States—Biography.   6. African American intellectuals—
Biography.   7. African American leadership—History—20th century.
8. African Americans—Civil rights—History—20th century.
9. African Americans—Intellectual life—20th century.   10. Plural-
ism (Social sciences)—United States—History—20th century.   I. Title.

E185.97.D73   2002
305.896′073′0092—dc21
[B]

                                                    2002017951

⊚™ This paper meets the requirements of the
American National Standard for Permanence of Paper
for Printed Library Materials, Z39.48, 1984.

Text design: Elizabeth K. Young
Jacket design: Jennifer Cropp
Typesetter: The Composing Room of Michigan, Inc.
Printer and binder: The Maple-Vail Book Manufacturing Group
Typefaces: Diotima Roman and Berkeley Book

In Memory of My Mother and Father
and of
Five Capuchin Priests and Teachers at
St. Francis High School
LaCanada-Flintridge, California

•

Fr. Paul Barrett

Fr. Lawrence Caruso

Fr. Cyril Kelleher

Fr. Emilian Meade

Fr. Alphonsus O'Connor

Contents

Preface

This book was in preparation for a long time. When I was an undergraduate student, I was very much taken by Richard Hofstadter's collection of biographies, *The American Political Tradition*.[1] Ever since then I have wanted to write a collective biography. When I started my doctoral dissertation, I had it in mind to write about several southern demagogues of the 1930s. Yet I could not figure out how to combine the pace and scope of a group portrait with the quantity of new information that is expected of a dissertation. I was afraid that my project would not pass muster as an original contribution to knowledge. So I turned to a different topic and later to another book.[2]

In the 1970s I began to work on *Du Bois and His Rivals*. At the time the papers of W. E. B. Du Bois were owned by Du Bois's widow, Shirley Graham Du Bois, but were in the custody of the historian Herbert Aptheker. The papers were actually lodged in the basement of Dr. Aptheker's house in Brooklyn, but he periodically brought a briefcase full of Du Bois's letters for me to read in the Manhattan office of the American Institute for Marxist Studies. I appreciate Dr. Aptheker's getting me started on this project, although he will doubtless disagree with my departure from the usual depiction of Du Bois as a radical *par excellence*. He may even think it perverse for me to have portrayed our hero as a man who in at least some respects was a conservative: a man who believed in the conservation of races and who held traditional middle-class values with respect to art, the family, and sexual morality; a man who opposed Communism during most of his adult life and succumbed only when he was elderly, rejected by his former allies, and embraced by a new left-wing support network.

After reading several briefcases of documents, I knew that I should consult the entire collection of Du Bois's papers. At that point, however, the University of Massachusetts purchased the collection. The papers were then closed to scholars, to allow time for treatment with preserving chemicals and for microfilming. I was told that that would take a year or two, during which I traveled the country and did research in the manuscript collections of Du Bois's friends and rivals. I am grateful to the American Council of Learned Societies for a grant that gave me the time and money for several research trips. It turned out, though, that the microfilming project at the University of Massachusetts took much longer than the original estimate, and I turned to other projects, two books that had nothing to do with Du Bois.[3]

When I returned to Du Bois during a sabbatical leave that began in 1999, I discovered that in the interim there had been a renaissance in Du Bois studies—with David Levering Lewis having written a two-volume, Pulitzer Prize–winning biography and several other scholars having contributed valuable monographs, articles, and essays. In the meantime, I had joined with another professor to offer a large-lecture course on the American civil rights movement, and I wanted to begin that course with a book on the lives of several of the black leaders who came to the fore in the years before World War II. Finally, it seemed, the time had come for my collective biography. I would focus on Du Bois but would give sufficient attention to his friends and rivals to make the book a group portrait. My hope was that students and general readers would find the narrative interesting, and that scholars would understand that the book was based on extensive research in both primary sources and secondary literature.

The notes provide a good index to my indebtedness to other published works. But some comments are in order with respect to manuscript collections.

Throughout this book I have used the papers of W. E. B. Du Bois, which are at the University of Massachusetts and are also available now on microfilm. There are more than a hundred thousand letters in this collection and additional manuscripts, diaries, photographs, and miscellaneous documents. There are eighty-nine reels in the microfilm edition of these papers. Three volumes of the correspondence are also available in print: *The Correspondence of W. E. B. Du Bois*, edited by Herbert Aptheker.

When I first used the extensive papers of Booker T. Washington, they were collected in hundreds of containers at the Library of Congress. Since then most of the documents have been published in fourteen volumes edited by Louis R. Harlan and his associates, *The Booker T. Washington Papers*.

The papers of the NAACP were even more voluminous. I first used them in an untended records warehouse in New York City. Later they were carefully organized at the Library of Congress, and still later they were made available in a microfilm edition of more than fifteen hundred reels.

Because the papers of Marcus Garvey had been widely dispersed, special thanks are due to Robert A. Hill and his associates for collecting and editing nine large volumes of documents: *The Marcus Garvey and UNIA Papers.*

Many other collections have also been useful. The papers of William Monroe Trotter at the Boston University Library are not extensive, but there are several nuggets, and one box contains the notes and other research materials that Stephen R. Fox used for his biography of Trotter, *The Guardian of Boston.* The Freeman H. M. Murray Papers are a small collection at Howard University, but one that contains useful information on black leaders during the early years of the twentieth century. The papers of Oswald Garrison Villard, at Harvard University, are more extensive and especially valuable for the period from about 1903 to 1920. The papers of Archibald H. Grimke are at Howard University and are especially valuable for the period from about 1915 to 1925. The papers of J. E. Spingarn contain much important information, and in addition to his correspondence in the NAACP papers there are additional collections of Spingarn's papers at Howard University, the New York Public Library, and Yale University. Some of the papers of James Weldon Johnson and Walter White are also available at Yale, although most of their correspondence as civil rights leaders is in the NAACP papers. Most of the papers of Joel Spingarn's brother Arthur B. Spingarn are also in the NAACP papers, although there is a second collection of Arthur Spingarn papers at Howard University. The papers of Du Bois's Atlanta University friends John Hope, George Towns, and Edmund Ware are available at Atlanta University. At the National Archives, record groups 59 and 60 contain documents on Marcus Garvey. Two large manuscript collections that scholars have tended to neglect are the papers of Robert R. Moton, at Tuskegee Institute, and the papers of Emmett J. Scott, at Morgan State College.

Acknowledgments

I am pleased to acknowledge the assistance I have received while working on this book. For many years the University of Delaware has provided excellent working conditions. I have enjoyed teaching the students there, have received a sabbatical leave every seventh year, and am grateful for a second office for research in the Hugh M. Morris Library.

My colleagues at Delaware have helped in many ways. At a crucial early stage, David Allmendinger boosted my spirits when, after reading the first chapter, he assured me that I was on the right track. McKay Jenkins did the same after reading Chapter 6, as did Bill Boyer after reading the first draft of the entire manuscript. Peter Kolchin persuaded me to reshape the introduction and made valuable suggestions for revisions of specific statements throughout the book. Susan Brynteson offered good advice with respect to publishing, and two colleagues at other institutions, John McLarnon and Paul Moreno, told me what I wanted to hear when they said they would assign this book to their students.

I am especially indebted to Professor Gerard Mangone. Because he is the most widely read and broadly educated person that I know, I expected Gerard to give sage advice about shaping the manuscript. But when he returned his copy I discovered that he had done much more than that. He had gone over every line with a fine editor's eye. His comments amounted to what used to be called a work of supererogation. It was much more than anyone has a right to expect from a friend or colleague. It is customary for an author to take responsibility for any errors that remain in his work, but in this case I am not sure about that. Another reader later wrote that he was well into the manuscript before he encountered "the first infelicity of expression ('to barely eke out a living'—not only a split infinitive but also a redundancy, for *to eke* means 'barely'"). I then blamed Gerard Mangone. "How did a mistake like that escape the attention of your eagle eyes?" I asked.

It has been a pleasure to work with Beverly Jarrett, the director and editor-in-chief of the University of Missouri Press. I sent her the manuscript because, of the several editors with whom I spoke on the telephone, she seemed the most enthusiastic and knowledgeable about W. E. B. Du Bois. "We could have your book ready for the centennial anniversary," she said at one point during our first conversation. "What do you mean?" said I; "Du Bois was born in 1868." "I know," she replied, "but the one-hundredth anniversary of the publication of *The Souls of Black Folk* [1903] is looming." She then handled everything with professionalism and dispatch. I also benefited from three readers' reports from scholars who were later identified as James W. Ely Jr., Forrest McDonald, and Arvarh Strickland. In the course of final editing, Julie Schroeder asked many trenchant questions and did an especially good job of bringing order to the endnotes.

As always, my wife, Mary, has been a constant source of love and support. Our summer house at Long Point on the Bohemia River has also spurred my writing, for it is easy to compose for a few hours each morning when one can look forward to an afternoon of boating on the waters of the Chesapeake Bay. Two of our three sons have moved on to careers of their own, but our youngest son, Tom, is still at home and still listening with good grace to what at times must seem like interminable stories about Du Bois and his rivals. The same can be said of my colleagues who meet for lunch every Tuesday at the Blue and Gold Club. I must have tried their patience by repeating some of the same anecdotes, but they too have endured with good grace and encouragement.

Du Bois
and His Rivals

Introduction

On August 28, 1963, some 250,000 people gathered in front of the Lincoln Memorial and heard Martin Luther King's famous "I Have a Dream" speech. But the dream of racial justice began long before, and earlier in the twentieth century no civil rights leader stood taller than W. E. B. Du Bois. Just the day before King's speech, Du Bois died in his sleep at the age of ninety-five. The vast assembly observed a moment of silence when Roy Wilkins, the head of the National Association for the Advancement of Colored People (NAACP), announced Du Bois's passing and recalled that "at the dawn of the twentieth century [Du Bois] was the voice calling you to gather here today in this cause." In 1903 Du Bois had predicted that "the problem of the twentieth century" would be "the problem of the color-line,—the relation of the darker to the lighter races."[1] He was the preeminent black scholar of his era and also a principal founder and for twenty-eight years an executive officer of the nation's most effective civil rights organization, the NAACP. Du Bois was the great pioneer of the American civil rights movement.

Du Bois was a man of many parts—a prophet and an organization man, a scholar and a poet, an intellectual who championed the cause of common people. While celebrating the dignity and accomplishments of the black masses, he also emphasized the importance of developing a black elite—a Talented Tenth—to provide leadership for blacks in America and throughout the world. Du Bois condemned the white world for its discrimination against black people, but he also berated African Americans for mistakes of their own. Significantly, he opposed segregation but also had reservations about integration. Today he would be known as a pluralist.

Pluralism is central to understanding Du Bois. Du Bois differed from separatists who accepted formal, legal segregation and, in some instances, urged blacks to go back to Africa. Instead, he insisted that African Americans should enjoy all the rights of other American citizens. But that was not all. Du Bois was proud to be a Negro and, unlike some integrationists, he did not think that the solution to America's major race problem lay in the disappearance of black people through assimilation, dispersion, and intermarriage. He insisted that "self-obliteration" was not "the highest end to which Negro blood dare aspire." He urged African Americans to maintain their racial identity. "Their destiny," he said, was "not a servile imitation of Anglo-Saxon culture, but a stalwart originality which shall unswervingly further Negro ideals."[2] He celebrated a sense of "double-consciousness" and insisted that most American blacks, while resenting and opposing compulsory segregation, also wanted to preserve and develop enough racial distinctiveness to enable them to maintain and foster a sense of racial identity, community, and pride.[3]

Du Bois's pluralism was not without ambiguity and paradox, but he resolved contradictions by urging his fellow blacks to practice voluntary in-group cooperation even as they insisted on equal rights. He envisioned a system of parallel development, with the black and white people of the United States living "side by side in peace and mutual happiness," with each developing its own "peculiar contribution . . . to the culture of their common country."[4]

In addition to being a pluralist, Du Bois was a protest leader who insisted that black people should complain whenever they encountered unjust racial discrimination. There were occasions, however, when Du Bois flirted with conciliation, accommodation, and cooperation with influential whites.

This book focuses on Du Bois's relations with other black leaders during the "forgotten" years of the civil rights movement, the years before World War II. It especially emphasizes Du Bois's stance with respect to protest and accommodation and Du Bois's pluralism as he steered clear of both integration and separatism. Early in the twentieth century Du Bois challenged Booker T. Washington because he could not abide Washington's conciliatory approach toward powerful whites. At the time of the First World War, however, several African American critics found fault with Du Bois for being too accommodating to the powers that ruled. In the 1920s, the pluralist Du Bois challenged the leading black separatist of the decade, Marcus Garvey. And throughout his career with the NAACP, but especially during a bitter dispute with Walter White in 1934, Du Bois's pluralism put him in opposition to integrationist colleagues who touted assimilation and dispersion as the best way to promote the advancement of black people.

The first biographies of Du Bois, by Francis L. Broderick and Elliott M. Rudwick, were harshly antagonistic toward Du Bois. Published in 1959 and 1960, near the height of the Cold War and during the integrationist phase of the civil rights movement, they criticized Du Bois for flirting with and eventually embracing Marxism, and they also alleged that Du Bois's emphasis on racial pride crossed over the line and was a form of Negro chauvinism if not outright black racism. Manning Marable's biography of 1986, on the other hand, celebrated Du Bois as a radical democrat who moved steadily from protosocialism in his youth to the Far Left after World War II. Meanwhile, Julius Lester (1971), Arnold Rampersad (1976), and Jack B. Moore (1981) wrote perceptive books that focused on Du Bois's writings, and Herbert Aptheker not only republished Du Bois's many books but also did invaluable work in collecting and publishing three volumes of Du Bois's correspondence and a bookshelf of additional tomes that contain Du Bois's articles, essays, research reports, and fugitive manuscripts. Most recently, in 1993 and 2000, David Levering Lewis published the preeminent work in Du Bois studies, a full-scale, two-volume biography that covered Du Bois's life in Pulitzer Prize–winning style.[5] In addition to these general works, there are many articles, books, and monographs that deal with discrete aspects of Du Bois's life.

This book is written for a general audience and is more sympathetic to pluralism than the works of Broderick and Rudwick, less comprehensive than that of Lewis, and less concerned with Du Bois's writings than the books by Lester, Rampersad, and Moore. In some ways it is a counterpoise to Manning Marable's biography. Where Marable saw socialism as a central component of Du Bois's thought, I have found only traces of radical economic thinking in the years when Du Bois was a civil rights leader, the period from about 1900 to 1934. Instead of emphasizing Du Bois's radicalism, I have stressed his pluralism, his double-consciousness, his insistence that blacks wished neither to Africanize America nor to bleach their Negro blood, but simply "to make it possible for a man to be both a Negro and an American . . . "[6] "We want to be Americans, full-fledged Americans, with all the rights of other American citizens," he wrote.[7] But he also insisted that African Americans should proudly develop their unique talents so that someday, "among the gaily colored banners that deck the broad ramparts of civilization," there would be one that was "uncompromising[ly] black."[8]

Although pluralism has enjoyed a resurgent popularity in recent years, another aspect of Du Bois's thought has become more controversial than ever. Throughout his life, Du Bois emphasized the importance of self-improvement and conventional morality. In an essay of 1897 he noted that blacks had "a vast work of self-reformation to do. . . . Unless we conquer our present vices they will conquer us."[9] When Du Bois reread this statement thirty-seven years later, he was "rather pleased to find myself still so much in sympathy with myself."[10] Du Bois criticized his fellow blacks for insufficient cooperation with one another and for failing to internalize middle-class standards with respect to marriage and the family. He identified "sexual looseness" and "lack of respect for the marriage bond" as "the great weakness of the Negro family."[11] Some contemporary writers on the Left have rejected Du Bois's moralism, while at least one writer on the Right has mistakenly concluded that Du Bois's emphasis on protest prevented him from emphasizing the importance of hard work and conventional morality.[12]

My goal has been to apprehend key aspects of Du Bois by describing the controversies that pitted him against the other civil rights leaders of his day, while at the same time providing enough information so that readers can follow the outline of his life. Thus this book explains Du Bois by showing how he differed from his principal rivals. Du Bois was *not* Booker T. Washington, *not* Oswald Garrison Villard, *not* Robert Russa Moton, *not* Marcus Garvey, and certainly *not* Walter White. He was known above all for his protests against racial oppression, but he stood for much more. Du Bois was committed to pluralism, and his pluralism emphasized the importance of both traditional moral standards and internal cooperation within the black community.

One Du Bois

Boyhood in the Berkshires

Du Bois's pluralism was reflected in his lineage. As he wrote in a letter applying for a college scholarship, Du Bois was "in blood, about one half or more Negro." His mother, Mary Silvina Burghardt, was a member of a black family that had lived in the Berkshire Mountains of western Massachusetts since before the American Revolution. His father, Alfred Du Bois, was a mulatto born in Haiti but with so little Negro ancestry that he could pass for white.[1]

The black Burghardts were descended from Tom Burghardt, a slave who was born in West Africa about 1730. As a reward for serving with Colonel John Ashley's regiment during the American Revolution, Tom and his family were freed from slavery. One of Tom's sons, Jack, later participated in Shays's Rebellion (1786) and helped in the War of 1812. One of Jack's sons then became Du Bois's maternal grandfather Othello. For several years Othello Burghardt earned a comfortable living as a farmer, but by the time of Du Bois's birth changes in the economy were undermining the independence of the family. With agriculture languishing, and with industrial jobs often restricted to whites, many of the Burghardts made their way to towns where they found work as barbers, waiters, cooks, housemaids, and laborers.[2]

Although the Burghardts had suffered economic reverses, they embraced conventional standards of respectability. They were hardworking, churchgoing people. Du Bois recalled that the family also "had a New England strictness in . . . sex morals. So far as I ever knew there was only one illegitimate child throughout the family." That child, however, was Du Bois's older half brother, Adelbert, the child of an illicit union that "no one talked of . . . in the family."[3] After giving birth to Adelbert, Du Bois's mother, Mary Burghardt, left the family farm and moved to nearby Great Barrington, Massachusetts, where she worked as a housemaid. Then, in 1867 when Mary Burghardt was in her middle thirties, she met Alfred Du Bois, a light mulatto newcomer to the region who had recently served in the U.S. Army. Because of Mary's compromised situation, she could hardly expect more from a fiancé. The couple eloped to the nearby village of Housatonic—"a runaway marriage, but one duly attested and published in the *Berkshire Courier.*"[4] William Edward Burghardt Du Bois was born a year later, on February 23, 1868.

The Burghardts were respectable black yeomen, but the Du Boises traced their ancestry back to Geoffroi Du Bois, who emerged from the French forest (the *bois*) to sail with William the Conqueror in 1066. Although the family was of French origin, W. E. B. Du Bois insisted that his name should be pronounced "Du-Boys" rather than the Gallic "Du-Bwah."[5]

The first American member of the Du Bois family came from France early in the seventeenth century. Five generations later James Du Bois, a wealthy white physician in New York, emigrated from America to the Caribbean after siding with England during the American Revolution and receiving as a reward a large plantation in the Bahama Islands. There he fathered several colored children by a common-law wife. When his wife died, James Du Bois returned to the United States about 1812 and enrolled his light-skinned son Alexander (the grandfather of W. E. B. Du Bois) in an exclusive private school. However, when James Du Bois died suddenly in 1820, his white New York family apprenticed Alexander to a shoemaker. Because he was the son of a wealthy physician and planter, and had the beginnings of a gentleman's education, Alexander refused to become a shoemaker and went to Haiti to seek his fortune in the shipping trade. In the 1830s Alexander Du Bois returned to the United States with a five-year-old son of his own, Alfred, who would become the father of W. E. B. Du Bois.

Du Bois's father, Alfred, did not get along with grandfather Alexander. As a young man Alfred bounded around in New England and New York and even traveled to New Orleans. He also served in the United States Army before arriving in Great Barrington. Du Bois later wrote that his father was "small and beautiful of face and feature, just tinted with the sun, his wavy hair chiefly revealing his kinship to Africa. In nature, I think, he was a dreamer—romantic, indolent, kind, unreliable." He had "r[u]n away [from his own father] and rioted and roamed, and loved and married my brown mother."[6]

Unfortunately, when Du Bois was only two years old, Alfred Du Bois deserted his family, and young Willie never saw his father again and knew not where or when he died. Du Bois later wrote that his father was "gallant" and "charming" but also "irresponsible."[7] At various times Alfred Du Bois worked as a barber, merchant, and preacher, but he refused to settle for long at any one place or job. He had accepted marriage to please the Burghardt family, but he bolted after only three years of wedlock.

Du Bois's principal biographer has ascribed the father's desertion to flaws of character—mentioning that Alfred Du Bois apparently fled a previous marriage and at one time was listed as a deserter from the U.S. Army.[8] Du Bois, however, blamed the departure, at least in part, on the color consciousness of the black Burghardts. The Burghardts thought Alfred Du Bois was "too good looking, too white," and they looked askance at him because he would not work on the Burghardt family farm but instead insisted that he and Mary Burghardt should live in the town of Great Barrington.[9] The Burghardts "carried on a more or less open feud," Du Bois recalled, and one day some of the Burghardt cousins fired pistols from a riverbank near the Du Boises' house.[10] The incident was probably just a prank, but Alfred thought his life was in danger. "Without a word, he went into the house and packed some things and left," never to return.[11]

The story of Alfred's desertion alerted Du Bois to the importance of color consciousness and discrimination within the black community. Yet from his youth Du Bois also recognized that some of the tensions in his family were rooted in class differences. "I don't suppose it was simply a matter of color," he once said. "It was a matter of culture." Du Bois's father had come "from a different world."[12]

In 1883 Du Bois learned just how different that world was when, at age fifteen, he visited his grandfather Alexander Du Bois. After returning from Haiti, Alexander had worked as a steward on a ship that ferried passengers between New York and New Haven, Connecticut. By the time young Will met his grandfather, however, Alexander Du Bois had retired to spend his days in New Bedford, Massachusetts. This grandfather, Will reported, was "'colored' but quite white in appearance," "a short, stern, upstanding man, sparing but precise in his speech and stiff in manner."[13] He was also well educated and told Will about "schools and books and far-off places, of a world quite different from the Burghardt farms."[14]

Grandfather Du Bois stood in marked contrast to Grandfather Burghardt. The Du Boises were professional people of light complexion, not farmers and manual laborers. There was a hint of aristocracy in their French ancestry. Grandfather Du Bois owned some property, read Shakespeare, wrote poetry, and yet was more militant than any of the black Burghardts. "He held his head high [and] took no insults. . . . He was not a 'Negro'; he was a man!"[15]

Grandfather Du Bois's style and class were exemplified on one occasion that made a lasting impression. On this day young Will noticed that Grandfather Du Bois's table was set for visitors, with a cut-glass decanter of wine atop a fine linen cloth. His grandfather was dressed in a long black coat, with vest and gold watch chain. After some conversation with his guest, his grandfather served the wine, raised his glass, touched the glass of his visitor and uttered a toast.

Will had read about such ceremonies in books, but he had never observed anything of the sort in Great Barrington where, he said, blacks and whites alike were given to "casual greetings [and] sprawling posture."[16] In Grandfather Du Bois's parlor, Will suddenly sensed what manners meant and how people of breeding behaved. He never forgot that toast. He sensed that there was a wider world that he might one day enter.

But that day was still some years distant. In the meantime there was a struggle to survive. After being deserted by her husband, Mary Burghardt Du Bois lived on the Burghardt family farm until Grandfather Burghardt died when Du Bois was about five years old. Then Mary Burghardt Du Bois returned to Great Barrington, where she and her two sons were three of about fifty Negroes living in a town of some five thousand people. At first, they lived in servants' quarters on an estate, and then in a dilapidated house in the worst section of town, before settling in a five-room cottage that was near the Congregational Church and the local public school. Mary found work as a housemaid, and the family income was supplemented by taking in a boarder (Mary's brother Jim, a barber). Du Bois's half-brother, Adelbert, went to work as a waiter when he was quite young, and Will chipped in with money from odd jobs—delivering newspapers, selling tea, splitting kindling, and stoking the furnace at a local millinery shop.

As an adult Du Bois recognized that his family had lived near the edge of poverty, and their fortunes were further damaged in the mid-1870s when his mother suffered a paralytic stroke that left her with a lame left leg and a withered left hand. Nevertheless, Mary Burghardt

Du Bois still found occasional day work as a maid, and after school Will would meet his mother to help with bundles and to offer a supporting shoulder. In Great Barrington, many observers commented on the mutual devotion of mother and son. "I just grew up that way," Du Bois later said. "We were companions."[17]

Although Du Bois and his mother were hard-pressed, Will thought they were living in simple comfort rather than mired in poverty. He had enough food and suitable clothing and was not made to feel deprived in the company of his fellow students. On the contrary, he was frequently entertained at the larger homes of white friends but observed no conspicuous exhibition of wealth. "In general," Du Bois wrote, "the contrast between the well-to-do and the poor was not great." "Great Barrington was a town of middle-class people."[18]

Du Bois always remembered Great Barrington with warm feelings. "The town and its surroundings were a boy's paradise," he wrote. "There were mountains to climb and rivers to wade and swim. . . . My earlier contacts with playmates and other human beings were normal and pleasant."[19]

To be sure, the color line intruded on occasions. As a youth Du Bois sensed that "some folks, a few, even several, actually considered my brown skin a misfortune."[20] Years later he still recalled one instant of recognition: "In a wee wooden schoolhouse something put it into the boys' and girls' heads to buy gorgeous visiting-cards—ten cents a package—and exchange. The exchange was merry till one girl, a tall newcomer, refused my card—refused it peremptorily, with a glance. Then it dawned on me with a certain suddenness that I was different from the others."[21]

In response, Du Bois withdrew into himself. Thereafter his companions would have no chance to reject him. "They must seek me out and urge me to come . . . When my presence was not wanted they had only to refrain from asking."[22]

Despite this withdrawal, the white youths of Great Barrington did seek Du Bois. Du Bois was not particularly good at baseball and football, but he was popular with schoolmates because he excelled at running, exploring, telling stories, and planning intricate games. "In the ordinary social affairs of the village—the Sunday School with its picnics and festivals; the temporary skating rink in the Town Hall; the coasting in crowds on all the hills—in all of these, I took part with no thought of discrimination on the part of my fellows, for that I would have been the first to notice."[23]

At Great Barrington High School the boys and girls did not date, for "dating" at that time was usually considered serious courtship. There were no social clubs, no school dances—nothing to trouble anyone concerned about miscegenation. In these circumstances, Du Bois became friendly with fellow students of both sexes. There was Mary Dewey, who surpassed Du Bois in mathematics but did not do as well in history and English. There were Sabra Taylor and Minnie Crissy, two good students whom he liked. And there was a small gang of teenage boys: George Phelps, with whom Du Bois walked to school; Ned Kelly and George Beebee, for swimming; and Mike Gibbons, for playing marbles.[24]

All things considered, Du Bois enjoyed an idyllic youth in Great Barrington. He recalled that he was "born by a golden river in the shadow of two great hills," in a middle-class democracy where there was "almost no . . . segregation or color discrimination."[25]

Some critics have suggested that Du Bois's autobiographical recollections were colored by the romanticism of old age. But Du Bois said much the same in columns he wrote for the New York Globe when he was a teenager. There Du Bois described the First Congregational Church, where he and his mother were the only black members, as "the handsomest church in the county." He described a strawberry festival at the A.M.E. Zion Church, and he noted that Miss Lizzie Lee had "very agreeably entertained" her friends at "a candy-puller and supper." He mentioned a number of public debates, one of which (on the policy of forcing Indians to resettle on reservations) featured Du Bois as a participant.[26]

At Great Barrington High School, Du Bois was especially fortunate in having Frank Hosmer as school principal. If Hosmer had been another sort of man, a man with definite ideas as to the inferior place of black people in American society, he would have recommended that Du Bois study something practical, like carpentry or agriculture. But Hosmer suggested instead that Du Bois should take the college preparatory course—Greek and Latin as well as science, history, and English—and arranged to have the textbooks purchased for Du Bois.[27]

Du Bois was only sixteen when he graduated from high school in 1884. When he then went to work for a year and to live with his aunt

Minerva after his mother died of an apoplectic stroke, Principal Hosmer stepped in to make sure that Du Bois got the chance to go to college. He arranged for four Congregational churches to pledge one hundred dollars a year to cover the cost of young Will's education at Fisk University, a Congregational school for African Americans in Nashville, Tennessee. Moreover, because the standards at Great Barrington High School were higher than those in most southern high schools, young Du Bois was admitted to the sophomore class at Fisk.[28]

Some of the Burghardts resented the idea of sending Will away. "They said frankly that . . . I was Northern born and bred and instead of preparing me for work and giving me an opportunity right there in my own town and state, [the white benefactors] were bundling me off to the South."[29]

This was true. But Du Bois recognized that there were more opportunities for college-educated African Americans in the South. He thought the freed slaves had a great future, if they were properly led. Besides, although Du Bois's life in Great Barrington had been comfortable, as a teenager he began to feel lonesome in New England. He recognized that as he grew older the cordial intermingling with white people would be restricted. He knew that as young people approached the age of courting and marriage, "There would be meetings, parties, clubs, to which I would not be invited." A black college like Fisk University, on the other hand, would give Will the opportunity "to meet colored people of my own age and education, of my own ambitions."[30] Thus Du Bois hardly noticed the "irony by which I was not looked upon as a real citizen of my birth-town, with a future and a career, and instead was being sent to a far land among strangers who were regarded as (and in truth were) 'mine own people.'"[31] When he left for Fisk in 1885, Du Bois was thrilled at the prospect of being for the first time among so many people of his own race.

Fisk, Harvard, and Berlin

At Fisk Du Bois discovered two worlds. White Nashville was a hostile society of racism and segregation, for which nothing in Great Barrington had prepared him. The dark side of this world was displayed on one occasion when Du Bois accidentally bumped into a white woman as they passed on a Nashville street. The woman was not hurt in the slightest, but when Du Bois raised his hat and begged her pardon, she replied with scorn, "How dare you speak to me, you impudent nigger!"[32] From his fellow students, Du Bois learned that incidents such as this could get out of hand, and for that reason many of the young men at Fisk carried firearms. Some of them had faced mobs and seen lynchings. "You don't need [a pistol] often," G. D. Field told Du Bois, "but when you do, it comes in handy!"[33]

Yet there was another, uplifting aspect of life at Fisk. Despite feeling the need to be on guard, the black students at the university were not a dispirited group of lost souls but a company of self-assured young men and women. On the train to Nashville, Du Bois chanced to meet Otho Porter, who would become Du Bois's college roommate for three years and later one of the leading physicians in Kentucky. At his first supper on campus, Du Bois was seated near two of the most beautiful young women he had ever seen. He was infatuated with Lena Calhoun (whom Du Bois considered even more beautiful than her grandniece, the famous singer and movie star Lena Horne). Eventually, Du Bois lost his Lena to an upperclassman named Frank Smith. But he never lost his enthusiasm for Fisk. After graduating from Fisk in 1888, Du Bois spent six years at Harvard and the University of Berlin, but he always considered Fisk his alma mater. "I was at Harvard but not of it. I was a student of Berlin, but still the son of Fisk."[34]

Fisk University was one of the schools that the Congregational American Missionary Association had established for freedmen after the Civil War. Unlike many other schools for African Americans, Fisk had no courses in industrial education. Rather than train laborers and workers for the white South, Fisk was educating leaders of the black race. All but one member of the faculty were white, but, according to Du Bois, they "believe[d] in the possibilities of the Negro race and the reality of the broader humanity taught by the Christian religion."[35] Du Bois's three years at Fisk were a time "of splendid inspiration and nearly perfect happiness, under teachers whom I respected and amid surroundings that inspired me."[36]

Du Bois's course work was common for a college student of the 1880s. He studied ethics and philosophy with the president of the university, Erastus Milo Cravath; Greek and choral music with Dean Adam Spence; Latin with Professor Helen Morgan; German with Henry S. Bennett; and chemistry and physics with Frederick A. Chase.

More important than the specific courses, Du Bois discovered his purpose; or perhaps one should say he found himself by losing himself. At Fisk Du Bois replaced his hitherto egocentric world with a world focused on his race. At Fisk he found a university that was training leaders who would uplift the black masses. The faculty and students were "very close to each other," he recalled, and had "a oneness of object that I'd never had before." As David Levering Lewis has noted, for Du Bois "Fisk was basic training for combat, and Fiskites were to provide the officer corps. If [Du Bois] had not yet coined his most famous term, the concept of the 'talented tenth' must already have been gestating."[37]

Feeling as he did, during the summers after his first two years at Fisk, Du Bois went to rural Wilson County in East Tennessee, where he taught school in log cabins built before the Civil War. It was a fascinating experience, one that enabled Du Bois to travel back in time and to touch "the very shadow of slavery."[38] He discovered that some black people were sunk "into listless indifference, or shiftlessness"; but there were others "whose young appetites had been whetted to an edge by school and story and half-awakened thought."[39]

For Du Bois the lesson was clear. Educated African Americans had a responsibility to provide leadership for the black masses. This was a message that Du Bois set forth when he became editor-in-chief of the college newspaper, the *Fisk Herald.* It was a point he emphasized in occasional speeches. Addressing his classmates as "ye destined leaders of a noble people," Du Bois declared that he was "a Negro, and I glory in the name! I am proud of the black blood that flows in my veins. From all the recollections dear to my boyhood have I come here, not to pose as a critic but to join hands with this, my people."[40]

Du Bois touched on this theme again at Fisk's graduation ceremonies of 1888 when he was chosen as one of the class speakers. There he took "Bismarck" as his subject, not because he was especially familiar with German politics but because Otto von Bismarck had created a nation by uniting groups that had previously been bickering. In Du Bois's mind, "this foreshadowed . . . the kind of thing that American Negroes must do, marching forth with strength and determination under trained leadership."[41]

One of the first tasks of black leaders, as Du Bois saw it, was to discredit the prevailing white racism—the then widespread belief that black people as a group were inferior in intellect and morality. As long as educated white people subscribed to this belief, it would be hard for blacks to progress. Therefore, Du Bois set for himself the lofty goal of "prov[ing] to the world that Negroes were just like other people."[42] And, as noted, Du Bois focused especially on the role of educated Negroes who had the training and knowledge to lead the black masses.

But to discredit racism, black leaders needed the best possible education. For Du Bois, Fisk had been a good college. He liked it. But it was a small school, with a limited curriculum, and therefore not entirely adequate for training someone with towering aspirations. Moreover, as a native of Massachusetts, Du Bois was under the spell of Harvard's prestige. Harvard, after all, was the oldest university in the United States, the largest in Massachusetts, and the best known. Consequently, when he was about to graduate from Fisk in 1888, Du Bois applied for admission to Harvard. In response, Harvard admitted Du Bois on the condition that he enter as a junior, even after receiving his B.A. degree from Fisk. Some people might have considered this a condescending condition, but Du Bois thought it justified because the academic standards at Fisk were not as high as those at Harvard and because Du Bois had spent only three years at Fisk. To sweeten its offer, Harvard also gave Du Bois a Price Greenleaf fellowship that covered most of his expenses.

Thus in the fall of 1888, Du Bois matriculated at Harvard. Unlike many students, however, Du Bois was not interested in social clubs like Hasty Pudding. He ate at Memorial Hall, where students of modest means boarded; and later he became a member of the even more modest Foxcroft Eating Club. Du Bois also made a point of not living in the dormitories but instead rented a bedroom from a black couple, John and Mary Taylor. "Following the attitudes which I had adopted in the South," Du Bois wrote, "I sought no friendships among my white fellow students, not even acquaintanceships."[43]

This withdrawal from white society was reinforced by an unfortunate instance that occurred on one occasion when Du Bois departed from his usual custom and did seek membership in a white group. Du Bois was proud of his singing voice. In fact, during the summer of 1888, just before he left for Harvard, he and some friends from Fisk had earned a tidy sum singing at parlor concerts at a hotel on the shore of Lake Minnetonka, Minnesota. Nevertheless, the Harvard

Glee Club rejected Du Bois—and Du Bois berated himself for not recognizing all along that "Harvard could not afford to have a Negro on its Glee Club traveling about the country."[44]

Du Bois then withdrew into his shell, later acknowledging that he came to know fewer than a dozen of the three hundred members of his class of 1890. By his own admission, Du Bois was afraid of intruding where he was not wanted; of appearing without invitation; of showing a desire for the company of people who did not welcome him. Something of an inferiority complex might have been at work. After all, Du Bois was not just a black man at a white school; he was a poor man at a school where most of his classmates were well-to-do. On the other hand, Du Bois never lacked self-confidence. The absence of company did not make him unhappy, he recalled, for he had his "'island within' and it was a fair country."[45]

Yet all social life was not lost. Although Du Bois ignored the white world as much as possible, he became actively involved in the social life of black Boston. Shortly after enrolling at Harvard, Du Bois became a regular visitor at the Charles Street home of Josephine Ruffin, the light mulatto widow of a municipal judge who in 1869 had been the first black man to graduate from the Harvard Law School. At Mrs. Ruffin's home, Du Bois met several intelligent and companionable young women who were as white as it was possible to be and still be known as Negroes. For Du Bois—with his plans for leading the Negro race—these women had the handicap of being too light-skinned. "I could not let the world even imagine that I had married a white wife," he later wrote.[46] In the short term, however, they were good company in staging theatrical productions in black Boston and on trips to visit African American students at Amherst and other colleges in New England.

Fortunately for Du Bois, another of Mrs. Ruffin's guests was Maud Cuney, a tall brunette with gold-bronze skin and coils of black hair. Du Bois was smitten, and before long he and Maud were engaged to be married. Eventually, the romance fizzled—a casualty, apparently, of conflicting career trajectories when Du Bois went to Germany for graduate work in 1892 and Cuney moved on to a successful career as a singer, folklorist, teacher, and historian of music. Yet Maud and "Du" (Maud's term of endearment) remained friends and correspondents.

Meanwhile, Du Bois did not neglect his studies. He recalled that he "burned no midnight oil," but he planned his days almost to the minute, spent a great deal of time in the library, and did his assignments thoroughly.[47] One paper on ethics for Professor William James ran to fifty-two handwritten pages.

As an undergraduate at Harvard, Du Bois majored in philosophy. He was repeatedly invited to the home of William James, his favorite professor, attended evening meetings of the Philosophical Club, consulted with the eminent philosophers Josiah Royce and George Palmer, and read Kant with George Santayana. During his senior year, however, Du Bois came under the influence of a young history professor, Albert Bushnell Hart. In some ways, Du Bois acknowledged, Hart was "as dry as dust."[48] But Hart had just returned from Germany with a new methodology that before long would become dominant in academic history. Instead of rehashing tales for a popular audience, Hart insisted that historians should immerse themselves in original sources and look for new information. They should spend less time in the library reading and interpreting one another's books, and more time in the archives working with documents. They should be accurate, objective, and restrained; above all, they should provide ample documentation for their statements.

With Hart's support, Du Bois examined documents pertaining to the African slave trade. Eventually, this research culminated in a doctoral dissertation and Du Bois's first book, *The Suppression of the African Slave Trade to the United States* (1896). In the process, Hart directed Du Bois away from philosophical speculation and toward a program of investigation. Hart "brought me down to earth," Du Bois recalled, "by making me study documents and look up facts pretty carefully."[49] As an undergraduate, Du Bois majored in philosophy; but he chose history for his specialty in graduate school. For Du Bois, abstract thought gave way to the accumulation of information.

The transition from philosophy to history was one of two major intellectual developments that Du Bois experienced at Harvard. The other involved English composition and writing style. As a high school student in Great Barrington, Du Bois published several news stories in the *New York Globe*. As an undergraduate at Fisk, he had been the editor of the college newspaper, the *Fisk Herald*. Nevertheless, one of Du Bois's early undergraduate papers at Harvard—a critique of a racist senator from Alabama—"came back marked 'E'—not passed!" It was the first time in his life that Du Bois had experienced such a failure. He was "aghast," but, surprisingly, he "did not doubt but what my instructors were fair in judging my English technically even if they did not understand the Negro problem."[50]

Du Bois then went to work on his English and by the end of the semester had improved his grade to a C—the only C that would besmirch a record of As and Bs in all other courses at Harvard. Yet, in terms of influence on Du Bois's subsequent career, that C was especially significant. It made Du Bois recognize that "while style is subordinate to content, and that no real literature can be composed simply of meticulous and fastidious phrases, nevertheless that solid content with literary style carries a message further than poor grammar and muddled syntax."[51]

To improve his style of writing, Du Bois enrolled in English 12, an advanced course taught by one of Harvard's most fastidious masters of composition, Barrett Wendell. Here again there were difficulties, for Wendell was very particular about grammar and favored the English style of understating rather than overstating a thesis. One of Du Bois's papers was returned with the biting comment, "Such truculence as yours is thoroughly injudicious. Nothing could more certainly induce an average reader to disagree." But Du Bois persevered. In an essay entitled "Something about Me," Du Bois wrote, "In early youth a great bitterness entered my life and kindled a great ambition." Therefore, Du Bois explained, he decided to go to college, partly because other youths did but also because college would prepare him for leadership. Du Bois then concluded, "I believe, foolishly perhaps but sincerely, that I have something to say to the world, and I have taken English 12 in order to say it well."[52] Professor Wendell liked that sentence so much that he read it to the class.

As he was about to receive his second B.A. degree in 1890, Du Bois was overflowing with confidence. Because his grades placed him near the top of his class at Harvard, he had been chosen as one of six students to speak at the commencement. Moreover, Du Bois's plans for the future were coming together. For the next few years, he would continue as a graduate student, working on a doctoral dissertation on the African slave trade; in the longer term, he hoped for a professorship that would allow him to combine scholarship with leading his people.

Du Bois was so set on his future that he found it hard to understand that other members of his class still remained uncertain and

conflicted. He was astonished when, in the spring of 1890, just before graduation, he chanced to meet one of his white classmates while
waiting for a streetcar. As they talked, the classmate acknowledged
his own ambivalence about the commencement, for he did not know
what he would do after graduation. "There's nothing in which I am
particularly interested," the classmate confessed. Du Bois was "astonished [and] almost outraged to meet any human being of the ma-
ture age of 22 who did not have his life all planned before him—at
least in general outline; and who was not supremely, if not desperately, interested in what he planned to do."[53]

It was not until some time later that Du Bois recognized that
most college seniors are not certain of what they want to do or can
do with life; they stand uncertainly on a threshold, awaiting direction, chance, or opportunity. Because he had a sure sense of his own
life's work, and probably because he had not mingled socially with
his Harvard classmates, Du Bois did not realize at the time that his
own sense of purpose was unusual.

For Du Bois, the path ahead led to graduate school and a Ph.D.
in history. But even this was not enough for someone with the lofty
ambition of both discrediting racism and leading his people out of
the wilderness. For this, Du Bois thought he would need further
training in Europe, for the German universities were then considered
superior to the American, just as Harvard was regarded as better than
Fisk. Thus in 1892, when the opportunity presented itself, Du Bois
sought to matriculate at the University of Berlin.

To study in Europe was problematical, for Du Bois was a poor or-
phan with no means of his own. While he was a graduate student at
Harvard, however, Du Bois chanced to come upon a newspaper article that stated that former president Rutherford B. Hayes, who then
was the chairman of the Slater Fund for the Education of Negroes,
which had previously focused on the vocational education of African
Americans, had said that the fund would finance an advanced education in Europe "if there is any young colored man . . . whom we
find to have a talent for art or literature."[54]

Du Bois applied, but his hopes and the hopes of all the applicants
were dashed. President Hayes said that the original press report was
in error, that the Slater Fund had no plans to send any Negroes
abroad.

Du Bois then sat down and wrote Hayes a letter that Du Bois acknowledged "could be described as nothing less than impudent"—a letter that stands as an early example of the sort of protest for which Du Bois would later become famous. Du Bois began by saying that he had expected all along that his application would be rejected, for he never really believed that the Slater Fund, which in the past had focused its philanthropy on "training plowmen," would now finance an advanced education for any black youth. Du Bois then noted that the rejection, coupled with the original announcement that the fund would give assistance "if there is any young colored man . . . whom we find to have a talent for art or literature," left the impression that there were no African Americans with an aptitude for advanced education in art or literature. For this, Du Bois concluded, "I think you owe an apology to the Negro people."[55]

To his credit, President Hayes did not take offense but encouraged Du Bois to apply again. The Slater Fund then looked with favor on Du Bois's appeal, giving him $1,500 (half of which was a loan) to finance two years of graduate study in Europe. Du Bois was ecstatic, and in his application and subsequent reports he explained why. To properly finish the education he had begun at Fisk and Harvard, he deemed further education in a European university indispensable. For a prospective black leader who inevitably had suffered some scars as a result of racial discrimination in the United States, the contact with European culture would be of great value. By giving him "a broad view of men and affairs," Du Bois told the Slater Fund, the scholarship would enable him "to view the problems of his race in their true perspective."[56]

In one important respect, Du Bois's education in Germany had an effect that was the opposite of his education at Harvard. At Harvard, as noted, Du Bois had few friendships among his white fellow students. In Germany, on the other hand, Du Bois enjoyed a great deal of social intermingling with Europeans of education and manners and, as a result, he emerged from the extremes of his racial parochialism.

Ever since he had gone South to Fisk—perhaps ever since the white girl peremptorily refused to accept his card in Great Barrington—Du Bois had been suspicious of whites. "I had reached the habit of expecting color prejudice," he acknowledged. Consequently, when Du Bois was on a steamship approaching Germany and happened to see a Dutch woman with two grown daughters, he "proceeded to put as much space between us as the small vessel allowed."[57] The daughters nevertheless approached Du Bois, and before long they were happy companions who ate and sang together while speaking English, French, and German. Du Bois was so moved by this cordiality across the lines of race and sex that there were tears in his eyes when he bade the Dutch women good-bye.

More fraternization followed in the German town of Eisenach. On one occasion in the summer of 1892, Du Bois attended a dance where, according to the local custom, the girls went with their parents, the boys went alone, and the dancers twirled by under the watchful eyes of mothers and fathers. When the time came for the *Damen Wahl* (the Ladies' Choice), Du Bois drew back, with the memory of the old visiting-card business in Great Barrington perhaps troubling him for a moment. But there was no reason to fear, Du Bois later recalled, "for my card was filled for every dance."[58]

In Eisenach, Du Bois also fell in love with blue-eyed Dora Marbach, the daughter of the rector of a local church. After Du Bois serenaded Dora in his strong baritone voice, Dora "said she would marry [him] *gleich* [at once.]"[59] But an interracial marriage was out of the question for a prospective race leader like Du Bois, who had previously spurned Negro girls in Boston for being too light. Sixty years later Du Bois still spoke with feeling when he said, "Dora never understood why I could not marry her, why I could not bring her back to the United States as my wife. How could she imagine the United States, or why the work to which I have dedicated my life could not be shared with her?"[60]

Du Bois's affair with Dora Marbach was closely chaperoned, but at the University of Berlin he lived with a white shopgirl named Amalie. Du Bois was ashamed of the relationship, however, perhaps because of the difference in class standing as well as misgivings about fornication.[61]

While in Europe, Du Bois also mixed with white men. At the university he was something of a loner, although he had some student companions. He traveled through much of Europe with two white fellow students and followed "the political movements of [Germany], the rise of anti-Semitism, which has much in common with my own race question and therefore is of considerable interest to me; the socialist movement, the new agrarian movement, etc."[62] He attended political rallies, read the newspapers, and conversed with Germans in restaurants and beer halls.

Du Bois's experience in Europe did much to counter the suspicion of white people that he had developed in Nashville and at Harvard. Because of his cordial relations with white people in Europe, Du Bois wrote, "I became more human; learned the place in life of 'Wine, Women, and Song'; ceased to hate people simply because they belonged to one race or color."[63]

Du Bois's academic work in Germany simultaneously reinforced and modified some of the lessons he had learned at Harvard. At the University of Berlin, he attended some twenty hours of weekly lectures, but his major scholarly work involved research for a seminar with Professor Gustav Schmoller. Schmoller was one of the most prominent figures in a new German specialty, a field known as historical economics. As much a sociologist as an economist or historian, Schmoller emphasized the importance of collecting empirical information through close observation of particular situations. Once sufficient information had been accumulated, Schmoller said, it could be used as a guide for state intervention in the economy on behalf of poor people.

Schmoller's influence steered Du Bois away from the theoretical free market economics that had been taught at Harvard. But Schmoller's insistence on careful investigation reinforced the lessons that Du Bois had learned from the Harvard historian Albert Bushnell Hart. Like Hart, Schmoller discounted deductive speculation and emphasized the importance of pure research, the inductive accumulation of facts. For Schmoller, however, the goal was not knowledge for its own sake, but knowledge as the basis for reform policies that would be instituted by college-educated government officials. Thus Schmoller showed Du Bois how to combine objectivity and activism, how to use his training to improve the lot of the black masses. First, there would be the "accumulation of accurate information; then social policy based on that information; the whole suffused with the ideal of justice."[64]

As a student in Schmoller's seminar, Du Bois compared American sharecropping with peasant proprietorship in Germany. The work evolved into a statistical report on the relative economic advantages of large and small farms. As such it was approved as a German doctoral dissertation, and Du Bois's major professors wrote letters urging the University of Berlin to give Du Bois a doctorate. Du Bois did not receive the degree, however, because he could afford to spend only two years in residence at the university—not the three years then required for a German doctorate. Consequently, Du Bois had to settle for having a Ph.D. only from Harvard![65]

Although Du Bois's academic work in Germany reinforced his commitment to inductive research, in some ways his studies also reinforced his pluralism. Once again, as at Fisk and Harvard, Du Bois enjoyed good personal relations with the faculty. However, some of the unspoken assumptions in Germany differed from those at Fisk and Harvard. In America, Du Bois had been given to understand that educated intellectuals should be above national and color prejudice. In Germany, on the other hand, the tacit understanding was that professors should not be deracialized intellectuals who lived in a world that transcended considerations of race and nationality. The previously independent German states had only recently joined together to form a new nation, and a spirit of patriotism was rife. One of Du Bois's professors, Adolf Wagner, praised Bismarck for uniting the Germans. Another, Heinrich von Treitschke, proclaimed that national and racial groups were separated by irreducible differences—and was open in showing "pity for France [and] hearty dislike for all things English" and in criticizing the extent of Jewish influence in Germany.[66]

In addition, Du Bois wrote, "the pageantry and patriotism of Germany in 1892 astonished me." It was quite unlike anything he had experienced in the United States, where most people loved their country with restraint and reason rather than with emotional passion. In Germany, even Du Bois was stirred by "the march of soldiers, the saluting of magnificent uniforms, [and] the martial music." He was thrilled when he saw the kaiser ride through the Brandenburg gate "ahead of his white and golden troops on prancing chargers, . . . 'with banners gaily flying, with trumpet and with drum!'" Du Bois was so inspired that thenceforth he trimmed his beard and mustache after the fashion of the German leader. He envied his fellow German students because he recognized that "they felt something I had never felt" when they sang, "Deutschland, Deutschland uber Alles, uber Alles in der Welt."[67]

Influenced by these notions and his earlier experience, in 1893 Du Bois held a special ceremony to celebrate his twenty-fifth birthday. He knew that his years of preparation and study were coming to an end and that his years of adult work were about to begin. So, with candles burning in his private quarters, Du Bois rededicated himself to using research to uplift his race. He recognized that a life of scholarship and service would entail some sacrifice of financial gain and personal comfort. Yet Du Bois confided to his diary that he was determined to make his life all that life may be—by "work[ing] for the rise of the Negro people, taking for granted that their best development means the best development of the world."[68]

In more prosaic language, Du Bois explained his program to the trustees of the Slater Fund: "My plan is something like this: to get a position in one of the Negro universities, and to seek to build up there a department of history and social science, with two objects in view: (a) to study scientifically the Negro question past and present with a view to its best solution, and (b) to collect capable young Negro students, and to see how far they are capable of furthering, by independent study and research, the best scientific work of the day."[69]

Professor Du Bois

Upon his return to the United States in 1894, Du Bois hoped for a position at Howard University in Washington, D.C. When that did not materialize, he applied to other colleges and received offers from Wilberforce University in Ohio, from Tuskegee Institute in Alabama, and from Lincoln Institute in Missouri. Du Bois chose Wilberforce.[70] The school had been established in 1856 by a group of white Methodists interested in the education of blacks. In 1863, Bishop Daniel Alexander Payne purchased the institution for the African Methodist Episcopal Church, and since then blacks have managed Wilberforce. More than a century later, the official stationery featured the inscription, "America's First College Owned and Operated by Negroes."

Wilberforce impressed Du Bois initially as a good place to try his plan of racial uplift through education and research. After all, Wilberforce was the flagship campus of the nation's most influential African American church, and Du Bois was well aware of the importance of religion in black life. It turned out, however, that the religious fervor at Wilberforce was too intense for Du Bois. He refused to attend the annual revival meetings that interrupted schoolwork every year. In fact, on his birthday in 1896, Du Bois noted in his diary that although he kept to his rooms, he was "driven almost to distraction by the wild screams, cries, groans, and shrieks" reverberating from the campus chapel.[71] Also, Du Bois nearly lost his job on one occasion when he refused to lead a class in a spontaneous prayer. He recalled that "it took a great deal of explaining to the board of bishops why a professor in Wilberforce should not be able at all times and sundry to address God in extemporaneous prayer."[72]

As a youth Du Bois had attended the Congregational Church, where he happily taught Sunday school. In addition, as noted, Du Bois had attended Fisk University (which was founded by the American Missionary Association) with the aid of a subvention from four Congregational churches. However, unlike Du Bois's almost all-white congregation in Great Barrington, the black Congregationalists at Fisk prohibited dancing. Du Bois was so outspoken in opposing this stricture—another early indication of his disposition toward protest—that church leaders eventually tried to reconcile matters. But in the process the patriarchs so annoyed young Du Bois that thereafter he refused to join any organized church.[73]

David Levering Lewis has written that the controversy over dancing set Du Bois on "an intellectual journey that would end, after a very short time, in serene agnosticism." However, at Harvard Du Bois attended church on Sundays, taught Sunday school, and criticized fellow students who were blasphemous. In Germany, he tended to ignore religion and to focus on economics, sociology, and travel; but he continued to write warm letters to the Congregational Sunday school in Great Barrington, and when he returned to the United States, he chose to work at a religious college. "I'm a Christian," Du Bois confided to his diary when he was at Wilberforce. Although the revival meetings at the college were not to his taste, Du Bois supported them "somewhat—that is, I suppose there are times when all earnest workers in any cause need re-consecration to their ideals." His writings were suffused with allusions to religion and later, when he became a father, he saw to it that his daughter, Yolande, was baptized. Du Bois's "Credo," published in 1904, and republished in 1920, began with the statement, "I believe in God."[74]

Yet Du Bois's religious style was less emotional than the approach that was in vogue at Wilberforce in the 1890s. He had to explain to the bishops that where he was reared, in the Congregational Church of Great Barrington, "the ordinary layman doesn't lead in prayer. He sits and listens and that sort of thing, but . . . he doesn't take active part in any religious exercises." Because Du Bois was uncomfortable offering spontaneous prayers, a compromise was worked out whereby Du Bois read from the prayer book. Sometimes he would comment on the formal prayers, a practice he continued at Atlanta University between 1898 and 1910, where the president of the institution reported that "some of the deepest and most vital expressions of the religious life came from [Du Bois's] lips as he conducted evening devotions at the University."[75]

Du Bois's commitment to Wilberforce was further shaken by the intrusion of religious politics on campus. When Ben Arnett, the son of a bishop but a young man with inadequate academic training, was appointed to a professorship, Du Bois organized a faculty strike. In the short term, the professors won. "Young Ben Arnett never became a professor at Wilberforce." But no professor who challenged Bishop Arnett could stay long at the university. By the middle of his second year on the faculty Du Bois knew that his days at Wilberforce were numbered, that his dreams would not be fulfilled there. Early in 1896, Du Bois informed Booker T. Washington that he was looking for another position.[76]

While he was still at Wilberforce, however, Du Bois fell in love with one of the students, Nina Gomer, a "slender, quiet, and dark eyed girl" with "an hourglass figure."[77] In complexion, Nina resembled Will, her father being a black chef at a leading hotel in Iowa and her mother a German woman from Alsace. Later Du Bois recalled that Nina was so pretty that people would "stop and stare at her in the street."[78] Will was twenty-eight years old when the couple were married on May 12, 1896.

The marriage lasted for fifty-four years, until Nina's death in 1950. Although Nina was a remarkable beauty, Du Bois insisted that her looks were not her chief attribute. Her great gifts were honesty and loyalty, which, according to Du Bois, made their marriage "happier than most." Yet Du Bois acknowledged that the marriage suffered from "a difference in aim and function between its partners."[79] His work was out in the world, and sometimes Will and Nina would be apart for months at a time, with Nina busy tending to their home and two children while Will was on the road doing research and, later, working for the NAACP. Nina supported Du Bois's work, but Du Bois recognized that "she must often have been lonesome and wanted more regular and personal companionship." "Poor Nina," he said after her death, "I should never have left her so much."[80]

As his two-year stay at Wilberforce was nearing its end, Du Bois also put the finishing touches on a revised version of his Harvard doctoral dissertation. It was published in 1896 as the first volume in what would become a well-regarded series of books, the Harvard Historical Studies.[81] Based on thirty months of research in legal records and government documents, *The Suppression of the African Slave Trade to the United States of America* combined the investigative skill that one would expect of a scholar trained by Albert Bushnell Hart and Gustav Schmoller with an interpretive flair that was distinctively Du Bois. *The Suppression of the African Slave Trade* was considered a standard work on the African slave trade for more than fifty years. It was cited thousands of times.

Du Bois chose not to describe the bloody excesses of the slave trade. He would leave that for others. Instead, in restrained and sober language, Du Bois summarized the restrictions the various colonies placed on the transatlantic slave trade. Then he discussed the debate over the trade at the Constitutional Convention of 1787 and the outlawing of the trade by legislation enacted in 1808. One of his main conclusions was that the prohibition was not enforced. Despite laws that condemned the trade as piracy, the slavers smuggled "not less than 250,000" Negro slaves into the United States after 1808.[82]

Du Bois was correct, but only partially. His research in the legal records established that the prohibition was not enforced conscientiously. Du Bois showed that the United States continued to receive slaves from Africa and the West Indies long after 1808. However, Du Bois was mistaken to base his estimates of the extent of the smuggling on legal records. In 1969, Philip Curtin examined bills of lading, ship manifests, and other economic records, and came up with the now prevailing estimate that "only" 54,000 slaves were smuggled into the United States after 1808.[83]

Curtin's revision was important because it suggested that the growth of the American slave population (from 1,191,354 in 1810 to 3,953,760 in 1860)[84] was not due to lax enforcement of the laws against slave trading. It was, rather, testimony to a high birth rate and a declining rate of mortality among American slaves. American slaveholders apparently provided living conditions that were good enough to allow their human property to stay healthy and increase in value.[85]

Although Du Bois was mistaken in his estimate of the extent of smuggling, in several other respects he was right on target. He was prescient in noting that a fear of slave rebellions, especially after the Haitian uprising of 1791, had made many southerners fearful of importing still more slaves. He astutely noted that slaveowners in the Upper South had been selling many of their own slaves to the Deep South; they therefore opposed the African trade, for, they recognized, importing more slaves from Africa would drive down the price of the slaves that they were exporting to the Cotton Kingdom. In addition, Du Bois's discussion of the 1850s campaign to reopen the transatlantic slave trade was so good that seventy-five years would pass before there would be a better book on the subject.[86]

When it was published, *Suppression of the African Slave Trade* was widely reviewed and favorably received. In 1954 Du Bois expressed regret that he had used what he called "the monographic method" to thoroughly examine a discrete topic. Yet, although much of the book is dry, this was the price that modern, "scientific" history exacted for depth and accuracy. Du Bois also wished that he had made more use of the insights of Sigmund Freud and Karl Marx.[87] However, considering the recent decline in the reputation of these worthies, Du Bois was well-served by sticking close to his sources. As it was published, *Suppression of the African Slave Trade* was not a monumental book,[88] but it was a very good piece of work. It broke new ground, was scrupulously documented, and was generally sound.

Most important in terms of Du Bois's immediate future, *Suppression of the African Slave Trade* established his reputation for scholarship and led to his appointment as a researcher for the University of Pennsylvania and the College Settlement Association. His assignment was to investigate social conditions in the predominantly black sections of Philadelphia. The hope was that reliable scientific information could be used as the basis for reform.

Du Bois welcomed the chance to study race relations in Philadelphia. He was eager to leave Wilberforce, and the new research was in line with his plan to establish a factual, scientific basis for uplifting his race. Nevertheless, Du Bois had some reservations about moving his bride of three months into an economically depressed, crime-ridden slum. Neither Nina nor Will had previously lived in an area "where kids played intriguing games like 'cops and lady bums'; and where in the night when pistols popped, you didn't get up lest you find you couldn't."[89]

In fact, the Du Boises' apartment in Philadelphia was so small that Nina and Will found it difficult to hide gifts from one another. When Nina fell asleep on Christmas Eve 1896, Will slipped out of bed and tiptoed across the floor to find an umbrella that he placed in Nina's stocking. Then, after falling half asleep, he awoke to find Nina retrieving presents for him. Finally, Christmas "came in with laughing over the night's adventure, the revealing of hiding places and enjoyment of the umbrella, suspenders, and neckties. . . . The whole day melted away in misty happiness."[90] Before long, Nina was pregnant, and on October 2, 1897, a son was born, Burghardt Gomer Du Bois.

With things going well at home, Du Bois threw himself into a truly prodigious work of investigation. For some fifteen months, Du Bois scoured through the libraries and archives of Philadelphia. He gathered statistics and made maps, charts, and graphs. Rather than use canvassers, he personally visited and talked with five thousand people. He assayed a thorough piece of work because he thought the Negro problem was "a matter of systematic investigation and intelligent understanding. The world was thinking wrong about race, because it did not know. The ultimate evil was stupidity. The cure for it was knowledge based on scientific investigation."[91]

Du Bois understood that his idea of reform differed from that of his sponsors. Like many progressives elsewhere, the leaders of the University of Pennsylvania and the College Settlement Association were opposed to what was called "machine politics"—rule by politicians who did not give government construction contracts to low bidders, or appoint the best-trained people to jobs in the civil service, but instead gave the business and the patronage to people who had supported the machine on election day. In Philadelphia, the Republican machine had withstood challenges from reformers, in part because African American voters, in return for various sorts of patronage, had supported the machine at the polls.

When it was published in 1899, Du Bois's book, *The Philadelphia Negro*, substantiated the expectations of its sponsors. It showed that the forty thousand African Americans of Philadelphia cast almost all their votes for the candidates of the machine. "There can be no doubt but that corrupt and dishonest white politicians have been kept in power by the influence thus obtained to sway the Negro vote." Some Negroes sold their votes for small change or for the proverbial bottle of whiskey. Others, "while not open to bribery, accept[ed] the indi-

rect emoluments of office or influence in return for party loyalty."
Only a small minority were independent voters who sought to use
their vote to improve the conditions of municipal life. "There can be
no doubt," Du Bois concluded, "but that the wisest provision would
have been an educational and property qualification impartially enforced against ex-slaves and immigrants."[92]

To this point, Du Bois was telling the sponsors what they wanted to hear from a black scholar. But Du Bois had much more to say
and, to their credit, the sponsors asked for more. In authorizing the
research, C. C. Harrison, the provost of the University of Pennsylvania, explained: "The University . . . wishes to make the investigation
as thorough and exact as possible. We want to know precisely how
this class of people live; what occupations they follow; from what occupations they are excluded; how many of their children go to
school; and to ascertain every fact which will throw light upon this
social problem; and then having this information and these accurate
statistics before us, to see to what extent and in what ways, proper
remedies may be applied."[93]

With meticulous detail, Du Bois showed that the vast majority of
black workers were restricted to menial service or unskilled labor.
Machine politicians were just about the only whites who would work
with blacks. Hardly anyone else would give a well-educated black
man a job above the level of porter at six or eight dollars a week. But
if the black man went into politics, blindly supported the candidate
of the party boss, and by hard work persuaded most of the voters in
his precinct to do the same, he had the chance of becoming a city
clerk with a salary of sixty or seventy-five dollars a month.[94]

By way of contrast, Du Bois's progressive sponsors proposed to
give government jobs to candidates whose formal education would
enable them to do well on civil service examinations. Since many
worthy black people would lose their jobs in the process, it was hardly surprising that most blacks looked askance at reformers "who did
not apparently know there were any Negroes on earth until they
wanted their votes."[95]

Just as Du Bois developed an economic explanation for black voting, so he also probed the complex roots of crime and family insta-
bility. Excluded from most good jobs and facing discrimination along
the color line, many blacks turned to crime. In fact, after reviewing
police reports and other evidence, Du Bois concluded that the blacks

of Philadelphia, who made up only 4 percent of the city's total population, committed 22 percent of the serious crimes.[96]

The situation with respect to the black family was also bad. White racism and discrimination made it hard for black men to support their families and, Du Bois also maintained, the legacy of slavery "still show[ed] itself in a large amount of cohabitation without marriage." Especially among recent immigrants from the South, there was "much sexual promiscuity and the absence of a real home life." Because Philadelphia did not have a reliable registration of births, Du Bois could not ascertain the incidence of illegitimacy; but he judged it to be high and found evidence of "the unchastity of a large number of women." "The great weakness of the Negro family," he concluded, "is . . . lack of respect for the marriage bond. . . . Sexual looseness then arises as a secondary consequence, bringing adultery and prostitution in its train."[97]

Du Bois emphasized that white racism was ultimately responsible for the blacks' high crime rate and broken families. "The centre and kernel of the Negro problem . . . is the narrow opportunities afforded Negroes for earning a decent living." Whites were at fault because of discrimination in the past and because they continued to bar black men and women from most good jobs. The whites' duty was to "stop it." "Talent should be rewarded, and aptness used in commerce and industry whether its owner be black or white." "The same incentive to good, honest, effective work [should] be placed before a black office boy as before a white one." Many blacks admittedly lacked the skills needed for economic success. But if discrimination ended, "it would make one vast difference: it would inspire the young to try harder, it would stimulate the idle and the discouraged and it would take away from [blacks] the omnipresent excuse for failure: prejudice."[98]

Although Du Bois thought that whites were largely responsible for racial problems, he also insisted that many necessary reforms could be undertaken only by blacks themselves. "The Negro race has an appalling work of social reform before it," Du Bois wrote. "The amount of crime that can without doubt rightly be laid at the door of the Philadelphia Negro is large and is a menace to a civilized people." "The homely virtues of honesty, truth and chastity must be instilled." Black youth should be taught that "it is a greater disgrace to be idle than to do the humblest labor."[99]

Du Bois distinguished between fault and responsibility. Whites were at fault, but blacks had a responsibility to undertake "a vast amount of preventive and rescue work." Indeed, according to Du Bois, "the bulk of the work of raising the Negro must be done by the Negro himself, and the greatest help for him will be not to hinder and curtail and discourage his efforts."[100]

"Above all," Du Bois wrote, "the better classes of the Negroes should recognize their duty toward the masses." Throughout *The Philadelphia Negro* Du Bois noted the existence of a professionally trained, conventionally moral black elite. Unfortunately, there were strong forces that kept this Talented Tenth from lending a hand to their fellows. Some felt a genuine revulsion from the rougher, uneducated, and sometimes crude immigrants from the South. Moreover, because many whites assumed that blacks as a group were inclined toward crime and sexual promiscuity, many aristocrats of color kept their distance from lower-class blacks. Du Bois nevertheless insisted that the better classes had "their chief excuse for being in the work they may do toward lifting the rabble."[101]

David Levering Lewis has characterized *The Philadelphia Negro* as a "great, schizoid monograph." On the one hand, Du Bois ascribed the Negro problem to white racism and, in the process, shifted a paradigm. Earlier, the dominant literature had attributed poverty, crime, and indolence to deficiencies in the character and genetic inheritance of black people. Later, enlightened opinion came to regard these phenomena as symptoms of complex social conditions. At the same time, as the *American Historical Review* noted, Du Bois was "perfectly frank, laying all necessary stress on the weaknesses of his people."[102]

Although Du Bois's twin premises are complementary, some writers have criticized Du Bois for candidly discussing black weaknesses and for subscribing to a moral code they consider hopelessly bourgeois. Going beyond Arnold Rampersad, who accused Du Bois of "prissiness when the subject is sex," Allison Davis pronounced Du Bois guilty of narrow, middle-class bias, because Du Bois "renounce[d] the magnificent sexual vitality and sensualism of the underclass Negroes." And David Levering Lewis scoffed that Du Bois was urging black people "to behave like lending-library patrons."[103]

To rescue Du Bois from appearing to be too middle class, Lewis suggested that Du Bois's statements about moral uplift were included in *The Philadelphia Negro* for tactical reasons. To gain a respectful hearing for the major premise of the book—the one that emphasized the importance of white racism rather than innate defects of character—Du Bois, according to Lewis, calculated that it was necessary to affirm the conventional morality of the Victorian era.[104]

Yet this interpretation is questionable. When Du Bois spoke to black audiences, and no whites were present to be influenced, he also emphasized the black community's need for moral reform. In fact, in an 1897 address to the American Negro Academy, an exclusive organization of black intellectuals, Du Bois reversed the priorities of *The Philadelphia Negro.* "The second great step" toward solving America's racial problems, Du Bois said, "should be a more impartial selection of ability in the economic and intellectual world, and a greater respect for personal liberty and worth, regardless of race." But "the first and greatest step . . . [is] the correction of the immorality, crime and laziness among the Negroes themselves." "We are diseased, we are developing criminal tendencies, and an alarmingly large percentage of our men and women are sexually impure." *"Unless we conquer our present vices they will conquer us."* Du Bois said it was the duty of black leaders "to keep black boys from loafing, gambling, and crime; . . . to guard the purity of black women and to reduce that vast army of black prostitutes that is today marching to hell."[105]

This address was published as an occasional paper of the American Negro Academy. Although "The Conservation of Races" ran to only fifteen pages, it was one of Du Bois's most important publications. In it he synthesized his philosophy. He called for a "Talented Tenth" to lead blacks toward high standards and in a distinctive, pluralist direction.

"The history of the world," Du Bois told the American Negro Academy, was "the history not of individuals, but of groups, not of nations, but of races." The English-speaking people were justly renowned for constitutional liberty and commercial freedom; the Germans for science and philosophy; the Mediterranean nations for literature and art. Other races had "not as yet given to civilization the full spiritual message which they are capable of giving," but Du Bois was confident that "the Negro people, as a race, have a contribution to make . . . which no other race can make." He envisioned a not-too-distant day when, "among the gaily-colored banners that deck the broad ramparts of civilization" there would be one that was "uncompromising[ly] black."[106]

Du Bois explained that American Negroes were "not simply Americans or simply Negroes," but a distinct minority group with a unique culture and history "which they cannot escape because it is in the marrow of their bones."[107] This duality inevitably led to identity diffusion: "Am I an American or am I a Negro? Can I be both?" Some black leaders thought that white racism was so deeply entrenched that blacks would never receive fair treatment in America; they must separate to achieve the freedom needed for self-fulfillment. Others thought the "sole hope of salvation lies in our being able to lose our race identity in the commingled blood of the nation."[108]

Du Bois had to choose among three conflicting black political and cultural traditions. In the nineteenth century, Martin R. Delany and Edward Wilmot Blyden had espoused racial solidarity, glorified Africa, and looked with favor on an exodus of African Americans back to the Motherland. Frederick Douglass, on the other hand, basically accepted the goal of racial integration and assimilation. And Alexander Crummell, while insisting on equal rights for blacks, urged African Americans not to forget that they were "colored people" and to cooperate together "as colored men, in schools, churches, associations, and friendly societies."[109]

Du Bois could not evade an agonizing question: "Have we in America a distinct mission as a race, . . . or is self-obliteration the highest end to which Negro blood dare aspire?"[110] He sided with Crummell and answered in terms of what today is called cultural *pluralism*. Rejecting the melting-pot idea, which looks toward a blending of different cultures into one, Du Bois envisaged the coexistence of distinct groups. According to Du Bois, blacks wished neither to Africanize America nor to bleach their Negro blood, but simply "to make it possible for a man to be both a Negro and an American." "We want to be Americans, full-fledged Americans, with all the rights of other American citizens," Du Bois insisted.[111] But more was needed. African Americans should fight for equal opportunities and also proudly develop certain aspects of their unique heritage and subculture.

Du Bois further insisted that it was "the duty of the Americans of Negro descent, as a body, to maintain their race identity until this mission of the Negro people is accomplished."[112] In the fullness of time, Du Bois thought that widespread miscegenation was inevitable. Yet Du Bois also thought that the amalgamation of the races in America would be harmful if it occurred before African Americans had developed special qualities that were generally recognized as valuable contributions to the larger society. There was, he wrote, "a very grave problem as to how fast and under what conditions this amalgamation ought to take place."[113] For the foreseeable future Du Bois favored separate racial development and opposed amalgamation because he thought that if blacks amalgamated quickly they would suffer the fate of the blacks of ancient Egypt, who had lost their identity and had been denied credit for contributions to their civilization.

Du Bois was treading on dangerous ground. The argument for preserving races could also be used against blacks. Many whites, in fact, regarded segregation as essential for the conservation of their race. Left to themselves, it seemed, many whites would cross the color line. "This mixing was so common," two African American women have written, "that there was a saying among poor whites. They used to say, 'Takes a little bit of nigger blood to bring out the beauty.'"[114]

Many whites were aghast at this attitude, and concluded that widespread intermarriage could not be prevented unless there was segregation and, in addition, frequent statements about the "inferiority" of black people. "The superiority of [the white] race cannot be preserved without pride of blood and an uncompromising attitude toward the lower races," wrote one of Du Bois's white correspondents. Without white supremacy, the Caucasians of North America "would be swallowed up in a mongrelization on the pattern of Latin America."[115]

Even whites who saw no need to disparage Negroes often favored social separation as a bulwark against racial intermarriage. Thus Charles W. Eliot, the longtime president of Harvard University, wrote that the goals of those working for the advancement of African Americans should be twofold: "first, the social separateness of the negroes as a race, and secondly, the opening to negroes of education of all grades from bottom to top, and the admission to all trades and employment." Eliot then explained the reason for social separation: "on grounds of experience the world over, anthropologists and naturalists are convinced that intermarriages between the negro race and the white race are physiologically and economically inexpedient as a rule, and therefore that the two races had better live side by side in harmony, but without mixing in any way which could promote intermarriages."[116]

In *The Philadelphia Negro,* Du Bois acknowledged that whites had a "duty . . . to guard their civilization against debauchment." But he insisted that to do this it was not necessary to discriminate against black workers, or to sneer, or to be unkind or insulting. "The little decencies of daily intercourse can go on, the courtesies of life be exchanged even across the color line without any danger to the supremacy of the Anglo-Saxon or the social ambition of the Negro." There was little danger of widespread miscegenation, Du Bois said, because "natural pride of race, strong on one side and growing on the other, may be trusted to ward off such mingling as might in this stage of development prove disastrous to both races."[117]

Thus Du Bois's opposition to miscegenation was a useful tactic. By reassuring whites, it improved the chances for ending job discrimination and the insult of legally enforced segregation. However, Du Bois's comments about the conservation of races were not primarily a matter of tactics. Above all, Du Bois had faith in black people. He was confident that, in time, they would make a distinctive contribution to world civilization.

There was an additional consideration. Personally, Du Bois thought the problems of African Americans were caused by white racism and not by any inherent lack of talent. But among educated white people the consensus of his era was that as a race blacks were inherently inferior, especially with respect to intelligence and sexual morality.[118] In Germany, the prominent philosopher Georg W. F. Hegel had maintained that blacks were a primitive, "infantile nation," a "Kindernation."[119] In one of Du Bois's classes at the University of Berlin, Professor Heinrich von Treitschke had declared, "Mulattoes are inferior; they feel themselves inferior."[120] At Harvard, another of Du Bois's professors, Nathaniel Shaler, had warned that free blacks might relapse into barbarism and said that even under the best conditions black people should remain the wards of civilization.[121] Even Du Bois's mentor, Albert Bushnell Hart, had written that the experience of blacks in the North led "rather to negative than to positive conclusions as to their intellectual and moral power."[122]

. Du Bois conceded, "behind the thought lurks the afterthought." What if the others were right? What if "somewhere between men and cattle, God created a *tertium quid,* and called it a Negro,—a clownish, simple creature, at times even lovable within its limitations, but straitly foreordained" for inferiority? It was almost too much even to entertain such questions: "to doubt the worth of his life-work,—to doubt the destiny and capability of the race his soul loved because it was his."[123] Yet there was only one way to down the suspicions. Blacks must remain united until their achievements were sufficient to discredit racism.

By the end of the nineteenth century, Du Bois had emerged as an intellectual as well as a scholar. As the author of two large, well-regarded research monographs, he should have been in line for an appointment at a leading university. But most white universities, like most white employers, never dreamed of hiring any blacks for professional positions. Fortunately for Du Bois, an offer came from Atlanta University, which, like Fisk University, had been established for blacks by the American Missionary Association. Du Bois probably would have chosen Atlanta in any case. But he was miffed not to receive any offers from leading white universities. He knew an insult when he saw it.

From 1898 to 1910 Du Bois was a professor of sociology and history at Atlanta University. At first, he was the only black professor on the faculty but Du Bois said that, as at Fisk, "the relations [among the professors] were very good. There was a complete academic democracy."[124] Because Du Bois was stern in battling racism, and because of his disputes with other black leaders, which will be described in the chapters that follow, many people thought Du Bois must be intransigent and pessimistic in his personal relations. One of Du Bois's friends recalled, however, that when Du Bois was among friends he was a "light-hearted man, . . . abundantly endowed with the gift of laughter."[125] The president of Atlanta University described Du Bois as "the jolliest member of our faculty."[126]

At first Du Bois's relations with the students were strained. Some of the students had known inferior Negro teachers in their high schools and questioned whether any black professor, even a Harvard man, should be entrusted, as one put it, with "our 'higher education.'" Perhaps to compensate, Du Bois had long reading assignments and demanding standards. (Twenty years later, one of the students reminded Du Bois that "we 'talked you over' and decided if lessons were to be slighted it would not be [your class on] Civil Government.") In addition, whenever he was on campus, Du Bois was quite formal. Students remembered him as a fastidious dresser whose wardrobe was not flashy but rather of quality and style; and they remembered that he always carried a walking cane—a habit he had acquired during his student days in Germany. One said Du Bois was unsociable, and others remembered that sometimes he would walk past students without speaking. Only when he played tennis did the students see anything other than "that formal dignity we knew indoors."[127]

Nevertheless, Du Bois taught five or six classes each year, and in time the students took to him. In this respect, Nina was a real helpmate, for she made warm friends at social events. One coed also recalled baby Burghardt as "our baby, how pretty we thought him, how we were drawn to you through interest in his growth."[128] Most importantly, the students recognized that Du Bois knew his subject and that he was a good teacher. Although Du Bois did most of the talking in his classes, his courses were well enrolled. Eventually, the students made him one of the most popular professors at the University. In fact, attendance at the weekly prayer meeting was especially large when it was known that Du Bois was to be the speaker.

Du Bois's smaller seminars were especially popular. These he held at his residence, where he served cookies and a special blend of coffee in Harvard cups. Students reported that these evenings were "perfectly delightful. . . . The atmosphere was different from the classroom [it was more intimate]. We were special and he let us know it." When he was at home, Du Bois usually wore his smoking jacket and was a "charming host . . . thoughtful and entertaining. He told anecdotes and showed that he did understand his students . . . he seemed very relaxed in his apartment, very witty and permissive."[129] On many of these occasions students were offered special cigarettes that Du Bois smoked—cigarettes imported from Cuba, Russia, and Turkey.

On the other hand, Du Bois was a strict disciplinarian who would report students who were caught smoking in places where smoking was prohibited. And when it came to schoolwork Professor Du Bois was a stern taskmaster. On one occasion when a coed feigned illness as an excuse for bad grades, Du Bois assured the girl's mother that "there is nothing the matter with her except she is suffering from a very bad attack of laziness. She is smart and can do good work if she chooses, but she is very irresponsible and cuts class whenever she feels inclined. . . . Your daughter has deceived you concerning her state of health and she has got the idea that the students of Atlanta University do not have to work in order to pass. I am sorry to make this unfavorable report but it is, I am convinced, true."[130]

But Du Bois was a scholar first and foremost, and at Atlanta University he continued the sort of work he had pioneered with *The Philadelphia Negro*. That, indeed, was the main reason for his appointment.[131] Each year about one-half of Du Bois's time was devoted to organizing and publishing the results of a conference on a particular aspect of African American life. In 1899 the focus was on "The Negro in Business," and in other years Du Bois concentrated on black workers, colleges, churches, and families.[132]

The Atlanta monographs were competent rather than outstanding. Their importance lay in the fact that, because no other institution was sponsoring research on African American life at the time, they were the preeminent scholarly studies of the era. As Du Bois noted, "between 1896 and 1920 there was no study of the race problem in America made which did not depend in some degree upon the investigations made at Atlanta University."[133]

The Atlanta monographs, like *The Philadelphia Negro*, pointed to an environmental rather than a racial explanation of social problems. As with *The Philadelphia Negro*, the Atlanta report on the black family distinguished between upper-class African Americans whose marital fidelity was above question and the "more primitive, less civilized" blacks whose "sexual immorality is probably the greatest single plague spot among Negro Americans." Some modern scholars have decried this moralism. Kevin K. Gaines, for example, has criticized Du Bois for emphasizing the class differentiation in moral values, and Robin D. G. Kelley has rejected the idea that there is anything wrong with the moral standards of lower-class blacks.[134]

While Du Bois was a professor at Atlanta University, he also began to write essays for several journals of national circulation: the *Atlantic Monthly*, *Harper's Weekly*, the *Independent*, the *Nation*, and the *Outlook*. In these essays Du Bois developed a distinctive voice. His academic writing had always been clear, but now, in the essays, his prose was also passionate, poetic, and spiritually elevated. Of pluralism, he wrote:

> One ever feels his two-ness,—an American, a Negro; two souls, two thoughts, two unreconciled strivings; two warring ideals in one dark body, whose dogged strength alone keeps it from being torn asunder. The history of the American Negro is the history of this strife.[135]

Then, in 1902, the A. C. McClurg Company of Chicago asked Du Bois if they might publish some of the essays in book form. At first

Du Bois hesitated because, he said, "books of essays almost always fall so flat." Eventually, however, he collected several essays and added a chapter on Booker T. Washington. As Du Bois told the story, it sounded easy; but, as David Levering Lewis has noted, before Du Bois allowed the essays to be republished, "they were cut, polished, and mounted with a jeweler's precision."[136]

The result was a classic of American literature, *The Souls of Black Folk* (1903). According to James Weldon Johnson, the leading black literary critic of the era, that volume "had a greater effect upon and within the Negro race in America than any other single book published in this country since *Uncle Tom's Cabin*."[137] It did so because Du Bois had mastered both substance and style. As a student, Du Bois had known that he had something to say. Now, with *The Souls of Black Folk*, Du Bois was using the English language to make a lasting impression.

With the essays in journals of large circulation, and especially with *The Souls of Black Folk*, Du Bois was no longer just a prominent African American scholar. By 1903, Du Bois was the second most influential black man in the United States. But, as we shall see in the next chapter, he was on a collision course with the nation's most influential African American, Booker T. Washington.

Two
Du Bois and Booker T. Washington

Up from Slavery

To understand a person, one must know something of the times in which that person lived. Booker T. Washington was born in 1856 and died in 1915.

Washington was born a slave and became free at the end of the Civil War. He passed his teenage years during the Reconstruction era, when blacks emphasized education, voting, and politics as the keys to improving their position. Washington celebrated his twenty-first birthday in 1877, the year Reconstruction officially ended and southern whites gained full control of their state governments. When Washington was an adult, southern whites closed some of the schools that had been established in the black South during the era of Reconstruction; they also manipulated poll taxes, literacy tests, and primary elections to disfranchise most black voters. In addition, in *Plessy v. Ferguson* (1896) the U.S. Supreme Court held that formal, legal segregation was constitutional as long as the separate facilities for blacks were theoretically equal to those provided for whites. The challenge for Booker T. Washington was to devise a strategy that would help blacks survive and even prosper during hard times.

Although Washington eventually became the nation's most prominent black leader, he never forgot that his life began as a slave in Franklin County, Virginia. With his mother, Jane, and brother, John, Washington lived in a small cabin that had no windows but "large cracks . . . [that] caused us to suffer with cold in the winter." He did not wear shoes until he was eight years old, and his only clothing was a single shirt made of flax so rough and coarse that it seemed like a hundred pinpoints pricking his skin. Although his mother was a plantation cook, Washington never sat down at a table to eat with his family. Instead, he and his brother ate their meals in haste, snatching what they could from the kitchen fire.[1]

Washington had no schooling when he was a slave, but he remembered that he sometimes went "as far as the schoolhouse door with one of my young mistresses to carry her books. The picture of several dozen boys and girls in a schoolroom engaged in study made a deep impression upon me, and I had the feeling that to get into a schoolhouse and study in this way would be about the same as getting into paradise."[2]

Washington knew almost nothing of his ancestry. He praised his mother for her good common sense and for having high ambitions for her children, but he knew little of her origins—of where she came from or who her parents were. He never met his grandmother and had no knowledge of uncles, aunts, or cousins. Later, Washington sometimes imagined himself as W. E. B. Du Bois was in fact, as the possessor of a distinguished ancestry that could be traced back through several generations. Washington recognized that it would be a spur to achievement, and of great help in resisting temptation, if his own children recognized that failure would reflect badly on their entire family. He therefore "resolved that because I had no ancestry myself I would leave a record of which my children would be proud, and which might encourage them to still higher effort."[3]

Of his father, Washington knew nothing. He did not even know his name. Gossip had it that he was a white man who lived on one of the nearby plantations but, whoever he was, Washington "never heard of his taking the least interest in me or providing in any way for my rearing." Yet Washington expressed no resentment of his father. "I do not find especial fault with him," Washington wrote. "He was simply another unfortunate victim of the institution which the Nation unhappily had engrafted upon it at that time."[4]

Despite the hardship that slavery entailed, Washington did not regard enslavement as an unmitigated evil. Slavery was morally wrong, to be sure. It was established for selfish reasons. Yet in some ways slavery in the United States had been a school that left American blacks "in a stronger and more hopeful condition, materially, intellectually, morally and religiously, than is true of an equal number of black people in any other portion of the globe."[5] Sometimes Providence worked in mysterious ways.

After emancipation, Washington moved with his mother and brother to Malden, West Virginia, where his stepfather, Washington Ferguson, found a job working at a salt furnace. Although Washington was only ten years old, his stepfather put him to work packing salt barrels with the crystals that remained after water from a salt spring had been boiled. Washington's workday usually began before dawn and continued until dark. Later, the stepfather made Washington take a higher-paying job as a coal miner—a job that Washington detested because of the dirt, the darkness, and the danger. Almost as distasteful were the living conditions. The family's new house was no better than the one they had left on the old plantation, Washington recalled; and many of the neighbors were ignorant and degraded people who engaged in "drinking, gambling, quarrels, fights, and shockingly immoral practices."[6]

Washington resented his stepfather for making him work and live in these conditions, and the disaffection increased when the stepfather decided that the family was too poor to allow Booker to attend the local elementary school. Instead, Booker had to trudge to the salt-packing shed, where he saw other children walking back and forth to school. He obtained a copy of Webster's "blue-back speller" and tried to learn how to read on his own. Finally, after much pleading, the stepfather allowed Booker to attend school if he would agree to work at the salt furnace for five hours each morning and for two more hours after school.

Washington's larger education began when he was about twelve years old and found work as a houseboy for Lewis Ruffner and his wife, Viola. After retiring from Civil War service as a major general in the U.S. Army, Ruffner had devoted himself to a family-owned salt furnace and coal mine as well as a thousand acres of farmland. Viola, his young second wife, was in charge of their large house in Malden and had such a reputation for strictness in household management that, at first, Washington trembled whenever he saw her. Before long, however, Booker Washington came to understand Viola Ruffner. He learned that "first of all, she wanted everything kept clean about her, that she wanted things done promptly, [and that] nothing must be sloven or slipshod; every door, every fence, must be kept in repair."[7]

Before long a bond of affection developed between young Washington and his white mistress. In later years Washington wrote that the lessons that he learned from Viola Ruffner were "as valuable to me as any education I have ever gotten anywhere since."[8] At the Ruffners' house Washington learned about the importance of manners and style as well as cleanliness and punctuality. Observing the

Ruffners kindled an ambition to escape from the lower standards, hard labor, and poor pay of the salt packers and coal miners.

Viola Ruffner also encouraged Booker Washington to get an education, giving him hours off to attend school in the middle of the day and providing books that young Washington read at night, "burning dear old Mrs. Ruffner's oil."[9] Then, after he learned how to read, write, and do basic arithmetic, Washington resolved to attend a secondary school for African Americans, the Hampton Normal and Agricultural Institute in Virginia, although he had no idea where Hampton was or how he was going to get there.

The distance from Malden to Hampton was about five hundred miles, and Washington did not have enough money to pay for transportation. Yet by walking and begging rides in wagons, he made his way across Virginia. When he reached Richmond, still eighty-two miles distant from Hampton, Washington had no money and could afford neither food nor lodging. After walking the streets for hours, he noticed a portion of the street where the board sidewalk was above the ground. When it was quite dark and he was sure that no passersby could see him, Washington "crept under the sidewalk and lay for the night upon the ground, with my satchel of clothing for a pillow. Nearly all night I could hear the tramp of feet over my head."[10]

When Washington awakened the next morning, he discovered that he was near the city dock and that a large boat was unloading a shipment of pig iron. He went at once to the vessel and got a job as a stevedore. His work so pleased the captain that Washington continued to work for a few more days, all the while saving money by sleeping under the board sidewalk. Finally Washington arrived at Hampton Institute on October 5, 1872, shortly after the school year had begun. Although he needed a haircut and had gone a month without a bath, he was admitted to the school and given a job as a janitor. Most of the seventy-dollar annual tuition was paid by a general scholarship provided by a benefactor from Massachusetts, S. Griffitts Morgan.

Hampton Institute had been established in 1868 with funds from the American Missionary Association and from individuals in New England and New York. Yet from the outset the school was shaped by the distinctive personality, character, and leadership of its founding principal, Samuel Chapman Armstrong. After graduating from Williams College, Armstrong had distinguished himself for skill and valor at the Battle of Gettysburg and later served as an army officer with the Ninth U.S. Colored Troops. There he developed a sympathetic concern for the black soldiers he commanded. He was promoted to the rank of brigadier general when he was discharged, and after the war he served with the Freedmen's Bureau in Virginia.

At Hampton, Armstrong established a distinctive system of industrial education. Students were taught the standard subjects of the high school curriculum, but they were also expected to work at a trade for a few hours each day, and there was an additional hour of daily military drill. From 5:00 in the morning until 9:30 at night, the ringing of a bell told students when to get up, go to classes, go to meals, go to work, and go to bed. In addition, students were expected to conform to the canons of Victorian morality. Attendance at chapel was compulsory, relations between the sexes were closely supervised, and janitors and matrons were authorized to inspect the students' rooms at any time of the day or night.

Armstrong established this regimen because he was a devout Christian who believed that character and moral virtue were more important than either intellectual education or training for a trade. He also thought that slavery (and perhaps the Negro's own nature as well) created some special problems. Slavery had encouraged laziness and given free rein to sensuality, he said, adding that the Negro was "a child of the tropics, and the differentiation of races goes deeper than the skin."[11] "The north," Armstrong said, "generally thinks that the great thing is to free the negro from his former owners; the real thing is to save him from himself."[12]

The implications of the Hampton curriculum are still the subject of debate. Critics have said that vocational training was not intended to uplift blacks to the point where they could compete for professional positions, or even for the best technical jobs, but rather to train them for effective service in the humbler walks of life. Behind the emphasis on vocational training for blacks, the critics say, lay the belief that blacks were incapable of higher learning and should instead be trained as useful workers.[13]

This was not the intent of many of those who gave money to Hampton, and probably not of General Armstrong, either. As Louis R. Harlan has noted, "Armstrong would not discourage a bright young dark man from higher education and higher aspirations." Nevertheless, some white southerners regarded the Hampton curriculum as a way to keep blacks in what was called their "place" and to supply a pool of useful servants. "Since the South would not accept any other kind of Negro education," Henry Allen Bullock has written, "especially education aimed at developing the race for general participation in Southern society, [Armstrong and other educators] struck a compromise with the South and settled for a special kind of education that would prepare Negroes for the caste position prescribed for them by white Southerners."[14]

Other writers have been more favorable to Armstrong and to industrial education. They have noted that during the twenty-five years when Armstrong was the principal, Hampton was essentially a normal school preparing teachers for work in the black South. The emphasis on teacher training was supplemented with a work program that enabled some students to support themselves and made it easier for the school to raise and save money, but prior to the 1890s Hampton was primarily concerned with general education. Moreover, given the widespread belief that blacks should be kept in subordinate roles, it may be that some emphasis on vocational training was needed to prevent the total eradication of black schools. If schools for blacks had not been made to appear as nonthreatening as possible, there would have been fewer schools.[15]

Whatever the intent and implications of industrial education, Booker T. Washington thrived at Hampton. In Armstrong, the mulatto boy found the father he never knew, and he worked diligently to win the general's approval. By 1875, when Washington had completed a three-year course that qualified him to be an elementary teacher, he was one of the honor students who spoke at the commencement. Four years later he was invited to return to Hampton as a teacher. Then, when Hampton admitted some one hundred Indian students from the West, General Armstrong chose Washington to preside over their acculturation and to be the house father at the Indian dormitory (the "Wigwam"). Armstrong also chose Washington to head the night school at Hampton.

For his part, Washington regarded Armstrong as "a great man— the noblest, rarest human being that it has ever been my privilege to meet."[16] At Hampton, Washington said, General Armstrong developed a system of education that taught students that "all forms of labor were honorable and all forms of idleness a disgrace." According to Washington, industrial education was finely attuned to the requirements of "a race that had little necessity to labor in its native land before coming to America, and after coming to this country was forced to labor for two hundred and fifty years under circumstances that were not calculated to make the race fond of hard work."[17] Later, when Washington was offered the opportunity to set up his own school in Tuskegee, Alabama, he chose Hampton as the model.

Immediately after graduating from Hampton, Washington returned to Malden for three years to teach in the public elementary school. Washington later remembered these years as some of the happiest of his life, and certainly they were among the busiest. In addition to teaching during the day, he established a night school, gave private lessons, organized a debating society, and introduced the Hampton practices of morning inspection and military drill. He also fell in love with one of his students, Fanny Smith, but marriage had to be postponed for a while because teaching in the colored public schools of West Virginia was not so much a career as a way to eke out a living. If Washington was to support Fanny and to do more for his race, he would have to find another career.

Since the church was a key institution in most black communities, and since Washington had been a Sunday school teacher in Malden, it probably was inevitable that the ambitious young man would consider a career as a clergyman. With that in mind, Washington attended the Wayland (Baptist) Seminary in Washington, D.C., for most (or perhaps all) of the 1878–1879 academic year. There he met some strong men and women, but on the whole Washington considered the education at Wayland far inferior to that at Hampton. He wrote that the seminarians knew much about Latin and Greek but little about the actual lives of working-class blacks. Indeed, the very experience of the seminary students, living for several years in comfortable surroundings and observing and envying the social life of urban aristocrats of color, seemed to distance the seminarians from the masses of blacks. The seminary students wore stylish clothes but seemed more concerned with a life of ease than with taking up work for the black race. According to Washington, their goal was to succeed one-by-one, "a rather selfish kind of success—individual success at the cost" of neglecting the black masses.[18] In addition, the location of the seminary in the nation's capital fostered a dependence on government rather than self-reliance.[19] In less than a year, Washington decided that he was not cut out to be a minister. Ever after, he remained suspicious of the clergy, of cities, and of the government's ability to uplift his race.

In 1877, Washington worked for three months as a spokesman for interests that wanted to move the capital of West Virginia from Wheeling to Charleston (which was only a few miles from Malden). The successful campaign boosted Washington's confidence that he had a special talent for public speaking and for influencing people. This led him to consider a career as a lawyer, and after Washington left the seminary he read law under the direction of a white lawyer named Romeo Freer. Yet Washington was never truly committed to a career in law. When General Armstrong invited Washington to go back to Hampton as a teacher in 1879, Washington returned to his alma mater.

In May 1881, while Washington was teaching at Hampton, three Alabama state commissioners asked General Armstrong to recommend someone to head a normal school that was to be established for Negroes in the small town of Tuskegee. "The only man I can suggest," Armstrong answered, "is one Mr. Booker Washington, a graduate of this institution, a very competent capable mulatto . . . the best man we ever had here." The commissioners had expected Armstrong to recommend a white man, but they replied, "Booker T. Washington will suit us. Send him at once."[20] In that fashion, Washington embarked on his career as principal of the Tuskegee Normal and Industrial Institute.

Before opening the new school in July 1881, Washington sought to understand the background and home conditions of his students. To this end, he spent a month touring the surrounding countryside, and what he saw was deeply troubling. Although Washington had grown up in difficult conditions in Virginia and West Virginia, he was shocked by what he saw of life in rural Alabama. He expected poverty but was surprised to find conditions that were truly primitive. On some farms the children and even adolescents went naked, while the entire family slept in one room. Yet, although much of the black population was in dire straits, there were surprising inconsistencies. One family had purchased a rosewood piano on installments but had only one fork in the kitchen. On another farm, Washington observed "a young man . . . sitting down in a one-room cabin, with grease on his clothing, filth all around him, and weeds in the yard and garden, engaged in studying a French grammar."[21]

After his tour, Washington was all the more committed to the sort of education that General Armstrong had established at Hampton. "To take the children of such people as I had been among for a month, and each day give them a few hours of mere book learning, I felt would be almost a waste of time." Instead, Washington proposed to supplement the standard courses with trades and farming, with compulsory chapel, daily inspections, and military drill. Washington knew that most of his students eventually would become teachers, but he wanted to educate them "to return to the plantation districts and show the people there how to put new energy and new ideas into farming, as well as into the intellectual and moral and religious life of the people."[22]

At first, Washington was the only teacher, and classes were held in a shanty next to the A.M.E. church in Tuskegee. The building was so dilapidated that whenever it rained one of the older students would hold an umbrella over Washington while he continued to teach. Subsequently, a stable and henhouse were used as recitation rooms. "Washington later had a large fund of henhouse stories, too many for the taste of some."[23]

However difficult the early years at Tuskegee, Washington's progress was unmistakable. Before long he had made friends with the leading white businessmen of Tuskegee and for only two hundred dollars had purchased a farm for a campus just outside of town. Additional teachers had to be employed when, within a year, enrollment increased from about thirty-seven students to eighty-eight. New buildings were erected, some with bricks made by students in the school's own kiln. Enrollment steadily increased to about fifteen hundred students in 1915, and, thanks to contributions from Andrew Carnegie, George Eastman, and other wealthy philanthropists, Tuskegee became one of the best-endowed schools in the country. Meanwhile, to Washington's delight, his hometown sweetheart, Fanny Smith, graduated from Hampton, and she married Washington in 1882. A daughter was born one year later.

Yet the course of Washington's life did not proceed easily. In 1884 Fanny died from internal injuries after falling from a farm wagon. A year later Washington married Olivia Davidson, a New England–educated teacher and fund-raiser who had been instrumental in launching Tuskegee Institute. Olivia bore two sons, but in 1889 her life was cut short by anemia and tuberculosis. In 1892, Washington took a third wife, Margaret Murray, a Fisk University graduate who had been a teacher and the Lady Principal at Tuskegee.

It was no easy task for Margaret Murray to succeed the sweetheart (Fanny) and the helpmate (Olivia), and Washington's principal biographer has suggested that this third marriage was not an ideal love match.[24] Yet "Maggie"—as the new Mrs. Washington was known to her friends—turned out to be just what Washington prescribed. Washington told students that education should fit them for the work that was available and help them adjust to the times in which they lived. It seemed appropriate, then, that Maggie Washington was well suited to the requirements of the situation. She was a good wife for the thirty-five-year-old widower. "She provided the well-ordered household lacking for several years, gave a mother's care to the children, provided abundant hospitality to the constant stream of black and white visitors to Tuskegee, and, with an energy that matched Booker Washington's own, continued as head of one of the principal departments of the school."[25]

Booker Washington insisted that black students should make the best of the circumstances in which they found themselves. In the past, he said, much valuable time had been lost because many students had not been educated with the idea of training them to do the work that was available in the South. To avoid repeating this mistake, Washington emphasized practical training at Tuskegee. He proposed to educate black youths in fields where there was strong demand. Most of Tuskegee's graduates would become teachers. In addition, for the young men, there was a farm, a printing office, a blacksmith's shop, and a brickyard; for the women, sewing, laundry, and home economics.

Critics have said that Washington was preparing black people for efficient service in subordinate positions. Washington insisted, however, that his goal was *not* to have blacks continue on the same level on which they had worked during the era of slavery. He said that African Americans should prepare for higher stations. "But the surest way for the Negro to reach the highest positions is to prepare himself to fill well at the present time the basic occupations. This will give him a foundation upon which to stand while securing what is called the more exalted positions."[26]

For Washington, success in the world of work was a prerequisite for racial progress. If a black man succeeded in business or farming,

Washington wrote, he would eventually win the respect of his neighbors. He told of a Tuskegee graduate who, thanks to his knowledge of soil chemistry and improved agricultural methods, had produced 266 bushels of sweet potatoes per acre in a county where the average production had been only 49 bushels. That man, Washington wrote, won the respect of his white neighbors because he had contributed something to the wealth and comfort of his community. Similarly, he said, whenever a Tuskegee-trained brickmaker went into a community and made a contribution by plying his trade, "pleasant relations between the races have been stimulated."[27]

Washington said there were two keys to racial progress. One was developing skills that were useful to the larger community. As Washington saw it, "No man who continues to add something to the material, intellectual, and social well-being of the place in which he lives is long left without proper reward."[28] "Almost without exception," Washington wrote, "whether in the North or in the South, wherever I have seen a Negro who was succeeding in business . . . that man was treated with respect by the people of both races."[29] There was something in human nature that made people recognize and reward merit, "no matter under what color of skin merit is found." "No race that has anything to contribute to the markets of the world is long in any degree ostracized."[30]

The second key to progress was interracial harmony. Washington said that during the era of Reconstruction, African Americans had placed too much emphasis on voting and politics. "We made a mistake at the beginning of our freedom. . . . Politics and the holding of office were too largely emphasized, almost to the exclusion of every other interest."[31] It was a mistake to elect freedmen to public offices, since whites understandably resented being governed by former slaves, many of whom were illiterate and ignorant. It would have been better "if some plan could have been put in operation which would have made the possession of a certain amount of education or property, or both, a test for the exercise of the franchise."[32] Washington insisted, however, that any tests for voting should be applied honestly to both whites and blacks. He also asked for more funding for education, pleading "that in the degree that you close the ballot box against the ignorant you will open the school-house door."[33]

Instead of fostering self-reliance, Washington wrote, Reconstruction caused blacks to depend upon the federal government, "very much as a child looks to its mother."[34] He also said that the black vote had been used to elect white politicians who had their own self-ish and partisan agendas, and sometimes to empower northern whites who had gone to the South after the Civil War with revenge on their minds. In the end, though, blacks suffered most from the in-crease in racial and sectional tensions.

Washington thought black people eventually would enjoy full political rights in the South. But progress in this direction would not begin until the white South got over the Reconstruction-born feeling that it was being forced to do something it did not want to do.

Because he thought that no movement for the elevation of south-ern blacks could succeed without the support of southern whites, Washington tried to reconcile the races. In his own personal life, he had learned that it was hard to win the support of people that one criticized—that making friends was "more often accomplished by giving credit for all the praiseworthy actions performed than by call-ing attention alone to all the evil done."[35] Consequently, Washington pointed to examples of interracial cooperation and focused on the progress that blacks were making, the improvements in education and land ownership, the establishment of black-owned businesses, and a decline in illegitimacy. Only occasionally did he mention an-other side of the story—the increases in segregation, disfranchise-ment, and lynching.

Washington explained his social philosophy in speeches given throughout the country and in articles that had a mass circulation in journals like the *Atlantic Monthly* and the *Independent*. Most famous-ly, he summed up his views in a widely publicized speech at the open-ing of an exposition (or trade fair) in Atlanta in September 1895. The speech was especially memorable because of a striking story and an unforgettable metaphor.

At the outset of his Atlanta address, Washington told of a ship that had been lost at sea for several days when it sighted another craft. When the distressed ship signaled that its crew was dying of thirst, the other vessel signaled back, "Cast down your bucket where you are." The lost ship then signaled a second time, "Water, water; send us water!" and was answered: "Cast down your bucket where you are." After a third and fourth signal were answered the same way, the captain of the distressed ship did as he was told, cast down his buck-et, and it came up full of fresh water that was fit for drinking. It turned out that the ship, although well off the coast of South America, was within the two-hundred-mile-wide mouth of the Amazon River.

The story was a parable. Washington counseled blacks to reject any dream of returning to Africa, and he advised against moving to the North as well. Instead, he urged them to cast down their buckets where they were in the South, to cultivate friendly relations with white people, and to make the best of their situation by developing skills in agriculture and business. Washington also pleaded with white industrialists not to rely on immigration to supply a workforce for their factories. It was not necessary to recruit workers in foreign lands when America itself contained a large pool of black workers. He urged the industrialists to cast down their buckets among the Negro people—a people who would "stand by you with a devotion that no foreigner can approach."[36]

Then Washington made a dramatic gesture. Holding up his fist, he said that "in all things essential to mutual progress," blacks and whites should be "one as the hand." But, opening his palm to the assembly, Washington also insisted that "in all things that are purely social we can be as separate as the fingers."[37]

In essence, Washington accepted separation. He said that "the wisest among my race understand that the agitation of questions of social equality is the extremest folly." He decried "artificial forcing," and he reiterated that "no race that has anything to contribute to the markets of the world is long in any degree ostracized." Washington said that "the opportunity to earn a dollar in a factory just now is worth infinitely more than the opportunity to spend a dollar in the opera house."[38]

Washington's Atlanta address was a triumph. According to one press report, "the whole audience was on its feet in a delirium of applause" when Washington "held his dusky hand high above his head, with the fingers stretched wide apart, and said to the white people of the South on behalf of his race: 'In all things that are purely social we can be as separate as the fingers, yet one as the hand in all things essential to social progress.'"[39] At the close of the speech, the white governor of Georgia, Rufus B. Bullock, rushed across the stage to congratulate Washington, while other whites shook his hand and said, "Good bless you" and "I am with you."[40]

The black response to the speech was more varied. Washington acknowledged that some African Americans felt that he had not spoken out strongly enough for the "rights" of his race.[41] However, several prominent Negroes also congratulated Washington. Edward Wilmot Blyden, one of the pioneers of Pan-Africanism, found "delight" and "inspiration" in the speech. And in a personal note to Washington, W. E. B. Du Bois characterized the Atlanta address as "a word fitly spoken." When Washington said that blacks and whites could be as separate as the fingers socially and yet united as one hand, Du Bois "rather agreed with him. I thought that was a good general statement." Du Bois even wrote to the *New York Age* suggesting that "here might be the basis of a real settlement between whites and blacks in the South, if the South opened to the Negroes the doors of economic opportunity and the Negroes co-operated with the white South in political sympathy."[42]

Most important of all, from the standpoint of the history of American race relations, the Atlanta Exposition address catapulted Washington into national prominence as a black leader. Washington doubtless benefited from good timing. The death of Frederick Douglass only a few months earlier had left a vacuum in the leadership of the black race in America. But Washington owed his ascendancy primarily to the artful way in which he shaped rhetoric to meet the requirements of his time. In the long term, Washington sought full equality for his race, but he effectively masked the ultimate implication of his social philosophy. He did so by criticizing Reconstruction, by discounting the importance of politics and mass voting, and by emphasizing the importance of interracial cooperation, trade training, and practical self-help.[43]

Even before his Atlanta Exposition address, Washington had enjoyed considerable success in raising funds from northern businessmen and philanthropists. The buildings on the Tuskegee campus were testimony to this. One had been named for Andrew Carnegie, another for Collis P. Huntington, and a third for John D. Rockefeller. In 1899, William H. Baldwin helped Tuskegee Institute obtain twenty-five thousand acres of farm and timberland, and four years later Andrew Carnegie gave the school a stupendous grant of six hundred thousand dollars.[44]

In 1901, Washington's status as the nation's preeminent black leader was confirmed when President Theodore Roosevelt invited Washington to be his guest for dinner at the White House. Yet Washington's dinner with President Roosevelt eventually turned out badly for both men. Since Washington was well regarded in the white South, Roosevelt had not expected the dinner to cause political problems. However, several southern newspapers took strong exception, on the grounds that such dining was at odds with southern mores and inconsistent with the belief that the races should be "separate as the fingers . . . in all things that are purely social." The editors expressed the fear that social mixing in the dining room might lead eventually to interracial marriages and miscegenation.[45]

In addition to concern about the long-term ramifications of social mixing, southerners also objected to the political implications of the dinner. They correctly understood the dinner to signify that President Roosevelt would consult with Washington before appointing people—whites as well as blacks—to federal offices in the South.

Many blacks further understood that Washington would now decide which blacks were appointed to federal offices in the North as well as the South. They understood the dinner to signify that henceforth Washington's role in politics would be similar to the part he already played in the realm of philanthropy (where men of wealth seldom contributed to a black institution without first asking for Washington's advice). Washington doubtless savored the influence, but he should have considered the matter more carefully, because the distribution of patronage and philanthropy led to strife and contention. When Washington dispensed jobs and gifts, he had to choose among many worthy institutions and ambitious candidates. Predictably, those who were rejected came to resent Washington and to question his views. As one of his correspondents noted, Washington was put "into the untenable position of being the political clearing house for the colored race, a position no one can fill in the long run with success, or without causing the most intense hostility on the part of your colored fellow citizens."[46]

To be sure, Booker Washington had a following among northern blacks who recognized that Reconstruction had ended and that it was necessary to try something else. Many blacks were willing to give Washington's approach a try, at least until it proved itself to be ineffective as a method for uplifting the race. But the mantle of Washington's leadership was bestowed upon him largely by whites. He was never a leader who inspired hope, passion, or intense devotion in a large following. He offered jobs and grants and practical advice rather than glad tidings. As his correspondent had warned, when Washington started dispensing philanthropy and political patronage to some blacks but not to others, it was inevitable that those who had been passed over would challenge Washington's leadership and social philosophy.

The Road to Niagara and the National Association for the Advancement of Colored People

W. E. B. Du Bois eventually became the most influential critic of Booker T. Washington. Since both men were educators, it is not surprising that some of their differences touched on educational philosophy. Du Bois stressed the importance of a college-educated Talented Tenth, while Washington emphasized vocational training for the black masses. Without well-educated black leaders, Du Bois said, African Americans would have to depend on whites for guidance, and Du Bois thought no race should depend on outsiders for its own leaders. Washington, on the other hand, sometimes disparaged the importance of higher education and said that skill in business, farming, or the trades was the best foundation for progress in the future.

Du Bois agreed with Washington's emphasis on personal responsibility and self-help, but he was put off by Washington's tendency to minimize racial grievances and to emphasize the weaknesses and mistakes of black people. Instead, Du Bois favored a more open and forceful protest against racial injustice. By 1905, he had abandoned his previous support for nondiscriminatory literacy and property tests and demanded the unqualified right to vote. Without full manhood suffrage, Du Bois said, blacks could not protect their right to work and to lift themselves up from poverty. In addition, Du Bois thought that the silence of black people in the face of racial insult and oppression was too high a price to pay for conciliating white people. Judging from the historical experience after the end of Reconstruction, Du Bois thought that silence had emboldened whites to proceed with disfranchisement and segregation. Du Bois also feared that black submission in the face of white injustice demeaned African Americans and led to a sense of helplessness and to a loss of the pride, initiative, and self-reliance that Booker T. Washington himself had called for.

Du Bois acknowledged that his and Washington's theories of racial progress were not absolutely contradictory. "I recognized the importance of the Negro gaining a foothold in trades and his encouragement in industry and common labor. Mr. Washington was not absolutely opposed to college training, and sent his own children to college."[47] In some of his comments, however, Washington had intimated that he disliked Negro colleges. And his emphasis on the mistakes and shortcomings of blacks suggested that Negroes themselves were responsible for their status.

The dispensing of patronage at Tuskegee Institute was another bone of contention. Because of Washington's influence with government officials and private philanthropists, Washington had the power to reward some blacks and to punish others. He used this power to promote conformity among black leaders and to stifle those who did not subscribe to his own approach to race relations. "I was greatly disturbed at this time," Du Bois recalled, "not because I was in absolute opposition to the things that Mr. Washington was advocating, but because I was strongly in favor of more open agitation against wrongs and above all I resented [the way Tuskegee used its influence to suppress] even mild and reasonable opposition to Mr. Washington."[48]

Principled opposition to what Du Bois called the "Tuskegee Machine" eventually led to a civil war among black leaders. Yet, at first, Du Bois did not take part in this combat. Instead, Du Bois initially sought Washington's support. This gives rise to a suspicion that Du Bois's later move to opposition was influenced not only by principle but also by the fact that Washington slighted Du Bois personally and professionally.

From 1897 to 1910, while he was a professor at Atlanta University, Du Bois proceeded with his plan to use sociological and historical research to uplift African Americans. His annual reports on black life were well received, with the philosopher William James describing one of the studies as "splendid scientific work" and the economist Frank W. Taussig judging that "No better work is being done in the country, and no better opportunity is afforded for financial support on the part of those who wish to further the understanding of the negro problem." Nevertheless, no large foundation grant ever materialized, and Du Bois had to soldier on with an annual budget of about two thousand dollars.[49]

Because the philanthropists of the time favored Booker T. Washington, Du Bois recognized that the great research center he envisioned was more likely to become a reality if he moved to Tuskegee

Institute. And Washington knew that criticism of his leadership could be nipped in the bud if the nation's foremost African American scholar was affiliated with Washington's school. Each man had good reasons for maintaining cordial relations with the other.

Yet the friendship between Du Bois and Washington was not simply a matter of convenience. Du Bois appreciated the insight with which Washington intuitively understood the spirit of the age. He admired the way Washington had mastered the speech and thought of the nation's business leaders. Du Bois knew that some blacks were suspicious of Washington for being on good terms with southern whites. But Du Bois also knew that while Washington was publicly conciliating the white South, he challenged some sorts of racial injustice.[50]

In 1899, Washington and Du Bois had cooperated in working against the Hardwick disfranchisement bill in Georgia, which provided for a white primary and racially discriminatory "grandfather" and "understanding" clauses. Later, after an instance in which Du Bois was denied a railroad berth because of his race, Washington secretly assisted Du Bois in a contemplated lawsuit and in a protest to Robert Todd Lincoln, the president of the railroad and the son of Abraham Lincoln. Du Bois probably also knew what later scholarship has demonstrated, that Washington asked philanthropists for money to fight voting discrimination in other states and that he engineered lawsuits to test the constitutionality of peonage, the exclusion of blacks from jury panels, and Jim Crow railroad facilities.[51]

Thus Du Bois knew that Washington had reason to say that while he sought the approval of the white South, he also "at the proper time and in the proper manner, . . . call[ed] attention . . . to the wrongs which any part of the South has been guilty of." To critics who found fault with Washington for being too cautious, Washington explained that timing was crucial. Washington said "the world would pay no attention to my words" if he criticized all the injustices that occurred along the color line—but that "whenever . . . the proper time has come for utterance upon any subject concerning my race I have never hesitated to give that utterance."[52]

When the National Afro-American Council met in Chicago in 1899, Du Bois defended Washington against criticism from what Du Bois called "hot headed members of his own race, who accomplished no great thing . . . and who have neither the capacity nor force to ac-

complish anything."[53] At this conference, Du Bois endorsed a resolution that supported Washington and said that he personally would
be "very sorry if it went out into the world that this convention had
said anything detrimental to one of the greatest men of our race."[54]

Because Du Bois and Washington had much in common, and because Du Bois's affiliation with Washington's school might lead to
generous foundation support for Du Bois's research program, Du Bois
seriously considered moving to Tuskegee Institute. Twice in 1897 Albert Bushnell Hart asked Washington to find a place for Du Bois on
the Tuskegee faculty, and finally, in 1899, Washington made an attractive offer. If Du Bois would come to Tuskegee and teach one class
a year, Washington promised that the rest of Du Bois's time would be
left free for research and whatever writing and speaking Du Bois
wished to do.[55]

Washington courted Du Bois assiduously. He gave Du Bois a tour
of Tuskegee's red-brick campus, which was far more impressive than
the campus at Atlanta University. Thirteen new buildings had been
erected between 1895 and 1900, buildings that bore the names of
wealthy northern benefactors. Washington also offered Du Bois a
comfortable house and a salary that was 14 percent more than Du
Bois was earning at Atlanta. One of Tuskegee's wealthy benefactors
also entertained Du Bois at an estate where Du Bois found himself
"looking through a great plate glass window with two butlers at my
back." "Oh," Du Bois recalled, "every courtesy and kindness was paid
to me."[56]

Yet Du Bois finally decided against going to Tuskegee. He recognized that Tuskegee had more money than Atlanta, but the insistence
that Du Bois ought to go to Tuskegee made Du Bois suspicious. It reminded him that however much he understood Washington, there
was an essential difference between schools like Hampton and
Tuskegee, schools that emphasized vocational training, and colleges
like Fisk and Atlanta, with their emphasis on higher education. Du
Bois sensed that he would be out of place at Tuskegee, that his research program would be at odds with the Tuskegee idea. He wondered if Washington would continue to fund sociological research
when Washington no longer felt the challenge of the chase.[57]

In addition, because of segregation, Du Bois was weary of the
South. He refused to ride on Atlanta's segregated street cars, prefer-
ring instead to walk or to take a cab. Because of segregation, he nev-

er attended the theaters or the opera house. His world was on the university campus, and as his fame spread he would occasionally receive visitors from the North and from abroad. Yet these visitors, if they were white, would stay at hotels where Du Bois was not allowed to set foot. "In Atlanta, they would observe a caste system as rigid as if a Brahmin had laid out the city. And to acquire wisdom they went up the hill to see this colored 'untouchable.'"[58]

Moreover, Nina Du Bois was a midwesterner who never adjusted to the requirements of life in the Deep South. Like her husband, she refused to use segregated public transportation and instead walked the two miles for shopping in downtown Atlanta. But she resented every step of the trek. "Nothing in provincial Iowa or backward Wilberforce had prepared her for the stinging apartheid in the capital of the so-called New South."[59]

In May 1899, baby Burghardt Du Bois died of diphtheria when he was only two years old. In a moving tribute, Du Bois recalled how he loved Nina, the "girl-mother," who, with her baby, "unfold[ed] like the glory of the morning—the transfigured woman." And he recalled how, after Burghardt's death, Nina was "the world's most piteous thing—a childless mother." Fifty years later, Du Bois remembered that with the death of Burghardt, "in a sense my wife died too." After the passing of her first-born, Nina was "never . . . quite the same in her attitude toward life and the world. . . . Even when our little girl came two years later, she could not altogether replace the One."[60]

The Du Boises sent Burghardt's body North for burial in Great Barrington—a decision that one of Du Bois's perceptive students correctly understood as evidence that the couple did not "feel at home among [their] adopted friends."[61] Nina, especially, wanted to leave the South. For her, Tuskegee—despite what its financial resources might do for her husband's research program—was not a satisfactory alternative to Atlanta, and she knew how to appeal to Du Bois's self-respect. Nina planted the suspicion that at Tuskegee, Du Bois would "sink to the level of a ghostwriter.'" "Oh," she said, "all they want you at Tuskegee for is to write Mr. Washington's speeches."[62]

With that, Du Bois decided to look for work in the North, but that made it all the more important that he not alienate Booker T. Washington. Thus before declining the offer from Tuskegee, Du Bois told Washington that he might do more for "both your cause & the general cause of the Negro" if Du Bois was stationed in the national capital.[63] He explained that a position in one of the nation's leading cities would make it easier for Du Bois to write and to influence public policy.

In 1900, a position was available in the District of Columbia, where George Cook was retiring after more than thirty years as the superintendent of Washington's black schools. Du Bois wanted that job and recognized that Washington's support "would go further probably than anyone's else." "Could you conscientiously give it?" Du Bois asked. "If . . . you could endorse me I shall appreciate it."[64]

Washington endorsed Du Bois, but after doing so learned that his own supporters in the District of Columbia favored the appointment of Robert H. Terrell, a Harvard graduate who was the principal of the highly regarded M Street High School (later known as Dunbar High School). Washington had no idea that the matter would become so important to his supporters. In an attempt to extricate himself from the situation, Washington asked Du Bois *not* to use the letter of recommendation that Washington had written. Washington tried to sugarcoat the pill, saying that he had already "recommended [Du Bois] as strongly as I could" in a personal conversation with a member of the board of education, and that Du Bois would seem unreasonably persistent if he personally presented a letter from Washington.[65]

Washington did not mean to rebuff Du Bois. He probably did not know about Du Bois's domestic situation, and the offer of a faculty appointment at Tuskegee was still open to Du Bois. Nevertheless, Du Bois wanted that job in the North. When the D.C. board of education instead chose a pleasant but undistinguished man (Winfield Montgomery), Du Bois must have been discouraged. Du Bois knew that Washington had the power to make or destroy careers, and he must have resented the fact that he had lost out to a patronage operation. Du Bois sensed, too, that he and Washington had clashing temperaments. During one of his meetings with Washington, Du Bois had been quick and fast-speaking, while Washington seemed wary and unresponsive. At the end of the meeting, Du Bois realized that he had done "practically all the talking" while "Mr. Washington had said about as near nothing as was possible."[66]

Still, because of Washington's influence with President Roosevelt and with organized white philanthropy, Du Bois did not want to alienate Washington. The aborted negotiations over the jobs at

Tuskegee and in Washington had caused some tensions, but Du Bois was careful to maintain friendly relations with Washington. In 1901 he accepted Washington's invitation to go camping and fishing in West Virginia,[67] and in 1903, four months after Du Bois published *The Souls of Black Folk,* which contained a celebrated but measured critique of Washington's leadership, Du Bois dined with Washington at Washington's estate, The Oaks, and taught students in the summer session at Tuskegee Institute.

While Du Bois was socializing with Washington and teaching at Tuskegee's summer school, several well-educated blacks in Boston had been taking strong exception to Washington's leadership. The leader of this opposition was William Monroe Trotter, and Trotter, as it happened, was not personally vexed by any loss of patronage or preferment. On the contrary, Trotter had been doing well financially until, out of heartfelt conviction, he took up the cudgels against Washington. Then he became almost obsessed with discrediting Washington, neglected his business interests, and eventually wound up living in genteel poverty.

Trotter was born in 1872 and was the first black student to be elected to Phi Beta Kappa at Harvard College. After graduating, Trotter became an insurance agent and mortgage negotiator, working with whites and only occasionally dabbling in racial matters. Within a few years, Trotter had prospered to the point where he owned several properties. At age twenty-seven, he married Geraldine ("Deenie") Pindell—one of the light-skinned mulattoes Du Bois had known when he was at Harvard in the 1890s but whom he considered too white for a wife. The young couple settled into a handsome house in Boston where Trotter could look out "from the sitting room window over all the county as far as Blue Hill and from my bed-room window over all the bay down to . . . Deer Island."[68]

Yet Trotter sensed that something was wrong. "[P]ursuit of business, money, civic or literary position was like building a house upon the sands, if race prejudice and persecution and public discrimination for mere color was to spread up from the South."[69] Trotter thought Booker T. Washington should protest forcefully against racial injustice. He was not at all satisfied when Washington explained that he had "kept silent because I wanted to wait until I knew the white people of the South were in that frame of mind where they were willing to listen to what I had to say."[70]

No such caution constrained many blacks in Boston. In 1899, the mere mention of Washington's name at a meeting of colored men elicited hissing, and in 1901 Trotter and a friend, George W. Forbes, began to publish a weekly newspaper, the *Guardian*. The general themes of the paper were that Washington's policy had failed and that a policy of aggressive protest should be tried. More particularly, the *Guardian* insisted:

1) That Washington should protest against poll taxes and literacy tests. Washington said that he accepted these disfranchising provisions only if they were applied equally to blacks and whites, but Trotter sensed that the provisions would never be enforced equally—that the very purpose of the provisions was to stop African Americans from voting.

2) That Washington was wrong to apologize for the moral shortcomings of black people and for the mistakes they supposedly made during the era of Reconstruction.

3) That vocational education, although theoretically useful for many people of all races, was suspect when it came to African Americans, because "the idea lying back of it was the relegating of a race to serfdom."[71]

4) That Washington, when he distributed patronage and philanthropy, was driven by "his lust for power, his desire to be a czar"; that he was using "clandestine methods . . . to crush out all who will not bow to him"; that he aspired to "rule the race with an iron hand."[72]

The *Guardian's* tone was as important as its message. And the tone was personal, scurrilous, even vicious. When it came to biting invective Trotter had few equals. In 1902, the *Guardian* jubilantly reported that Washington's daughter Portia had flunked out of Wellesley College. On another occasion, the *Guardian* described Washington as a man whose "features were harsh in the extreme," with "vast leonine jaws," "mastiff-like rows of teeth," "an enormous nose and mouth," and "eyes [that] were dull and absolutely characterless."[73]

The *Guardian's* invective alienated some readers who sympathized with the newspaper's policies but took exception to the vitriol. The African American novelist Charles W. Chesnutt complimented the newspaper for its "uncompromising stand on all questions pertaining to the rights of the Negro" but also said that he could not "see [his] way to adopt the extreme position" of the *Guardian*.[74] Chesnutt told Trotter that the "impulsive disposition to make the matter a personal one" had "injure[d] your own influence." Similarly, Du Bois said there was a "vast difference between criticizing Mr. Washington's policy and attacking him personally."[75]

Ironically, Du Bois was teaching summer-session classes at Tuskegee when Trotter's campaign to discredit Washington came to a head. After learning that Washington had accepted an invitation to speak at a church in Boston on July 30, 1903, Trotter prepared nine truculent questions, including, for example: "Don't you know you would help the race more by exposing the new form of slavery just outside the gates of Tuskegee than by preaching submission?"[76] Then Trotter packed the audience of some two thousand with as many anti-Washington people as he could rally.

When Washington's name was mentioned at the meeting, there were hisses from the audience; and when Washington spoke, Trotter stood on a chair and read his questions while the crowd disintegrated into confusion and fistfights. The police were called to restore order, and Trotter, his sister Maud, and two other supporters were arrested for disturbing the peace. The next morning, the *Boston Globe* gave a full account of what it called the "Boston Riot." Amidst the scuffling, one man had been cut with a knife, another's coat was torn, and a policeman was jabbed in the side with a woman's hatpin. Throughout the country, the white press covered the story, with the *New York Times* reflecting the prevailing opinion when it called the melee "a most disgraceful and lamentable episode."[77]

The Boston Riot was basically a brawl and, superficially, Washington was the victor. After the scuffle, Washington finished his speech while Trotter, as Washington described the scene to a friend, "was taken out of the church in handcuffs, yelling like a baby."[78] Yet the press coverage of the incident damaged Washington, for it forced whites to recognize that many well-educated African Americans did not accept Booker T. Washington as their leader. Whites also learned that some black newspapers blamed Washington for the riot, saying that Washington's "political dictatorship and methods" were "at the bottom of the whole affair," that Washington and his friends were "trimmers and apologists" for racial injustice, that however much wealthy whites supported Washington, "they can never ram him down the throats of the Afro-Americans as their new Moses."[79]

Washington made the situation worse by overreacting to the

provocation. Instead of dismissing the incident as a small matter, he allowed his friends to press charges against Trotter, who in due course was found guilty of disturbing the peace and sentenced to thirty days in jail. Many blacks regarded the punishment as too severe, but Trotter rather enjoyed the confinement, for he continued to edit the *Guardian* from his cell in the Charles Street Jail and could now describe himself as one of the early martyrs "in the cause for redemption from Booker Washington."[80]

Du Bois arrived in Boston while Trotter was in jail. During the early summer, Du Bois had been teaching at Tuskegee Institute, while Nina and their baby daughter, Yolande, had escaped the heat of Tuskegee to live in Boston as the houseguests of Du Bois's old Harvard friend, Deenie Pindell. By then, however, Deenie Pindell was Mrs. Monroe Trotter.

The Boston Riot had occurred while Du Bois was aboard a steamship traveling to meet Nina and Yolande. Du Bois had known nothing of Trotter's plans and learned of the riot only when he read the accounts in the newspapers. The situation epitomized Du Bois's ambivalence. In addition to the ideological dichotomy of pluralism— "an American, a Negro, two unreconciled strivings in one dark body"—Du Bois found his sympathies suspended between his recent employer, Washington, and his wife's hosts, the Trotters.

This ambivalence was also reflected in Du Bois's book *The Souls of Black Folk*, which had been published a few months earlier. On the one hand, the book contained a persuasive critique of Washington's approach to race relations. And yet it was also a balanced assessment that gave Washington a good measure of credit. Du Bois acknowledged that Washington was a "distinguished Southerner" and "the one recognized spokesman of his ten million fellows." He said that "so far as Mr. Washington preaches Thrift, Patience, and Industrial Training for the masses, we must hold up his hands and strive with him." But Du Bois also said that "Washington's counsels of submission overlooked certain elements of true manhood" and that "his educational programme was unnecessarily narrow." Du Bois called for "the right to vote" and "the education of youth according to ability," and he insisted that "the way to truth and right lies in straightforward honesty, not in indiscriminate flattery."[81]

Even after the Boston Riot, Du Bois maintained a balanced viewpoint. He condemned Trotter for "lack of judgment" in disrupting

Washington's speech, but he also admired Trotter's "unselfishness, pureness of heart and indomitable energy even when misguided."[82] Trotter then published a statement in which Du Bois expressed admiration for Trotter's "single hearted earnestness & devotion to a great cause."[83] This, in turn, led Washington to conclude mistakenly "that Dr. Du Bois is very largely behind the mean and underhanded attacks that have been made upon me . . ."[84]

Washington retaliated. Du Bois was given to understand that because of his support for Trotter, there would be no philanthropic support for his research work at Atlanta University. Nor was this all. Du Bois also learned that he "had become *persona non grata* to powerful interests, and that Atlanta University would not be able to get support for its general work or for its study of the Negro problem so long as I remained at the institution."[85] In 1910 Washington told the editor of the *Atlanta Constitution* that it was "too bad that an institution like Atlanta University has permitted Dr. Du Bois to go on from year to year stirring up racial strife in the heart of the South."[86]

Washington also cracked down on other critics. In Boston, Washington's wealthy backers tried to drive Trotter's *Guardian* into bankruptcy by funding rival black newspapers. In New Haven, a Yale student, William Pickens, was aided in suing the *Guardian* for libel. And in Georgia, the trustees of Atlanta University were pressured to rebuke George W. Towns, a black professor at the university, for supporting Trotter and for making intemperate and discourteous statements about Washington.[87]

Washington's overreaction to the Boston Riot—his retaliation against Du Bois and others—was the final nudge that caused Du Bois to oppose Washington openly. A few years later, Kelly Miller, a professor at Howard University, offered a conspiracy theory to explain the development. "Conscious of his own lack of attractive personality and felicity of utterance," Miller wrote, " . . . Trotter began to cast about for a man of showy faculties who could stand before the people as leader of his cause." Trotter "wove a subtle net . . . and gradually weaned [Du Bois] away from his erstwhile friendship for Mr. Washington, so as to exploit his prominence and splendid powers in behalf of the hostile forces."[88]

This theory is interesting but probably gives Trotter too much credit. In the twentieth century, the leaders of the civil rights movement (and of many other causes) learned that they would benefit if their opponents could be provoked into responding with excessive reprisals. But there is no evidence that Trotter counted on Booker T. Washington to overreact.

In any case, while Du Bois condemned Trotter's disruptive action, he also thought it was wrong for Washington to retaliate "to the extent of actual imprisonment" and outrageous "to treat as a crime that which was at worst mistaken judgment."[89] Moreover, because Du Bois personally had begun to feel the force of the Tuskegee Machine, it was no longer possible for Du Bois to occupy middle ground and get along simultaneously with both Washington and the *Guardian*.[90]

By 1905 black leaders were divided into two camps, and the breach became official when Du Bois and fifty-eight other black men called for a meeting to organize in opposition to Washington. Originally the meeting was scheduled for a hotel in Buffalo, New York, but Du Bois changed the site to the Canadian side of Niagara Falls after he encountered discrimination at the American hotel. The Niagara Movement was born on July 10, 1905, when twenty-eight blacks gathered at the Erie Beach Hotel.[91]

The Niagara Movement emphasized protest above all else— protest against racial insult, against the denial of civil rights, and against discrimination in the world of work. "Of [our] grievances we do not hesitate to complain, and to complain loudly and insistently. To ignore, overlook, or apologize for these wrongs is to prove ourselves unworthy of freedom. Persistent manly agitation is the way to liberty, and toward this goal the Niagara Movement has started and asks the cooperation of all men of all races."[92]

True to Du Bois's pluralism, the Niagara Movement also promoted support for black businesses and colleges. As Leroy Davis has noted, the movement worked to build institutions within the black community. Thus it did not insist on integration or even desegregation but instead called for more government support for black schools. In early-twentieth-century America, building black institutions signified more than an accommodation to segregation; it was a form of racial self-assertion.[93]

Most of all, the Niagara Movement opposed Booker T. Washington's compromising, conciliatory style of leadership. "I bow to no Boss" was one of the movement's published slogans, and the point was reiterated in Du Bois's private correspondence. In one letter Du Bois insisted that he would "no longer wear Mr. Washington's livery or put on his collar," and in a handwritten comment added to the bottom of a letter he received from his Harvard mentor, Albert Bushnell Hart, Du Bois wrote that Washington had "done the race infinite harm & I'm working against [him] with all my might."[94]

By 1905 Du Bois had come to think that criticism of Washington involved more than opposition to one man and his patronage machine. "It was opposition to a system and that system was part of the economic development of the United States at that time."[95] As Du Bois saw it, after Reconstruction the economic growth of the United States was based on a corrupt bargain. The magnates of industry and commerce in the North recognized that sectional reconciliation with the states of the former Confederacy was a prerequisite for doing profitable business in the South; and since the dominant elements in the South insisted on racial segregation and white supremacy, the men of business needed a black leader like Booker Washington.

According to Du Bois, schools like Tuskegee and Hampton were training teachers who were going throughout the South telling blacks not to repeat the mistakes of the era of Reconstruction—to stay out of politics and to prepare themselves for efficient work in subordinate jobs. In one of its official resolutions, the Niagara Movement condemned efforts "to educate black boys and girls simply as servants or underlings,"[96] and in a speech at Hampton Du Bois candidly said it was educational heresy to train blacks "not with reference to what we can be, but with sole reference to what somebody wants us to be."[97] "Every energy is being used to put black men back into slavery," Du Bois wrote, "and Mr. Washington is leading the way backward."[98]

Once Washington was exalted, the magnates of business meant to keep him ascendant—and to squelch any black leaders who challenged the racial and sectional compromises that undergirded the American economy. In one letter Du Bois wrote, "Mr. W. is today [the] chief instrument in the hands of a N.Y. clique who are seeking to syndicate the Negro & settle the problem on the trust basis." In *Dusk of Dawn,* he explained that the Tuskegee Machine was not just the creation of black folk at Tuskegee. It was also encouraged and received financial support from northern capitalists who regarded race relations as a matter of business.[99]

Because so much seemed to be at stake, there was enormous hostility between Washington's Tuskegee Machine and Du Bois's Talented Tenth. James Weldon Johnson noted that it was "hard to imagine the bitterness of the antagonism between these two wings." Kelly Miller described the feud as "war to the knife, and knife to the hilt."[100]

Washington's private correspondence supports these assessments. In one letter, the New York editor T. Thomas Fortune assured Washington that he was ready to squash the critics—that, as Fortune put it, he was "out for scamps . . . with blood in my eyes and a chip on both shoulders." Charles W. Anderson, another of Washington's supporters in New York, described the opposition as "young upstarts" who deserved "a good thrashing." Wilford H. Smith, a lawyer for Washington, similarly noted that "Trotter and Forbes must be muzzled and at once," and Washington's personal secretary, Emmett J. Scott, observed that "the dirty gang needs to be thoroughly repressed."[101]

Washington himself vacillated in assessing the critics. On one occasion he acknowledged that, because African Americans were "smarting under wrongs and injustices inflicted from many quarters, it is but natural that they should look about for some individual on whom to lay the blame for their seeming misfortunes, and in this case I seem to be the one."[102]

Most of the time, however, Washington refused to concede anything to his critics. It was a great mistake, he wrote, to assume "that those connected with the Niagara Movement are honest."[103] Rather, the critics felt "jealousy over what they consider my success." That envy was compounded because most of the critics had graduated from some of the best universities in the country—and had done nothing else. Washington said that the critics, "in most cases, have not had to work their way up from the bottom through natural and gradual processes. Their growth has been artificial rather than natural. They have not paid the price for what they have gotten."[104] Emmett Scott made the point succinctly: "[The critics'] program is insincere, and petty spite against one individual of the race actuates them."[105]

Because they questioned the motives of their critics, Washington and his followers did whatever they could to put down the opposition. A man named Melvin Chisum was employed as a spy, with instructions to work his way into and report on the inner circle of Trotter's friends in Boston. Another spy, Clifford Plummer, was sent to

Buffalo to report on the first meeting of the Niagara Movement. Plummer, however, did not realize that Du Bois had moved the conference
to Canada and mistakenly informed Washington that no one came
except Du Bois. With greater effect, Plummer later persuaded the Associated Press not to circulate an account of the meeting.[106]

The espionage enabled Washington to identify his friends and
opponents—and to follow up with appropriate rewards and punish-
ments. An appointment as Assistant U.S. Attorney helped Washington to peel William H. Lewis away from his previous support for Trotter, and James Weldon Johnson was kept away from the opposition
(for a while) with an appointment as U.S. Consul in Venezuela and
Nicaragua.[107]

Washington also revved up the Tuskegee Machine to combat his
opponents. On learning that L. M. Hershaw, an Atlanta University
graduate who held a clerical position in the Department of Interior,
had attended the Niagara conference, one of Washington's confidants
advised Washington "to make an effort to have that man Hershaw removed."[108] It turned out that Hershaw was protected by civil service
regulations, but another Niagara man, a twenty-seven-year-old journalist named J. Max Barber, was not so fortunate. The Tuskegee Machine not only cracked down on Barber's magazine, *Voice of the Negro,* but also, after the magazine failed, got Barber removed from his
position as a teacher in a vocational school. Barber then left public
life, worked his way through dental school, and established a practice in Philadelphia.[109]

Because of Washington's influence and willingness to engage in
reprisals against the Niagara Movement, many potential members refused to join the organization. One young man, David Wallace, "resign[ed] from membership . . . for the reason that I am about to begin work." Wallace praised "those who dare speak and act" but felt
that he could not afford "to be associated with [Niagara] openly." "You
shall have a secret comrade in me," Wallace wrote to Du Bois. "My
private prayers shall go up for you who dare, and when opportunity
affords, I shall be a secret subscriber to our common cause."[110]

Despite the opposition of the Tuskegee Machine, for a while the
Niagara Movement did well. By the end of 1905, there were 150
members, and in 1906 a second conference was held at Storer College in Harpers Ferry, West Virginia. With a flair for drama, Du Bois
organized a barefoot, silent procession from the college dormitories

to the arsenal where John Brown had made his famous raid of 1859. Later in the day, Du Bois eulogized Brown and the conferees sang "The Battle Hymn of the Republic." Then, with ringing rhetoric, the Reverend Revardy Ransom summarized the significance of the Niagara Movement:

> Today, two classes of Negroes . . . are standing at the parting of the ways. The one counsels patient submission to our present humiliations and degradations; it deprecates political action and preaches the doctrine of industrial development and the acquisition of property. . . . The other class believes that it should not submit to being humiliated, degraded, and remanded to an inferior place. It believes in money and property, but it does not believe in bartering its manhood for the sake of gain.[111]

Yet within a few years the Niagara Movement foundered. Part of the reason was the opposition from Tuskegee, and in this regard Washington's master stroke was using his influence to prevent the establishment of a well-edited journal of opinion. For some time Du Bois had thought that blacks needed a first-rate journal that would uplift African Americans while also educating influential whites. To establish such a journal, Du Bois needed money, and one well-to-do benefactor, Jacob Schiff, expressed interest in the project. Before proceeding, however, Schiff asked permission to discuss Du Bois's proposal with men "whose opinion in such a matter I consider of much value."[112] That almost certainly meant consultation with Tuskegee and, not surprisingly, in the end Schiff decided against funding Du Bois's project. Du Bois's appeals to other potential benefactors also came to naught.[113]

Thus the Niagara Movement was denied its voice. Du Bois and two partners invested about three thousand dollars in a printing plant and did the best they could with a journal called the *Moon*. Yet the circulation was small, and by the end of 1906 the *Moon* was bankrupt. Another Niagara journal, the *Horizon*, also proved to be underfunded and short-lived. To add to Du Bois's discomfort, in 1906 the Tuskegee Machine again used its influence to prevent Du Bois's appointment to a government position in the District of Columbia, and in 1909 Washington prevented Du Bois's appointment to the faculty at Howard University.[114]

The Niagara Movement also suffered from internal weaknesses

and fissures. From the outset there were problems with Du Bois's style of leadership. One observer took exception to the traces of New England in Du Bois's accent, complaining that Du Bois pronounced *Niagara* as "Neeagara," and saying that Du Bois, although "a bright, intellectual fellow," did not possess "any of the elements of leadership." Another noted that Du Bois's formal and reserved manner, his inability "to unbend in his relations with people outside [a] small circle," gave rise to the suspicion that Du Bois was "cold, stiff, [and] supercilious." This was cause for concern even among Du Bois's adherents. The Cleveland journalist Harry Smith asked Trotter why Du Bois couldn't "'warm up' to the fellows," and Du Bois himself recognized the problem. "I was not what Americans called a 'good fellow.'" "I was no natural leader of men. I could not slap people on the back and make friends of strangers. I could not easily break down an inherited reserve."[115]

If Du Bois was taciturn and withdrawn, Trotter was mercurial and, at times, obstinate. One of Trotter's principles was that, to avoid compromising themselves, race leaders should not seek or hold public office. This put Trotter into conflict with Clement Morgan when Morgan, another black member of the Niagara Movement, sought a seat in the state legislature. In 1908, the quarrel evolved into a bitter dispute for control of the Massachusetts branch of the Niagara Movement, and when Du Bois supported Morgan, Trotter quit the movement. "How happy [Booker] Washington must be over this," one of Du Bois's correspondents wrote. "I can see him rubbing his hands with glee, and calling on the good work to go on."[116]

Money was another problem. Many members fell behind in their dues, and in 1905–1906 the Niagara Movement raised only thirteen hundred dollars. One of Washington's confidants called the men of Niagara "a lot of 'unmoneyed' patriots,"[117] and Washington did his best to keep it that way. He knew that the Niagara Movement, however annoying it might be, could not rival Tuskegee as long as it lacked money.

For Tuskegee, the danger was that wealthy whites might supply Du Bois and the Niagara Movement with the funds that one of Washington's correspondents called "the necessary implements of war." When the Niagara Movement began in 1905, the most likely white backers were Andrew B. Humphrey and John E. Milholland, two New York entrepreneurs and civil rights activists. However, because most of Milholland's income came from manufacturing pneumatic message cylinders for the Post Office, Washington was confident that he could use his political connections to exercise leverage. "I know the principal sources from which they get their money," Washington wrote in one letter, "and can come pretty near closing up these sources at any time." For the nonce, it seemed sufficient "to let men like Humphrey and Milholland understand that if they are to take up such scoundrels as Trotter and Du Bois that we can have nothing to do with them."[118]

By 1908, the Niagara Movement was moribund. Washington even wrote an obituary of the movement for publication in the *New York Age*.[119] Additional meetings took place in 1909, but the movement was expiring—a casualty of determined opposition from Tuskegee, internal wrangling, and insufficient funds. Yet the Niagara Movement showed that the spirit of protest persisted in black America even during the age of Booker T. Washington. Moreover, the movement allowed protest-minded civil rights leaders to assemble, to know one another, and to plan for the future.

These personal connections were exemplified in Du Bois's relations with his closest black friend, John Hope. Hope was born in the same year as Du Bois, 1868, also graduated from an Ivy League college (Brown), and joined the faculty of Atlanta Baptist (later Morehouse) College in 1898. By chance, Hope had been present for Booker Washington's Atlanta Exposition address, and he became an early critic of Washington's views. In November 1895, Hope gave a speech in which he said, "I regard it as cowardly and dishonest for any of our colored men to tell white people or colored people that we are not struggling for equality." Five months later Hope anticipated Du Bois's concept of the Talented Tenth when he said that "we ourselves will never be possessed of conscious self-respect until we can point to men in our own ranks who are easily the equal of any race."[120] Hope was one of those who signed the original call for the Niagara Movement.

After he became president of Atlanta Baptist–Morehouse College in 1906, Hope toned down his rhetoric. While continuing as a member of the Niagara Movement, Hope became more active with the YMCA and the Commission on Interracial Cooperation. He also mended his fences with Booker T. Washington, and in time the two men and their families exchanged visits and enjoyed the rivalry between their schools' football teams. With assistance from Washington (and from Washington's successor at Tuskegee, Robert R. Moton), Hope eventually persuaded Andrew Carnegie and the Rockefeller General Education Board to give generously to Atlanta Baptist–Morehouse.

As the president of a black college, Hope could no longer speak like a militant. Nevertheless, he always regarded himself as a Niagara man, and he was deeply troubled when friends, even in jest, chided him for being too conciliatory toward whites or too close to Booker T. Washington. Hope understood that he was being "roasted" with "perfectly pleasant joking," and yet it was "unpleasant to be charged with apostasy even in joke."[121]

"What would Du Bois think?" Hope asked himself. Du Bois was "the one man to whom I thought I might owe an explanation. Why to Du Bois? Because I have followed him; believed in him; tried where he was not understood to interpret and show that he is right; because I have been loyal to him and his propaganda—not blatantly so, but, I think, really loyal; and because, in spite of appearances, I am truly as ever a disciple of the teachings of Du Bois regarding the Negro problem."[122]

Hope acknowledged that the needs of his college made him think carefully about public statements and try to get along with wealthy whites and with Tuskegee. Yet Hope could not bear to be estranged from Du Bois, and so in 1910 he asked Du Bois "whether you have me in your heart—not on your calling list or your mailing list but in your heart[?]" Hope put the question "as a strong man would ask his chieftain." Whatever the answer, Hope concluded, "I shall be loyal to my chieftain still."[123]

For Du Bois, Hope's letter stimulated "greater feelings than I dare express." Du Bois understood that Hope had to weigh the interests of his college and said he never doubted Hope's "loyalty to the principles which we both so sincerely believe."[124] Du Bois assured Hope that their friendship would endure—and it did, until Hope's death in 1936.

The relationship between Du Bois and Hope was the special bond of best friends. But the Niagara Movement was also the catalyst for other warm friendships. In retrospect, the significance of these personal connections looms large, for the Niagara Movement was a foundation for the modern civil rights movement. For years to come, Du

Bois would command the support of most of the men in the movement—men like J. Max Barber, L. M. Hershaw, and George A. Towns.

Meanwhile, Du Bois himself had encountered gross examples of
racial discrimination and oppression. Mention has already been
made of Du Bois's being denied a Pullman berth simply because of
his race and of his being unable to set foot in the Atlanta hotels where
his white guests stayed. In addition, on two occasions Du Bois personally came into contact with white mobs. The first instance occurred after a black farmer named Sam Hose was charged with killing
his landlord in a dispute over debts, and then with raping and killing
the landlord's wife. When Hose was captured, he confessed to the first
murder but refused, even after being beaten, to confess to the second
crime. Du Bois wrote an account of the case and was actually walking to the offices of the *Atlanta Constitution* with his story in hand
when he learned that Hose had been lynched and burned at the stake,
and that Hose's knuckles were being displayed at a grocery store on
the very street where Du Bois was walking. The shock of this experience caused Du Bois to question his approach to racial uplift—to
wonder whether detached research and reasoned writing could ever
turn the tide of racial animosity.[125]

The Atlanta Riot of 1906 brought these questions to the fore once
again. Here a variety of groups concocted a witches' brew. Prohibi-
tionists said that black men had a biological craving for whiskey laced
with cocaine, and argued that to protect blacks from degeneracy and
whites from black villains, the manufacture and sale of alcoholic bev-
erages should be criminalized. Meanwhile, advocates of disfranchisement said that denying blacks the vote would purify politics by
reducing the influence of saloons on election day. In addition, moral
reformers censured the interracial debaucheries that supposedly
were commonplace in the saloons and brothels that lined Atlanta's
Decatur Street. Some concerned women also said that black-on-
white rapes were occurring with appalling frequency and challenged
white men to do their duty. "[I]f it takes lynching to protect woman's
dearest possession from drunken, ravening human beasts," declared
Rebecca Felton, who later became a U.S. senator from Georgia, "then
I say lynch a thousand a week if it becomes necessary."[126]

The Atlanta press chimed in with allegations that black men
raped twelve white women during the spring and summer of 1906.
Only half this number of assaults actually occurred,[127] but "many At-

lantans began to believe that a 'torrid wave of black lust and fiendish-ness' placed them 'in a state of siege.'"[128] Politicians then fanned the fears as two white candidates for governor, Hoke Smith and Clark Howell, tried to outbid one another in promising to protect white women from assault.

On September 22, 1906, some ten thousand whites went on a rampage. Twenty-five blacks were killed after being caught in white sections of the city, and the black community reacted by organizing for self-defense. They shot out the electric lights, stationed snipers in darkened windows, and telephoned the governor: "Don't send the police to us, *send the mob.*" The white media minimized Caucasian casualties, although Du Bois wrote that at least a hundred persons died, "most of whom were Negroes, although a very large proportion of both the dead and maimed were white, the exact number on ei-ther side being unknown."[129]

When the Atlanta Riot began, Du Bois was doing research in Lowndes County, Alabama. As soon as he heard about the violence, he caught a train to Georgia and bought a Winchester double-barreled shotgun and two dozen rounds of shells filled with buck-shot. Then he proceeded to Atlanta University to protect Nina and Yolande. "If a white mob had stepped on the campus where I lived I would without hesitation have sprayed their guts over the grass," he recalled.[130]

The image of Du Bois standing guard with a shotgun is symbol-ic. At the end of the twentieth century's first decade, Du Bois was on defense. His research program at Atlanta University was barely sur-viving on a pittance, and he had begun to question his youthful, ide-alistic assumption that solid scholarship would establish a founda-tion for better race relations. In addition, Du Bois had failed in his search for a suitable position outside the South. The Niagara Move-ment was disintegrating, and its journals, the *Moon* and the *Horizon,* were bankrupt. Meanwhile, segregation and disfranchisement were becoming more entrenched with each passing year.

Ironically, another race riot touched off a chain of events that eventually saved Du Bois. In Springfield, Illinois, eight blacks were killed and fifty people injured during two days of mayhem in August 1908. The roots of the conflict were complex and tangled, but there were shades of Atlanta at the outset of the riot. A black man had sup-posedly raped a white woman, and a mob took to the streets after a white woman called out: "What the hell are you fellas afraid of? . . . Women want protection."[131]

The Springfield Riot shocked many whites. Not only did it occur in the North, but in Abraham Lincoln's town. In response, the millionaire writer William English Walling organized a conference in New York to plan for a national, biracial organization of fair-minded whites and well-educated blacks. Several influential whites were involved from the outset, and Du Bois was consulted immediately. This conference led to the establishment of the National Association for the Advancement of Colored People (NAACP) in 1909, with Du Bois as one of the five original incorporators of the new organization. A year later Du Bois moved to New York and became the NAACP's director of research and publications and the editor of a new, nationally circulated journal, the *Crisis*.[132]

In 1906 Booker T. Washington observed that "When [Du Bois] stuck to the business of scientific investigation he was a success." But Washington predicted that Du Bois would be "a failure as an agitator," that he was going to "make a fool of himself."[133] For once, Washington's calculation was wrong. Moving to New York was a great risk for Du Bois. Although his $2,500 salary would be double what he had earned at Atlanta University, it was guaranteed for only one year. Nevertheless, Du Bois had been stymied in Atlanta and understood that there are critical moments when risks should be taken. In his *Autobiography*, Du Bois noted that his "career as a scientist was to be swallowed up in my role as a master of propaganda."[134] In fact, the move to the NAACP was the key turning point in his life. Within a decade, the NAACP would supplant Tuskegee as the capital of black America, and Du Bois would displace Washington as the nation's most influential black leader.

Three
Du Bois and the National Association for the Advancement of Colored People

Du Bois, the Crisis, and Oswald Garrison Villard

Because The National Association for the Advancement of Colored People is a lengthy name, the organization became well-known by its initials. During the first half of the twentieth century the NAACP waged one of the most effective reform campaigns of the era.

At the outset the NAACP was an advocacy and antidefamation society that incorporated a central defense committee to receive gifts and bequests to further its work. The new association had only limited funds and lacked the strength that comes from a large membership, but its founders were clear about their goals. In 1911 in its first annual report, the association sought "to uplift the colored men and women of this country by securing to them the full enjoyment of their rights as citizens, justice in all courts, and equality of opportunity everywhere." The NAACP said democracy was stymied if people were denied benefits solely on the grounds of race or color. The "underlying thought," Du Bois wrote, was that "any discrimination based solely on race is fundamentally wrong."[1] The goal was "equal rights and opportunities for all," and the organization was so committed to the principle of nondiscrimination that it maintained that governments should not even keep statistics about the race of citizens.[2]

In waging war against racial discrimination, the NAACP deployed several weapons. Agitation and publicity were used to describe the injustice of discrimination and to expose the contradiction between America's principles and its mores. Carefully planned lawsuits challenged the constitutionality of discrimination, and voters were organized to encourage officials to treat blacks fairly. In addition, the leaders of the NAACP recognized that the aims of the association could never be realized by only criticizing white people. It would also be necessary to awaken blacks to a sense of their rights. Regardless of what might be done *for* blacks, another important part of the work had to be done by blacks themselves.[3]

Du Bois's main job from 1910 to 1934 was editing the *Crisis,* the monthly magazine of the NAACP, and as an editor, he enjoyed spectacular success. In November 1910 the first issue of one thousand copies sold out completely. The circulation then went up like a rocket: by 1912, 22,500 copies were being sold; by the end of 1917, 50,000; and at the end of the First World War, 100,000.[4] To put these figures in perspective, by the turn of the twenty-first century the population of the United States had almost tripled since Du Bois started the *Crisis,* but only one of the nation's three leading journals of opinion had a circulation of more than 100,000.[5]

Du Bois's achievement with the *Crisis* was remarkable. As Du Bois's friend Albert E. Pillsbury reminded him in 1910, "periodicals are as numerous and as pestilential nowadays as flies were in Egypt, and most of them meet with the same reception."[6] Du Bois knew this for a fact, since two of his own magazines had previously gone bankrupt. In the process Du Bois had learned something about editing. And now, with the NAACP, he also had the support of a few white philanthropists.

Nevertheless, the *Crisis* would not have succeeded as it did if it had been simply a journal of record—the sort of magazine that many organizations sponsor to catalog their activities. A few pages of each *Crisis* provided such information, but the magazine was a journal of opinion—mostly Du Bois's opinions, conveyed with his flair, style, and personality. As Du Bois noted, the *Crisis* was "a personal organ . . . the expression of myself." Had it been otherwise, the magazine would not have enjoyed great popularity. "It would have been the dry kind of organ that so many societies support for purposes of reference and not for reading."[7]

In the annals of leadership, Du Bois is unusual because he rose by dint of editing a magazine. It was the dynamic force of his editorials and articles for the *Crisis* that catapulted Du Bois to the fore as a leader of the civil rights movement. He did not have the friendliness of approach or the adaptability that usually are prerequisites for leadership; but he wrote eloquently, surpassed others in knowledge of American race relations, and impressed his personality upon others by means of the written word.

After 1910, reading the *Crisis* became de rigueur for members of the Talented Tenth. Just as the *New Republic* gave a sense of purpose and common identity to liberal reformers during the years of Franklin D. Roosevelt's New Deal, while the *National Review* served the same purpose for conservatives in the days of Barry Goldwater and Ronald Reagan, the *Crisis* inspired the fledgling civil rights movement. Marie Brown, the daughter of a black clergyman and later the wife of the sociologist E. Franklin Frazier, recalled that she grew up reading the *Crisis*, which "was just like a Bible to me." The writer and literary critic J. Saunders Redding recalled that his father, a postal worker in Delaware, read *Crisis* editorials to his children when the children were too young to understand. He also remembered the ritual in his boyhood home. When the *Crisis* arrived in the mail, it was placed on the table next to his father's reading chair, and there it was to remain untouched until father had finished with it. "We could child-handle the *Pathfinder,* the *Literary Digest,* and the *National Geographic* without fear of reprimand, [but] the *Crisis* was strictly inviolate until my father himself had unwrapped and read it—often . . . aloud. Afterwards it was turned over to us."[8]

Yet for all the success, Du Bois and the *Crisis* were also sources of controversy within the NAACP. William English Walling, the millionaire journalist who started the NAACP, had persuaded Du Bois to leave Atlanta by assuring Du Bois that the "whole effort and hope" of the organization was "built almost exclusively on obtaining you as our director of investigations."[9] But in 1910 Walling became involved in a scandalous breach-of-promise lawsuit in which he was sued for $100,000 for making false promises of marriage. He resigned as chairman of the NAACP's board of directors when the case went to trial.[10] Meanwhile, Du Bois never got along well with Oswald Garrison Villard, who succeeded Walling as chairman of the board.

Villard was the grandson of William Lloyd Garrison, the editor of the *Liberator,* the journal that had inspired many abolitionists during the years before the Civil War. Villard was also the owner, publisher, and editor of an influential newspaper, the *New York Evening Post,* and of the *Nation,* a leading journal of opinion, both of which he had inherited from his father, Henry Villard, a wealthy financier and railroad magnate. Given this background, Oswald Garrison Villard recognized the power of the press. Within the NAACP he had favored establishment of the *Crisis.*

Du Bois and Villard both saw the value of protest and agitation.

Earlier in his career, Villard had supported Booker T. Washington. But by the time of the founding of the NAACP, Villard had become quite critical of the principal of Tuskegee Institute. In 1910, Villard wrote directly to Washington, saying that his philosophy was wrong, that he should speak out against racial discrimination, that he was not helping the race by portraying the conditions as favorable. Villard went on to say:

> If my grandfather had . . . dwelt in his speeches on slavery upon certain encouraging features of it, such as the growing anger and unrest of the poor whites, and stated the number of voluntary liberations and number of escapes to Canada, as evidences that the institution was improving, he never would have accomplished what he did, and he would have hurt, not helped, the cause of freedom. It seems to me that the parallel precisely affects your case.[11]

Despite their agreement about Washington (and many other matters), Du Bois and Villard did not get along personally. In fact, tensions between the two antedated the time when they worked together at the NAACP. As early as 1905 there was some unpleasant correspondence between the two men.[12]

Then, in 1909, Villard published an unfairly critical review of Du Bois's biography, *John Brown*. Du Bois had previously told Villard that the biography was "going to be an interpretation, and I am not trying to go very largely to the sources"; that for factual information he would rely primarily on Franklin B. Sanborn's 1885 biography of Brown.[13] Yet when Villard reviewed Du Bois's book for the *Nation*, Villard did not mention Du Bois's interpretations but instead denounced the book for "abound[ing] in inaccuracies"—inaccuracies that were mostly the result of Du Bois's reliance on the earlier biography. Villard said nothing about Du Bois's effort to place Brown in the context of racial egalitarianism and slave resistance, which are two themes that later historians have developed and reinforced. Instead, Villard faulted Du Bois for mistakenly accepting the statement that one of Brown's ancestors had traveled to America on the *Mayflower;* for repeating that one man was a Canadian when he had been born in the United States; and for misstating the number of black people who were killed during Brown's raid on the arsenal at Harpers Ferry. In conclusion, Villard wrote that "a page of the *Nation* would not suffice to record the other slips which make it impossible to accept this volume, readable as it is, as a reliable contribution to American history."[14]

In response, Du Bois noted that it was possible, when reviewing most books, "to pick numberless immaterial flaws in absolute accuracy." But Du Bois considered it "contemptible" for Villard to have "savagely . . . emphasize[d] these so as to give an impression of total falsity." Du Bois said "the very least reparation which can be made and a thing which courtesy among gentlemen has a right to demand is the printing of [a] reply of the attacked party." But the *Nation*, which Villard owned, refused to publish Du Bois's reply, which led Du Bois to conclude that Villard had written an unfair review of the book because Villard himself was about to publish his own biography of John Brown. "When an author about to publish a book . . . give[s] a supposedly rival book an unfair drubbing it certainly does not improve the appearance of his 'intentions.'"[15]

Personal relations between the two men were further strained because Villard, who was strongly opposed to any official or governmental discrimination, himself discriminated when it came to private social life. Du Bois noted that Villard "had married a wife from Georgia, a former slave State, and consequently I could never step foot in his house as a guest, nor could any other of his colored associates."[16] This discrimination annoyed Du Bois, although as a youth Du Bois himself had also discriminated when it came to dating and marriage (but not to other social relations).

Other tensions between the two men stemmed from financial matters. Du Bois's education had been in the liberal arts and social sciences, not in accounting or marketing. He acknowledged that his work at the *Crisis* was "impaired first and last by lack of trained business management." As a professor at Atlanta University and as the editor of two previous magazines, Du Bois had acquired some familiarity with the world of publishing. But his experience paled in comparison with Villard's, and Villard grumbled that the *Crisis* did not have accurate advertising records, did not know "what news dealers are in arrears, what the amount of bad debts are, whether the paper costs are as low as they should be, etc."[17] The situation was aggravated because the *Crisis* had its offices, during its first four years, in the *New York Evening Post* building that Villard owned.

Villard was also accustomed to command. As the chief executive officer at the *New York Evening Post,* he gave orders to scores of employees, and he expected to do likewise as chairman of the NAACP board. Du Bois, however, was used to the independence that is customary for professors. For fifteen years at Wilberforce and Atlanta, Du Bois had been required to teach a few classes each week, but the rest of his time was free for research, writing, and public speaking. As the NAACP's director of research and publications, Du Bois had expected to continue with a variety of activities. Before joining the NAACP, Du Bois had arranged that he would be the only employee of the organization who was also a member of the board of directors. Du Bois had demanded a great measure of freedom and the right to report directly to the board.[18]

In addition to editing the *Crisis,* Du Bois continued to write for other journals. In 1910 *The American Historical Review* published his prescient essay, "Reconstruction and Its Benefits." A year later, *The Sociological Review* published Du Bois's substantial work, "The Economics of Negro Emancipation," and in 1913 "The Negro in Literature and Art" appeared in *Annals of the American Academy of Political and Social Science.* Du Bois also continued to write for the popular press—for the *Independent,* the *New York Times,* the *Boston Globe.* In 1915 the *Atlantic Monthly* published Du Bois's important article on the origins of the First World War, "The African Roots of the War." Du Bois also had an active schedule of public speaking—with seventy-two lectures to 41,000 people in 1913 and forty-five lectures to 70,000 people in 1914.[19]

This outside activity led Villard to question whether the NAACP was getting full value for the salary it paid Du Bois.[20] Villard was also concerned with what today might be called "the chain of command." Du Bois was an employee of the NAACP but, as he stated in one memorandum, "I did not come to this organization as a clerk." He was also a member of the board of directors. He wanted his work for the NAACP to be "perfectly definite and to consist of the editing and managing of *The Crisis.*"[21] Any activities beyond that Du Bois expected to undertake as he saw fit. He let it be known that while he would promote the NAACP in a general way, direct fund-raising was not a job for which he was suited. "It called for a friendliness . . . which I did not have."[22]

To Du Bois, the allocation of his work time was a matter of executive discretion and independence, which he felt he deserved as a prominent African American scholar and writer. But Villard insisted that "the Chairman of the Board of Trustees is *the* executive of the Association and must exercise certain authority over the paid employees of the Board, whether they be editors or clerks." In March 1913 an angry exchange between the two men at a board meeting led Villard to conclude that "[no] further co-operation between us in the work of the association is possible." In April, Villard demanded that his name no longer appear on the masthead as a contributing editor to the *Crisis*. In 1915 Villard threatened to turn his wealthy friends away from the NAACP. "My name has brought in a good deal of money from people who give liberally because of their faith in me, and I cannot be in that position of trust and see *The Crisis* conducted as it is."[23]

In private correspondence, members of the NAACP reacted with alarm. Board member Mary White Ovington noted that "there was a strong desire on the part of some . . . to get rid of [Du Bois]." She explained that "Mr. Villard had always been opposed to [Du Bois] being here. He had not wanted him in the beginning and he had never been convinced that our choice of a Director of Publicity & Research had been wise." May Childs Nerney, the executive secretary of the NAACP from 1912 to 1916, similarly reported that Villard was "determined to dominate everything, particularly *The Crisis*." Nerney was not especially close to Du Bois and acknowledged that Villard had some strong points, saying that Villard was "a magnificent worker and such a fine man." But Nerney also noted that Villard was cursed with an imperious disposition which, she speculated, might have been inherited from William Lloyd Garrison. "Dear me," she wrote, "isn't it a terrible thing to have both a personality and a grandfather?"[24]

Given his desire to dominate the *Crisis*, Villard tried to take advantage of any complaints about the magazine. And because the *Crisis* was a journal of strong opinions, there inevitably were complaints. Professor Kelly Miller complained when Du Bois wrote that in some respects the academic work at Howard University was only "fair."[25] President William Scarborough complained when Du Bois praised some new, state-supported programs at Wilberforce but said nothing about the traditional programs at the school.[26] Monroe Trotter grumbled about the way the *Crisis* downplayed Trotter's work against the segregationist policies of President Woodrow Wilson.[27] And members of the NAACP in Washington were miffed when Du Bois did not publish essays by the president of their branch chapter, Archibald Grimke.[28]

Nor was that all. Black editors were furious when Du Bois wrote that "some of the best of colored papers [were] wretchedly careless in their use of the English language."[29] Black clergymen took offense when Du Bois wrote that the Negro church was "choked with pretentious ill-trained men."[30] And a subscriber from Tacoma, Washington, complained when Du Bois not only refused to publish his letter to the *Crisis* but gratuitously stated that the letter was full of "narrow-minded foolishness."[31]

Occasionally Du Bois was tactless, but the success of the *Crisis* derived from his combination of editorial judgment and straight talk. Du Bois did not become the nation's most influential black writer simply because he was educated at Harvard and Berlin. One observer noted that Du Bois succeeded because he "believed in certain things and he doggedly refused to recede from his position." Another observer—Du Bois's friend John Hope—told Du Bois, "Intellectual honesty and moral courage, not Massachusetts or Germany, account for your getting a hearing from foes as well as friends." Hope expressed the wish that "nothing will ever come to you so tempting as to make you swerve in the least."[32]

Villard tried to use the complaints to oust Du Bois or, failing that, to curb the independence of the editor. He argued that controversy over the *Crisis* was distracting the NAACP from the important work of lawsuits and establishing local branches.[33] On one occasion Villard took particular exception to a *Crisis* cover that he considered unpleasantly suggestive. It showed an attractive black woman in a dress with a neckline that was cut low, but not so low as to reveal any cleavage.[34] When Villard protested, Du Bois gave further offense by simply leaving the room—"without excusing himself . . . a fine attitude for an employee," Villard huffed.[35]

At one point Du Bois wrote a letter of resignation, but the board refused to accept it. William English Walling was no longer chairman but still was a member of the board, and Walling insisted that the NAACP should "make the most sweeping concessions in order to give [Du Bois] free play to exercise all his abilities and energy and enthusiasm." Mary White Ovington agreed. "The rest of us on the Board are able journeymen," she wrote, "doing our day's work to be forgotten tomorrow." But she thought that Du Bois was a tremendous figure. "He is head and shoulders above any other colored man we could find to fill his place, his reputation as a writer grows with every year, and he gives to our little magazine a distinction that we should find the public missed did we once remove it."[36] J. E. Spingarn, another member of the board, also weighed in, taking "the position that there must be at least one publication in the country in which a Negro could say what he wished without any interference whatsoever from any white person."[37]

As a result of the controversy over the *Crisis,* Villard resigned as chairman of the board in 1913. To a friend Villard confided that he could "not . . . be connected with the Association as long as Dr. Du Bois is connected with it."[38] He was convinced that "The National Association will never do its duty to itself until it removes a man of Dr. Du Bois' spirit from all connection with it." Board member Mary White Ovington was "sick at heart" over this development, which she interpreted as "a confession to the world that we [whites] cannot work with colored people unless they are our subordinates."[39]

For Du Bois, Villard's resignation provided welcome security. At the time of Villard's resignation, Du Bois was in his late forties, and it was both unsettling and unseemly for a man of Du Bois's stature to have had to endure years of wrangling and job insecurity with the NAACP. After all, the NAACP's leaders had known who Du Bois was before they hired him. They had known that Du Bois enjoyed considerable independence as a professor, and they should have expected him to insist upon similar freedom and discretion at the NAACP.

Du Bois, J. E. Spingarn, and Mary White Ovington

In 1914 J. E. Spingarn became the chairman of the NAACP's board, a move that must have pleased Du Bois, for Du Bois and Spingarn were personal friends. Joel Spingarn was a prominent and independently wealthy literary scholar who had resigned from the faculty at Columbia University in 1911 after a dispute over academic matters. Spingarn then retired to a large family estate where he became a gentleman farmer and a reformer. He served the NAACP in various capacities from 1911 to 1940, but, unlike Villard, whose family background was Christian, Spingarn was of Jewish ancestry, and his ascendancy at the NAACP coincided with the rise of Jewish philanthropy. By 1920 Julius Rosenwald, Jacob Schiff, and Edwin Seligman were contributing to the NAACP, and Joel Spingarn's brother, Arthur B. Spingarn, handled much of the organization's legal work. Neoabolitionists from New England—people like Mary White Ovington, Charles Edward Russell, and Moorfield Storey—also supported the association, but Jews contributed a significant part of the eleven- to fifteen-thousand-dollar annual income that the NAACP received between 1912 and 1917.[40]

Like Du Bois, Joel Spingarn publicly criticized Booker T. Washington. In fact, Spingarn's rise at the NAACP was facilitated by three speaking tours where he promoted the association to audiences that totaled about seventy thousand people. "I let myself go about Washington tonight," Spingarn reported after one speech in 1914—so much so that an Urban League official in St. Louis "said he would not allow me to speak at [the] St. Louis City Club if I did not promise silence on that subject."[41] Like Du Bois, Spingarn believed in agitation and protest. His faith in pro-black literature, and especially in the *Crisis,* was such that he sent as many as fifty copies of the magazine to influential white southerners.[42]

Yet after he became chairman of the NAACP's board, Spingarn, like Villard, tried to subordinate Du Bois to the work of the association. Spingarn also wanted to organize local branches, and he winced when the *Crisis* published what one of Spingarn's correspondents called "bitter and sarcastic expressions" that alienated people whose support would have been valuable. There should be "no Crisis and no non-Crisis," Spingarn told Du Bois. "Both must be one. You must cooperate with us. . . . The time has come when we must 'hang together or be hanged together.'"[43]

Du Bois, on the other hand, said that his editorial policy was shaped by a larger vision. He knew that most members of the NAACP disagreed with an occasional editorial or phrase or picture. But Du Bois insisted that he was using the *Crisis* to impart the inspiration that was needed for the success of the NAACP and of the larger movement for civil rights. Because the *Crisis* was thought-provoking and alive, because its prose was straightforward and forthright, and sometimes brusque and abrupt, thousands of black people read it. And Du Bois considered these thousands "as soil being prepared for seed of permanent organization."[44]

Du Bois was using the *Crisis* to give the NAACP the magnetism and presence without which the organization could not succeed. Without the *Crisis,* Du Bois said, the NAACP would "piddle on . . . do[ing] a few small obvious things." But the great goal—"the freeing of ten million"—could not be achieved without organization on a tremendous scale, and if the NAACP lacked charisma large numbers of blacks would never join.[45] As Du Bois saw it, the *Crisis* was imparting the personality, spirit, and inspiration that would make the NAACP possible.

There was much truth in this assessment. But after Spingarn became chairman of the board, he told Du Bois that the NAACP could not work effectively unless Du Bois's talents were subordinated to the general welfare of the organization. Unlike Villard, Spingarn did not wish to create a scene and drive Du Bois from the NAACP. But he warned Du Bois that some board members felt that the association could not avoid friction and operate effectively unless Du Bois was eliminated. Spingarn advised Du Bois to be less obstinate and more cooperative, if only for the sake of Du Bois's career.[46]

In response, Du Bois conceded that his temperament could be a difficult one to endure. "In my peculiar education and experiences it would be miraculous if I came through normal and unwarped," he told Spingarn.[47] Ever since the boyhood incident in Great Barrington, when the white girl refused to accept Du Bois's calling card, Du Bois had refused to push himself forward. Although Du Bois's reticence grew out of a certain shyness and insecurity, others often mistook Du Bois's reserve for arrogance. A case in point occurred at about the time Spingarn was urging Du Bois to be less abrasive. The incident involved John Milholland's extraordinarily beautiful daughter, Inez, whom Du Bois passed on the street without even a perfunctory greeting. A few minutes later, Inez Milholland charged into Du Bois's office and demanded an explanation. "You didn't speak to me!" she exclaimed, as a surprised Du Bois fumbled for an answer: "I didn't know whether she would dare to speak to me. . . . It wasn't up to me," he said.[48]

Du Bois conducted himself similarly when he was with members of the NAACP board—"like a wary lion concealing uncertainty and sensitivity behind a proud tread." As a result, Spingarn wrote, "even some of your most intimate friends feel toward you a mingled affection and resentment." "They have come to feel that you refused the alternative of cooperation . . . that you would not 'play the game,' at least with others."[49]

Du Bois's enemies made much of his aloofness. On one occasion, for example, the *New York Age* criticized Du Bois for refusing to join any church, for having little to do with the social life of his race, and even for not joshing with other blacks when he visited the barber shop. This was admittedly a diatribe from a newspaper that Booker T. Washington subsidized, but in a personal letter to one of his closest friends Du Bois himself confessed that he was "a wretched mixer and have an unfortunately difficult time adjusting myself to new acquaintances."[50]

Yet more was involved than simply Du Bois's temperament. Du Bois thought the *Crisis* could become one of the great journals of the world. It could become a center of black enterprise and cooperation. But this would be possible only if Du Bois was freed from petty criticisms and annoyances and interferences. Some board members, on the other hand, wanted to change the *Crisis* into a periodical that said almost nothing that anyone would take exception to. This Du Bois would not allow. He demanded "a full man's chance to complete a work without chains and petty hampering," and he was confident that the NAACP would benefit if he had real editorial freedom.[51]

Du Bois also thought that some of the criticism of his editing was rooted in racism. Of course, the NAACP's white leaders professed that they had no color prejudice, but Du Bois noted curious paradoxes. One concerned May Childs Nerney, whose work for the association focused on administration and organizing branch chapters. Du Bois said that if Nerney consulted Spingarn as an authority on some point where Spingarn was learned, Nerney would accept Spingarn's judgment without question. But "If she consults me on a point where I have knowledge she feels quite at liberty to oppose her judgment to mine because none of my type ever spoke to her or her friends with authority."[52] According to Du Bois, Villard was "the same way, only more so."[53] "He is used to advising colored men and giving them orders and he simply cannot bring himself to work with one as an equal."[54]

As the NAACP's only black officer, Du Bois was understandably concerned about white domination of the association. He must have been troubled by the knowledge that the success of the NAACP depended (at least during the early years) on financial support from wealthy whites. And Du Bois's difficulties with the overbearing Villard doubtless heightened this concern.

Spingarn, however, was a man of a different sort—one who was so free of racial prejudice that Du Bois said there was "no shadow of the thing in [his] soul." "The same is true," Du Bois wrote, of his other favorite board member, Mary White Ovington. But for that very

reason, Spingarn and Ovington failed to recognize that color prejudice intruded even in the work of the NAACP. To solve this problem,
Du Bois developed a pluralist plan for the NAACP to have "two
branches of the same work, one with a white head and one with a
colored; working in harmony and sympathy for one end."[55] In 1914,
he recommended that whites should control the administrative office
of the NAACP, where they would lobby for favorable laws, organize
legal cases to defend victims of injustice, and challenge the constitutionality of racial discrimination. Meanwhile Du Bois would devote
the *Crisis* to agitation and protest as well as to providing inspiration
and direction for the civil rights movement.

To this end, Du Bois proposed to take personal charge of the *Crisis*. Since he had developed the journal, he asked the NAACP to give
it to him with a condition: that in return for the *Crisis* remaining
the official publication of the NAACP, a committee selected by the
NAACP's board would have the right to veto the publication of articles that might damage the organization. In return for the independence of the magazine, Du Bois offered to assume the magazine's
debts and to pay his salary from its receipts.[56]

Du Bois's proposal was never formally adopted. As the new chairman of the board, Spingarn was opposed to reducing the range and
functions of the NAACP. He did not think the *Crisis* could remain the
official publication of the association if the board had only a veto
power. Spingarn and Du Bois remained friends who accompanied
one another on speaking tours. But the cordial relations of the two
men were tested when Du Bois proposed that the *Crisis* be established
as an independent entity. Spingarn's biographer has written that "Spingarn had no sympathy with any plan to accord [Du Bois] so much
autonomy that the *Crisis* . . . would be separated from the Association."[57]

Nevertheless, something close to Du Bois's proposal became the
NAACP's actual method of operation. Although the board of directors theoretically controlled the policy and management of the *Crisis*, the NAACP and the *Crisis* occupied different offices across the hall
from one another. Mary White Ovington recalled that "Du Bois was
a member of the [NAACP] board, careful in his judgment and scrupu-
lous in never demanding his way in matters that pertained to the
NAACP."[58] Du Bois allowed a special NAACP committee to veto stories that might damage the organization, but otherwise he wanted

complete freedom in editing the *Crisis*. It was probably inevitable that this unusual partnership would dissolve—as it eventually did in the 1930s. For two decades, however, the *Crisis* was Du Bois's domain.

The question arises as to why Du Bois did not take control of the NAACP as well as the *Crisis*. David Levering Lewis has written that Du Bois secretly harbored a desire to head the entire organization. Du Bois, however, insisted that all he wanted was the freedom to edit the *Crisis*. In 1910 Du Bois refused an offer to become the chief executive of the organization, and in 1916 he told a friend that he never had a desire to lead the NAACP—that he was not a "'mixer' and there is no use in my trying to be a popular leader."[59] In 1930 Du Bois stated that editing the *Crisis* was "the only work" at the NAACP "which attracts me."[60]

Thus Du Bois came to control the *Crisis*. He proceeded to lay down for the NAACP a clear, strong, and distinct body of doctrine that could not have been achieved by a majority vote. Not surprisingly, most black readers cheered when Du Bois openly condemned white injustice and oppression. After all, "Who would freely choose accommodation, compromise, and cast-down buckets if they could vicariously soar with Du Bois and say boldly to the Man things only whispered previously?"[61] By 1919, there were sixty-two thousand members of the NAACP, the great majority of them blacks. Du Bois "thank[ed] God" that by then most of the NAACP's money came "from black hands." "We must not only support but control this and similar organizations," Du Bois wrote, "and hold them unwaveringly to our objects, our aims and our ideals."[62]

At the same time, Du Bois received candid but friendly criticism from Mary White Ovington. Because Ovington was close to Du Bois and influential in the NAACP, her criticism should be understood in context. Born to a comfortable, upper-middle-class New York family and educated in private schools and at Radcliffe College, Ovington gave up the social life of a debutante and became "the first professionally trained social worker in the United States to devote her career and personal fortune to the cause of the Negro."[63] After college, she lived in tenements and wrote a book on social conditions among black New Yorkers. Published in 1911, Ovington's *Half a Man: The Status of the Negro in New York* was a standard reference work for more than half a century; in some ways it was similar to Du Bois's book of 1899, *The Philadelphia Negro*. Ovington continued to live among and write about northern blacks and also traveled and commented on race relations in the South. In 1904 she attended a conference at Atlanta University and by chance found herself seated next to Du Bois, whose work she had long admired. "My cup of happiness was full," Ovington later wrote, recalling that Du Bois's head was "like Shakespeare's, done in bronze."[64] More than most white social workers, Ovington recognized "that the Negroes aren't poor people for whom I must kindly do something. . . . [T]hey are men with the most forceful opinions of their own."[65]

Du Bois immediately took to Ovington. Departing from his customary aloofness, Du Bois was lighthearted and unpedantic. At their first dinner together, Ovington recalled that Du Bois did not hold forth on matters of philosophy or race relations but instead proceeded with pleasant banter throughout the meal.[66] Perhaps Du Bois was smitten with the beautiful, well-educated author and social worker from New York.

Smitten or not, Du Bois and Ovington became lifelong friends. At Du Bois's invitation in 1908, Ovington became the only white woman ever to address the Niagara Movement,[67] and the teasing comments that Du Bois and Ovington often exchanged led some observers to suspect that the two were or wished to become lovers.[68] Although this suspicion was probably unfounded, Ovington was certainly protective of Du Bois. At one NAACP meeting, she bristled with anger when Villard called Du Bois "childish and insubordinate";[69] at another she stated that if she had to choose between supporting the Crisis and the other work of the NAACP, she would choose the Crisis.[70]

Yet Ovington also thought there was something wrong with the Crisis. She understood that it was necessary to shake the nation out of its complacency and "to superimpose on the picture of the black brute . . . the picture of the white brute."[71] But sometimes Du Bois's jeremiads against whites went too far. When Du Bois edited the Crisis, Ovington said, he had in mind a black audience, and consequently he condemned white discrimination, promoted black racial consciousness, and seemed to teach blacks to regard whites as the enemy. "You offend the white people," Ovington told Du Bois, "by calling them hogs, by saying that they are reactionary heathen." (In one editorial for the Crisis, Du Bois had opined, "It takes extraordinary training, gift and opportunity to make the average white man anything but an overbearing hog, but the most ordinary Negro is an instinctive gentleman.")[72]

Ovington's criticism was perceptive. In the past, Du Bois had called upon blacks to uplift themselves, and throughout his career he would mention the need for high standards and moral reform. After about 1900, however, Du Bois's emphasis was on white racism. At the outset of his public career, he had written that "a little less complaint and whining, and a little more dogged work and manly striving, would do us more credit than a thousand civil rights bills."[73] But later, Du Bois focused on the depredations of whites. "A Southerner," Du Bois wrote in the *Crisis*, "must be a man who has assimilated no new ideas as to democracy and social class since 1863. . . . [H]e hates niggers; he pursues them vindictively; he chases a drop of Negro blood like a sleuth. He makes it his chief business in life to hound, oppress, and insult black folk, and to tell them personally as often as he can how utterly he despises them—except their women, privately."[74]

Du Bois especially questioned the "assumption that of all the hues of God whiteness alone is inherently and obviously better than brownness or tan." According to Du Bois, Western civilization was "built on black and brown and yellow slavery." Who raised whites to their glory, Du Bois asked, "But black men of Egypt and Ind, Ethiopia's sons of the evening, Indians and yellow Chinese, Arabian children of the morning, And mongrels of Rome and Greece."[75] Moreover, Du Bois predicted that someday in the fullness of time the colored races would pull the whites down from their perch, "Down with the theft of their thieving, And murder and mocking of men." As for whites:

> I hate them, Oh!
> I hate them well,
> I hate them, Christ!
> As I hate hell!
> If I were God,
> I'd sound their knell
> This day![76]

Living in segregated Atlanta for thirteen years left its mark on Du Bois. Especially after the violence of 1906, when reports of black crime set the stage for a riot, Du Bois sided with blacks and treated evidence of black weakness circumspectly. Thereafter he would protest and agitate and demand justice for his downtrodden race, but he feared that "a moment's let up, a moment's acquiescence, means a chance for the wolves of prejudice to get at our necks."[77] Consequently, Du Bois rejected Oswald Garrison Villard's suggestion that the Crisis should balance its articles on lynching with accounts of crimes committed by African Americans.[78] Nor was Du Bois willing to concede a point made by a friendly white journalist, Ray Stannard Baker: that whites, and especially white women who lived in the vicinity of blacks, had good reason to fear crime in general and rape in particular.[79] If whites moved away from black residential areas, Du Bois insisted, it was not because they feared black crime. "The reasons for the white people leaving . . . are social and economic and not criminal," Du Bois wrote. The whites simply wanted to have more social contact with other whites. To the extent that whites feared blacks, it was "the fear the oppressor has of the oppressed; the fear of the man who is always looking for insurrection from beneath because he knows that the lower class have been wronged." "That same fear existed during slavery time," Du Bois told Baker, "that same vague apprehension that some insurrection might take place. But it is not a fear of the crime of rape."[80]

Why did Du Bois change his emphasis? It seems that while Du Bois always acknowledged the importance of skills and character, after the Atlanta Riot he feared the consequences of dwelling on black weakness. He came to think that press reports about black crime and other problems set the stage for white discrimination and oppression. Du Bois also insisted that blacks must have rights and opportunities if they were to develop their capacities and realize their potential. Thus Du Bois affirmed what might have been a motto for the Crisis: "To those people who are saying to the black man today, 'Do your duties first and then clamor for rights,' we have a right to answer and to answer insistently, that the rights we are clamoring for are those that will enable us to do our duties."[81]

Du Bois and Booker T. Washington, Again

Establishing his independence as editor and developing rapport with the Crisis's black audience were crucial for Du Bois. But there were additional battles with Booker T. Washington before the NAACP became the nation's most influential black organization and before Du Bois became the country's most prominent black leader.[82]

In theory, the strife between Washington and Du Bois might have been avoided. Of course the two men had different emphases, with Du Bois demanding rights and Washington stressing the importance of skills and moral character. But each recognized the legitimacy of the other's points. On one occasion Washington conceded "that there is a work to be done which no one placed in my position can do, which no one living in the South perhaps can do." And Du Bois would have accepted Washington's additional point: that "there is a work which those of us who live here in the South can do, which persons who do not live in the South cannot do."[83]

Nevertheless, Washington and Du Bois had a "history," and each doubted the sincerity of the other. Washington was convinced that his own approach—with its emphasis on conciliating whites while acquiring property, education, and character—would lead to equality and citizenship rights for blacks. The NAACP's agitation and protest, on the other hand, was a delusion and a snare because it neglected the importance of skills and "deceiv[ed] the colored people into the idea that they can get what they ought to have in the way of right treatment by merely making demands."[84]

In addition, Washington feared that Du Bois and other critics would undermine Washington's own power and influence. The real effect of the NAACP, Washington predicted, would not be to uplift blacks but to destroy Tuskegee. "As a matter of straight fact," Washington wrote to one Tuskegee graduate, the NAACP "is for the purpose of tearing down our work wherever possible."[85]

Therefore, Washington tried to stifle the new organization. He sent subsidies and instructions to the *New York Age,* hoping that this newspaper would become a rival to the *Crisis.* In addition, Washington persuaded one black college president not to serve on the NAACP's board, and he urged a black judge to get his wife to back away from the NAACP. NAACP leaders were convinced that Washington also used his influence to shape the press coverage of the NAACP and to discourage his wealthy friends from supporting the association. Washington's supporters also did what they could to discredit Du Bois. One sent black editors a copy of Villard's scathing review of Du Bois's book on John Brown.[86]

In addition, Du Bois alleged that Washington put detectives "on my track looking for . . . white women with whom I was going, and various other things."[87] Yet the most the detectives could report was that while Du Bois was starting the *Crisis* during his first months with the NAACP in New York, he stayed at the Hotel Marshall while his wife and daughter stayed behind in the family's apartment in Atlanta. In a confidential letter to Booker T. Washington, Charles W. Anderson described the Marshall as "the favorite rendezvous for 'ladies' of both races"—and professed surprise "that so fastidious a gentleman as the Atlanta Professor would deign to make [the Marshall] his domicile."[88]

In fact, the Marshall bordered on the bohemian but was not a disreputable place. It served dinner to music and was frequented by black and white writers, actors, and musicians. Du Bois, however, recognized that the absence of Mrs. Du Bois had led to endless talk and speculation. Consequently, when he met with women either socially or for business, Du Bois was careful to have the meetings in public "where everybody could see."[89] The detectives never discovered Du Bois in a cheating situation.

Having found nothing untoward about Du Bois's sex life, Washington and his supporters turned to other members of the NAACP. One easy target appeared when William English Walling was sued for reneging on a promise of marriage. Washington then instructed the Tuskegee-subsidized *New York Age* to "burn Walling up." In due course an *Age* editorial expressed the hope that "no colored man or woman will in the future disgrace our race by inviting Mr. Walling in their home . . . "[90]

Mary White Ovington also came in for rough treatment after she attended an interracial dinner where Du Bois, attired in his formal tuxedo, was one of the principal speakers. Washington's lieutenants arranged for a pro-Washington reporter to cover the event and, as Washington's secretary confided, the reporter "served up . . . a particularly savory article."[91] Readers were informed that "Although there was no direct reference to marriage between whites and blacks, the speakers strongly intimated that miscegenation was inevitable and not undesirable." During the dinner, the reporter wrote, "White women, evidently of the cultured and wealthier classes, fashionably attired in low-cut gowns, leaned over the tables to chat confidentially with negro men of the true African type. . . . [T]he broad smiles of the negroes as they leered surreptitiously across the room at their Caucasian friends made one feel their inner ecstasy."[92] Afterwards, Ovington received so many obscene letters that she asked male relatives to open her mail.[93] "My mail is interesting," Ovington wrote, "more than interesting."[94]

Although Washington and his liege men never found evidence

that Du Bois was involved in illicit love affairs, they concocted other false stories to put Du Bois in a bad light. Thus Washington told a black editor that Du Bois ran away from Atlanta during the riot of 1906 and hid at a school in Alabama, when in fact (as noted in the previous chapter) Du Bois rushed from Alabama to Atlanta as soon as he heard of the riot and then armed himself with a shotgun to protect his family and Atlanta University.[95]

Washington also had one of his supporters check the voting records to see if Du Bois actually bothered to vote. Even though the supporter reported that "the registration list shows that Dr. Du Bois is a voter,"[96] Washington told the journalist Ray Stannard Baker that Du Bois, "who tries to lead in the matter of agitation [for] the franchise, has never voted . . . or attempted to register." Washington further told Baker that there was "practically no trouble in any colored man registering and voting," if the man was willing to pay the poll tax. "Notwithstanding this is true," Washington continued, "you would be surprised at the large number of educated colored people who have never attempted to register to vote."[97] According to Washington, this was especially true of those who had graduated from college.

Du Bois retaliated. He was convinced that the success of the NAACP depended on destroying the influence of Washington and his patronage machine. In his *Autobiography*, Du Bois recalled that the "controversy between myself and Booker Washington . . . became more personal and bitter than I had ever dreamed."[98]

Du Bois sent a shot across the bow in March 1910, when he accused Washington of being "the political boss of the Negro race in America." Ever since Washington's dinner with Theodore Roosevelt in 1901, Du Bois said, few blacks had been appointed to public office without Washington's consent—an ironic development since Washington had become "the sole referee for all political action concerning 10,000,000 Americans" at the very time that he also "counselled his race to let politics alone, acquiesce temporarily in disfranchisement and pay attention chiefly to industrial development and efficiency."[99]

A few months later, when Du Bois heard that Washington was painting pleasant pictures of American race relations in speeches to English audiences, Du Bois circulated a protest that eventually was signed by twenty-three prominent African Americans. The statement asserted that "if Mr. Booker T. Washington . . . is giving the impression abroad that the Negro problem in America is in process of satisfactory solution, he is giving an impression which is not true." Racism and oppression were still the order of the day, the statement said, and it was "like a blow to the face" to have a fellow African American "give the impression that all is well. It is one thing to be optimistic . . . and forgiving, but it is quite a different thing . . . to misrepresent the truth."[100]

These comments naturally infuriated Washington, but a modicum of harmony between the warring groups was achieved in 1911 after a white man brutally assaulted Washington in New York City. The details of this matter are still shrouded in mystery. Suffice to say that while tarrying near an apartment house in a predominantly white neighborhood of dubious reputation, Washington was beaten so severely that sixteen stitches were required to close the wounds. Washington's biographer placed the building "near but not in the Tenderloin, an 'easy-morals' section of the city," but Du Bois called the area a "neighborhood of high class prostitutes."[101]

The white assailant, a man by the name of Henry Ulrich, may have mistaken Washington for a burglar, or perhaps he simply took exception to a black man being near a white building; but when Washington's identity was revealed (and thus the suggestion of burglary discredited), Ulrich's wife said her husband had defended her honor after Washington "looked me right in the face . . . and said, 'Hello Sweetheart.'"[102] This belated explanation was obviously contrived, but it acquired a patina of credibility because Washington himself was unable to offer a believable explanation of his presence in a disreputable area. Some police thought Washington had been intoxicated. Among newspapermen the story "floating around" was that Washington "really went to the place to meet a white woman."[103]

Among themselves, Washington's black critics probably exchanged a good deal of ribald banter. Yet although they must have found it hard not to enjoy Washington's predicament, the critics knew that publicizing a story of illicit interracial sex could backfire against all blacks. Thus the reports in the *Crisis* were brief,[104] while Monroe Trotter's *Boston Guardian* also aimed at restraint, "although somewhat less convincingly, having told readers it had 'no desire to take any advantage of [Washington's] present troubles. We want to fight men when standing up.'"[105]

After the assault, Washington received dozens of letters of sympathy, many of them from people he considered his enemies. Even the NAACP passed a resolution of sympathy and support.[106] Since "practically every one of our enemies . . . had his heart softened," Washington adopted a conciliatory policy.[107] Arrangements were made for the exchange of fraternal delegates between the NAACP and Washington's own National Negro Business League. "The time has come," Washington said, "when all interested in the welfare of the Negro people should lay aside personal differences and personal bickerings. . . . [D]eep down in the heart of all of us, there is a feeling of oneness and sympathy and unity."[108]

Yet Du Bois remained wary.[109] After conversations with his table mates at the Hotel Marshall, Du Bois concluded that Washington probably had been searching for a brothel near the Tenderloin.[110] In any case, the fundamental points at issue between the two men had not been resolved. Three months after the assault, the *Crisis* censured Washington for still thinking that "it is not well to tell the whole story of wrong and injustice in the South, but rather one should emphasize the better aspects." On the contrary, Du Bois insisted, blacks should face "race prejudice, lawlessness and ignorance" with "unflinching firmness" and should "set our faces against all statesmanship that . . . dodge[s] and cloud[s] the issue."[111]

Any reconciliation after the assault was only partial. Relations between the NAACP and Tuskegee remained strained until Washington died in 1915. Then, finally, better relations were established. Du Bois led the way with a tactful obituary. The statement reiterated Du Bois's belief that Washington's conciliatory approach made it easier for whites to disfranchise blacks and to expand segregation. Yet Du Bois also asserted that Washington "was the greatest Negro leader since Frederick Douglass, and the most distinguished man, white or black, who has come out of the South since the Civil War." In particular, Du Bois praised Washington for directing the attention of blacks "to the pressing necessity of economic development."[112]

The trustees at Tuskegee Institute then promoted cordial relations between the two factions by choosing Robert Russa Moton, rather than Washington's close associate Emmett J. Scott, to succeed Washington as the principal of Washington's school. Scott had worked closely with Washington in directing the machinations of the Tuskegee Machine. Moton, on the other hand, had spent twenty-five years as the commandant of cadets at his alma mater, Hampton Institute. Moton's loyalty to Hampton's approach to education was beyond question, for he had spoken on behalf of Hampton throughout the United States and had also led the school's singers on tours all over the country. Yet most significantly in terms of developing a rapprochement, Moton and Du Bois were friends. Du Bois had personally invited Moton to become a member of both the Niagara Movement and the NAACP;[113] and in the past Moton had urged Booker Washington to cooperate with the NAACP.[114]

Du Bois, The Amenia Conference, and James Weldon Johnson

With the death of Booker T. Washington, Du Bois recognized that the moment was opportune for uniting the black factions. Thus he recommended that the annual meeting of the NAACP be postponed because it fell on the same day as a Tuskegee-sponsored memorial ceremony for Washington. For the summer of 1916, Du Bois then proposed a reconciliation meeting for black leaders of various persuasions.[115] J. E. Spingarn sent the invitations, and in August 1916 a three-day conference was held, not at the headquarters of the NAACP in New York City but at Spingarn's country estate at Amenia in upstate New York. Du Bois attended the conference but was careful not to appear on the program itself. In private correspondence, an NAACP officer explained that Du Bois was concerned lest people think they were "being called together simply to subject them to the Du Bois yoke."[116]

Du Bois took extraordinary precautions—perhaps because, after his recent struggles to establish editorial independence from the NAACP's mostly white board of directors, the prospect of black unity must have seemed especially desirable. Reconciliation with Washington's faction was another way to augment the power of blacks in the civil rights movement.

Du Bois wanted reconciliation on his terms. Consequently he divided the guests into three categories: "Niagara" men, "Washington" men, and others whose loyalties were "Questionable."[117] Superficially the factions appeared to be roughly equal, but Du Bois must have known that his side would have the advantage. As it turned out, seventeen of the eighteen "Niagara" men actually attended the Amenia Conference, while only eight of the fifteen "Washington" men showed up. Of the twenty-one invitees who were listed as "Questionable," only thirteen attended, and some of them were sympathetic to Du Bois. James Weldon Johnson, for example, was listed as "Questionable" because in the past he had maintained cordial relations with Booker Washington; but Johnson had joined the NAACP in 1915 and would become an officer of the organization in 1916.

The purpose of the Amenia Conference, Du Bois wrote, was "to gloss over hurts and enmities" and "to bring about as large a degree as possible of unity of purpose among Negro leaders." The animating idea was that everyone would benefit if the leaders of the different black factions got together and came to know one another personally. The official program stated that the time had come "to ascertain the most advanced position that all can agree upon."[118]

The conference was planned carefully, for Spingarn and Du Bois knew that it would not be easy to reconcile people who for years had been saying harsh things about one another. Spingarn insisted, "it is a conference—no speeches—more than 10 or 15 minutes is a speech."[119] Some topics were listed on the program, but discussion leaders were urged to keep the talks on a familiar plane.

Pleasant surroundings also fostered camaraderie at Amenia. To promote informality, tents were set up near a lake on the grounds of Spingarn's Tudor manor house, and the fifty-five guests were well fed. Du Bois recalled that

> Promptly at meal time food appeared, miraculously steaming and perfectly cooked. . . . We ate hilariously in the open air . . . and then filled and complacent we talked awhile of the thing which all of us called 'The Problem,' and after that we . . . broke up and played good and hard. We swam and rowed and hiked and lingered in the forests and sat upon the hillsides . . . [120]

Over the course of three days in August 1916, the conferees learned what many of them had suspected all along: that "none of us held uncompromising and unchangeable views. It was all a matter of emphasis. We all believed in thrift, we all wanted the Negro to vote, we all wanted the laws enforced, we all wanted assertion of our essential manhood; but how to get these things,—there of course was infinite divergence of opinion."[121]

The formal resolutions of the Amenia Conference were predictable. They affirmed that all forms of education were desirable for

the Negro; that voting was of crucial importance; that outdated suspicions and factional alignments should be eliminated and forgotten;
and that special circumstances in the South created a particular need
for sympathetic understanding between black leaders who lived in
the South and those who lived elsewhere.[122]

Even the most devoted supporters of Booker T. Washington
praised the Amenia Conference. Washington's chief assistant, Emmett Scott, was "pleased that we came together in that thoroughly in-
formal way to discuss the problems which are of such great moment
to us." Washington's favorite editor, Fred Moore, assured his friends
in Tuskegee that "the Conference was fine. Nothing happened that
would have been embarrassing." An editorial in Moore's newspaper,
the *New York Age,* described the meeting as epoch-making; "it marks
the birth of a new spirit of united purpose and effort that will have
far-reaching results." Mary Church Terrell, whose husband had been
appointed a judge thanks to Booker Washington's patronage, praised
Spingarn and Du Bois for "call[ing] together a group of representa-
tive people, some of whom have misunderstood and misjudged each
other, so that meeting face-to-face they may discuss and adjust their
differences."[123]

Most NAACP members were also enthusiastic about the conference, and many returned to their homes with, as one put it, the "determination that the NAACP will be a success . . . "[124] This, indeed,
was a principal consequence of the conference. In addition to establishing a truce among black leaders, the Amenia Conference marked
a shift in the balance of power in the Negro world. Du Bois had
"hoped that some central organization and preferably the NAACP
would eventually represent this new united purpose,"[125] and after
the Amenia Conference this hope became a reality. Among African
Americans, the influence of Tuskegee was waning while that of the
NAACP was ascending.

The NAACP received an additional boost later in 1916 when it
made one of its most important appointments, that of James Weldon
Johnson as National Organizer and Field Secretary. Johnson had been
born in 1871 in Jacksonville, Florida. His mother was a school-
teacher, and his father was the headwaiter at the luxurious St. James
Hotel. After receiving his primary education at Jacksonville's segregated Stanton School, Johnson spent seven years in the preparatory
and college divisions of Atlanta University. Thereafter he worked for

eight years as the principal of a black school, during which time he passed the bar and published a local black newspaper. Then he went to New York City, where he joined with his brother Rosamond and Bob Cole to form one of the nation's most popular songwriting teams.[126]

Thanks to support from Booker T. Washington's Tuskegee Machine, Johnson joined the State Department in 1905 and served for more than eight years as an American consul in Venezuela and Nicaragua. Upon his return to the United States, he worked for a few years as a contributing editor at the Washington-subsidized *New York Age*. In addition to these careers, Johnson also found time to write poetry, many articles, and a well-regarded novel, *The Autobiography of an Ex-Colored Man*. Later he would publish additional books on American Negro poetry, history, and music and a classic autobiography, *Along This Way*.

Since 1912 the NAACP's national organizer had been a black woman, Kathryn M. Johnson, who was fired in 1916 after there were complaints that she did not get along with well-educated blacks and with well-to-do whites.[127] At Du Bois's behest, the NAACP offered the position to Du Bois's friend from Atlanta, John Hope, but Hope, after carefully considering what he called "one of the most attractive offers that can come to a colored man at this time," decided to stay in Atlanta as the president of Morehouse College.[128]

After receiving the letter in which Hope declined the appointment, J. E. Spingarn wrote a note across the bottom of the page. "Has it ever occurred to you," he asked his NAACP colleagues, "that James W. Johnson might be the right sort of man?" Spingarn acknowledged that it would "seem strange to have us go to Fred Moore's office [at the *New York Age*] for a man," but the fact that Johnson had previously been part of the Tuskegee Machine only made Johnson seem all the more attractive. According to Spingarn, the appointment of Johnson "would be a *coup d'etat*."[129]

NAACP staff member Roy Nash promptly endorsed Spingarn's recommendation. "Jim Johnson would be better than . . . [John] Hope or . . . anyone else," Nash replied. "He is not academic, is a good mixer with a social bent that Du Bois and Hope lack. He is . . . a good talker and would offend no group."[130]

Du Bois also thought Johnson would be "entirely desirable," although Du Bois added that it would be "a pity to take a poet and literary man away from leisure and New York."[131] As it happened, for some time Johnson and Du Bois had admired one another. Johnson had asked Du Bois to autograph Johnson's copy of *The Souls of Black Folk* (and Johnson later wrote that Du Bois's book was the most influential volume about blacks that had been published since *Uncle Tom's Cabin*).[132] For his part, Du Bois published some of Johnson's poetry in the *Crisis* and once featured a photograph that made Johnson appear so handsome that, Johnson joked, "I gazed . . . in reverent admiration for some moments before I read the nice things you had said about me."[133]

After considering the NAACP's offer "up and down," Johnson accepted the new position. He "could not think of any other field which would allow me the opportunity to do something for the advancement of my race."[134] Of course the new job would take Johnson away from writing and put him on the road explaining the NAACP's program and helping local blacks organize branches of the association. But Du Bois reconsidered his earlier remarks about the "pity" of taking a poet away from his "real life work of literature" and strongly encouraged Johnson to take the position, saying that "contact with human beings will be an incentive rather than a drawback to your literary work."[135]

Du Bois went on to say, prophetically, "there is no telling what your wide acquaintance as organizer might not lead to."[136] As it happened, Johnson was phenomenally successful as an organizer. When Johnson joined the NAACP in 1916 the association had about 70 branches and 9,000 members—"a figure large in comparison to earlier civil rights groups but small given the number of blacks in the country."[137] Thanks in large part to Johnson's work in the field, by the end of 1918 there were 165 branches and 44,000 members. By 1920, membership had grown to 62,000.[138] Johnson had the attributes required for success as a national organizer: "great tact, executive skill, eloquence, sympathy, and . . . unswerving loyalty to the main purpose of the Association."[139]

Thanks to the popularity of the *Crisis,* the harmony achieved at the Amenia Conference, and the success of Johnson's organizing work, by the time of the First World War the NAACP had replaced the Tuskegee Machine as the most influential organization in black America.

The rise of the NAACP was due to more than the hard work of a few individuals. As usually is the case with success in history, the individual leaders benefited from being in touch with the trends of their time. In this instance, the ascendancy of the NAACP was facilitated by an important historical trend—the Great Migration of blacks from the rural South to the urban North. As early as 1903, Du Bois noted that "the most significant economic change among Negroes in the last ten or twenty years had been their influx into northern cities."[140] Between 1900 and 1910, the black population of New York City increased by 51 percent, while Philadelphia and Chicago each reported increases of more than 30 percent. Conditions in the northern ghettos often were difficult, but as black people left the rural plantations of the South they acquired new attitudes and new rights—including the right to vote—that made them more responsive to the NAACP's message.

After the death of Booker T. Washington, many people wondered, "Who will be the next great Negro leader?" They remembered that Washington had replaced Frederick Douglass as "the one great leader" after Douglass's death in 1895. When Washington died twenty years later, people expected another individual to excel all others.[141] Yet it turned out that an organization—the NAACP— emerged as the preeminent center of African American ideals and influence.

From about 1915 to 1931 the NAACP was a tetrarchy—that is, an organization dominated jointly by four rulers: W. E. B. Du Bois, J. E. Spingarn, Mary White Ovington, and James Weldon Johnson. In some ways, a cooperative form of leadership seemed especially appropriate at a time when organization men were also coming to the fore in big business. As the historian Glenn Porter has noted, the size and complexity of many large corporations called for large managerial bureaucracies.[142] In the case of the NAACP, however, bureaucratic leadership was a function of the personalities involved rather than a response to the demands of an impersonal and increasingly complex economy.

As the editor of the *Crisis,* Du Bois was the most widely known of the four tetrarchs—so widely known that many people considered Du Bois and the NAACP synonymous. Yet Spingarn and Ovington dominated the board of directors, with one or the other serving as chairman of the board between 1914 and 1940. And Johnson (and, after 1930, Johnson's successor, Walter White) were the national organizers and chief administrative officers.

Yet within the tetrarchy Du Bois was *primus inter pares*—the first among equals. And, ironically for someone who was aloof and uncomfortable in the company of many people, Du Bois developed close personal ties to Spingarn, Ovington, and Johnson. When Du Bois was with his close friends, Johnson recalled, Du Bois was easygoing and affable. In public, he was "a stern, bitter, relentless fighter." But when he "put aside his sword" and was among his particular friends, Du Bois became "the most jovial and fun-loving of men."[143]

In *Dusk of Dawn* (1940), Du Bois identified Spingarn as his "nearest white friend" and dedicated the book to Spingarn's memory.[144] He knew that, as Spingarn had once written to Du Bois, "because of the friendliness of our relations, and my constant championship of you, I have been thrust forward by your friends and enemies as intermediary and arbiter in their disputes with you."[145]

Had Du Bois thought it prudent to mention his closest friendship with a white woman, the distinction might have gone to Mary White Ovington. "You think I idolize [Du Bois]," Ovington wrote in a letter to Spingarn, "and perhaps I do. I do worship genius. . . . Du Bois is the master builder whose work will speak to men as long as there is an oppressed race on the earth."[146] For many years, Ovington used her position on the NAACP's board to support Du Bois. Moreover, judging from the tone of familiarity and bantering in the Du Bois–Ovington correspondence, Du Bois and Ovington were more than collegial fellow workers. They genuinely liked one another.

Du Bois's relationship with Johnson was also friendly but more formal, with letters usually addressed to "Dear Mr. Johnson" or, on especially familiar occasions, "Dear Johnson." As noted above, Du Bois admired Johnson's literary work and encouraged Johnson to join the NAACP. The admiration was mutual, and in later battles Johnson would take up the cudgels in defense of Du Bois. Johnson's biographer noted that Du Bois "looked upon Johnson as a kind of protector, as a man who understood him and whom he could trust."[147]

The friendship of the tetrarchs was also based on shared principles. They were determined to protest and to assail the ears of white America with the story of its shameful treatment of black people. They thought conditions would improve if the NAACP put the essential facts before the American people. Like the muckraking journalists and other progressive reformers of their era, the leaders of the NAACP wanted to expose wrongdoing. They assumed that when Americans knew of injustice, they would demand reform.

In addition, Du Bois and Ovington shared an economic radicalism that will be discussed later. They sympathized with working people and thought the national economy should be reorganized to help the poor.

Du Bois, Johnson, and Spingarn also shared pluralist convictions about cultural dualism and ethnic identity. They sought a middle ground between black separatism and integration. Thus Spingarn fostered cultural nationalism among blacks through annual literary prizes given in his wife's name and through his work as an editor at Harcourt, Brace and Company. In the 1920s he became one of the major patrons of the Harlem literary renaissance. His biographer has written that Spingarn adhered "to the concept of cultural pluralism, the belief that a given race or ethnic group should preserve its unique cultural heritage, while, at the same time, seeking full integration into all other facets of the larger society. Preservation of the black cultural heritage remained one of Spingarn's concerns throughout his life. . . . [He] insist[ed] that a greater emphasis upon black cultural nationalism must be a vital aspect of any new direction taken by the Negro."[148]

Johnson's biographer also noted that there was "a deep-running dualism in [Johnson's] thought." Johnson believed that blacks eventually would meld into a fully unified national culture, and in the process they would lose their racial identity. But Johnson hoped blacks would first develop special qualities that were generally recognized as valuable contributions to the larger society. He did not think it would be necessary to maintain a unique black culture in perpetuity, but he saw the need for doing so in America during his lifetime. He championed the race-conscious black writers of the Harlem literary renaissance and emphasized the importance of black achievement as necessary to repair a damaged group psychology and to pave the way toward eventual assimilation.[149]

Du Bois was fortunate in his colleagues. Because the tetrarchs were compatible, Du Bois was able to compensate for the limitations of his own personality. Although Du Bois was widely respected for his writings in the *Crisis* and other publications, his personal magnetism never transcended a small group of close friends. Yet Johnson,

Ovington, and Spingarn protected Du Bois and allowed him to continue with candid comments from his editorial perch. In the process they enabled the NAACP to become the nation's most influential African American organization and facilitated the emergence of Du Bois as the country's most prominent black leader.[150]

Four
Du Bois and the First World War

On the eve of the First World War, Du Bois had achieved a degree of prominence that only Frederick Douglass and Booker T. Washington had hitherto attained. He was the most prominent spokesman for his race in the United States. Yet Du Bois had no sooner risen to this pinnacle than he suffered a physical collapse. First, there was an operation for kidney stones in 1916. Then, in 1917, another exceedingly risky operation was needed to remove a kidney—an operation that took Du Bois "down into the valley of the shadow of death."[1]

One year later, after Du Bois had recovered his health, his reputation was damaged when several prominent African Americans denounced him for urging blacks to suspend their protests and rally around the American flag during the First World War. Eventually Du Bois regained his standing, but his rehabilitation took time and was marred by his own unfair criticism of other black leaders. Du Bois later confessed that he had second thoughts about his course during the First World War. He wrote in 1940 that he was "less sure now than then of the soundness" of his stance; and in his posthumously published autobiography, Du Bois confessed that he was "not sure that I was right."[2]

Du Bois at Fifty

Du Bois's life-threatening illness touched off an avalanche of letters and praise. Many correspondents shared the sentiments of Clark University president W. H. Crogman, who said that "to lose [Du Bois] would be . . . a racial calamity." John Haynes Holmes of the National Urban League "tremble[d] to think what it would have meant to the members of your race . . . had you been taken from us." J. E. Spingarn was so concerned that he asked his family physician to be present as an observer at Du Bois's second operation. Mary Church Terrell, an old friend from Washington, was one of only a few people who affected a lighter touch; a few days after Du Bois had finally left the hospital, she recalled that she had also had a similar operation and "if anything had happened to you I should have felt largely responsible for such a calamity to us all, because I would have had the uncomfortable feeling that you had met your fate in a reckless effort to keep up with me!!!"[3]

Du Bois was "glad to learn how important I am," and his recovery was rapid and complete.[4] To a friend who urged him to take it easy during recuperation, Du Bois answered: "Do not be afraid of my overdoing. . . . I retire at nine and rise at nine; get to my office at twelve, read the newspapers and sit around until I feel like going and then go. As a result I am feeling tip-top."[5]

A year after the second operation, J. E. Spingarn and other friends hosted a fiftieth birthday party for Du Bois at the Civic Club in New York City on February 25, 1918. It greatly boosted Du Bois's spirits, as best wishes came in from all over the country. From New England, Du Bois's high school principal, Frank Hosmer, recalled the pleasure he had "in introducing [Du Bois] to the expeditions of Caesar, to the speeches of Cicero, and the great power of Virgil."[6] A friend from Tennessee recalled their first dinner together at Fisk University.[7] From Boston, Du Bois heard from his Harvard fiancée, Maud Cuney Hare, who after twenty-nine years still recalled being with Du Bois on his twenty-first birthday; she told "Du" that she was still keeping "a remembrance" of the earlier birthday "safe in lavender and rosemary."[8]

Du Bois also heard from former colleagues and students. In response to congratulations from George Towns, who for a while was the only other black professor on the faculty at Atlanta University, Du Bois acknowledged, "It was a great privilege to know you and the other fellows at Atlanta. I have neither before nor since met so goodly a company." Bessie Taylor Page, a former student at Atlanta University, recalled cozy seminars in Du Bois's apartment, while Sadie Conyers fondly remembered the meals she had shared with Du Bois in the university's dining hall. "You were always kind to me at school and tolerant and I was impudent enough not to feel the difference [in status]," Conyers wrote. Conyers said there was "nothing original I can say," but she said it well: "I am thankful that there has been and is a Du Bois."[9]

Du Bois also received commendations from others, who knew him from his writing. J. Max Barber remembered that he "first became acquainted with you thru an article in *The Atlantic Monthly*" and then traveled "more than half across the continent to attend the formation of the 'Niagara Movement.'" Mrs. N. J. Burroughs similarly noted that Du Bois's work had been "an inspiration . . . ever since I, a nineteen year old girl, one day chanced on an essay of yours."[10]

Most of the birthday greetings expressed support for Du Bois's principles and especially for his outspoken opposition to racial injustice. "When sycophants . . . were fawning you stood up like a man, bravely, uncompromisingly for our rights," one friend wrote from Boston. "You have not been silent in the midst of the wrongs which we have suffered."[11] A comrade from Baltimore praised Du Bois for throwing himself "athwart the tide of subserviency that was gripping our people,"[12] while a well-wisher from Washington lauded Du Bois for defending the "most despised and persecuted people upon whom the sun shines."[13] From Georgia, the principal of an industrial school "thank[ed] God that you are free to let the world know that everything isn't all right."[14]

Du Bois was celebrated above all as a *protest* leader. The president of the NAACP noted that "What [Du Bois] has written in defense of [African American] rights will rank high among the most eloquent appeals for justice."[15] That was why one government worker regarded Du Bois as "the ideal leader of the Negro race in America,"[16] and why other correspondents repeatedly identified Du Bois as "the foremost leader of the Negro race today."[17] Estelle Matthews, a reader of the *Crisis* from Philadelphia, expressed the sentiments of Du Bois's partisans when she wrote: "I would that our country had a thousand brave, noble-minded men like [Du Bois]. Men who dare to speak the truth . . . Men who can look the blue-eyed Anglo-Saxon in the face and let them know there are true hearted black men and women."[18]

Within months of the fiftieth birthday party, however, Du Bois was condemned as an "accommodationist," a "quitter," and a "traitor to his race." As surely as it destroyed millions of lives, the First World War, reaching the United States in 1917, gravely damaged Du Bois's reputation as a protest leader.

The Black World and the Great War

Historians have not reached a consensus about the causes of the First World War. In our own day, "nationalism" is often mentioned as a culprit—with the Serbs and Austrians blamed for trying to increase their strength and territory at the expense of the disintegrating Ottoman Empire. The English have also been censured for their envy of the German economy and their alarm over a new German navy. The Germans have been faulted for building a strong navy and for resenting their failure to do well in the scramble for colonies. Several other nations have been reproached for fearing that another state would get the better of them as the balance of power shifted, with the militant rivalries compounded by a system of "entangling alliances."

At the time of the war, economic interpretations of its causes were also in vogue. Thus Lenin blamed the war on capitalists who coveted foreign markets and raw materials. Even Woodrow Wilson, on one occasion, said the war resulted from the conflict of competing imperialisms. "The seed of war in the modern world is industrial and commercial rivalry," Wilson asserted. "The real reason [for the war] . . . was that Germany was afraid her commercial rivals were going to get the better of her, and the reason why some nations went into the war against Germany was that they thought Germany would get the commercial advantage of them. . . . This war in its inception was a commercial and industrial war."[19]

Du Bois also offered an economic explanation of the war, but one that brought Africa into the equation. He insisted that "the dream of exploitation abroad included "the gold and diamonds of South Africa, the cocoa of Angola and Nigeria, the rubber and ivory of the Congo, and the palm oil of the West Coast."[20] As Du Bois saw it, it was not merely national jealousy and not just the competition for profits that led to the war. More fundamentally, the war resulted from "the color line"—from the theory that darker people were inferior and that Caucasians had the right "to confiscate [the] land . . . [of] black, brown and yellow peoples, . . . work the natives at low wages, make large profits and open wide markets for cheap European manufactures."[21]

Du Bois further said that white workers were complicit in the imperialism. Although they did not receive a full share of the wealth, that was a matter for bargaining. "The loot was ample for all."[22] According to Du Bois, the war was "engendered by . . . armed national associations of labor and capital whose aim is the exploitation of the wealth of the world mainly outside the European circle of nations."[23]

For Du Bois it was merely coincidence that the shot that sparked the war was fired in the Balkans—for the Balkan region was only one of several areas where rival imperialisms were wringing wealth from underdeveloped nations. The conflagration might as easily have been ignited by an incident in one of the other colonial areas—in Africa, Asia, or the South Seas. Du Bois traced "the real cause of this war to the despising of the darker races by the dominant groups . . . and the consequent fierce rivalry among European nations . . . to use darker and backward people for purposes of selfish gain."[24]

Despite his bitter assessment of the origins of the war, once the fighting began Du Bois quickly sided with England. This was surprising because Du Bois fondly remembered his years as a student in Germany, and he wrote that he still loved the German people, who showed him "the essential humanity of white folk twenty years ago when [I] was near to denying it."[25] But even in the 1890s Du Bois had noted that militarism cast a spell over Germany, that the strutting Prussians thought they were superior to other human beings.

England, on the other hand, impressed Du Bois as "an angel of light . . . as compared with Germany." Despite England's past complicity with slavery and a lingering disdain for colored people, Du Bois wrote, England had "the ability to learn from her mistakes." "Today no white nation is fairer in its treatment of darker peoples than England."[26]

When the United States entered the war in 1917, on the side of England and at the behest of President Woodrow Wilson, Du Bois urged African Americans "to join heartily in this fight." "Absolute loyalty in arms" was his watchword.[27] In part this was because Du Bois thought blacks would forfeit their claim to equal rights if they refused to perform the duties of citizenship. In addition, Du Bois hoped that unstinting patriotism would lead to "the right to vote and the right to work and the right to live without insult."[28] He recalled that after some five thousand African Americans fought in the American Revolution, the transatlantic slave trade was criminalized. He also remembered that slavery was abolished and the civil rights amendments added to the Constitution after two hundred thousand blacks served in the Union armed forces during the Civil War. He hoped for a similar "reward" after World War I.[29] The United States, after all, claimed to be fighting to make the world safe for democracy, and democracy implied an equality of privilege as well as an equal obligation of service.

Du Bois harbored these hopes despite hard experience that had led him to conclude that President Woodrow Wilson was hopeless as far as the African Americans were concerned.

For many years Du Bois and most other blacks had supported the Republican Party. The Democratic Party at the time took its cues from the white South and was firmly committed to segregation and disfranchisement. Du Bois thought the Republicans should have done more than they did for blacks, and he had misgivings about the Republicans' decision to funnel patronage for blacks through the Tuskegee Machine. Nevertheless, some patronage was better than none.

Yet Du Bois became angry in 1908 when the Republican presidential candidate, William Howard Taft, announced that in deference to the wishes of southern whites he would no longer appoint blacks to offices in the South. Du Bois then declared that he would "vote against Taft . . . even if I have to vote for [the Democrat William Jennings] Bryan."[30] He told one acquaintance that he was "a Republican, and I believe in Republican principles, but when the Republican party is false to those principles then I think it is time . . . to bring it to senses by refusing to vote for the candidates who stand especially for injustice and wrong."[31] Du Bois thought blacks would benefit if neither political party could take the black vote for granted. He wanted blacks to control the balance of power by switching back and forth from one party to another.

Du Bois tested this theory in 1912 when the *Crisis* endorsed the Democratic presidential candidate, Woodrow Wilson, after Wilson signed a statement expressing his "earnest wish to see justice done the colored people in every matter; and not mere grudging justice, but justice executed with liberality and cordial good feeling." Wilson went on to assure African Americans that they could "count upon me for absolute fair dealing."[32] Then, according to Du Bois, "in the North a hundred thousand black voters . . . supported Wilson . . . and [were] so distributed as to do much to help his election."[33] Although the black vote was not decisive, this amount of African American support for Wilson was greater than most prognosticators had thought possible.

Yet, after being elected, Wilson disregarded his promises and presided over the most antiblack administration of the twentieth century. By executive order, the Wilson administration introduced segregated cafeterias and rest rooms. Some departments put up chicken-wire partitions to separate black and white workers. The civil service employment of blacks was curtailed, and many already-employed

African Americans were phased out.[34] For a while Du Bois accepted Wilson's assurances of goodwill and blamed Wilson's southern subordinates. By 1915, however, two years before American intervention in the World War, Du Bois gave up on the president. He wrote that Wilson was "either not daring or not caring," that he was a man who contented himself "with shifty and unmeaning platitudes." For Du Bois, the whole affair was "one of the most grievous disappointments that a disappointed people must bear."[35]

For black Americans there were additional sources of discontent. When the war began, many whites were opposed to arming blacks, some because they thought blacks lacked the discipline required for effective military service and others for fear that blacks would be rewarded with equal rights if they fought well. In due course Congress had before it a bill to prevent the enlistment of Negroes in the military service.[36] Many African Americans consequently feared that they would be drafted only for service in labor battalions, and the NAACP was put in the unseemly position of having to plead for the right to fight. Ultimately some 367,710 blacks were conscripted into the armed services; but the army brass thought most blacks were better suited for work than combat and only 50,000 African Americans were organized into combat units.

In addition, Du Bois noted, "the opposition to Negro officers was intense and bitter."[37] "By a queer twist of American reasoning," the conventional wisdom held that black troops were "best known and best 'handled' by white [officers] from the South."[38]

African Americans thus faced a difficult choice. Since the army was segregated, there was no chance that black officers would be trained alongside whites. African Americans would have to endure the insult of requesting a separate camp for training black officers, or there would be no black officers. "We did not make the damnable dilemma," Du Bois wrote. "Our enemies made that. We must make the choice else we play into their very claws. It is a case of [a separate] camp or no officers. Give us the officers. Give us the camp."[39] "Give us Negro officers for Negro troops."[40]

Several black newspapers—the *Baltimore Afro-American,* the *Boston Guardian,* the *Chicago Defender,* the *New York Age*—assessed the situation differently. Instead of regarding segregation as preferable to exclusion, they considered it unseemly to accept separation. "No, thank you, Doctor!" the *Cleveland Gazette* wrote. "There is enough governmental segregation already." "We fail to enthuse over [the] suggestion that we fight SEGREGATION with a segregated volunteer officer school." When Du Bois said that segregation was the order of the day, and that drafted blacks would have no black officers unless a separate training camp was established, the *Gazette* answered: "when the government needs us bad enough, it too will quickly drop its segregation nonsense and train and treat our men in common with all other classes of Americans."[41]

Joel Spingarn, on the other hand, once again agreed with Du Bois, and because Spingarn had enlisted and had become a major in the army even before the United States declared war on Germany, he was in a position to take action. Working with administrators and professors at several black colleges, as well as with Du Bois and the *Crisis*, Spingarn first persuaded hundreds of blacks to volunteer for a separate officers training camp. Then for several months he pressed a reluctant army to set up a Colored Officers Training Camp at Fort Des Moines, Iowa. Ultimately more than a thousand African Americans were commissioned as officers during World War I.[42] These officers became a source of pride and inspiration in black America, but they did little to alter a great racial imbalance. "African Americans comprised 13 percent of the active-duty military manpower during the war, but only seven-tenths of 1 percent of the officers."[43]

Blacks were not just underrepresented in the officer corps. They were also confined to the lower ranks of lieutenant and captain and excluded from higher positions. This was evident in the case of the most prominent black graduate of West Point, Lieutenant Colonel Charles Young. Young had an outstanding record in the regular U.S. Army, where he had recently received a commendation for his service in a Mexican borderlands foray against Pancho Villa. Young was strong, fit, only forty-nine years of age, and the logical candidate to head the segregated officers training camp at Fort Des Moines. In the accelerated promotion of wartime, it seemed certain that Young would become a general by 1918. Instead, the army placed Young on inactive service after a physical exam indicated that he had high blood pressure. Young denied any ailment, stating that he had "[no] aches or pains of any kind and no medical history or sick record whatever." To prove his fitness, he carried a petition with him on a dramatic horseback ride to Washington from his family home in Ohio. "I am not sick, never felt more in condition than at this minute," Young insisted. Writing to Du Bois, Young's wife confessed that the relegation to inactive service made her "so mad [that] I can hardly write." She was convinced that her husband was the victim of "a dirty black trick."[44]

Du Bois knew all about this. He and Young had been good friends ever since they had served together on the faculty at Wilberforce in the 1890s. In some ways it was an unlikely friendship—a classically trained professor of history, Greek, and Latin, and a macho West Point graduate who was in charge of the university's military training program. But Du Bois and Young remained lifelong friends, and so did their wives. Of all Du Bois's comrades, none save John Hope was a closer friend. Thus the mistreatment of Young outraged Du Bois. In a private protest to a government official, Du Bois condemned the effort "to get [Young] out of the army by unfair means." In public, the Crisis demanded "that Colonel Young be restored to 'active service.'"[45]

When it came to discrimination against black soldiers, the mistreatment of Young was only the tip of the iceberg. When black and white troops mixed, epithets like "nigger" and "coon" were voiced frequently. Some white soldiers refused to salute African American officers, and a few refused to take orders. At the same time, in response to pressure from southern whites, previously desegregated, off-base facilities in the North began to separate the races.[46] In Kansas, when a black sergeant complained that a theater refused to sell orchestra seats to colored soldiers, the commanding general waffled. The general conceded that the sergeant was "strictly within his legal rights and the theater manager is legally wrong" but, the general continued, "the sergeant is guilty of the greater wrong in doing anything no matter how legally correct that will provoke race animosity." The general then issued a directive that advised "all colored members . . . and especially the officers . . . [to] refrain from going where their presence will be resented."[47]

The discrimination against black soldiers gave Du Bois pause. In the Crisis he expressed his indignation at "the shameful treatment which these men, and which we, their brothers, receive all our lives, and which our fathers received, and our children await."[48] Nevertheless, Du Bois remained optimistic about the future for African Americans. Secretary of War Newton D. Baker was a fair-minded man who tried to stop the petty discrimination that undermined military morale and effectiveness. To that end, Baker appointed a black man, Booker T. Washington's former executive secretary, Emmett J. Scott, as his special advisor and troubleshooter on racial matters.[49] Most significantly for Du Bois, more than a thousand African Americans were commissioned as officers in the U.S. Army.

Du Bois's spirits were also buoyed by what has come to be known as the Great Migration. As he noted in the *Crisis,* during the war there was "an immense migration of Negroes from the South to Northern cities and industrial centers."[50] Between 1915 and 1920 about one-half million African Americans left the rural South for the urban North, while a like number moved from southern farms to southern cities. Some of the migrants were fleeing from the discrimination and disfranchisement that were especially pronounced in the rural South, while others sought refuge from falling cotton prices, infestations of boll weevils, and floods. At the same time, the urban areas experienced an economic boom fueled in part by the war and suffered a labor shortage due to a pause in immigration from Europe and the departure of many workers for the war. Upon arriving in the cities, the new black immigrants found better wages, less discrimination, and the freedom to vote.

Du Bois knew white racism had not ended, but the Great Migration and the commissioning of black officers led him to believe that "after . . . years of oppression which at times became almost unbearable, the tide against the Negro in the United States has been turned." In the future Du Bois expected to see "the walls of prejudice gradually crumble."[51] Racists had not wanted blacks to fight, but they had failed in their efforts to keep them out of the army, and they could not stop other blacks from migrating. "We'll fight and work. If we fight we'll learn the fighting game and cease to be so 'aisily lynched.' If we don't fight we'll learn the more lucrative trades and cease to be so easily robbed and exploited." "We will walk into the industrial shoes of a few million whites who go to the front. We will get higher wages and we cannot be stopped."[52]

Du Bois's optimism was probably influenced as well by a spirit of excessive patriotism that was at large in the United States. During the war, the Wilson administration censored criticism and organized a propaganda campaign that was without precedent in American history. A special "Committee on Public Information" stressed two key points: that the United States was fighting for freedom and democracy, and that the Germans were diabolic Huns who perpetrated atrocities in their campaign to conquer the world. Later, Du Bois came to think that "the triumph of Germany in 1918 could not have had worse results than the triumph of the Allies." But at the time he was swept up in the prevailing sentiment and "felt for a moment during the war that I could be without reservation a patriotic American."[53]

Du Bois's personal regard for J. E. Spingarn also contributed to his euphoria. Despite occasional quarrels at the NAACP office, Du Bois recalled that "[no] other white man ever touched me emotionally so closely as Joel Spingarn." And Spingarn "was fired with consuming patriotism. [H]e believed in America and feared Germany." Du Bois later wrote that "it was due to [Spingarn's] advice and influence that I became during the World War nearer to feeling myself a real and full American than ever before or since."[54]

"Close Ranks"

While he was buoyed by this spirit of patriotism, Du Bois wrote the most controversial editorial of his long career, "Close Ranks." "While this war lasts," he wrote in the July 1918 issue of the *Crisis*, "let us . . . forget our special grievances and close our ranks shoulder to shoulder with our own white fellow citizens and with the allied nations that are fighting for democracy."[55]

Previously Du Bois had supported the war but also demanded the redress of "justifiable grievances" that had produced "not disloyalty but an amount of unrest and bitterness." He knew that many problems could not be settled immediately, but he demanded "that minimum of consideration which will enable [the African American] to be an efficient fighter for victory." Specifically, Du Bois wanted an end to lynching, the desegregation of public travel, and equal opportunity for employment. "All these things" were "matters not simply of justice, but of national and group efficiency." They were needed "to still the natural unrest and apprehension among one-eighth of our citizens so as to enable them wholeheartedly and unselfishly to throw their every ounce of effort into this mighty and righteous war."[56]

"Close Ranks," on the other hand, asked blacks to forget their special grievances for the duration of the war. This was something that many African Americans would not do.

Byron Gunner, an old friend from the Niagara Movement, spoke for many blacks when he told Du Bois that they "should do just the reverse of what you advise. Now, 'while this war lasts,' is the most opportune time for us to push and keep our 'special grievances' to the fore." Monroe Trotter agreed with Gunner. Before "Close Ranks," Trotter and Du Bois had thought alike: They both supported the war but also asked for democracy at home. Afterwards, Trotter called Du Bois "a deserter" and "a rank quitter in the fight for equal rights." "[W]hen the greatest opportunity [was] at hand," during "the war for democracy for all others," Du Bois had "weakened, compromised, deserted the fight, betrayed the cause of his race."[57]

Other editors and columnists were equally severe in criticizing "Close Ranks." The New York News accused Du Bois of "crass moral cowardice,"[58] and the Cleveland Gazette said it would be "many a year, if ever, before [Du Bois] will enjoy the full confidence of the majority of our most loyal people."[59] Columnist William A. Byrd acknowledged that Du Bois had previously been regarded as "the one fearless and uncompromising champion of the rights of our people." But now, because of "Close Ranks," Du Bois had forfeited "the confidence of those who once implicitly trusted his leadership."[60] Harry Smith, the editor of the Gazette, lamented that even "Booker T. Washington in the heyday of his 'doctrine of surrender' . . . would have dared no such a thing."[61]

Nor was the criticism of Du Bois limited to the black press. One meeting of the Washington branch of the NAACP became so stormy with denunciations that the local leader feared the organization would split up.[62] And one of Du Bois's supporters in the Cleveland NAACP was asked to leave a meeting when he tried to answer allegations that Du Bois had become a disloyal traitor to his race.[63]

Many people suspected at first that Du Bois had succumbed to pressure from the government. Because about one hundred newspapers and magazines had been denied mail privileges for questioning government policies during wartime, Du Bois knew he had to tread carefully in his editorials. This point was brought home when U.S. Attorney Earl Barnes asked for a complete file of the Crisis and then complained that the tone of some articles seemed "calculated to create a feeling of dissatisfaction among colored people." Barnes insisted that changes should be made, and an attorney for the Crisis gave assurances "that we would do everything within our means to meet the views of the Government."[64]

But the initial disappointment with Du Bois turned to outrage when the public learned that at the very time when "Close Ranks" was published, Du Bois had been considering a captaincy in the U.S. Army. Some critics then accused Du Bois of trying to serve two masters, and even of shifting his allegiance from the Negro people to the U.S. government.

The captaincy episode emanated from Du Bois's friendship with Joel Spingarn. In 1917, Spingarn had left New York to become a major in the army's Military Intelligence Branch (MIB). Among other activities, the MIB kept an eye on the black population, looking for evidence of pro-German activity; and in the fervid climate of World War I there was a tendency to look with suspicion on any outspoken attempt to combat racial discrimination. Germany was accused of exploiting racial tensions, of tempting blacks with offers of social equality, and even of planning a Negro uprising in the South. President Wilson himself said Germany had "filled our unsuspecting communities with vicious spies and conspirators [who] sought to corrupt the opinion of our people."[65]

After he was put in charge of a "Negro Subversion" subsection in 1918, Spingarn proceeded to redirect the MIB away from surveillance and toward redressing grievances. He reasoned that black loyalty could best be bolstered by using the federal government's enormous wartime powers to combat unfair discrimination. He therefore developed an ambitious program to suppress racism in the press and cinema, drew up plans for a committee of blacks to advise the army's chief of staff, and organized a conference of black editors. In addition, Spingarn persuaded the House Judiciary Committee to hold hearings on an anti-lynching bill.[66]

As Spingarn's work got under way, he also made a decision that almost wrecked Du Bois's career. On June 4, 1918, after telling Du Bois about the work being done to win the war for democracy in Europe and for civil rights in the United States, Spingarn gave Du Bois "the shock of his life by offering him a commission" as a captain in the Military Intelligence Bureau.[67] Spingarn then pressed Du Bois for an immediate answer, and Du Bois agreed to take an army physical exam on June 15. When Du Bois failed the physical (probably because of his kidney operations), Spingarn persuaded the War Department to waive the requirement. To Du Bois, Spingarn confided that Spingarn's "whole constructive programme" depended upon Du Bois's "joining forces with me now."[68]

Spingarn had proceeded with the best of intentions, but once knowledge of the captaincy became public the criticism of Du Bois mounted to the point where, as Du Bois noted, "the colored people . . . have got it into their heads that either I have sold out to the Government or that the Government is about to capture and muzzle me."[69] One journalist noted that just at the point when Du Bois was poised to assume the mantle of race leadership, he "lost the high regard our people in large numbers held him in."[70] Because of the captaincy, "Close Ranks" seemed to involve something worse than lowering sails during a wartime storm. Du Bois was accused of being party to a corrupt bargain. He was called a "traitor" and a "Benedict Arnold."[71] He was condemned, not because "Close Ranks" could not be defended in its own terms "but because what he wrote was written in large part to consummate [a] bargain."[72]

In private correspondence, Du Bois denied that there was any connection between "Close Ranks" and the captaincy. He told friends that the editorial was already in print before he was "summoned to Washington and to my great surprise asked if I would accept a captaincy in a new bureau to work among colored people."[73] Du Bois's friends accepted his word. One of them assured Du Bois that the suggestion of a bribe "imput[ed] to you motives beneath your type of manhood."[74] Indeed, because any such deal would have been out of character for Du Bois, early biographers rejected the suggestion that Du Bois wrote "Close Ranks" in order to secure a position in military intelligence.[75]

In the 1990s, however, two scholars indicted Du Bois. Mark Ellis showed that Du Bois wrote "Close Ranks" *after* Spingarn mentioned the captaincy and concluded that "the editorial crucially influenced the War Department when it was considering the commission." And biographer David Levering Lewis concluded that Du Bois "struck a deal" with the army to write "Close Ranks" in exchange for a captaincy. After reviewing the same evidence, however, William Jordan, another scholar of the 1990s, concluded that "Du Bois did not write 'Close Ranks' to qualify for a commission."[76]

Different conclusions are possible because the evidence is circumstantial and can be interpreted differently. Spingarn and Du Bois both agreed that Du Bois was taken by surprise when Spingarn first mentioned the captaincy on June 4, 1918. Yet when Spingarn pressed for an answer Du Bois agreed, although with reservations. Apparently he could not say "no" to a man he called his "nearest white friend," a man who had loaned him money in the past and even sent his personal physician to keep watch when one of Du Bois's kidneys was removed.[77] Therefore, rather than reject the captaincy outright, Du Bois agreed but with conditions. He said he would accept the captaincy *if* he could keep general control of the *Crisis* and *if* the NAACP would give him an annual subvention of a thousand dollars so that he would not earn less as a captain than he had as editor.[78] This sort of financial arrangement was not unusual at the time.

Because Spingarn was away on military service, he missed the meeting at which Du Bois presented his conditions to the NAACP's board of directors. But Du Bois made no effort to encourage the attendance of other board members who were known to favor the plan and, remarkably, some of those who did attend the meeting noted that Du Bois made the case in a perfunctory manner that suggested that he was ambivalent about the captaincy. After discussion, the board decided that it was "inadvisable that Dr. Du Bois undertake to combine the duties of . . . editor of *The Crisis* with . . . service as a commissioned officer in the Army Intelligence Bureau."[79]

Four days after the board meeting, Du Bois confided to John Hope that it would have been possible, by encouraging the attendance of sympathetic board members, "to get the consent of the Board."[80] But he also recognized that such maneuvering would polarize the NAACP—and Du Bois wanted to avoid "the disruption of this organization so painfully built up through the years of travail."[81] Consequently, Du Bois decided against accepting the captaincy. Writing to Spingarn, he said he was "sorry for this outcome because I know you will be disappointed and that I will miss a great opportunity for service, but I am convinced that even with a full board the proposition could be only carried by a sharp and unsatisfactory division."[82]

In reply, Spingarn practically begged Du Bois to reconsider.[83] But Du Bois had no enthusiasm for Spingarn's plan. He had considered the captaincy because it was hard for him to refuse Spingarn. But Du Bois would not campaign for the conditions he attached from the outset and, as he told Spingarn, he was "all at sea and disposed simply to sit and wait in order to get the inspiration to see my duty clearly."[84]

Two days after the NAACP board rejected Du Bois's conditions, Mary White Ovington wrote to Du Bois, reiterated her opposition to the captaincy, and further said that she suspected Du Bois was "probably glad" about the board's decision. In response, Du Bois told Ovington that he had "decided not to go to Washington."[85] Before departing from New York to join Nina and Yolande for three weeks of vacation at the New Jersey shore, Du Bois even wrote a draft of the official statement of the NAACP Board: "The Board . . . wishes in the present crisis to render to the country every patriotic service and it believes that the presence of Dr. Du Bois in New York City, giving his whole time to the conduct and editing of *The Crisis,* is a service of far greater national importance than the proposed commission in the Military Intelligence Bureau."[86]

While Du Bois was on vacation, the army reached a decision that was definitive but anticlimactic. From the outset some white officers had scoffed at Spingarn's plan to promote black loyalty by removing racial grievances, and others had warned that Spingarn's program would take the army beyond the proper limits of military activity. Finally, in late July 1918, the army formally rejected Du Bois's application for a commission, ostensibly for medical reasons but also because of the controversy over "Close Ranks." The controversy, after all, had demolished the argument that Du Bois would be especially effective in persuading black "radicals" to support the war. When it turned out that "the captaincy" was agitating and dividing black public opinion, Du Bois lost his value to military intelligence. After rejecting Du Bois, the army also closed Spingarn's office and sent him to France, where Spingarn saw military action on the western front.[87]

Du Bois backed away from the captaincy but not from "Close Ranks." The *Crisis* for August 1918 carried another ringing editorial, one that began by asserting that because the United States was "our country," this was "our war." Although the country was "not perfect," Du Bois again insisted that African Americans should not bargain with their loyalty. He called for "patience . . . without compromise; silence without surrender; grim determination never to cease striving until we can vote, travel, learn, work and enjoy in peace—all this, and yet with it and above it all the tramp of our armies over the blood-stained lilies of France to show the world again what the loyalty and bravery of black men means."[88]

Over There

After the armistice, Du Bois returned to his former emphasis on agitation. He sensed that the time had arrived "to bring the attention of the world to the Negro problem," and he wanted to do so by attending the Paris Peace Conference, which would influence "the destinies of mankind for a hundred years to come."[89] But traveling to Paris was not to be taken for granted, since the Wilson administration had denied passports to its critics. Monroe Trotter, for example, had to travel abroad without papers as a second cook on a small freighter and then jump ship after being allowed to go to a wharf to mail a letter.[90]

Du Bois therefore proceeded cautiously. Rather than announce his plans, he talked his way onto the fifty-two-member press delegation. First he persuaded President Wilson's press secretary that it was desirable for the *Crisis* to be represented because the president had already decided to send the Tuskegee principal Robert R. Moton to speak to the returning black soldiers. Then he enticed the secretary of war with vague comments about a Pan-African conference to discuss the application of Wilsonian self-determination to the former German colonies in Africa. Thus Du Bois and Lester Walton of the *New York Age* were the only black journalists to travel on board the official press boat, the *Orizaba*, where they shared a cabin with Moton and Moton's secretary, Nathan Hunt.

Du Bois was more candid in divulging his plans to colleagues at the NAACP. In 1918 the board of directors gave Du Bois two thousand dollars to investigate and collect documents pertaining to the treatment of black soldiers, and additional funds were earmarked for representing African Americans at the Paris Peace Conference and for discussing the problems of Africa. James Weldon Johnson explained that African Americans were "fully alive to the urgency of having not only their own cause but the cause of all colored people . . . brought to the attention of those who are to make the peace settlement."[91]

Upon arriving in France, Du Bois turned to the French government, particularly to the six black deputies in the French parliament. During the war, the French army had called up thousands of black troops from colonies in Africa, and in gratitude the French prime minister, Georges Clemenceau, gave permission to hold a conference in Paris. To readers of the *Crisis,* Du Bois explained that a meeting on the disposition of the former German colonies in Africa would serve, "better than any other means that could be taken, to focus the attention of the peace delegates and the civilized world on the just claims of the Negro everywhere."[92] He therefore set himself to the task of organizing a meeting that he called the Pan-African Congress.

In February 1919, fifty-seven delegates, including a number of native Africans who had been educated abroad, met at the Grand Hotel on the Boulevard des Capucines. There Blaise Diagne, a black deputy from Senegal, began the discussions with praise for French colonial rule. Later, however, the delegates passed a number of resolutions that called for better treatment of the African colonies.[93]

At the time, some African Americans thought Du Bois and the NAACP should focus on the betterment of African Americans within the United States. "Why 'democracy in Africa' alone?" asked Chandler Owen, one of the editors of the black socialist monthly, the *Messenger.* "Why not 'American democracy' too?"[94] Similarly, A.M.E. Bishop C. S. Smith acknowledged that work on behalf of Africa was important but added: "it ought not be done by the NAACP because the NAACP has its hands full with its American program."[95] In the *Kansas City Call,* Roy Wilkins complained that Du Bois was "gallivanting over the country from the Atlantic to the Pacific talking Pan-Africanism when he should have been using his talents to aid degraded America." Harry Smith of the *Cleveland Gazette* also complained that while Du Bois was getting "worked up" over the treatment of colored colonies, he had said "not a word" about "his own suffering (Afro-American) people."[96]

Du Bois's comments about Africa were cautious—at least by comparison with the opinions that would prevail in later generations. At the outset, Du Bois insisted that "Africa must *ultimately* be returned to the Africans."[97] But the devil was in the adverb, for Du Bois also conceded that the principle of self-determination could not be wholly applied to "semi-civilized [African] peoples."[98] He asked not for independence but for assistance in "strengthening the forces of Civilization."[99]

Yet, as Du Bois saw it, this assistance was not likely to come from the leading nations, for these nations were themselves not civilized. "Outside of cannibalism," Du Bois wrote, there was "no vice and no degradation in native African customs which can begin to touch the horrors thrust upon [Africa] by white masters. Drunkenness, terrible diseases, immorality, all these things have been the gifts of European civilization." "White men are merely juggling with words . . . when they declare that the withdrawal of Europeans from Africa will plunge that continent into chaos. What Europe, and indeed only a small group in Europe, wants in Africa is not a field for the spread of European civilization, but a field for exploitation."[100]

To make matters worse, Du Bois wrote, the whites were deluded by racism. They had forgotten that world history had once centered in Africa. They mistakenly assumed that the present status of Africa and its native races would be permanent. Rather than recognize that "the development of the uncivilized native is a simple problem of time, education, and fair economic treatment," the colonial powers assumed that black people were incapable of development and unworthy of education—fit only for exploitation.[101]

Du Bois insisted that "the twelve million civilized Negroes of the United States," as well as "educated people of Negro descent in South America and the West Indies," and educated blacks from Africa itself, should be given more say over the development of Africa.[102] The Pan-African Congress had "nothing to do with any 'Africa for the Africans' movement," Du Bois wrote.[103] Rather, the Congress defended the prerogatives of an international Talented Tenth. An official resolution asserted that "Whenever persons of African descent are civilized and able to meet the tests of surrounding culture, they shall be accorded the same rights as their fellow citizens; they shall not be denied on account of race or color a voice in their own Government."[104] The Pan-African Congress, in short, brought together educated representatives of the various peoples of African descent with the hope that their acquaintance would lead to progress in the future.

Later, the Pan-African Congress of 1919 would become an important symbol. It would be regarded as a harbinger of a new consciousness that eventually percolated through the African diaspora. Coming just a few months after the controversy over "Close Ranks," the congress was also important for more immediate reasons. Although Du Bois had received some additional criticism for focusing on the problems of Africa, as distinguished from the concerns of African Americans, his organization of the Pan-African Congress helped restore Du Bois's reputation as a race leader. The congress also lifted Du Bois's spirits, introduced him to new friends, and gave him an international perspective. Du Bois admitted that the concrete results of the congress were small, but the meeting loomed large in his memory.[105]

The second part of Du Bois's mission, investigating the treatment of black soldiers, did not go so well. Du Bois had supported the United States during the war because, despite all his country's faults, he deemed it "capable of realizing our dreams and inspiring the greater world."[106] When he investigated the actual treatment of African

American soldiers in Europe, however, Du Bois recoiled in anguish. He had expected some discrimination, but the reality was worse than anything he had imagined. "Within a month after landing he was utterly amazed and dumbfounded at the revelations poured upon him. He heard of conditions, acts, conspiracies, wholesale oppression and cruelty of which he had no previous inkling."[107]

Three-fourths of the two hundred thousand African American soldiers in France had been assigned to labor battalions—something that Du Bois accepted because he understood that America's great contribution was in mobilizing its enormous economic resources to support the Allied cause. The Allies needed stevedores, road builders, wood choppers, and railroad hands. Uniformed black laborers made a crucial contribution to the war effort, and Du Bois saluted them as "the best workers in France, . . . acknowledged by everybody [for] their efficiency."[108] He knew that many of the men who helped win the war never saw action on the battlefields.

Yet Du Bois was disturbed when he learned that blacks in the "services of supply" were generally mistreated, overworked, and almost enslaved. The army brass assumed that black workers were best "handled" by white people from the South and often turned for noncommissioned officers to southern whites who had previous experience managing gangs of Negroes on plantations, turpentine farms, and construction projects. Du Bois acknowledged that some of these supervisors were good men, but he insisted that "the majority were 'nigger' drivers of the most offensive type." They imposed long hours and confined black soldiers to barracks while white soldiers had the privilege of the town. "Worked often like slaves, twelve and fourteen hours a day, these [black workers] were well-fed, poorly clad, indifferently housed, often beaten, always 'Jim-Crowed' and insulted." Nevertheless, "they worked—how they worked! Everybody joins to testify to this: the white slave-drivers, the army officers, the French, the visitors—all say that the American Negro was the best laborer in France." "If American food and materials saved France in the end from utter exhaustion, it was the Negro stevedore who made that aid effective."[109]

About fifty thousand African American soldiers also served in combat units, and here the record was mixed. One of the two African American divisions, the Ninety-third, was incorporated into the French army. For seven months these black soldiers served as replacements in badly decimated French divisions, "partaking of the same activities, sharing the same hardships and the same dangers." Because "they were from the first treated on such terms of equality and brotherhood," Du Bois wrote, "they were eager to fight."[110] Five hundred and eighty four men of the division were killed in front-line service and 2,582 wounded. Special kudos went to the 369th Regiment from Harlem, which "was under fire 191 days—a record for any American unit" and received "over 170 citations for the Croix de Guerre and Distinguished Service Cross."[111]

On the other hand, the record of the Ninety-second Division—all black except for its high command—was undistinguished. One of its regiments, the 368th Infantry Regiment, broke when it received fire in the vicinity of barbed wire fences. Four of the unit's black officers were later convicted of cowardice, although the convictions were overturned when it was learned that the quartermaster had mistakenly failed to provide the troops with wire cutters.[112] Nevertheless, this incident was often mentioned to discredit the service of the African American officers and soldiers in France.

Du Bois detected a white conspiracy to set up black officers for failure. He remembered that many in the army had not wanted black officers in the first place. They had openly said that blacks were not capable of military leadership. After sending the 368th Regiment into battle without proper equipment, they had justified their hostility by publicizing the failure of the unit. Some white officers made no attempt to disguise their hostility. Brigadier General William H. Hay, for example, stated his views bluntly: "In my opinion there is no better soldier than the Negro, but God damn a 'nigger' officer."[113] And Colonel Allen J. Greer, the chief of staff of the Ninety-second Division, reported that black officers did not train, control, or command their units because they were "engaged very largely in the pursuit of French women, it being their first opportunity to meet white women who did not treat them as servants."[114]

Believing that black men lusted for white women, and impressed by what they called the "unbridled sexuality" of the black troops, Greer and others in the Ninety-second's high command did what they could to prevent racial mixing. To this end, they put into effect a series of orders that Greer called "drastic preventative measures." First, off-base freedoms were curtailed, with "no passes . . . issued except to men of known reliability." Then men of the Ninety-second were ordered "to stay out of French homes under penalty of twenty-four hours on bread-and-water followed by an eighteen-mile hike with full pack." Finally, bed checks were ordered "every hour daily between reveille and 11 p.m., with a written record showing how each check was made."[115]

Nor was this all. In rural areas, it was difficult for black troops to leave the cantonments and go into town except by stealth. In cities, black workers rarely received passes after their day's work was finished, and cafés and other public places were off limits to blacks. Talking to white women or entering a French home were regarded as serious offenses for colored soldiers. Black soldiers who broke the rules could expect abuse from the M.P.'s and punishment from their commanding officers. If M.P.'s were not available, white soldiers would take matters into their own hands, with barroom fights likely to occur if black soldiers tried to pick up white girls or were thought to be trying to do so.[116]

In addition, as official documents attested, the French were urged to segregate the races in France and above all prevent "any public expression of intimacy between white women and black men." U.S. officials understood that the French considered American segregation a matter of prejudice, but white Americans said they faced a prospect that did not exist in France—a future in the United States of widespread miscegenation. They said that "the increasing number of Negroes in the United States (about 15,000,000) would create for the white race in the Republic a menace of degeneracy were it not that an impassable gulf has been made between them." American whites especially feared that French women would "spoil" the African American soldiers—that they would "inspire in black Americans aspirations which to them [the whites] appear intolerable."[117]

In addition, myths were fostered to keep the races apart. Although blacks were more likely than whites to have venereal diseases, it was false to suggest, as rumor had it, that the great majority of black soldiers were infected.[118] Nor was it fair to insinuate, as rumors did, that the higher incidence of venereal disease was due to the fact that Africa lagged behind Europe in evolutionary development and that black people consequently were controlled by brutal instincts. Nevertheless, American army officers repeatedly told the French that it was not safe for white women to associate with primitive soldiers who were lacking in self control.

Rumors of rape were also used to discourage interracial liaisons. One investigator noted that "the report was current in France that the committing of the 'unmentionable crime' was very common, and according to the rumors, Negro officers, as well as privates in all branches and grades of the service, were guilty of this crime."[119] Another investigator reported that "The 92nd Division had not been in France long before it was charged with committing 'more rape than any division in the American Expeditionary Force.'"[120]

The reports were a slanderous effort at social control, for only a dozen black soldiers were ever indicted for rape in France—and only three were convicted.[121] As one scholar has noted, this was "an enviable record for any army in any war."[122] Du Bois understandably took umbrage at the "open reiteration of unfounded charges of . . . [the] infamous crime." For him, it was proof "that many Americans would rather have lost the war than to see a black soldier talking to a white woman."[123]

For four months in 1919, Du Bois heard stories and received documents that substantiated this mistreatment. Hell seemed to be loose in France. Black laborers were subjected to near-slavery. Black soldiers were accused of immorality. Black officers were court-martialed for cowardice. And black people were described as members of an inferior race. Despite their support for the war, African Americans had been the victims of "one of the bitterest and most stinging campaigns of personal affront and insult ever attempted."[124]

What could be done? In the short term, nothing; for Du Bois had been required to sign a pledge that while he was in France he would "not . . . publish any written statements, or give out any interviews, except through the censorship of the Intelligence Section of the General Staff."[125] Upon returning to the United States, however, Du Bois's indignation boiled over. During the next three months he published the documents he had acquired as well as an extended essay, "The Black Man in the Great War."

Understandably, Du Bois felt betrayed. At his behest, blacks had rallied around the flag, and their country had responded by organizing "a nation-wide and latterly a world-wide propaganda of deliberate and continuous insult and defamation of black blood."[126] This was the country to which the soldiers of democracy had returned. This was the fatherland for which they had fought. In especially stinging editorials, Du Bois issued a new call to arms:

To your tents, O Israel!
And fight, fight, fight for Freedom!

[B]y the God of Heaven, we are cowards and jackasses if now
that war is over, we do not marshal every ounce of our brain
and brawn to fight a sterner, longer, more unbending battle
against the forces of hell in our own land.
   We *return.*
   We *return from fighting.*
   We *return fighting.*[127]

Robert Russa Moton and Emmett J. Scott

Du Bois's truculent editorials made most white readers either
angry or miserable with guilt. In contrast, Robert Russa Moton, who
succeeded Booker T. Washington as the principal of Tuskegee Institute, had a knack for uplifting the spirits of white people. "If a vote
were taken . . . to determine the best-loved Negro in the United
States," Mary White Ovington wrote, "the choice would fall upon
Robert Russa Moton.[128]

Du Bois and Moton were good friends. "I always liked 'Major' Moton," Du Bois wrote. "He was one of the few persons with whom I
loved to spend a day or more in close companionship and conference." As mentioned in Chapter 3, Du Bois had personally invited
Moton to become a member of the Niagara Movement, and Moton
had encouraged Booker T. Washington to cooperate with the NAACP.
The friendship of Du Bois and Moton deepened in December 1918
when the two men traveled together to France. "We had a most en-
joyable passage," Du Bois wrote, "full of the pleasantest companionship."[129] Du Bois and Moton got along so well that, after sharing a
ship's cabin on the *Orizaba*, they stayed at the same Paris hotel with
rooms across the hall from one another.

And yet Du Bois and Moton were different. Moton towered well
over six feet while Du Bois reached a height of only five feet, seven
inches. Du Bois was a colored man of light complexion and one who
was fastidious about his appearance, while Moton was a *black* man
who wore standard clothing. Most importantly, Du Bois and Moton
approached whites differently. Du Bois condemned discrimination
and demanded equality—"political equality, industrial equality, and
social equality"—and insisted that African Americans would "never

. . . rest satisfied with anything less."[130] Moton took a more conciliatory approach.

Du Bois acknowledged that he and Moton agreed on the basic
questions. They both wanted African Americans to enjoy every right
of citizenship. They differed only in emphasis. But sometimes the difference led Du Bois to criticize Moton openly and bitterly. Du Bois
later recalled that there were instances when Moton "became to me
a symbol of 'Uncle Tom' and a 'white folks' nigger.' I thought he was
surrendering our rights and compromising with our enemies. . . .
The editorial pages of *The Crisis* attacked him without mercy."[131]

These attacks were especially sharp in 1919 during the months
just after Du Bois and Moton had visited France. To understand this
criticism, one must know more about Robert Russa Moton.

Moton was six months older than Du Bois, having been born in
Virginia in August 1867. Family tradition held that Moton's great-
great-great-grandfather was an African prince who was tricked into
boarding a slave ship after selling about a dozen blacks who had been
captured in a tribal battle. Then the prince was drugged and awoke
to find himself in the hold chained to one of the captives he had sold.

This ancestral prince never liked white people. But his great-great
grandson, Moton's father, came to differentiate between "quality"
whites and "poor white trash" when a master supported him after
Moton's father had thrashed a white overseer who tried to adminis-
ter an unauthorized whipping. During the Civil War, Moton's father
served as a body servant to a Confederate colonel. When Moton's father was captured by the Northern army near Petersburg he was told
that he might remain with the Yankees if he wished; "but he told them
that he could not do so at the time because he had given his definite
promise that he would stand by his [colonel] until the war was
over."[132]

By the time Robert was born, his father had settled in Virginia,
married a cook, and become the foreman on a large plantation.
Through his parents, Moton became a houseboy and waiter at the Big
House on the plantation. The mistress of the plantation taught Moton and his mother to read, and later Moton attended a free elementary school that had been established for African Americans in the
neighborhood.

Yet Moton's youth did not pass without incidents of discrimination. As a young boy, Moton was especially friendly with one of the

white scions of the plantation. The two lads "fished and hunted . . . and engaged in many boyish sports and pranks."[133] Yet when the white youth returned home after a semester at college, he refused to speak or shake hands with Moton—a snub that caused Moton to think more seriously about race relations than ever before.

This experience also awakened Moton's curiosity about education. After working for a few years in a lumber camp, Moton made his way to Hampton Institute where, like Booker T. Washington before him, he became a special favorite of General Samuel Chapman Armstrong. Shortly after he graduated from Hampton in 1890, Moton became Hampton's dean of students—a position that was known as the "Commandant of Cadets" at Hampton. For twenty-five years Moton made this his life's work, and he was widely known as the "Major" of the cadet brigade. He settled comfortably into the Hampton community, with a country home in Capahoosic as well as quarters near the campus. His first wife died in 1906 after only one year of marriage, but he had four children with a second wife, Jennie Dee Booth.

As the chief disciplinarian at Hampton, Moton was called upon to resolve many difficult problems. In addition to the usual situations that arose in a school that had an almost all-white faculty and mostly black students, there were special problems that involved some of the 150 Native American students on campus, and there was also the matter of reconciling the different aims of the white northern benefactors and the surrounding southern white community. It was no easy matter to harmonize all these groups, but Moton was so tactful and discreet that he eventually became one of the most popular members of the faculty.

When he was a student at Hampton, Moton initially had been ashamed of the black folk songs and plantation melodies that were popular at the time, saying that he had known such songs all his life and had gone to Hampton to learn something better. But after refusing to sing the songs for three years, Moton changed his mind and came to regard them as a priceless and distinctively Negro contribution to culture. This "readjustment of values . . . was not particularly easy for a raw country lad," Moton admitted,[134] but he was blessed with a deep and melodious baritone voice and in his senior year he toured the country with the Hampton Singers. Later, Moton accompanied Booker T. Washington on speaking and fund-raising tours.

Moton often began the meetings with songs, and then the two men would echo one another in promoting the Hampton-Tuskegee model of racial advancement through industrial training and interracial cooperation. Contemporaries noted that Moton had "a fine sense of humor" and was "a speaker of uncommon ability."[135]

When Booker T. Washington died in 1915, Moton became the principal of Tuskegee Institute. Other men would have sufficed if the principal had been required only to keep the affairs of the school running smoothly. But because the office carried with it implications of racial leadership, the trustees needed more than a prudent manager. They said they needed a man with a "forceful personality." "The man who is chosen to take Dr. Washington's place must be a man who as nearly as possible measures up to Dr. Washington's stature. He should not only be a man with the gift of organization and administration, . . . but he should be a man capable of shedding inspiration, arousing enthusiasm, and wielding influence."[136]

Yet Moton understood that he was not Booker T. Washington. He threw himself into a successful fund-raising campaign, but he downplayed efforts to control the patronage of philanthropists and politicians. He did not pay subventions to friendly editors, and he allowed someone else to succeed Washington as the president of one of the central cogs of the Tuskegee Machine, the National Negro Business League. "Moton had no relish for politics," one scholar concluded. "He thought of himself as a school principal. . . . He did not want to be the One Great Leader."[137]

Moton also became involved with "the interracial movement," an alliance with well-to-do whites who spoke out against racial discrimination even though they did not oppose segregation per se. Ever since his youth as a waiter at the Big House, Moton had cultivated friendships with upper-class whites, and as principal of Tuskegee he continued to proclaim a gospel that many whites found endearing. He said that "relations between black and white in America are more cordial than the relations between the white race and the darker races in any other part of the world."[138] And he insisted that blacks, if they were to make the most of their opportunities, should emphasize self-discipline, learn useful trades, and build up their own institutions.

Moton's popularity with whites inevitably aroused suspicions among blacks, especially those who thought their cause was best served by forcefully criticizing racial discrimination. Some blacks acknowledged, "If certain exigencies demand that R. R. Moton . . . make certain statements for the benefit of the institution he serves, we need no assurances where R. R. Moton, the man, stands on the same propositions." But others wondered if Moton's conciliation did not go too far. They sympathized with Du Bois, who wrote an open letter to Moton in 1916 expressing the "deepest solicitude in your case."[139]

Du Bois's open letter was precipitated by an incident that involved Moton's wife, Jennie, who was rudely ejected from a Pullman coach shortly after Moton was named as the principal of Tuskegee. The trustees of the Institute then rushed to the press with a statement announcing that Moton did not believe in social equality, did not encourage African Americans to ride in Pullman cars, and bore no resentment against anyone for the treatment accorded to his wife. The implications of this statement were certainly deceptive, for Moton himself traveled by Pullman, as had Booker T. Washington before him. Yet at the beginning of his career at Tuskegee, Moton could not rush into print and contradict the trustees. He remained silent and suffered the bitter criticism of the black press.[140]

Du Bois understood that Moton's views had not been correctly reported in the press. He knew that Moton never told members of his family not to ride Pullman cars. He knew "only too well the way in which Southern newspapers put such sentiments into the mouths of colored leaders." Nevertheless, Du Bois found fault with Moton for what he did not say. Du Bois did not expect Moton to spend valuable time correcting every misleading news story, but he insisted that "when so monstrous a statement is made, as in the case of the Pullman car, something besides silence and acquiescence is called for." "Such atrocious statements cannot be always passed in silence."[141]

Du Bois and Moton's different temperaments were also on display in France. Shortly after they arrived in Paris they met with John Hope, who had been in France for two months and who told them about the mistreatment of the black labor battalions, the rumors of rape and cowardice, and the orders that black men should not associate with French women.[142]

Du Bois and Moton reacted in ways that were characteristic of their differing personalities. Du Bois set out to investigate the complaints, to gather documents, and to write articles on the history of black soldiers in the World War. When the documents and articles were published in 1919, they created a sensation and drove up the circulation of the *Crisis* to more than a hundred thousand.

Moton, on the other hand, went quietly to leading officials with pleas that they end the discrimination and stop the rumors. First, he secured relief for the African American stevedores, whose workday was reduced to eight hours after Moton conferred with General John J. Pershing, the commander-in-chief of the American armed forces. Then, after discovering that the 368th Infantry Regiment had been sent into battle without proper equipment, Moton persuaded Secretary of War Newton D. Baker to set aside the court-martial convictions of four black officers.[143]

In addition, Moton squelched the rumors of rape. When the commanding general and two of the white staff officers of the Ninety-second Division said that rape was so common that they had considered either breaking the division into labor battalions or sending all the men back to the United States in disgrace, Moton asked if they would get the records. He explained that general statements were often damaging, and that, because the reputation of the Negro race was at stake, he needed to have exact facts for a report to the secretary of war. When the records were produced, it turned out that there were only seven allegations of rape against a division of more than twelve thousand soldiers—and "of those charged, only two had been found guilty and convicted, and one of the two convictions had been 'turned down' at General Headquarters."[144]

Moton also carried out another assignment that President Woodrow Wilson had given him. In June 1918, Moton told Wilson that there was "genuine restlessness . . . on the part of the colored people"—because their hopes about making the world "safe for democracy" had been dashed by a prevalent white desire to maintain the status quo in race relations. Later Moton informed Wilson that black soldiers, after surviving the shelling and the gas of the Germans, and after experiencing a measure of social equality in France, had developed a "revolutionary attitude . . . which shows itself in a reckless desire to have justice at any cost."[145]

Moton and Wilson both hoped to avoid conflict and bloodshed. To that end Moton agreed to tell the black troops to be realistic and not expect too much upon their return to the United States. Wilson then sent Moton to France as the president's personal envoy, with a special order that instructed army officers to render "all possible assistance in any visit or inspection Moton desires to make." By way of contrast, when Du Bois visited army cantonments, he was preceded by a quite different special order—one that instructed officers to report the "moves and actions" of "a man by name of DuBois."[146]

When addressing the troops, Moton made two points: He commended "the splendid record which they were making" but also mentioned "the danger that would attend any failure . . . to maintain [the] record untarnished." He said that despite special "privations" black soldiers had compiled a record that "sent a thrill of joy and satisfaction to the hearts of millions of . . . Americans." But he warned that when the soldiers returned to America they would face "prejudices and limitations just the same as before you left home." And he advised the troops to behave in a "manly [but] modest way," to "marry and settle down," and not "do anything in peace to spoil the magnificent record you have made in war."[147]

Moton also told the black soldiers that upon their return to America they should continue to fight. But unlike Du Bois, who urged the returning soldiers to struggle against racial discrimination and insult, Moton called for an "individual, personal battle [for] self-control." He called for a war against "passions and desires," "against laziness, shiftlessness, wilfulness." He told the soldiers to behave "in a manly, yet modest and unassuming manner." He said, "the best time to begin to show self-control . . . is right here in France by leading clean, pure lives."[148]

Some of the soldiers took exception to Moton's remarks. One wrote to Du Bois complaining that Moton had dwelt "almost entirely" on "the manner in which they should act upon their return to the United States," emphasizing above all that they should "not . . . be arrogant."[149] "Moton told us to go back South and be good 'niggers,'" was the way another writer put it.[150] Du Bois then published a *Crisis* editorial that, while not questioning "the personal integrity of Robert Russa Moton or his kindly disposition," nevertheless expressed "bitter disappointment."[151] To Du Bois, it seemed that Moton had joined forces with the government in an effort to make blacks submissive.

Other black newspapers echoed the *Crisis*. Before long Moton's friends were complaining that "Du Bois and his ilk" had mounted a "campaign of vilification against Dr. Moton." There were exceptions, however. The *Indianapolis Freeman* said it made good sense for returning black soldiers to be "dignified [and] self-respecting" rather than "belligerent [and] spoiling for a fight." The *New York Age* also commended Moton for recognizing that sometimes discretion was the better part of valor: "An incendiary speech about going back to America and starting a revolution to get their rights would have been popular and would have made Dr. Moton an idol for the moment. But Dr. Moton has had enough experience . . . to know just how far such inflammatory advice goes."[152]

Moreover, in response to Du Bois's criticism, Moton sent Du Bois a personal, not-for-publication letter. Moton began by saying that Du Bois's correspondents had misconstrued his remarks. Moton then emphasized that he was especially disappointed that Du Bois had rushed into print without "asking me directly." After all, Moton wrote, "our various conferences, both on board ship and in France, had been so free and frank that I was sure you would not hesitate a moment to consult me as to the truth of any statements . . . " In closing, Moton summoned a certain eloquence: "I appreciate your zeal and solicitude for the welfare of the twelve millions of our people in this country, in which however, I must protest, you are not alone."[153]

Moton made a good point. Before criticizing Moton, Du Bois should have checked with his friend. But one scholar has certainly rebuked Du Bois too severely when he concluded that criticizing Moton in the *Crisis* exposed Du Bois "as a petty, self-serving, uncharitable, and disloyal man, wholly unsuited for race leadership."[154] Although Moton's candid advice to the troops was defensible, it is easy to understand why many blacks resented Moton's remarks. If Moton had not told the black soldiers to be submissive, he had said they should "settle down," "show self-control," and "lead pure clean lives."

Du Bois's reaction had smacked of what might be called "defensive aggression." Moton and his friends noted that Du Bois himself had recently been vilified by critics who thought "Close Ranks" was too conciliatory. Now they thought Du Bois's criticism of Moton was motivated, at least in part, by a desire to regain his former position as a resolute protest leader. It was "not easy to understand" Du Bois's criticism, Moton wrote in his personal correspondence, especially coming so soon after "the pleasant, intimate personal association we had going over [on the *Orizaba*] and in Paris."[155] But Moton concluded that it was "part of the game."[156] At the time of "Close Ranks," Moton had told a friend that Du Bois had become "*persona non grata* with his own people," and Moton had wondered "what the end will be." Now he knew. The journalist Lester A. Walton also thought that "petty politics is being played to discredit [Moton]."[157] But it was not just politics. Moton's comments were shot through with offensive implications.

Committed to agitation as he was, Du Bois also took up cudgels against Emmett J. Scott, the black special assistant to Secretary of War Newton D. Baker. In the May 1919 issue of the *Crisis,* immediately after lambasting Moton, Du Bois put three truculent questions to Scott:

1. Did you know the treatment which black troops were receiving in France?
2. If you did NOT know, why did you not find out?
3. If you did know, what did you do about it?[158]

In posing these rhetorical questions, Du Bois was confronting a man who did not possess Moton's sweet disposition. This time the answer would not come by way of a friendly, personal letter. Scott replied forcefully and in public.

As one of five special assistants to the secretary of war, Scott's job had been to convey the policies of the War Department to African Americans and their responses to the War Department. By common consensus he worked conscientiously and effectively. During the war Du Bois had said that Scott was doing "as well as anyone could expect," and the *Crisis* thus "gave him every public and private aid and thanked him for his efforts."[159]

Scott's success was no surprise, for he had a well-deserved reputation as an able administrator and go-between. Born in Houston, Texas, in 1873, Scott left Wiley College after three years to become a journalist, first as a reporter for the white *Houston Post* and later as the publisher of his own newspaper for African Americans, the weekly *Houston Freeman.* After reading Booker T. Washington's Atlanta Exposition address, Scott was one of the first black men to recognize that Washington was destined to be a leader. In 1897 he accepted an offer to become Washington's personal secretary, a job for which he was suited by virtue of his intelligence and skill as a journalist.[160]

As Washington's secretary, Scott "subordinated his own ideas and interests to those of his superior so completely that it was almost impossible to tell which of Washington's communications was written by him and which by Scott."[161] Washington was so pleased with Scott's work that he eventually made Scott his chief deputy at Tuskegee Institute. As secretary and second-in-command of Washington's National Negro Business League, Scott also played a leading part in directing the operations of what Du Bois called "the Tuskegee Machine."

Some people expected Scott to succeed Washington as the principal of Tuskegee, but the trustees chose Moton, a man of more imposing public presence. Scott must have been disappointed at not receiving the promotion, but he continued as a loyal assistant to Moton. In private correspondence, he assured friends that he did "not feel bitter over the selection of Major Moton," and Moton confided that he was "surprised and pleased at the cordiality" he received from Scott.[162] Scott said that "Matters here [at Tuskegee] are going on quite pleasantly and the team work all along the line is effective and satisfactory."[163] Scott understood that Tuskegee Institute itself would suffer if factions "lin[ed] up . . . against each other."[164]

When the United States entered the war in 1917, Moton used his influence to get Scott's appointment in the War Department; and Scott then sent his own investigator, the black journalist Ralph Tyler, to France. Long before Du Bois reached Paris, Scott had learned about the special grievances of the black soldiers. Of course, he could not do everything, but it does not follow that he did nothing. He kept the secretary of war posted, and his files contain many letters from black soldiers thanking Scott for the assistance he gave them at home and abroad. Consequently, Scott was in no mood to suffer a scolding from Du Bois. He "refuse[d] to recognize [Du Bois's] puny right to call me to account."[165]

Even if Scott had not compiled a good record in the War Department, he probably would have lashed back. He had long resented Du Bois's criticism of Booker T. Washington, although that did not stop him from working hard to have Du Bois appointed as a captain in the army in 1918. Moreover, Scott, like Du Bois, was a short man who would not take any guff.

Scott struck back. In two articles, he summarized what he had done for black soldiers and, in addition, he questioned Du Bois's motives. Because of "Close Ranks," Scott wrote, Du Bois found himself "discredited . . . by a large portion of the Negro press." And now, by lashing out at Moton as well as Scott, Du Bois was "trying to rehabilitate himself in the eyes of the Negro world."[166] It was "difficult to deal with a man who dare not disclose the motives which underlie his criticisms," Scott told one friend.[167] Du Bois was "trying to rehabilitate himself . . . but I shall not permit him to do so at my expense."[168] "I will not permit Du Bois to get away with his mean, contemptible insinuations."[169] "I cannot . . . let Dr. Du Bois discredit my twenty-one months' record in the War Department."[170]

From the correspondence in Scott's papers, it is clear that many African Americans sided with Scott. And there is evidence that even some NAACP officials considered Du Bois's criticism of Scott unfair. In 1919 Neval H. Thomas, who would soon become the president of the NAACP's important branch in Washington, D.C., acknowledged that Du Bois had no right to criticize "a man who fought when [Du Bois] was silent."[171] At a time when Du Bois was advising blacks to "Close Ranks," Thomas noted, Scott had been working "day and night trying to lighten the burden of our suffering soldiers."[172]

Du Bois stopped the criticism when he sensed that it was doing him more harm than good. He lauded Moton later when the Major made a gallant stand against the Ku Klux Klan in the 1920s, and he also praised Moton for publishing two perceptive books. Moton continued at the helm of Tuskegee until 1935, and when Moton died in 1940 Du Bois acknowledged that "Robert Moton was a great and good man who suffered for a noble cause."[173]

After the war Emmett Scott continued to dispense patronage through what was left of the Tuskegee Machine. Meanwhile, he found new employment—at more than twice his Tuskegee salary—as the secretary-treasurer and business manager of Howard University. For several years Scott was content managing the business affairs of what he called "three great schools—the College, the School of Law, and the School of Medicine."[174] In 1926 he joined with two deans to engineer the appointment of Mordecai W. Johnson as the first black president of the university.

Scott and the deans had assumed that they could control Johnson, a thirty-six-year-old Baptist pastor who only one year before had been rejected for an appointment as an instructor on the faculty. Yet after Johnson became the president of Howard, one of the deans died, the other was ignored, and Scott was demoted from secretary-treasurer to secretary with no duties. For years he walked around the campus with nothing to do. Students said he was trying to figure out what had happened to all his power.[175]

During World War II Scott was put in charge of recruiting and hiring for an all-Negro yard at the Sun Shipbuilding Company. Later he retired to Washington, where he worked in public relations. Scott died in 1957.

And Du Bois? He continued as editor of the *Crisis*, but his reputation had been damaged by the controversies of the war years. It would take most of the next decade before Du Bois would regain the stature he had enjoyed on his fiftieth birthday.

Five
Du Bois and Marcus Garvey

Although African American soldiers in World War I had suffered from segregation, discrimination, humiliation, and slander, they assumed that things would be better in the United States when the war ended. After all, Du Bois and other black leaders had assured them that equality under the law would be the inevitable reward for bearing arms.

Many white people, on the other hand, feared that blacks had been "spoiled" by their experiences abroad. They insisted that the returning African American soldiers should be disabused of the belief that they would receive equal rights; they insisted that blacks should be kept "in their place."

To complicate the situation, about a million black people had moved from farms to cities during the war. These blacks found themselves in competition with urban whites for housing and the use of parks and other amenities. Under the circumstances, after the war there was a marked rise in friction between the races. The result was one of the two major clusters of race riots that the United States experienced in the twentieth century (with the other occurring during the 1960s). The summer of 1919 was aptly called the Red Summer. Twenty-five riots occurred between June and the end of the year. Some were large, others small. Hundreds of people were killed and thousands injured. The casualty rate was several times greater than that of the 1960s. Seventy blacks were lynched during the summer of 1919, ten of them soldiers recently returned from Europe, some of them still wearing their uniforms.[1]

African Americans did not react passively but organized for self-defense. They were determined to defend their lives and property against attacks, and several potential lynchings turned into race riots when blacks fought back. In some instances blacks also organized raids against innocent whites who owned stores or peddled merchandise in black neighborhoods.

Du Bois had reflected the postwar mood in his editorial, "Returning Soldiers," and the young black editors of the *Messenger* went Du Bois one better when they wrote "that *we return from fighting* is a fact. That *we return fighting* has been demonstrated . . . *[W]e return fighting like hell against the hell in this land.*"[2] Claude McKay later recalled that "the Negro people unanimously hailed me as a poet" when he wrote a famous sonnet, "If We Must Die."

> If we must die—let it not be like hogs.
> Hunted and penned in an inglorious spot,
> While round us bark the mad and hungry dogs,
> Making their mock at our accused lot.
> If we must die—oh, let us nobly die, . . .
> Like men we'll face the murderous, cowardly pack,
> Pressed to the wall, dying but fighting back.[3]

In this season of disillusionment and defiance, many African Americans were estranged from Du Bois. They welcomed the audacity of "Returning Soldiers," but they thought Du Bois had gone too far in his nationalistic call to "Close Ranks." In 1919 many blacks also sensed that interracial cooperation with liberal whites—the program of the NAACP—was not a realistic possibility. They turned instead to a black immigrant who touted racialism as an alternative to liberalism. They turned to Marcus Garvey, a remarkable, picturesque man who so profoundly stirred his fellow blacks that within a short time he had organized the largest mass movement in African American history.

Marcus Garvey and the Universal Negro Improvement Association

Marcus Garvey was born in 1887 in St. Ann's Bay, a small town on the northern coast of Jamaica, which was then a British colony. In some ways Garvey's youth was similar to that of Du Bois, but in other respects it was greatly different. It was alike in that Garvey's maternal grandparents had been small farmers. It was alike in that his father and paternal grandfather, after working as skilled stonemasons, were declining in status, losing property, and turning to common labor. The Garveys of St. Ann's Bay, like the Burghardts of Great Barrington, suffered as their society of artisans and peasants declined. Du Bois and Garvey also shared the experience of being reared by mothers who worked as domestic servants after their husbands fled their families as well as the stagnant local economies.[4]

Both men also felt pangs of rejection when white playmates of their youth later turned away from them. As noted, Du Bois first recognized the importance of race when a teenage white girl haughtily rejected his calling card in Great Barrington. And Garvey recalled that his closest boyhood friend, a white girl, was sent to Scotland at the age of fourteen and told by her parents "never to write or try to get in touch with me, for I was a 'nigger.'" Garvey's friendships with white male schoolmates lasted a while longer, but eventually they also drifted apart and Garvey came "to see the difference between the races."[5]

In other ways, Garvey's background was quite different from Du Bois's. Garvey's parents were of unmixed Negro stock, and Garvey was proud of the fact that he was a full-blooded black man without a trace of Caucasian ancestry. Garvey was also a man of limited formal education. He attended the elementary schools of St. Ann's Bay and the Church of England High School, but he never matriculated at a college—although in 1912 he attended some lectures at Birkbeck College of London University.

As a young man Garvey traveled widely, held several different jobs, and learned a great deal from a variety of experiences. In 1901 he moved to Kingston, took up the trade of printing, and became the foreman at a printing plant. After he joined other printers in an unsuccessful strike, Garvey left his homeland and took jobs as a timekeeper on a banana plantation in Costa Rica and as a newspaperman in Panama. In 1910 and 1911 he traveled and worked in several countries—Nicaragua, Honduras, Colombia, Venezuela, and Ecuador— all of which discriminated against black workers from the West Indies. When Garvey protested to the British consul in Costa Rica, however, he was told that nothing could be done to stop the mistreatment. This led Garvey to conclude that "white men did not regard the lives of black men as equal to those of white men, and had no intention of trying to protect blacks or giving them a square deal."[6]

In 1912 Garvey traveled to London, where he became an associate of Duse Mohammed Ali, the publisher of a monthly magazine, the *Africa Times and Orient Review*. There he became acquainted with many blacks who had emigrated from Africa. From them he learned about the conditions of black people throughout the world.

Returning to Jamaica in 1914, Garvey said his "brain was afire" with the desire to unite "all the Negro peoples of the world into one great body to establish a country and Government absolutely their own."[7] Yet when he traveled through rural Jamaica, Garvey observed "villainy and vice of the worst kind": "immorality, obeah [witchcraft], and all kinds of dirty things are part of the avocation of a large percentage of our people." To uplift these people, to "raise them to the standard of civilized approval," Garvey founded the Universal Negro Improvement Association (UNIA) and set for himself the short-term goal of establishing a Tuskegee-style vocational school for Jamaican blacks.[8]

Yet both the UNIA and plans for the school languished, despite the support of such eminent white citizens as the mayor of Kingston, a Roman Catholic bishop, and the governor of the island. They languished because the Negro majority of Jamaica—90 percent of the population of the island—was either indifferent or opposed to Garvey's program. Garvey blamed the failure on the opposition of what he called "the colored gentry," light-skinned mulattoes who considered themselves different from and better than black people; mulattoes who refused to associate with or support the development of Negro rights organizations. In a letter to Robert Russa Moton, Garvey confided, "whilst we have been encouraged and helped by the cultured whites . . . , the so-called representatives of our own people have sought to draw us down and . . . have been waging a secret campaign to that end."[9]

Many American citizens, including some African Americans, had returned home from visits to Jamaica talking of the easy acceptance of Negroes there. Yet Garvey knew that Jamaica had developed a system of racial discrimination that differed from that in the United States. What the American visitors had observed was the acceptance of mulattoes and not the acceptance of blacks. In the West Indies many white planters had cohabited with black women and, in a society where there were very few Caucasians, the mulatto children were regarded as whites, with the assumption that they would, through continued intermarriage, eventually "bleach out" the remaining traces of color. Thus the supposed disappearance of the color line in Jamaica involved erasing the line between whites and mulattoes, and not the boundary between whites and blacks or the gulf between mulattoes and blacks. "In the tropics," Garvey wrote, the mulattoes had "defeated the whites . . . and brought them to terms. . . .

In these places the hybrid may intermarry among the pure whites with all freedom, [and] after a generation or two the descendants boldly classify themselves as white."[10]

Garvey further recognized that the whites and mulattoes were dominant in Jamaica, while black people made up the great majority of both the rural peasantry and the urban working class. He also sensed that the black masses had been deprived of their natural leaders because black youths who showed initiative or talent were often incorporated into the society of whites and mulattoes. "Money whitens," was a popular saying, although it took a good deal of money to whiten a full-blooded Negro.[11]

Garvey recalled that as a young man and upon his return from England he "had to decide whether to please my friends and be one of the 'black-whites' of Jamaica, and be reasonably prosperous, or come out openly and defend and help improve and protect the integrity of the black millions and suffer."[12] Garvey chose to uplift the masses, and to emphasize this point he used the word *Negro,* not *colored,* in the title of his organization. But the colored elite regarded both the UNIA and a Tuskegee-style school as a challenge to the established order in Jamaican race relations. According to Garvey, the mulattoes then persuaded the tiny but wealthy Caucasian minority to reverse their previous support for the UNIA, making it necessary for Garvey to call upon black people in the United States to support his program in Jamaica.

With this in mind, Garvey wrote to Booker T. Washington in 1914 and 1915, explaining that he would be touring America to raise funds for his projects. Garvey had been profoundly affected by Washington's autobiography, *Up from Slavery,* and he also recognized that Washington was in a position to help him secure funds for the projects. In response, Washington offered polite assurance that he would make Garvey's stay at Tuskegee "pleasant" and "profitable," but he gave no definite commitment of financial aid.[13]

By the time Garvey reached the United States in 1916, Washington was dead and social conditions stemming from the Great Migration and the First World War had created a new mood in black America. At first, Garvey lodged with a Jamaican family in Harlem and found part-time work as a printer, but in 1917 he went on a tour that took him through thirty-eight states. During this tour Garvey observed a spirit of profound disillusionment among blacks as it became evident that despite their having rallied around the flag during the war, they were not going to receive equal rights. He also recognized that black workers, who initially were delighted by the better wages and treatment in the North, had become discouraged when returning white soldiers reclaimed their jobs, when blacks were restricted from moving into many neighborhoods, and when blacks discovered that even in the fabled North they would still be second-class citizens. Accordingly, Garvey modified his message to suit the requirements of a new era.

Instead of depending on whites for kindly and sympathetic assistance, Garvey called for self-reliance. Rather than appeal to the better nature of Caucasians or to egalitarian principles, Garvey urged blacks to rally together and help themselves. "Race First" was his motto—race above all else. This was the principal tenet in Garvey's creed and the key to his success in organizing the largest mass movement in African American history.[14]

In addition, Garvey was acutely aware of the importance of symbols, culture, and social psychology as tools for organizing the masses. Thus he designed a distinctive new flag for Africa (red, black, and green); organized a Black Congress in Harlem; and had his official historians and theologians delve into biblical writings and reconstruct the nativity of Jesus as a black (or at least colored) man. At a time when most whites considered blacks inferior, every aspect of Garvey's program was designed to build up the black man's self-esteem and to foster racial pride.

Many educated people laughed when they first heard about a black Jesus. But Garvey reasoned that "if man was made in the image and likeness of God, then black men should depict a God in their own image and likeness, which would inevitably be black."[15] Garvey acknowledged that God had no color, but since human beings thought in human terms, it was natural to think of God as a person. "God is not white or black," Garvey told one audience, "but if [whites] say that God is white, [the UNIA] says that God is black."[16]

Garvey also thought that secular programs, like those of Du Bois and Booker T. Washington, were not sufficient to inspire the masses of people to do all they could to uplift themselves. While the UNIA was never affiliated with any specific denomination, hymns and prayers were interspersed in its meetings, and every unit had a chaplain. An Episcopal priest named George Alexander McGuire became the chaplain general of the UNIA, whose liturgy and ritual were patterned after Roman Catholicism, to which Garvey had converted after being reared as a Methodist in St. Ann's Bay. As an organization, the UNIA was pro-religion but nondenominational. It endorsed all congregations that were led by black people. Christmas and Easter were celebrated, with the Blessed Virgin Mary depicted as a black madonna and Jesus as "the Black Man of Sorrow."

History was also used to boost racial pride. Garvey thought that one reason whites had achieved as much as they had was that they had been taught they were superior to other races. As he saw it, the standard school curriculum ascribed all worthwhile deeds to Caucasians and suggested that Negroes had not amounted to much and would never measure up to the standards of white people. Garvey, on the other hand, called for a new interpretation of history that would inspire confidence and rehabilitate blacks psychologically. If "the white man's history is his inspiration," Garvey said, so it should also be for blacks.[17]

Garvey conceded that blacks had "done nothing praiseworthy on their own initiative in the last five hundred years. . . . They have made no political, educational, industrial, independent contribution to civilization for which they can be respected by other races."[18] But Garvey insisted that it was not always thus. History moved in cycles and, although black people had fallen behind in the preceding few hundred years, in the ancient world Negroes had a glorious past. When the ancestors of the proud Caucasians were still living in caves and slinging stones at wild animals, the black people of Egypt were in the forefront of the arts and sciences. Indeed, Garvey said, the civilization of ancient Egypt was superior to that of either Greece or Rome.[19]

White writers had disseminated the myth that the blacks of antiquity were only hewers of wood and drawers of water, but Garvey insisted that this history was "written with prejudices, likes and dislikes; and there has never been a white historian who ever wrote with any true love or feeling for the Negro." In fact, the blacks of ancient Egypt "gave the first great civilization to the world; and for centuries Africa, our ancestral home, was the seat of learning."[20] Indeed, "3,000 years ago, [when] black men excelled in government and were founders and teachers of art, science and literature," the people of other races were "groping in savagery, darkness, and barbarism."[21]

Garvey did not deny the intrinsic importance of religion and history, but his primary goal was racial uplift. He urged black people to teach their children that they were direct descendants of the greatest race that ever peopled the earth. He said, in addition, that blacks were hated and oppressed by a jealous and prejudiced contemporary world that feared that once again a distinctively black civilization might outshine that of Asians or Caucasians.

Another cardinal tenet of the UNIA called for the redemption of Africa. Unlike Du Bois, whose Pan-African Congress recommended an international system of administration for the former German colonies of Tanganyika and German Southwest Africa, Garvey demanded self-determination for the entire continent. "If Europe is for the Europeans," Garvey said, "then Africa shall be for the black peoples of the world. We say it; we mean it. . . . The other races have countries of their own and it is time for the 400,000,000 Negroes to claim Africa for themselves."[22] Garvey insisted that the whites who controlled Africa should "clear out now" before the continent was awash "in blood," "because we are coming not as in the time of Father Abraham, 200,000 strong, but we are coming 400,000,000 strong, and we mean to retake every square inch of the 12,000,000 square miles of African territory belonging to us by right Divine."[23]

Garvey also used a great deal of pageantry to support his cause. The journalist Roi Ottley recalled that as a youngster he witnessed the UNIA's first annual convention in Harlem. "It was a monster affair, almost approaching medieval splendor in regalia of lush colors. During the whole month of August, 1920, delegates from all the states, the West Indies, South America, and Africa assembled in [Harlem]. . . . People were fascinated by all the bustle, color, and animation," and there was "a magnificent parade in which more than fifty thousand 'Garveyites' marched through Harlem. His Excellency, Marcus Garvey, Provisional President of Africa, led the demonstration bedecked in a dazzling uniform of purple, green, and black, with gold braid, and a thrilling hat with white plumes. . . . He rode in a big, high-mounted black Packard automobile and graciously, but with restraint becoming a sovereign, acknowledged the ovations of the crowds that lined the sidewalks. Behind him rode His Grace, Archbishop McGuire, in silk robes of state, blessing the populace. Then [came] the Black Nobility and Knight Commanders . . . properly attired in regalia drawn from a bold palette. Arrayed in gorgeous uniforms of black and green, trimmed with much gold braid, came the smartly strutting African Legion; and in white, the . . . Black Cross Nurses. Then came troops of kilt-clad Boy and Girl Scouts, trailed by a multitude of bumptious black subjects."[24]

At the conclusion of their 1920 Congress, twenty thousand Garveyites gathered in Madison Square Garden beneath the new African flag—black for the race, green for the vegetation of the motherland, and red for "the blood which men must shed for their redemption and liberty."[25] The *New York Times* reported that "for more than two hours [the crowd was] worked up to a high pitch of enthusiasm by a quartet, soloists, and a band. Then Marcus Garvey . . . stepped to the platform [and] received an ovation. Five minutes passed before he could raise his voice." When he did speak, Garvey proclaimed:

> We are the descendants of a suffering people. We are the descendants of a people determined to suffer no longer. . . . We shall now organize the 400,000,000 negroes of the world into a vast organization to plant the banner of freedom on the great continent of Africa.[26]

However, Garvey had only a hazy plan for reclaiming Africa. He proposed to make a start by settling pioneers—engineers, contractors, businessmen—in Liberia, the only black-governed country on Africa's west coast. The Liberian government needed funds desperately and initially looked with favor on the possibility of an infusion from the UNIA. But in 1920, after surveying conditions in Liberia, Garvey's commissioner Elie Garcia reported that the ruling aristocracy in Liberia was using the natives as slaves and suggested that eventually Garvey's colonists would have to overthrow the established government. Somehow the Liberian government got a copy of Garcia's report, whereupon Garveyites in Liberia were seized and deported. In 1924, the Liberian consul general announced that "no person or persons leaving the United States under the auspices of the Garvey movement will be allowed to land in the Republic of Liberia."[27]

Meanwhile, Garvey's emphasis on self-reliance led to the establishment of a number of small businesses: restaurants, a chain of cooperative grocery stores, a steam laundry, a dressmaking shop, a millinery store, a publishing house, and a toy company that manufactured black dolls. Garvey urged black people to build their own enterprises and become independent of white capital and white employers. He dreamed of "a self-contained world of Negro producers, distributors, and consumers who could deal with or be independent of the rest of the world as necessity and circumstances dictated."[28] If a black man needed a suit of clothes, there should be a black store for the purchase, a black tailor to take the measurements and to place the order with black agents, who represented the black farmers and ranchers, who produced the raw material, and the black truckers who transported it.

To emphasize the connections of black people and the UNIA's commitment to Africa, Garvey implemented a spectacular concept. He established an all-black steamship company, the Black Star Line, to link the commerce and industry of Negroes throughout the world. While critics complained that blacks would not stand a chance in this field of big business, Garvey proudly announced the purchase of his first ship, the *Yarmouth,* for $168,500. With much pageantry, the ship was rechristened the *Frederick Douglass,* and African Americans swarmed to Harlem to see the vessel. Thousands of people paid a half-dollar to go on board and shake hands with the black crew. Others purchased Black Star stock at five dollars a share. In one Louisiana college, students raised seven thousand dollars. The appeal of the great racial enterprise was not limited to the United States, either. From Panama one loyal shareholder wrote: "I have sent twice to buy shares amounting to $125. . . . Now I am sending $35 for seven more shares. You might think I have money, but the truth . . . is that I have no money now. But if I'm to die of hunger it will be all right because I'm determined to do all that's in my power to better the conditions of my race."[29]

The Black Star Line captured the imagination of Negroes everywhere. Before long there were about eight hundred branches of the UNIA in the United States and another three hundred abroad. In 1920 Garvey claimed a following of four million people, but his numbers were not reliable. The members who paid dues numbered in the thousands rather than millions—with estimates ranging from about eighteen thousand to more than eighty thousand. Whatever the exact membership, several million black people sympathized with Garvey, and his UNIA was the world's largest organization of Negroes.[30]

The people who joined the UNIA also tended to be younger, poorer, and darker than those who belonged to the NAACP. When the two organizations eventually clashed, there were decided elements of class in the conflict. Du Bois once said that Garvey's followers were "the lowest type of Negroes." And Garvey envied Du Bois's formal education and resented his elegant style.[31]

But Garvey's appeal transcended class. His meteoric success was based on an eclectic combination of charisma, oratory, and showmanship, as well as a timely message. As a public speaker, Garvey demonstrated that oratory could indeed be a form of art. As a young man, Garvey had visited several churches to observe the oratory and platform styles of various clergymen; then "he would spend long hours alone in his room reciting poetry and passages . . . and experimenting with different gestures." As an adult, he continued to hone his oratory, and Du Bois acknowledged that Garvey was "a facile speaker, able to express himself in grammatical and forceful English." James Weldon Johnson noted that Garvey possessed a "magnetic personality, torrential eloquence, and intuitive knowledge of crowd psychology. He swept the audience along with him."[32]

Garvey's message was as important as his presentation. His emphasis was on race, self-reliance, the connectedness of the African diaspora, and the liberation of the motherland. It was perfectly attuned to the postwar era, a time when blacks felt that they had been abandoned by whites, a time when President Wilson and other diplomats were calling for democracy and self-determination for the nationalities of Europe, for the yellow people of China and Japan, for the brown Hindus of India—for everyone, it seemed, except the black people of Africa, the West Indies, and the United States.

Garvey's success, however, proved to be short lived. The maiden voyage of the *Frederick Douglass* had begun auspiciously as thousands of people cheered its departure from the 135th Street pier in Harlem, but the ship got only as far as 23rd Street before authorities stopped the vessel for lack of proper insurance. When the *Frederick Douglass* resumed its voyage to Cuba, there was trouble with the boilers and the ship ran aground in soft sand in the Bahamas. During the ship's second voyage to Cuba, other problems developed and the cargo had to be jettisoned. A third voyage was less eventful but no more successful financially. Finally, to raise money to pay the many bills, the ship was sold in 1921 for $1,625, less than one-one hundredth of its original purchase price.[33]

The Black Star Line had no greater success with its second ship, rechristened the *Antonio Maceo* after the Cuban patriot. Garvey paid an excessive sixty thousand dollars for this converted millionaire's yacht, but it blew a boiler on its first voyage and was plagued thereafter with mechanical problems. Repairs came to about forty-five thousand dollars, but the ship was never seaworthy and eventually had to be declared a total loss. A third ship, the *Shadyside,* was purchased for thirty-five thousand dollars and carried passengers on excursions along the Hudson River. A fourth ship, one that was to be called the *Phyllis Wheatley,* never came into the possession of the Black Star Line, but its history was unfortunately similar to that of the *Frederick Douglass* and the *Antonio Maceo.* "It involved the loss of a large sum of money, entangled the company in litigation for over a decade, and was finally sold as scrap."[34] In the end, the Black Star Line went bankrupt, and stockholders lost all that they had invested in the company.

Thus Garvey's record was mixed. He was an extraordinary leader—one whose message of racial pride and self-help was always pertinent even if his inspiring but hazy vision of African redemption was historically premature by a generation or two. Some critics said that Garvey was a swindler who had devised an extraordinary scheme for exploiting the gullible masses. But there was never any proof that Garvey enriched himself or was anything other than an well-intentioned, sincere orator with a brilliant vision and an unselfish desire to uplift his race. Nevertheless, with the bankruptcy of the Black Star Line, it was evident that Garvey had no business sense. It would soon be apparent that he also had some serious defects of temperament and character.

Du Bois versus Garvey

Since the UNIA and the NAACP were both based in New York City, Du Bois had the opportunity to observe Garvey's movement closely, and from the outset, Du Bois was skeptical. When subscribers wrote to the *Crisis* with questions about Garvey, Du Bois at first "simply answered that we had no reliable information."[35] But when Jim Burghardt, Du Bois's uncle from Bennington, Vermont, asked if it was safe to invest money in the Black Star Line, Du Bois advised against doing so "under any circumstances" and added the suggestion that Garvey's methods might be "fraudulent."[36] Jessie Fauset, a coworker at the *Crisis,* recalled that Du Bois told her confidentially that, "while he was in accord with Garvey's main aspiration, he repudiated [Garvey's] methods, which . . . were lacking in plain sense, and he questioned the soundness of [Garvey's] financial enterprises."[37]

Nevertheless, Du Bois's public position was quite restrained. His first articles on Garvey, in 1920 and 1921, acknowledged that the Jamaican was "an extraordinary leader" and "essentially an honest and sincere man with a tremendous vision, great dynamic force, stubborn determination, and unselfish desire to serve."[38] Du Bois then added that when it came to Garvey's business enterprises there was "more ground for doubt and misgiving than in the matter of his character." Du Bois warned that Garvey's "financial methods [were] so essentially unsound that unless he speedily revises them the investors will certainly get no dividends and worse may happen." He concluded that Garvey was "a sincere, hardworking idealist" with "worthy industrial and commercial schemes" but also an "inexperienced business man" who might "overwhelm with bankruptcy and disaster one of the most interesting spiritual movements of the modern Negro world."[39]

Du Bois's assessment was accurate as well as balanced, but Garvey responded with vitriol. An FBI agent who was surveilling Garvey reported that shortly after Du Bois's articles appeared in *The Crisis,* "Garvey denounced Du Bois before a packed house in which there was not even standing room." Garvey "described Du Bois as the 'white man Negro,' who had never done anything yet to benefit Negroes, saying that while Du Bois was a friend of the upper 'tenth' Negroes, he, Marcus Garvey, was along with the working class Negroes."[40] These allegations resonated among rank-and-file blacks, many of whom had long considered the NAACP elitist and condescending.

Garvey also resented the fact that on several occasions Du Bois asked about the finances of the Black Star Line. One of these inquiries was addressed to Garvey personally, and others were sent to Lloyds of London, the Canadian Department of Corporations, the American Bureau of Shipping, and the U.S. Department of State. Du Bois said he was simply trying to answer questions that he had received from readers of the *Crisis.* Garvey, on the other hand, suspected that Du Bois's real intent was to discredit Garvey's organization.[41]

In addition, since Garvey wanted "self-determination" for Africa, not "internationalization," he thought Du Bois and the Pan-African Congress were "soft" on imperialism.[42] And Garvey also begrudged Du Bois's distinguished academic record. In one speech Garvey challenged Du Bois, "graduate of Harvard and Yale as you are, to meet me on the platform . . . at midnight, at noontime, or any time. . . . If you think your education so superior, this is your chance to defeat Marcus Garvey. . . . That is my challenge to Dr. Du Bois and the class of men who call themselves intellectuals."[43]

In addition to Garvey's envy of Du Bois, there was the matter of race, for in his mulatto body Du Bois encapsulated the colored leadership that Garvey had long criticized. This had been apparent to Garvey ever since his arrival in New York in 1916, when Garvey had visited the offices of NAACP and the *Crisis* to pay his respects. Garvey later recalled that he was "dumbfounded" when he discovered that only a few of the people in the offices were visibly Negroes. "The whole staff was either white or very near white, and thus Garvey got his first shock of the advancement hypocrisy. The advancement meant you had to be as near white as possible, otherwise there was no place for you as a stenographer, clerk, or attendant in the office of the National Association for the Advancement of 'Colored' People."[44] Before long, Garvey was referring to the NAACP as "the National Association for the Advancement of (Certain) Colored People."[45]

Garvey's suspicion of colored people was reinforced as he traveled through the United States. He observed that "In restaurants, drug stores and offices all over the nation where our people were engaged in business . . . those employed were the very 'lightest' members of the race—as waitresses, clerks, and stenographers." Garvey also noted that in some cities the light-skinned colored people had organized exclusive "blue vein" societies—organizations of mulattoes whose skin was light enough to show blue veins. In New Orleans there were "paper bag" parties where admission was denied to anyone whose color was darker than that of a paper bag from a grocery store. And in Detroit the Reverend Robert Bagnall, who would soon become an executive officer of the NAACP, allegedly barred black people from sitting at the front of his African Methodist Episcopal church. To test this report Garvey attended one of the Sunday services in disguise. He took "one of the empty seats . . . and the effort nearly spoiled the whole service, as Brother Bob, who was then ascending the pulpit, nearly lost his 'balance' to see such a face so near the 'holy of holies.'"[46]

These experiences reinforced Garvey's Jamaican-bred suspicion of colored people. At first Garvey must have thought that in the United States, as in Jamaica, the mulatto was not a Negro. But Garvey was a quick study. It did not take him long to recognize that most white Americans regarded anyone with visible traces of African ancestry as a black person. In the United States, whites did not distinguish between a light colored person with one Negro great-grandfather and a full-blooded Mandingo, and neither did many African Americans. Colored people of the lightest hue consequently considered themselves Negroes. When Garvey recognized this, he saw to it that several light-skinned mulattoes held influential positions in the UNIA. Membership in the organization was open to anyone who was one-sixteenth or more Negro.

Despite his accommodation to American conditions, Garvey could not resist the temptation to criticize Du Bois for his color. In fact, playing the race card became a staple of Garvey's comments. According to Garvey, Du Bois wanted to do what had already been done in the West Indies; he favored "racial amalgamation or general miscegenation with the hope of creating a new type of colored race by wiping out both black and white." According to Garvey, integrationists in general and Du Bois in particular wanted Negroes to "settle down in communities of whites and by social contact and miscegenation bring about a new type." Garvey said that Du Bois, in order to solve the race problem, was urging blacks "to commit [race] suicide by jumping over the white fence." Du Bois allegedly sought "a destruction of the black and white races by the social amalgamation of both."[47]

When it came to Du Bois's motives, Garvey mentioned two possibilities. One was that Du Bois was "a misfit, . . . neither a Negro nor a white man," who favored assimilation and miscegenation so that blacks would become "so mixed up with the white race as to produce a new type, probably like Du Bois himself, which will in time be the real American." A second possibility was that Du Bois and the other African Americans in the NAACP wanted to "associate with white women," while their white colleagues "only desire[d] easy contact with colored women." Garvey said the NAACP was an "immoral" organization that wanted to destroy both Caucasians and Negroes and "build up a mongrel America."[48]

It is hard to assess Garvey's allegations. In the fullness of time equality of rights may lead to widespread miscegenation and the disappearance of separate races. But this was not Du Bois's *conscious* strategy for racial uplift. On the contrary, for years Du Bois and the NAACP demanded political and civil rights for African Americans but deliberately avoided public discussion of "social equality."

Because of Garvey, after 1920 it was no longer possible to ignore the subject of social equality, but Du Bois's position was too nuanced for easy summation. On the one hand, Du Bois opposed laws against racial intermarriage, for he knew that such laws were based on the premise that people with Negro ancestry were inferior to Caucasians. He insisted that such laws were "a cruel insult" and that it was "a monstrous perversion of our proven scientific knowledge to assert that the white race is the physical, mental, and moral superior of other races." He upheld "the individual right of any two sane grown individuals of any race to marry."[49]

On the other hand, Du Bois wrote, "above the individual problem lies the question of the social expediency of the intermarriage of whites and blacks today." Because of the prevailing opposition to interracial marriages, among black people as well as whites, Du Bois advised "most emphatically . . . against race intermarriage in America." It simply was "not socially expedient today for such marriages to take place." The pressure against such unions "involve[d] too great a strain to evolve a compatible, agreeable family life and to train proper children."[50]

In addition, Du Bois returned to a point he had stressed in his 1897 essay "The Conservation of Races." Du Bois wanted African Americans to maintain their racial unity until they had disproved the suspicion of racial inferiority by "giv[ing] to civilization the full spiritual message which they are capable of giving." He continued to believe that "the Negro people, as a race, have a contribution to make . . . which no other race can make." In 1897 Du Bois had urged blacks to maintain their separate identity until "among the gaily-colored banners that deck the broad ramparts of civilization" there was one that was "uncompromising black." In 1920 he continued to oppose miscegenation until blacks had built "a great black race tradition of which the Negro and the world will be as proud in the future as it has been in the ancient world."[51]

Garvey, however, ignored Du Bois's carefully articulated opposition to racial intermarriage and continued to rant against the editor of the *Crisis*. As Elliott Rudwick noted, while Du Bois "showed remarkable temperateness" and his "comments about the Jamaican's program were usually calmly delivered and based on objective data," Garvey's assessment of Du Bois partook of "hysteri[a]." Garvey said Du Bois was the evil "genius" behind "that vicious Negro-hating organization known as the NAACP." According to Garvey, Du Bois and the NAACP were "as great Negro haters as the Southern crackers are, for the simple reason [that] their program is race assimilation which will in another hundred years wipe out this Negro race and make a new race which will not be Negro in any degree."[52]

Perhaps Garvey's vehemence was due to a peculiar reverse chemistry. He took an intense dislike to Du Bois from their first meeting—to his color, his formal education, his expensive clothes, his cultural tastes, his imported cigarettes. One of Garvey's associates reflected this attitude when he wrote that "The NAACP appeals to the Beau Brummel, Lord Chesterfield, kid-gloved, silk stocking, creased-trousered, patent leather shoe . . . element, while the UNIA appeals to the . . . hard-working man. . . . [Du Bois] appeals to the 'talented tenth' while Garvey appeals to the Hoi Polloi."[53]

There were other differences in addition to class-based resentment. Because Du Bois relied partially on interracial cooperation with whites and did not count on blacks alone to uplift the race, Garvey thought Du Bois had not placed enough emphasis on self-reliance. Garvey said that the UNIA sought "to prove to the world our ability as a race," but the NAACP was trying "to have the white race admit Negroes to the full enjoyment of all the privileges . . . without any exertion or effort on the part of the Negro to do for himself."[54] As Garvey saw it, Du Bois and the NAACP did not take account of deeply rooted racial instincts and naively overestimated the likelihood that whites would treat blacks on the basis of individual merit.

Garvey also regarded Du Bois as the leading member of a whole group of middle-class black intellectuals, many of whom went far beyond Du Bois's measured assessment of Garvey. Garvey "accept[ed] Dr. Du Bois as the leader of the opposition," "the most dangerous of the Mulattoes."[55] And while Du Bois's assessment of Garvey was calm and reasoned, many of the other critics of Garvey regarded him with contempt.

From the outset, many educated African Americans looked askance at the UNIA's gold braid and brass buttons, at the flowing colors of a United Africa. For them, Garvey resembled a comic figure from vaudeville. A. Philip Randolph, the young black editor of the

Messenger, was not content to write that Garvey was "misleading ignorant Negroes, wasting their money and making them the butt of ridicule and raillery."[56] Randolph added a personal insult, describing Garvey as a "half-wit, low grade moron, whose insufferable presumption is only exceeded by his abysmal ignorance."[57] The Reverend Robert Bagnall, the clergyman who according to Garvey almost stumbled from the pulpit when he saw Garvey sitting near the front of his congregation, penned an even more insulting portrait of Garvey: "a Jamaican Negro of unmixed stock, squat, stocky, fat and sleek, with protruding jaws, and heavy jowls, small bright pig-like eyes and rather bull-dog like face . . . prolix to the 'nth degree in devising new schemes to gain the money of poor ignorant Negroes . . . a lover of pomp and tawdry finery and garish display . . . a sheer opportunist and demagogic charlatan."[58]

As early as 1919 some blacks urged the Department of Justice to bring charges against Garvey. The business operations of the Black Star Line were fraudulent, one correspondent alleged, and, in addition, Garvey was said to have violated "the Mann White Slave Act . . . [by] travel[ing] out of New York with his secretary."[59] In 1922 a "Garvey Must Go" campaign was organized, and eight prominent African Americans urged the attorney general to prosecute and deport Garvey "for using the mails to defraud."[60] Three of those who signed the letter were editors, one was a prominent businesswoman, two were officials of the National Urban League, and two were from the NAACP.[61] Du Bois, however, refused to participate. He thought Garvey was "a thoroughly impractical visionary" but probably not a criminal and, in any case, Du Bois did "not . . . believe in deportation for [Garvey] or anybody else."[62]

Accounting for the hostility of the middle-class black leaders necessarily involves a degree of speculation. The critics said they wanted to protect the black masses from what the *New York Age* called "a gigantic stock jobbing scheme" that had been "put forth under the guise of racial improvement." They said Garvey was a demagogue who used a peculiar blend of psychology and pageantry to delude people and take their hard-earned money. The *Age* pointedly observed that selling stock for the UNIA gave some "vociferous agitators . . . the best jobs that they have ever had in their lives."[63]

Garvey, however, attributed the opposition to color prejudice. He said that five of the eight people who had written to the attorney general were "Octoroons or Quadroons," one was "a Mulatto," and the "two black Negroes . . . have married Octoroons." According to Garvey, his assailants considered black people "primitive and ignorant" and had "the hidden motive or intention . . . to set up a social caste as distinct from the Negro." They thought "the race problem is to be solved by assimilation, and that the best program for the Negro is to make himself the best imitation of the white man and approach him as near as possible."[64]

Scholars have mentioned other reasons for the hostility towards Garvey. They have noted that the black socialists who gathered around the *Messenger* magazine said that Garvey was misleading the black masses into thinking that racial unity, rather than interracial, working-class solidarity, was the key to progress. And they have speculated that the *Messenger* radicals became jealous when they recognized that Garvey was by far the most successful organizer of the masses of the black race of his generation. He accomplished this, moreover, on a nonsocialist basis and without resort to the rhetoric of class conflict.[65]

In addition, other black organizations found it harder to raise funds because, as one of Garvey's critics explained, Garvey was receiving money "in stacks" and thereby "killing . . . the contribution market."[66] To make matters worse, Garvey was using the money for what the most middle-class black leaders considered escapism. Instead of fighting against discrimination, segregation, and lynching, and instead of working to make a better future for the race in America, Garvey had focused on the liberation of the Motherland and the expatriation of African Americans to Africa.[67] "The present concern of the great mass of the American Negro is not with Africa," the *New York Age* insisted, "but right here in the United States. And it is bound to remain here."[68]

When the middle-class blacks urged the attorney general to prosecute Garvey, they also alleged that the UNIA was guilty of specific acts of coercion and violence. They said that Garveyite thugs had disrupted meetings in several cities and, in a particularly grisly attempt at intimidation, had sent A. Philip Randolph a package that contained a human hand.[69] In another instance, Garveyites were accused of assassinating James H. Eason, a Philadelphia minister who at one time had been second only to Garvey in the UNIA's chain of command. After leaving the UNIA and establishing a rival organization, Eason had been shot from ambush and murdered. Two Garveyites were indicted but eventually acquitted because of a legal technicality.[70] Whether or not Garvey was involved in any of the incidents, there was a widespread belief that the UNIA had resorted to acts of intimidation.

Garvey's middle-class enemies were also deeply troubled by Garvey's cooperation with white supremacists—a cooperation that was based on a shared belief in the importance of racial integrity. One early indication of this occurred in 1921 when Garvey congratulated President Warren G. Harding for a speech that Harding had made in Birmingham, Alabama. In the speech Harding said that blacks should be guaranteed political and economic equality, but he also maintained that the races possessed "widely unequal capacities and capabilities" and that, therefore, he was "uncompromisingly against every suggestion of social equality. . . . Racial amalgamation there cannot be."[71]

Garvey's insistence on racial purity eventually led him to cooperate with the Ku Klux Klan, for Garvey was as proud of being black as any Klansman was of being white. "Slavery brought upon us the curse of many colors within our Race," Garvey told his followers, "but that is no reason why we of ourselves should perpetuate the evil." Since membership in the UNIA was open to Negroes of all different hues, Garvey acknowledged that there were "about 200 different colors . . . all the colors of the rainbow" in the crowds that came to hear him speak. But enough was enough. Garvey insisted that it was "time we call a halt . . . [and] establish a uniform type among ourselves."[72]

In addition, Garvey thought that blacks would never receive fair treatment in the United States. In part, this was because of white bigotry. As his widow explained, Garvey believed "that the prejudice exhibited by the Klan in hysteria, hate, cruelty, and mob violence was the prejudice common to most white Americans."[73] "Between the Ku Klux Klan and the [NAACP]," Garvey said, "give me the Klan for their honesty of purpose towards the Negro. They are better friends of my race, for telling us what they are, and what they mean."[74]

But it was not simply a matter of white bigotry. Surely, Garvey thought, whites must be as proud of their race as he was of his. Rather than "lose their identities through miscegenation and social intercourse," whites eventually would "seek self-protection and self-preservation." They would never accept "the aggressive program of the National Association for the Advancement of Colored People," whose leaders "hanker[ed] after social equality" and sought "the impossible in politics and government." Instead of following Du Bois, who allegedly preferred "to fight and agitate for the privilege of dancing with a white lady at a ball," Garvey urged blacks to undertake the work of building a separate civilization.[75]

With such convictions, Garvey met with leaders of the Klan and other white supremacist organizations. In 1922 he conferred amicably with Edward Young Clarke, the acting imperial wizard of the Klan, and he later corresponded warmly with Earnest Sevier Cox of the White America Society and with John Powell of the Anglo Saxon Clubs of America. In the 1930s, Garvey also cooperated with Mississippi Senator Theodore G. Bilbo and others who proposed to give government money to African Americans who would resettle in Africa.[76] Of course Garvey did not agree with many of the supremacists' views—certainly not with their belief that blacks were inherently inferior or that ancient Egypt had originally been Caucasian and had subsequently declined because of the introduction of Negroid influences. But Garvey and the white supremacists shared a belief in the importance of race and a commitment to keeping the races separate.

After meeting with Imperial Wizard Clarke, Garvey made a statement that infuriated many established black leaders. "It is indeed unfair to demand equality," Garvey said, "when one of himself has done nothing to establish the right to equality."[77] Instead of trying to desegregate the whites' streetcars, Garvey advised blacks to build their own. "The white man built them for his own convenience," Garvey said. "And if I don't want to ride where he's willing to let me ride then I'd better walk."[78] On another occasion, he said that black people would be in darkness if "Edison turn[ed] off his electric light," and then added that the world despised black people "because the world knows the Negro has made absolutely no independent contribution to the civilization of the world."[79]

In making these statements Garvey had intended to spur his fellow blacks to greater achievement and self-reliance. Such statements, however, were not typical, for on most occasions Garvey condemned unjust racial discrimination. The UNIA's Declaration of Rights protested against "the wrongs and injustices [that blacks] are suffering at the hands of their white brethren." It condemned "inferior separate schools." It rebuked the southern states for making Negroes use separate, inferior Jim Crow public accommodations.[80]

Nevertheless, Garvey's critics made much of the fact that Garvey occasionally seemed to justify and grovel before white prejudice. The editors of the *Messenger* characterized some of Garvey's statements as "fool talk" that only strengthened their desire "to drive the menace of Garveyism out of this country." Du Bois complained that Garvey's "only attack is on men of his own race; . . . his only contempt is for Negroes."[81]

In the short term, cooperating with white supremacists turned out to be something of a boon. The Klan stopped its harassment of the UNIA, and thereby made it possible for the UNIA to establish additional chapters in the South. Some people even speculated that this was the real reason for Garvey's *entente* with the Klan. With the support of the Klan, they said, Garvey was able to establish UNIA chapters in the rural South, which had previously been off-limits to black organizations. William Pickens of the NAACP, for example, told a Harlem audience that Garvey was trying "to get on the right side of the Ku Klux Klan so he could go and collect money from Southern Negroes."[82]

But Garvey eventually paid a high price for this entrée, for his cooperation with the Klan did more to antagonize the black establishment than anything else. As E. David Cronon has noted, "The mere thought that a responsible Negro leader would collaborate with the leading avowed enemy of his race brought down a storm of criticism upon Garvey's head." And Garvey aggravated the situation when he said that "lynchings and race riots . . . work to our advantage by teaching the Negro that he must build a civilization of his own or forever remain the white man's victim."[83] Before long, press reports were saying that Garvey welcomed the success of the Klan because he thought its triumph "would drive Negroes to his program in despair."[84] Garvey's widow recalled that "the startling news was flashed that Garvey had become a member of the KKK, . . . that he would encourage the Klan to brutalize Negroes, and cause them to want to leave America for Africa."[85]

Garvey's cooperation with white supremacists also gave the black press an excuse for carrying on what became a campaign of vilification. Garvey should have known better than to treat with the Klan, for he recognized that his black enemies had been "plotting for some time to besmirch my character in order to hold me up to public ridicule and to cause me to lose favor among my people."[86] When he met with the Klan, Garvey gave these enemies a sword. More than that, as the black criticism of Garvey mounted, the U.S. Department of Justice was emboldened to prosecute Garvey for using the mails to defraud the stockholders of the Black Star Line.

In February 1922, Garvey and three of his associates were indicted on twelve counts alleging fraudulent use of the mails, but the trial was postponed until mid-May 1923. In truth, the government did not have a strong case. There was plenty of evidence that the Black Star Line had paid exorbitant prices for the purchase and maintenance of its fleet, and the salaries, advertising expenses, and promotional costs of the company had been excessive. There was also evidence that some employees had engaged in thievery and even sabotage. As a result, the company's forty thousand black stockholders had lost more than six hundred thousand dollars.[87]

Yet there was scant evidence of fraud—as distinguished from mismanagement. The crux of the government's case was that the directors of the Black Star Line knowingly used the mails to distribute circulars that promised dividends and profits when the directors knew that the financial condition of the company was hopeless. But only a few of those who had lost money testified for the government. Most of the spectators who crowded the court house sympathized with Garvey. It was the government, not stockholders, that was primarily responsible for the charges.[88] And the testimony of the government's chief witness, a janitor named Benny Dancy, was given hesitantly and riddled with inconsistencies. Dancy had kept an empty postmarked envelope that he had received from the Black Star Line. The prosecution said the envelope had originally contained a circular that had puffed up the value of the company's stock, but the government did not match the envelope with specific circulars, and Dancy was not sure about what he had received in the mail.[89]

Nevertheless, Dancy's claim of being defrauded was the one count on which Garvey was convicted, while three other directors of the Black Star Line were acquitted. The split verdict was probably due to the fact that Garvey had been the government's chief target all along. In addition, the other defendants retained their attorneys while Garvey fired his lawyer and insisted on representing himself.

At times, Garvey brought eloquence to the courtroom, as when he pleaded with the jury to consider what the Black Star Line sought to do for black people. "You will say it was bad business. But, gentlemen, there is something spiritual beside business."[90] Garvey acknowledged that the line had lost money, but he insisted that the investments had paid dividends by boosting the pride and confidence of a downtrodden race.

But Garvey also weakened his defense by routinely taking exception to rulings from the bench, by digressing about matters that were not relevant to the subject at hand, and by a general arrogance and belligerence that, according to one biographer, would have "prejudice[d] him in the eyes of any jury, white or black."[91] On several occasions Judge Julian W. Mack jokingly complained that he almost had to conduct a law school for Garvey's benefit.

At the end of the trial, the jury found Garvey guilty on one count of mail fraud, even as it acquitted his three fellow defendants. Judge Mack then sentenced Garvey to pay a fine of one thousand dollars and to serve the maximum term of five years in prison. On appeal, the second circuit court affirmed the conviction and sentence. Judge Charles M. Hough wrote:

> It may be true that Garvey fancied himself a Moses, if not a Messiah; that he deemed himself a man with a message to deliver, and believed that he needed ships for the deliverance of his people; but with this assumed, it remains true that if his gospel consisted in part of exhortations to buy worthless stock, accompanied by deceiving false statements as to the worth thereof, he was guilty of a scheme or artifice to defraud, if the jury found the necessary intent, . . . no matter how uplifting, philanthropic or altruistic his larger outlook may have been.[92]

When he was sent to the Atlanta penitentiary, Garvey insisted that he had been framed because the government feared the potential consequences of black pride in a white world. Even more, Garvey maintained that mulattoes resented him for his color and thought that "leadership should have been in the hands of a yellow or a very light man." According to Garvey, these "very light colored negroes" thought that "no black man must rise above them." His "success as an organizer was much more than rival negro leaders could tolerate." He was victimized by "wicked members of my own race."[93]

Many black people agreed, and for a while the UNIA continued to thrive. Garvey's conviction, however, cleared the way for deportation, for Garvey had become a resident alien with a felony record. In November 1927, when President Calvin Coolidge commuted Garvey's sentence, the Jamaican was sent back to his homeland, never to return to the United States. Garvey lived in Kingston and London for another thirteen years, but in the United States the UNIA declined steadily once it was deprived of its charismatic leader.[94]

Despite what Du Bois called "persistent and unremitting repetition of falsehood after falsehood as to [my] beliefs," the *Crisis* did not comment on Garvey's trial and conviction. Before the trial got underway, however, Du Bois had published two critical articles, one on the Black Star Line and the other on Garvey's "Back to Africa" program.

With respect to the Black Star Line, Du Bois acknowledged that Garvey was "brilliant" to develop a "plan to unite Negrodom by a line of steamships." But it was clear to Du Bois that Garvey did not have the business sense to execute the plan. Du Bois did not pronounce Garvey dishonest but calculated that the Black Star Line had collapsed at a cost of "at least $630,000 [in] the hard-earned savings of colored folk." He concluded with a letter from a widow who had asked "if it is wise . . . to continue to make the sacrifice by sending $5 per month on payment of shares in the Black Star Line . . . [when] I have an aged mother to support and I haven't one penny to throw away."[95]

Du Bois also questioned Garvey's African program. He noted that Garvey had raised hackles in the motherland because, without consulting anyone there, he had established a sort of African government in exile and pronounced himself "Provisional President of Africa." Then, without consulting anyone in Liberia, Garvey had foolishly made plans for establishing an autonomous enclave in that country. To complicate matters, Garvey's rhetoric about "forcing Europe out" led the colonial powers to make inquiries that compelled the Liberian government to repudiate Garvey. Thus Liberia's president, C. D. B. King, who previously had welcomed a UNIA delegation to his country, reversed the policy and announced that members of the UNIA would no longer be allowed to land in Liberia. King explained that his country respected "the integrity of the territory of her neighbors in the same way that they respect hers," and that "under no circumstances [would Liberia] allow her territory to be made a center of aggression or conspiracy against other sovereign states."[96]

After Garvey's conviction, Du Bois took off the kid gloves. With vituperation that matched anything Garvey had directed at the edi-

tor of the *Crisis,* Du Bois declared that Garvey was "either a lunatic
or a traitor." Du Bois condemned Garvey for squandering the investments of African Americans, for surrendering their claims to equal
rights, and for bullying his critics. "Everybody . . . who has dared to
make the slightest criticism of Garvey has been intimidated by threats
and threatened with libel suits," Du Bois wrote. "After my first and
favorable article on Garvey, I was not only threatened with death by
men declaring themselves his followers, but received letters of such
unbelievable filth that they were absolutely unprintable." Du Bois
said that, unbeknownst to him, his friends had "actually felt compelled to have secret police protection for me." "To such depths have
we dropped in free black America!" It was "time to tell the truth about
black traitors." "Garvey is, without doubt, the most dangerous enemy of the Negro race in America and in the world."[97]

Fisticuffs were barely avoided shortly after Du Bois called Garvey
"a lunatic or a traitor." As it happened, the two men were in Cincinnati's Hotel Sterling on May 19, 1924. Du Bois and his friend Wendell Dabney were waiting to take the elevator to the coffee shop.
When the door opened, an honor guard stepped out and then "a stout
dark gentleman, gorgeously apparelled in military costume." "Ye
Gods!" Dabney thought to himself; "'Twas Garvey. He saw me, a smile
of recognition, then a glance at Du Bois. His eyes flew wide open.
Stepping aside, he stared, while Du Bois, looking straight forward,
head uplifted, nostrils quivering, marched into the elevator. . . . A
sigh of relief escaped me. Immediately, I remarked, 'I must compli-
ment you upon your wonderful nerve, your coolness, your poise. The
only sign I saw of nervousness was the quivering of your nostrils.'

> "What are you talking about?" said [Du Bois].
> "Why about your meeting with Garvey, just now. I expected him to
> attack you at once."
> "Are you crazy? Garvey? Where is Garvey?"
> "Why, he stepped out of the elevator as we entered."
> "Stepped out of the elevator? Garvey? Why, I did not know it. I saw
> a man in uniform, but paid no attention. I was deeply thinking about
> something."
> "Well, if you did not know it was Garvey, why was your nose
> twitching so?"
> "That was caused by thought. You see, I smelled the breakfast and
> was wondering how soon we would reach the table."

We ate, he chuckling with laughter as he thought of the meeting, and I a little serious at the thought of what might have happened. But "All's well that ends well."[98]

With time, Du Bois's assessments of Garvey became more generous. In 1940, he acknowledged that Garvey had been "an astonishingly popular leader" whose influence had spread from the West Indies to the United States and eventually to "every corner of Africa." He admitted that the UNIA "was a mass movement that could not be ignored."[99] And near the end of his life, Du Bois reiterated that Garvey was "a sincere and hard-working idealist" with "a great and worthy dream."[100]

Some recent historians have been even kinder in dealing with Garvey. In a deeply researched monograph, Tony Martin defended Garvey on almost every point. And in a general survey of black leaders, John White depicted Garvey as a prophet and a visionary who was ahead of his time in dreaming about the expulsion of European colonial powers from Africa. White also saluted Garvey for, "more than any previous leader, stimulat[ing] racial pride and confidence" and for articulating "the grievances of those [lower-class] blacks for whom the civil rights goals of desegregation and political rights were largely meaningless."[101]

In his biography of Du Bois, David Levering Lewis has also sided with Garvey. After noting that Garvey's emphases on self-help and African independence were compatible with Du Bois's pluralism, Lewis concluded that Du Bois should have disregarded Garvey's comments about mulattoes and octoroons. The two black titans could have been allies, Lewis suggested, except for the fact that Garvey's "crude hyperbole and garish costumes" were too vulgar for the fastidious Dr. Du Bois, who wanted upper-class Negroes to maintain their "near monopoly in the leadership of black people."[102] The author of this book, on the other hand, believes that Lewis was mistaken to make little of Garvey's argument that brown-skinned mulattoes like Du Bois were too "light" to be trusted.[103]

For his part, Du Bois attached the greatest significance to the fact that black Americans eventually rejected Garvey. He admitted that in some cities Garvey had attracted a following that reached into the thousands. But in the end, "American Negroes stood the test well."[104] After comparing Garvey's results with his flamboyant promises, most African Americans recognized that the NAACP's focus on interracial cooperation and uplifting black people in the United States was more likely to lead to progress than was Garvey's program.

Indeed, as Du Bois saw it, his generation of black Americans had survived two grave temptations. "The greater one, fathered by Booker T. Washington, . . . said, 'Let politics alone, keep in your place, work hard, and do not complain.'" "The lesser, fathered by Marcus Garvey, said, 'Give up! Surrender! The struggle is useless; back to Africa and fight the white world.'"[105]

In opposing Garvey, Du Bois flirted with integration and appeared more optimistic about interracial relations than he actually was. However, as will be noted in the next chapter, in the 1930s Du Bois himself took up several black nationalist positions and Garvey was left sputtering that Du Bois "after he succeeded in killing [the UNIA] in the United States and ha[d] the field almost entirely to himself," was trying to persuade the NAACP to move toward Garvey's positions.[106] In the effort Du Bois would first split and then quit the NAACP, but in doing so he would show, once again, that he favored pluralism rather than either separatism or integration.

Du Bois, standing at left, and fellow members of the Great Barrington High School class of 1884. Principal Frank Hosmer is seated in the center of the first row. *Special Collections and Archives, W. E. B. Du Bois Library, University of Massachusetts Amherst.*

The graduating class of Fisk University, 1888. Du Bois is seated at left. *Special Collections and Archives, W. E. B. Du Bois Library, University of Massachusetts Amherst.*

The class day speakers at Harvard's commencement, 1890. Du Bois is at the far right. *Special Collections and Archives, W. E. B. Du Bois Library, University of Massachusetts Amherst.*

Du Bois, his wife, Nina Gomer Du Bois, and their infant son, Burghardt, about 1898. *Special Collections and Archives, W. E. B. Du Bois Library, University of Massachusetts Amherst.*

Du Bois in Paris, 1900. *Special Collections and Archives, W. E. B. Du Bois Library, University of Massachusetts Amherst.*

Du Bois in his office at Atlanta University, circa 1905. *Special Collections and Archives, W. E. B. Du Bois Library, University of Massachusetts Amherst.*

Booker T. Washington in his office at Tuskegee Institute, circa 1905. *Library of Congress, Prints and Photographs Division, LC-USZ62–119898.*

Du Bois, seated, with fellow members of the Niagara Movement, left to right: Freeman H. M. Murray, L. M. Hershaw, and William Monroe Trotter. *Special Collections and Archives, W. E. B. Du Bois Library, University of Massachusetts Amherst.*

John Hope at the time of World War I. Hope was Du Bois's closest personal friend. He was a professor and then president at Atlanta Baptist College, which later became Morehouse College. Still later, he was the president of Atlanta University. *Special Collections and Ar*chives, W. E. B. Du Bois Library, *University of Massachusetts Amherst.*

Oswald Garrison Villard, Du Bois's principal rival in the early years of the NAACP. *Special Collections and Archives, W. E. B. Du Bois Library, University of Massachusetts Amherst.*

The "tetrarchs" who dominated the NAACP in the 1910s, 1920s, and early 1930s. Clockwise from top left: W. E. B. Du Bois, James Weldon Johnson, Mary White Ovington, and J. E. Spingarn. *Du Bois, Johnson, and Ovington photos, Special Collections and Archives, W. E. B. Du Bois Library, University of Massachusetts Amherst; Spingarn photo, Library of Congress, Prints and Photographs Division, LC-USZ62–84498.*

Charles Young was the highest-ranking black army officer when the United States intervened in World War I. He had been a close friend of Du Bois's since the 1890s, when they were both members of the faculty at Wilberforce University. *Library of Congress, Prints and Photographs Division, LC-USZ62–62353.*

182

Robert Russa Moton was a friend of Du Bois's, but a friend who came in for criticism for allegedly urging black soldiers to be meek and subservient after the First World War. *Special Collections and Archives, W. E. B. Du Bois Library, University of Massachusetts Amherst.*

Emmett J. Scott was the principal assistant to Booker T. Washington at Tuskegee Institute. During the First World War he became a special assistant to Secretary of War Newton D. Baker. There was a lively controversy when Scott lashed back after Du Bois criticized Scott's work for the War Department. *Library of Congress, Prints and Photographs Division, LC-J601–266.*

Marcus Garvey, Du Bois's principal rival of the 1920s. Du Bois thought Garvey had "a great and worthy dream," but he questioned Garvey's tactics and especially the soundness of Garvey's financial enterprises. *Library of Congress, Prints and Photographs Division, LC-USZ62–109627.*

Walter White, Du Bois's nemesis within the NAACP. This photograph is from about 1930. *Library of Congress, Prints and Photographs Division, LC-USZ62–107019.*

Nina Du Bois in the mid-1930s. Mrs. Du Bois was constant in supporting her husband's causes, but she placed her emphasis on making a comfortable home and on caring for their two children and one grandchild. *Special Collections and Archives, W. E. B. Du Bois Library, University of Massachusetts Amherst.*

George W. Streator was Du Bois's ally in the NAACP's internal battles of the 1930s. In 1925 Streator had been a leader of a student rebellion at Fisk University. After leaving the NAACP in 1934, he became a reporter for the *New York Times*. *Special Collections and Archives, W. E. B. Du Bois Library, University of Massachusetts Amherst.*

Du Bois at seventy. *Library of Congress, Prints and Photographs Division, LC-USZ62–103164.*

Du Bois and Shirley Graham Du Bois at the time of their wedding, 1951. *Special Collections and Archives, W. E. B. Du Bois Library, University of Massachusetts Amherst.*

Du Bois remained active throughout his life; this photo shows him at about age eighty-five. *Special Collections and Archives, W. E. B. Du Bois Library, University of Massachusetts Amherst.*

Du Bois and Shirley Graham Du Bois in Communist China, 1959. Deng Xiaoping, who later became China's "paramount leader," is second from right. *Special Collections and Archives, W. E. B. Du Bois Library, University of Massachusetts Amherst.*

Six

Du Bois and Walter White

Du Bois at Sixty

By the time of his sixtieth birthday in 1928, Du Bois had regained his position as the nation's most prominent spokesman for African Americans. Marcus Garvey had been deported from the United States by then, and the NAACP had become the nation's most influential civil rights organization. With about 320 branches in all sections of the country, the NAACP was receiving dues that paid 80 to 90 percent of the national office's $50,000 to $55,000 yearly operating budget. Other NAACP executives were more active in organizing the branches but, because he was the association's best-known leader, Du Bois's influence increased as the organization developed strength at the grass roots.

Du Bois's reputation also benefited from the African American arts movement that became known as the Harlem Renaissance. At the time of his controversy with Booker T. Washington, Du Bois had famously asserted that the progress of black people depended on training a Talented Tenth to become "leaders of thought and missionaries of culture among their people." During the 1920s the talented elite were on special display as several black writers and artists gained recognition for the quality of their work: Countee Cullen and Langston Hughes in poetry; Nella Larsen, Zora Neale Hurston, Claude McKay, and Jean Toomer in fiction; Richmond Barthe and Sargent Johnson in sculpture. And there were many more.[1] This was in marked contrast to the situation a few years earlier when, as Du Bois wrote in 1911, "We have among ten millions today [only] one poet, one novelist, and two or three recognized writers of articles and essays. That is all."[2]

Du Bois himself wrote two novels, *The Quest of the Silver Fleece* (1911), a love story that dealt with several aspects of black life and race relations, and *Dark Princess* (1928), a melodrama that Du Bois once called "my favorite book." He also contributed greatly to the Renaissance through his work as editor of the *Crisis,* where he published a sampling of the works of most of the black writers of the 1920s. The poet Langston Hughes later recalled that the *Crisis* "mid-wifed the so-called New Negro literature into being," and the scholar Arnold Rampersad concluded that there was "no doubt that the *Crisis . . .* was the most important black magazine interested in the arts."[3] For a few years the *Crisis* also gave literary prizes for outstanding books, and in 1928 Du Bois's daughter, Yolande, wed the poet Countee Cullen in what turned out to be a short-lived marriage. The wedding was the social event of the Harlem season, a pageant of the African American aristocracy, with the fifteen hundred guests dressed in formal attire.

Du Bois hoped that high-quality African American art and literature would transform the negative images of Negroes that so many white people harbored. James Weldon Johnson also made this point when he wrote that "nothing will do more to change the mental attitude and raise [the] status [of black people] than a demonstration of intellectual parity by the Negro through his production of literature and art."[4] The two NAACP leaders wanted to use art to create a better society. According to Du Bois, "Fiction, in addition to being 'clear, realistic and frank,' should show 'the possible if not the actual triumph of good and true and beautiful things.'"[5]

Du Bois wanted literature and art to contribute to racial advancement. But because he was conventional and Victorian in his own personal tastes, Du Bois looked askance at some of the literature of the Renaissance. He took particular exception to the white writer Carl Van Vechten's novel of 1926, *Nigger Heaven,* a book that focused on the lower strata of black life and painted African Americans at their worst.[6] Two years later, Du Bois also criticized Claude McKay's novel, *Home To Harlem.* This was the first novel by a black writer to achieve best-seller status, but no graduates of Harvard or Howard graced its pages; instead, the book focused on the activities of what Du Bois called "the debauched Tenth"—"drunkenness, fighting, lascivious sexual promiscuity and utter absence of restraint."[7] After reading the book, Du Bois wrote, he felt "like taking a bath."[8]

Because tales of the black underclass reinforced prevailing stereotypes, Du Bois thought some writers had succumbed to white publishers and readers who considered blacks primitive and looked upon them with a combination of amusement, contempt, and pity. He also suspected that some publishers were encouraging the Talented Tenth to take up literature in order to entice them away from agitating the Negro question.[9] He criticized *Nigger Heaven, Home To Harlem,* and other novels not simply because they emphasized the decadent side of black life, but also because their authors, without recognizing it, allowed themselves to become the puppets of white racists. When one aspiring black novelist sought Du Bois's opinion of a manuscript, he replied: "This 'Nigger Heaven' stuff has . . . been done to death, and I do not think it is true to fact. Nevertheless, it is quite possible that you can get a publisher for it. Most of the publishers like this kind of thing . . ."[10]

Du Bois's criticism led some of the black writers to regard the editor of the *Crisis* as a fuddy-duddy. Thus after Du Bois wrote that a novel by Arna Bontemps was "of the school of 'Nigger Heaven' and 'Home to Harlem'—a "sordid" account of "crime, drinking, gambling, whore-mongering, and murder,"[11] Bontemps answered that Du Bois "leaned toward the tidy, the well-mannered, the Victorian— literary works in which the Negro puts his best foot forward, so to speak."[12] But Du Bois's criticism of the younger writers did not cause a lasting breach. In the 1930s, Claude McKay published essays in the *Crisis,* and in 1953 Bontemps confided that he remembered Du Bois's review "by heart" and had "forgiven it completely because the motive was pure."[13]

Moreover, most of the Renaissance artists fostered a positive impression of blacks. On balance, Du Bois wrote in 1927, "we Negroes are quite well satisfied with our Renaissance."[14] As the best-known patron of the black arts movement, Du Bois gained added stature and recognition. If the arts movement did not—and could not by itself— usher in a new era of egalitarian race relations, it by no means follows that it made no contribution to the advancement of civil rights.

Du Bois had no ambivalence at all when it came to another manifestation of "New Negro" action in the 1920s. He gave unqualified praise to the black students who organized strikes at Fisk, Howard, Hampton, and Florida A & M, and he commended the alumni for insisting on a larger role at these schools and also at Wilberforce and the two Lincoln universities (one in Pennsylvania, the other in Missouri).[15]

Du Bois's enthusiastic support for the black college rebellions of the 1920s should be understood in context. Ever since the turn-of-the-century controversy with Booker T. Washington, Du Bois had complained about a corrupt bargain that he thought involved the white South, northern secular philanthropy, and cooperating blacks. According to Du Bois, most white southerners feared that a college education would lead to increased dissatisfaction with the inferior economic and social status accorded to African Americans. Throughout the South, Du Bois said, planters feared that education would undermine black willingness to work in the fields and would make Negroes less deferential, submissive, and dependent. One editor in New Orleans openly proclaimed that "the higher education of the Negro unfits him for the work that it is intended that he shall do, and cultivates ambitions that can never be realized." A U.S. senator from Mississippi candidly asserted that "education is ruining our Negroes. They're demanding equality."[16]

It was against this background that some northern philanthropists came to regard vocational training as especially suited to the subordinate status that blacks were given in the South. By endowing the vocational programs at Hampton and Tuskegee, and by decrying and discouraging the work of the black liberal arts colleges, Du Bois said, secular philanthropists in the North made peace with the white South. They supported a form of black education that promised not to raise blacks out of their "place" but to make them more efficient servants and laborers. Then the federal government reinforced this trend with a land-grant program that gave money to black colleges that emphasized agricultural, mechanical, and technical studies— colleges whose names were followed by the letters "A and M" or "A and T." Du Bois complained that some of the vocational institutes were "not . . . our school[s]" but rather belonged to "the white South and the reactionary North." They were "center[s] of that underground and silent intrigue that is determined to perpetuate the American Negro as a docile peasant and peon."[17]

Fortunately there were a few Negro liberal arts colleges that rejected southern demands that they emphasize industrial and manual training. Most of these schools—Atlanta, Fisk, Howard, and some others—had been founded by Christian missionaries during the era of Reconstruction, and they endured in the twentieth century despite receiving little assistance from either secular philanthropy or from the federal land-grant program. Moreover, because segregation required that blacks provide their own leaders, a critical minority of African Americans had to be trained as doctors, lawyers, journalists, clergymen, and teachers. There were only 13,587 black college students in 1927.[18] But thanks to the missionary colleges, some of those black students were not steered into accepting subordinate roles. Instead, they demanded equal rights and the same sort of education that was thought to be effective in uplifting and civilizing white students.

In the early 1920s, students at Hampton Institute insisted that academic standards at their institution should be raised. They said that more college courses should be offered and that teachers should be required to have more formal education and advanced degrees. Finally, in October 1927, hundreds of students went on strike at Hampton, pledging not to attend classes until their demands were met. "The complaints with regard to education are possibly unique in the annals of student strikes," the Hampton administration noted, "demanding as they did more and better education."[19] One of the striking students declared that the students possessed "a Du Bois ambition" that would not mix with "a Booker T. Washington education."[20] Trustee George Foster Peabody confided to a relative, "Our friend Du Bois is at the bottom of this thing. . . . Scarcely any of the Hampton students fail to read the *Crisis* regularly and for ten years past it has been a real influence on the campus."[21]

At Fisk the situation was different, for Fisk never embraced the gospel of vocationalism. Its emphasis in the 1920s, as in earlier decades, was on the arts and sciences. Nevertheless, Fisk found other ways to socialize its students in the etiquette of American race relations. Thus the student newspaper, the *Fisk Herald,* was suspended; a request for a campus chapter of the NAACP was denied, and the librarian was instructed to inspect NAACP literature and excise articles deemed too radical; and a Draconian code of student discipline was rigorously enforced and justified with repeated statements that black youths were particularly sensuous beings who would abandon themselves to indulgence if they were not subjected to firm control. In addition, special Jim Crow entertainments were arranged for benefactors. On one occasion the president of the university led the girls' glee club up an alley and through a kitchen entrance into a smoke-filled room to sing plantation songs for the white Shriners of Al Menah Temple.[22]

Du Bois was outraged when he heard such stories from other alumni and from his daughter, Yolande, who was a student at Fisk from 1920 to 1924. Still, Du Bois hesitated and kept an uneasy silence because Fisk was trying to raise a one-million-dollar endowment, the first endowment of that size for any black *academic* institution. It seemed unwise to protest at so critical a time. Yet in his heart Du Bois agreed with those who gibed, "Yesterday Fisk had a president; tomorrow she will have a million dollars."[23] As soon as the endowment was obtained, Du Bois came forward to utter a protest, a plea, and a warning.

Du Bois issued his challenge on the Fisk campus in 1924, when he attended his daughter's graduation and addressed the alumni. After participating in the traditional baccalaureate procession, and without giving any warning of his intentions to the trustees or to Fisk's President Fayette Avery McKenzie, Du Bois announced that he had "never known an institution whose alumni on the whole are more bitter and disgusted . . . than the alumni of Fisk University today." Du Bois confessed that since he had "neither money nor monied friends" and since his thoughts were "distasteful to those from whom Fisk . . . was expecting financial aid," he had for some time "taken refuge in silence even when I sensed wrong." Yet he knew that "it would never do for purposes of expediency to lie to the world as Galileo once lied when he knew that his heart held the truth." So Du Bois went to Fisk "to criticize and to say openly and before your face what so many of your graduates are saying secretly and behind your back." Du Bois insisted that "of all the essentials that make an institution of learning, money is the least," and it was secured at too great a cost if, to win the favor of secular philanthropy, Fisk had to win the sympathy of southern whites by humiliating and repressing its students.[24]

To counter the philosophy and attitude of the Fisk administration, Du Bois personally revived and published the suppressed student newspaper, the *Fisk Herald*. His New York editions of the student paper featured articles from students and alumni throughout the country, and the picture that emerged was one of kowtowing to the white South, repressing student initiative, and enforcing disciplinary rules that undermined self-respect and taught black students to regard themselves as inferiors who should accept racial discrimination without complaint. Du Bois was convinced that the policies of the college administration were intended to persuade the elite of black youth to forsake egalitarian principles and adjust to the times; that students were being "humiliated and insulted in order to attract the sympathy of Southern whites."[25]

Du Bois promised to keep up the publicity. "Unless [President] McKenzie is removed from Fisk, I intend to publish every word of evidence I hold to prove he is unfit and a detriment to the cause of higher education for our race." Fisk, Du Bois said, had "fallen on evil days; it has gotten money and lost the Spirit. . . . This great institution must be rescued or it will die." "This fight is going on until McKenzie leaves Fisk." "We are not going to let up a single minute."[26]

Du Bois's publicity stiffened the attitude of the administration. One trustee confided that "the whole matter might have been argued out and diplomatized originally, but the virulence of Du Bois . . . [has] rendered it absolutely impossible to deal with conditions in that way."[27]

At the same time, students were emboldened. Twice in December 1924 there were impromptu after-curfew demonstrations, with students pounding on garbage cans and cheering for Du Bois. Then in February 1925, more than one hundred men of Livingstone Hall ignored the ten o'clock curfew and instead sang, yelled, smashed windows, and told the faculty that it would not be safe for any authorities and that they were "going to keep up this sort of thing until the President's hair was white." According to the dean of women, "The disorderly students overturned chapel seats, broke windows, . . . all the while keeping up a steady shouting of 'Du Bois!' 'Du Bois!'"[28]

Eventually police were called to the campus. The students then organized a remarkably effective strike of ten-weeks' duration, while Du Bois personally provided a subsistence allowance for George Streator, the leader of the striking students. Finally, the trustees recognized that it was impossible to operate a college without students. They accepted President McKenzie's resignation and changed the offensive policies.[29]

Du Bois was elated. For him, there had "not been a fight for academic freedom in a long time that approache[d] this in importance."[30] As Du Bois saw it, the protest at Fisk was essentially against a system whereby, in order to promote the economic growth of the United States, northern philanthropists and southern whites had reconciled their differences and come together to support a plan that was designed to educate blacks for subordinate service rather than for full participation in American life. According to Du Bois, the fight against secular philanthropy was "more than opposition to a program of education. It was opposition to a system and that system was part of the economic development of the United States at that time."[31] He hailed the student or alumnus who "hits power in high places, white power, power backed by unlimited wealth; hits it openly and between the eyes; talks face to face and not down 'at the big gate.' God speed the breed!"[32]

The rebellious students at Fisk, Hampton, and elsewhere probably did not dwell on the larger ramifications of their protests. Their concern was either with academic courses that were inferior to those at most white colleges of the day or with disciplinary rules that seemed designed to persuade the elite of black youth to accept a subordinate status. Nevertheless, the success of the black college rebellions of the 1920s—a new president at Fisk, college courses at Hampton, and greater alumni influence at Howard, Wilberforce, and Pennsylvania's Lincoln—were a triumph for Du Bois as well as for the rebellious students and alumni.

Bolstered by the growth of the NAACP, by the renown of the Harlem Renaissance, and by the victories on the black campuses, Du Bois was at the height of his popularity in the late-1920s. In 1927, as Du Bois's sixtieth birthday approached, some supporters even broached the possibility of establishing a private endowment to ensure that Du Bois would have the leisure and economic wherewithal to do whatever work he wished. Du Bois appreciated the offer but discouraged the campaign. He appreciated the fact that he had "a few fine and loyal friends," but he also recognized that many blacks did "not particularly like me personally" even though they applauded his work. He knew as well that most African Americans had "little surplus money." Thus the bulk of any private endowment would have to come from the very whites who had "borne the brunt of my attacks for thirty years." This was not likely for, as Du Bois noted, most white philanthropists were "sore and sensitive over my activity." Their ostracism was "the price that I must pay for speaking plainly . . ."[33]

Fortunately for Du Bois, no subvention was necessary. At the age of sixty he was still well and strong and optimistic. He hoped that "in some far off day much praise will come to my memory," but he knew "that is not certain, for history plays curious tricks."[34] Indeed it does. In the past Du Bois had triumphed over Booker T. Washington, gained ascendancy over Oswald Garrison Villard and others at the *Crisis,* attained primacy within the NAACP, and prevailed over Mar-

cus Garvey. He had survived the travail of the First World War, promoted the Harlem Renaissance, and inspired the black college rebellions of the 1920s. But he was about to fall victim to Walter White,
a small, unprepossessing young assistant secretary in the NAACP's
national office.

A Man Called White

Walter White was proof that appearances can be deceptive. To all
the world he looked like a white man; his skin was white, his eyes
blue, his hair blond. He was so pink-cheeked and non-Negroid in appearance that almost everyone who met him at first took him for a
white man. After assessing White's physical features, the Harvard an-
thropologist Ernest Hooten estimated that White's ancestry was only
one sixty-fourth Negro.[35] Others came up with different calculations,
but whatever the percentage, White was proud of his Negro ancestry.

Although he could pass for white—indeed, he was legally a white
man in areas that had miscegenation laws—White chose to be black
because his identity was formed as a child growing up in the South.
He was reared in a family of nine light-skinned African Americans,
and one of his early memories was of a day in 1906 when the infamous Atlanta Riot began. White was thirteen years old at the time,
and the experience affected his character indelibly.[36]

On that day, White happened to go on rounds with his light-
skinned father, a postal worker. As they went down Atlanta's main
business street, they witnessed a mob of whites beating a black man
to death. The Whites' skin color was so light that the mob mistook
them for Caucasians. But the Atlanta Riot of 1906 was just beginning
and as night fell the mob marched into the neighborhood where the
Whites lived. "We turned out the lights early," White recalled, and
"Father and I . . . took our places [with rifles] at the front windows
of the parlor. . . . A voice which we recognized as that of the son of
the grocer with whom we had traded for many years yelled, 'That's
where that nigger mail carrier lives! Let's burn it down! It's too nice
for a nigger to live in!' In the eerie light Father turned his drawn face
toward me. In a voice as quiet as though he were asking me to pass
him the sugar at the breakfast table, he said, 'Son, don't shoot until
the first man puts his foot on the lawn and then—don't you miss.'"[37]

Fortunately, some friends of the White family distracted the mob
by firing shots from a two-story brick building nearby. The Whites'

property was spared as the mob paused, swayed, and then broke up. But in those moments young Walter White learned as never before who he was. "I was a Negro." Thereafter, he insisted: "I am not white. There is nothing within my mind and heart which tempts me to think I am."[38]

Like Du Bois, who also guarded his residence with a rifle during the Atlanta Riot, White was reared within the orbit of the Congregational church. His parents were so religious that young Walter was forbidden from studying his school lessons on the Sabbath. Nevertheless, White eventually made his way to college and, again like Du Bois, it was a Congregational liberal arts college for Negroes—Atlanta University. White also shared Du Bois's high regard for the white missionary teachers who went to the black South. "It dawned upon me . . . how indebted I was to the unselfish and brilliant men and women who had forsaken their homes in New England to go south to teach in a school like Atlanta University. There they had been subjected to ostracism and sometimes insult from Southern whites for teaching and associating on a basis of complete equality with Negroes. Many of them were so well-trained and able that they could have earned much larger salaries and lived in far greater comfort in the North. They had been moved by a selfless devotion to a cause in which they passionately believed—education for the Negro on the same basis as for others. . . . It was they who saved me from the defeatist belief that all whites are evil and bigoted in their attitude toward dark-skinned peoples."[39]

After graduating from Atlanta University in 1916, White worked for an African American firm, the Standard Life Insurance Company. He also became active with civic groups that opposed the Atlanta school board's plan to save enough money to build a new high school for whites by eliminating the seventh and eighth grades from the Negro grammar schools. In the course of persuading the board to scrap this plan and eventually to float a bond issue to improve schools throughout Atlanta, White and others organized a local branch of the NAACP. Then, when James Weldon Johnson came to Atlanta to support the cause, White gave an impromptu introduction that White later described as "impassioned" and "rabble rousing."[40] Johnson was favorably impressed, and one year later he offered White a position as assistant secretary in the NAACP's national office. The job with the NAACP paid less than White had been earning at Standard Life, but White took it anyway.

Upon joining the NAACP in 1918, White made himself indispensable to Johnson. Johnson was an effective chief executive officer, but he was also a poet and writer who longed for leisure. White, on the other hand, was an indefatigable worker with boundless energy. Johnson's biographer has written that before long "Johnson . . . depended on the physically more vigorous assistant secretary to carry out field investigations as well as to handle a major share of the office work."[41] By the mid-1920s, White and Johnson were really co–chief executives, although White's official title remained assistant secretary.

White may have been kept at a low rank because physically he appeared to be an insignificant fellow. In addition to seeming to be a white man, White was short in stature, slight in build, and youthful in appearance. He tried to compensate by growing a mustache, but it turned out to be a delicate champagne color and never amounted to much. One colleague scoffed that "nobody but your sweetheart would ever know you had a mustache!"[42] Acquaintances frequently commented on White's unimpressive appearance. An article in *Ebony* magazine described White as "a dapper, highly-strung little intellectual who scurrie[d] about . . . with endless energy."[43] By 1929 White was virtually in charge of the NAACP, but when his second wife met him at a party she initially had no idea who he was. All she saw was "a slight, blond young man with blue eyes and a charming smile . . . making sandwiches."[44]

Once again, appearances were deceptive, for White's ordinary mein concealed an impressive combination of gregariousness, courage, and intensity. This was just what the NAACP was looking for when it hired White in 1918, for the organization wanted to bring the light of publicity to bear upon lynching. To do so the NAACP needed an investigator who could mingle freely with white people when mob action occurred. White's personal qualities as well as his ability to "pass" as a white man made him perfect for such assignments. Shortly after he went to work for the NAACP, White was sent to Estill Springs, Tennessee, where a gang of whites reportedly "had some fun with a Negro, their particular sport involving a use of red-hot pokers."[45] It was the first of more than forty incidents that White would investigate.

Sometimes White's investigations proceeded smoothly, even with touches of humor. In Tulsa in 1921, for example, White himself briefly served in a posse that was assigned to protect white neighborhoods. White had been sent to investigate a major race riot that had occurred in the Oklahoma city. Some whites feared that blacks would invade their neighborhoods, and local authorities tried to relieve this concern by augmenting the police force with enough temporary deputy sheriffs to make up several posses. "White happened along during the swearing-in ceremonies, and, being light-skinned and blond-haired, was adjudged to have all the necessary qualifications. . . . He was handed a revolver, assigned to an automobile with five other armed men, and authorized to shoot any Negro he thought obstreperous. The area their car patrolled proved to be a pacific one, so the six deputy sheriffs passed the time by discussing the lofty principles of the Ku Klux Klan and the nefarious ones of the NAACP."[46]

On other occasions, White came close to being killed. When he went to Chicago during the race riot of 1919, White recalled, "a Negro drew a bead on me with a revolver from behind a tree. I ducked as a bullet whanged into the side of the building exactly where my head had been a fraction of a second before."[47] Thereafter, White made sure that a dark Negro was with him whenever he had business in black Chicago.

White's most nerve-racking brush with death occurred in Phillips County, Arkansas, where he was almost lynched in the fall of 1919. During the summer, the county had been the scene of one of the bloodiest race riots in American history—a riot that claimed the lives of about two hundred blacks and perhaps scores of white people.[48] White was sent to Arkansas to investigate the situation, and he began in the state capitol, where he led Governor Charles H. Brough to think that he was a white reporter from a Chicago newspaper. White so charmed Brough that the governor said he was "delighted that a Northern newspaper has sent so able and experienced a reporter to answer the foul lies [of] the *Chicago Defender* [a black newspaper] and that infamous National Association for the Advancement of Colored People." Governor Brough then gave White a letter of introduction in case he ran into difficulties in Phillips County. The letter said that White was "one of the most brilliant newspaper men [the governor] had ever met."[49]

Armed with the governor's letter, White proceeded to the county seat in Elaine, Arkansas. There he interviewed many white people, including some who had participated in the riot. White eventually asked too many questions, and some whites became suspicious. As

White was walking on the street, a black man brushed against him and whispered, "Mister, I've got something important to tell you . . . I don't know what you're down here for, but I just heard them talking about you—I mean the white folks—and they say they are going to get you."[50]

White immediately walked to the railroad station and, as luck had it, a train was about to leave. White climbed aboard, paid his fare in cash, and told the conductor that he had important business and had not had time to buy a ticket. "But you're leaving, mister, just when the fun is going to start," the conductor said. When White asked about the nature of the "fun," the conductor replied, "There's a damned yellow nigger down here passing for white and the boys are going to get him. . . . When they get through with him he won't pass for white no more!"[51]

Thanks to his work as an investigator, White rose to prominence in the NAACP. After the press learned of his bravado and published his picture in newspapers and magazines, however, White had to shift his attention to lobbying and fund-raising, tasks for which he was well suited by virtue of a strong work ethic and an outgoing personality. At first the lobbying was for the Dyer Anti-Lynching Bill. Under the American constitutional system, police work is the responsibility of state and local governments but, with sixty-one lynchings in 1920 and sixty-four in 1921, many local communities obviously were not stopping mob violence.[52] The Dyer Anti-Lynching Bill, named for Missouri congressman L. C. Dyer, proposed to remedy this by making lynching a federal crime. Yet from the outset there was strong opposition to the Dyer Bill. The NAACP's own president, Moorfield Storey, was only one of several legal authorities who doubted the constitutionality of the bill. Others feared the danger of extending federal police power, and some people were indifferent to crimes against blacks.[53]

Nevertheless, during the 1920s James Weldon Johnson and Walter White worked hard to win support for the Dyer Bill, and White continued the effort for successor antilynching bills in the 1930s. By whatever standard one cares to measure—the amount of money spent, the amount of time consumed, the quantity of publicity given—the NAACP of the 1920s and 1930s devoted more attention to work against lynching than to any other subject. However, while the House of Representatives repeatedly voted to make lynching a federal crime, Johnson and White could not muster enough support to get a bill through the Senate, where a two-thirds vote was required to stop filibusters by southerners and strict constructionists.[54]

In retrospect it seems that there never was a realistic chance of passing an antilynching law, and one wonders why the NAACP placed so much emphasis on the effort. The campaign on Capitol Hill, however, was another way to publicize the horrors of mob violence. In fact, the publicity militated against the crime, for the incidence of lynching declined from more than sixty per year during the first three years of the 1920s to an average of only twelve during the last three years of the decade.[55] In addition, lobbying Congress also hearkened back to the era of Reconstruction and forward to the modern era of civil rights, in that black-led civil rights organizations regarded action by the federal government as the key to racial uplift. In this respect, the work against lynching portended the main emphasis of post-1960s civil rights activism.

But more was involved. Johnson and especially White focused on antilynching legislation because, for personal reasons, lobbying was an especially congenial activity. White was a gregarious, sociable man with a taste for fine food, expensive liquor, good parties, and beautiful women. Friends repeatedly noted that his wife, Gladys, was a breathtaking beauty,[56] and in the 1920s and 1930s the Whites hosted many parties, dinners, and dances at their large, exquisitely decorated apartment in the fanciest part of Harlem, Sugar Hill. They and their guests sometimes "closed the evening or began the morning, by all going to one of the Harlem cabarets to dance."[57] The Whites' daughter Jane later recalled that "The parties in Daddy's and Mother's apartment were formidable."[58]

In the 1920s, White's circle of friends included many of New York's leading writers and artists, and in the 1930s and 1940s he cultivated an even more influential circle of friends. In 1946 *Ebony* magazine quoted one acquaintance as saying, "I've never known anyone with so many distinguished friends," and in 1948 the *New Yorker* said White was "a first-name friend of at least five of the nine justices" of the Supreme Court.[59] White lived, and no doubt enjoyed living, in the world of well-to-do, stylish black and white intellectuals and reformers.

Because he had a special talent for cultivating influential people, White took to lobbying like the proverbial duck to water. He instinctively knew how to get along with intellectuals and reformers, and he threw himself wholeheartedly into the campaigns for anti-lynching legislation. These campaigns gave White the opportunity for frequent conferences with influential members of Congress (and later with President and Mrs. Franklin D. Roosevelt) and for close collaboration with leading lawyers, writers, and artists who also were working against lynching.

Yet White's sincerity was beyond question. He never forgot the night when he and his father had huddled behind windows and taken aim at an advancing mob, and in later years White often seemed preoccupied with lynching. In addition to his investigative work, he wrote a novel and a nonfiction book on the subject.[60] One of his friends of the 1930s recalled that whatever the topic of discussion, White generally turned the subject to lynching and famous instances of mob violence.[61] In public speeches, he often told the story of Mary Turner, a Georgia woman who was lynched in 1918. In fact, White told the story so frequently that once, as he prepared to speak to an audience, a man stood up and called out, "Please don't lynch Mary Turner tonight, Walter."[62]

The NAACP never succeeded in getting an antilynching law through Congress, but White was more successful in 1930 when his lobbying contributed to the defeat of Judge John J. Parker, a North Carolinian whom President Herbert Hoover had nominated for a seat on the U.S. Supreme Court. In 1920 Parker had made a speech that seemed to favor keeping blacks out of politics. But Parker did not expect the NAACP to oppose him because he had a good record as a judge on the Fourth Circuit Court of Appeals, where he had recently held that a segregation ordinance in Richmond was unconstitutional. White nevertheless saw an opportunity for the NAACP to flex its muscles. Soon the Senate was bombarded with telephone calls, telegrams, letters, and petitions urging the defeat of Judge Parker. In the end, Judge Parker lost by a vote of forty-nine to forty-seven. The defeat came as a surprise because at the time the Senate rarely rejected a president's nominee for the Supreme Court.[63]

The NAACP was not the only group that contributed to Parker's defeat. The American Federation of Labor also took exception to Judge Parker, because he had upheld the use of injunctions in labor disputes and had accepted the yellow-dog contract as a legitimate device. Some senators from the Democratic South were also retaliating against the Republican Hoover administration for political reasons. Still, White had demonstrated that a well-organized minority group could play an influential role in politics. Du Bois paid a special tribute to White, saying that the battle against Judge Parker was "conducted with snap, determination, and intelligence never surpassed in Colored America and very seldom in White."[64]

The successful campaign against Judge Parker reinforced White's belief that focusing on the government was the key to progress. After 1930 he marshalled not just the NAACP but also the Negro press and especially black voters against his special bête noire, racial segregation. He was convinced that segregation almost always meant inferior accommodations and limited opportunities for African Americans. As with his opposition to lynching, this conviction was reinforced by an unforgettable experience in White's own life.

In 1931 White's father had been walking home from a market when he stepped from the curb and was hit by a speeding automobile. The driver of the car assumed that White's light-skinned father was a Caucasian and rushed him immediately to the Henry W. Grady Hospital, where Atlanta's best doctors did all they could to save his life. When it was learned that George White was an African American, however, he was transferred across the street to inferior accommodations in a Negro ward. When Walter White reached Atlanta he found his father fighting desperately for his life in a dilapidated building that, despite constant scrubbing, was infested with cockroaches. When George White died, White cried not just for his father but for a race that had been relegated to second-class status.[65]

Thereafter, White redoubled his efforts to combat segregation. During World War II, for example, White strongly opposed the War Department's plan to set up a special training school for black pilots at Tuskegee Institute—a plan that many African Americans supported and that finally was put into effect. The Tuskegee airmen compiled a creditable war record; one of them was a nephew of White's who was killed in action. But White never wavered in his conviction that supporting a segregated institution of any kind, in any circumstances, was a bad policy.[66]

The postwar era saw White's two crowning achievements: the desegregation of the U.S. armed forces and of the public schools. Many people worked in these campaigns, but no one deserved more credit than Walter White. It was White who cultivated President Harry

Truman for the NAACP, and it was White who brought in Charles H. Houston and Thurgood Marshall to plan and direct the NAACP's campaign against school segregation.[67]

At first, when he was James Weldon Johnson's assistant, White also got along well with his coworkers at the NAACP. Du Bois recalled that White "investigated lynchings at great personal risk," "carried out the plans which Johnson laid down," and did so with an "appealing" approach, "a ready smile," and "a sense of humor."[68] By the mid-1920s Johnson recognized that White's help at the office was essential if Johnson was to have free time for writing. But in 1927–1928, White went to France on a year's leave of absence, and after he returned he no longer did as much work around the office. White did not refuse assignments, but he no longer did things on his own, as he had in the past.

Because he had to pick up the slack, Johnson was left with less time for his own literary work. According to his biographer, he had a strong desire "to be free from organizational demands, demands which, while in a good cause, seemed to be draining him both physically and mentally." Johnson told Du Bois that "White was not cooperating as usual" and intimated that "he would have to resign if he lost the cooperation of his executive helper." Du Bois thought "White had already concluded that he should be [the NAACP's chief executive] instead of working under Johnson." White's chief assistant, Roy Wilkins, reported that Johnson's wife, Grace Nail Johnson, also "thought Walter had pushed her husband out."[69]

Finally, Johnson resigned in 1931 to become writer-in-residence at Fisk University, and Walter White was chosen to succeed Johnson at the NAACP. White's assumption of office set off an explosion within a year. Unlike Johnson, who had consulted widely and acted with consummate tact, White pushed ahead willfully. At the end of 1931 Mary White Ovington resigned as chairman of the NAACP's board of directors, a position she had held ever since J. E. Spingarn went off to World War I. She complained to Spingarn that White rarely consulted with her and did not invite her to committee meetings.[70] Ovington later referred to White as "a dictator" who discouraged discussion within the NAACP and "maneuvered" the board into taking a "rubber stamp attitude."[71]

In 1931 White also incurred the wrath of his coworkers at the office. The occasion was a report that White had prepared that strongly criticized the NAACP's field secretary, William Pickens, and its director of branches, Robert W. Bagnall. According to White, Pickens and Bagnall had fallen down on the job of raising funds. To prove his point, White compared the amount of money contributed by branches within two months after a visit from either Pickens or Bagnall with the amount contributed after visits from White and another NAACP worker, Daisy Lampkin. White reported that he and Lampkin had "done very well," but Pickens and Bagnall's visits cost the NAACP more than seventeen thousand dollars while returning only fourteen thousand.[72] White then recommended that Pickens should be fired and that Bagnall should focus exclusively on raising money.

White's recommendations inevitably caused a stir. Pickens had worked for the NAACP for twelve years and Bagnall for eleven, and each was popular with his colleagues. White also aggravated the situation because he gave Pickens and Bagnall neither warning of his intentions nor any chance to comment or to provide additional information. In addition, the basis of White's comparisons was unfair. Pickens and Bagnall had visited 114 branches, while White and Lampkin visited only 34 of the larger and more prosperous branches that were located in the major metropolitan areas. It was also arbitrary to base comparisons on a two-month period, since such a short span obscured the results of campaigns and contests whose income was available only months after a visit.[73]

In response, four of the six NAACP executives—a small group that in 1931 included only Herbert Seligmann and Roy Wilkins in addition to Du Bois, White, Bagnall, and Pickens—asked Du Bois as the senior executive to lead a protest against White.[74] They also promised to maintain a united front. "It was understood that the statement would be made by all the men, or not at all," Pickens wrote in a letter. "All or none," was the way Bagnall put it.[75] Du Bois then wrote a stinging letter that he and the four other executives signed.

Du Bois began by saying it was "unfair" to "attack . . . a person's record behind his back," (that is, without giving Bagnall and Pickens a chance to comment or explain). Then, with an allusion to White's extravagant personal style, Du Bois called for "a thorough-going examination of the expenditures of [White's] office." He said the executives "all had considerable and varied experiences, but in our several careers, we have never met a man like Walter White who under an outward and charming manner has succeeded in antagonizing every one of his co-workers, including all the clerks in the office." Finally, Du Bois asked a rhetorical question: "How long can [White] remain in his present position and keep the NAACP from utter disaster?"[76]

Du Bois presented the protest to the NAACP's board of directors, but White almost immediately persuaded Wilkins, who had gone to work as White's assistant only a few months before, to break ranks and withdraw his signature. After White apologized profusely, Seligmann also withdrew his signature, and so did Pickens and Bagnall.[77] J. E. Spingarn then urged Du Bois, "as your sincere well-wisher, to retract every charge or innuendo against [White's] character, honesty, or motives." Yet Du Bois characteristically refused to budge and instead replied with a single sentence: "I will not retract or change a single word in the statement signed and read before the Board."[78]

White mended his ways for a while. He "abased himself before the Board and made every promise of reform," Du Bois wrote later. He "changed his attitude toward the staff. He became pleasant and approachable." But he also got even. "He worked hard and went underground to accomplish many of his aims. . . . Everyone who signed the protest except Wilkins, lost his position and Wilkins yielded to White in every request."[79] Seligmann quit in 1932 after the NAACP offered him only part-time employment.[80] Bagnall was fired in 1933.[81] Pickens hung on longer but was convinced that White was conspiring against him. After he was finally fired in 1942, Pickens told a friend that "Walter and I have worked in the NAACP together for twenty-two years and some weeks, and for twenty-two years of that time he has done all in his mortal power to destroy or hurt me in some way."[82]

Getting rid of Du Bois, however, was not so easy. White could not have done it save for an unusual combination of developments that occurred against the background of the Great Depression.

Du Bois, the Crisis, and the Great Depression

When Du Bois began the Crisis in 1911, he had a clear field. There was no other nationally circulated journal of African American opinion. During the 1920s, however, two other well-edited black monthlies, Opportunity and the Messenger, were circulated nationally, and so were several black newspapers. Then, with the Great Depression, the Crisis faced additional problems that had nothing to do with competition or the quality of the magazine. In 1931 James Weldon Johnson noted that "*The Crisis* is a better magazine today than it ever was," but economic conditions were so desperate that many blacks could no longer afford a subscription. During a field trip to Indiana, Mary White Ovington reported that local members of the NAACP were "interested all right, but the lack of money makes it impossible to get new subscribers and the old ones are compelled to give up the magazine." By 1932 the monthly circulation of the *Crisis* had fallen to about 15,000, and Du Bois reported that the magazine could not survive unless the NAACP paid his salary and provided an additional annual subsidy of a few thousand dollars.[83]

This put Du Bois in a difficult position. Ever since 1916, he had enjoyed a great deal of independence because income from subscriptions had paid for his salary and all other expenses of the *Crisis*. When this changed during the Great Depression, Du Bois became dependent not only on the NAACP but also on Walter White, who increasingly was raising the money that kept the NAACP alive. With the Depression, membership in the association declined to about 20,000, many of whom were behind in their dues, and the organization could not have survived without money that White raised from the Garland Fund and the Rosenwald Foundation, and from several bequests.

Despite the gifts, the NAACP had to cut the budget of its national office from almost $60,000 in 1930 to $38,000 in 1934. The salaries of all the NAACP executives were reduced by 10 percent in 1932, and when revenues continued to decline, an additional cut of 5 percent was imposed. When the NAACP still could not balance its budget, the salaries were reduced by an additional 16 percent. At about the same time, between 1930 and 1934, the NAACP had to provide more than $30,000 to keep the *Crisis* afloat.[84]

As long as the *Crisis* remained financially self-sufficient, Du Bois had been able to proceed with only a modicum of supervision. But when the journal became dependent on annual subsidies, it was difficult for Du Bois to maintain his previous independence. "Now that *The Crisis* cannot balance its books and . . . the Association is responsible for all its debts," Mary White Ovington wrote, it seemed only natural "to put the business management in the hands of the people who are ultimately responsible."[85]

Ovington also noted other ways in which the times had changed.

"In the early days [of the NAACP]," she told Du Bois, "the magazine amounted to more than the organization. [But] as time has gone on the organization has become increasingly important, and the *Crisis* less important, not just in relation to the Association but in relation to the Negro world. It is not unique as it once was. . . . It is doing a useful, interesting work, but it is not as essential to Negro progress and to radical Negro thought as it once was."[86] Since the *Crisis* had become an adjunct to the association, Ovington thought it was inevitable that Du Bois would eventually lose control of the journal. In these circumstances, Ovington advised Du Bois to anticipate the inevitable and become a semiretired editor emeritus who wrote occasional articles for the magazine while also traveling and giving lectures for the NAACP.

Du Bois, however, rejected Ovington's suggestion. "Either *The Crisis* is necessary to the work of the NAACP or it is not," he answered.[87] The board of directors then decided to continue the *Crisis* with Du Bois as editor but with the board taking control over financial matters.[88] In addition, since Walter White was increasingly raising the funds that kept the association and the *Crisis* alive, White was appointed to the *Crisis* editorial board.[89]

Du Bois, of course, opposed White's ascendancy. As noted, in 1931 Du Bois's protest on behalf of the other executive officers had concluded by questioning White's fitness to serve as the NAACP's chief executive officer. And this was only one of several instances in which Du Bois and White were at odds. In 1929, Du Bois had offered no objection when the board of directors resolved that the secretary was "the executive officer of this Association, and that all employees . . . shall be subject to his authority."[90] But that was because the office was held by James Weldon Johnson. After White succeeded Johnson as secretary, Du Bois persuaded the board to repeal the resolution.[91] In 1930 Du Bois told J. E. Spingarn that he would "withdraw from *The Crisis* and the NAACP" unless White's authority was limited.[92] In 1933 he said he "would not work under any Editorial Board of which Mr. White is a member, if that Board has authority which is more than advisory."[93] Nor, Du Bois added, would he work with Roy Wilkins, unless Wilkins was clearly under Du Bois's supervision. "You see," Du Bois told Spingarn, "Wilkins is White's errand boy," and for that reason Wilkins "does not have my confidence."[94] To another member of the NAACP board, Du Bois confided that he was "getting

terribly tired fooling away time and energy on Walter White. He's neither straight nor honest."[95]

Eventually, the battles in the office wore Du Bois down. He
thought some board members were "trying to put White and Wilkins
in control [of the *Crisis*] . . . and still carry my name on the flagpole,"
and he was "getting awfully tired of it."[96] He told a friend that he was
on the verge of leaving the NAACP because the board wanted "to use
my name and whatever reputation goes with it, and at the same time
have my power cut to a minimum."[97]

Nevertheless, Du Bois decided to stay on. He explained to his
wife that he did not want "to give up *The Crisis* . . . at this critical junc-
ture."[98] He regarded the magazine as "an independent organ leading
a liberal organization toward radical reform,"[99] and during the Depression he hoped that a campaign of constructive criticism would
lead to a realignment and reorganization of the NAACP. Du Bois was
convinced that the NAACP faced "the most gruelling of tests which
come to an old organization."[100]

In the past the association had emphasized the importance of civil and political rights, but with the Depression Du Bois thought the
time had come to develop a new program to improve the economic
condition of the black masses. At the NAACP's annual conference in
1932, he complained that the NAACP's attitude was to work for the
black masses but not with them. Then he presented a reorganization
plan whose goal was to transform the association from a top-down
organization that emphasized lobbying and legal cases to a bottom-
up society that enlisted the masses of black folk. He insisted that the
NAACP, in addition to fighting against segregation and discrimination, should also develop a positive program for improving the economic status of blacks.[101]

For years Du Bois had had reservations about capitalism. As a
student in Germany he had attended meetings of the Social Democratic party. In 1904 he had voted for the Socialist candidate for
president, Eugene V. Debs, and during a visit to Russia in 1926 he
celebrated the fact that the Soviet Union had renounced private ownership of the major means of production. Prior to the 1930s he had
insisted that union discrimination was no excuse for a blanket con-
demnation of the trade union movement, and he carried the union
label on the *Crisis,* even though it meant that no Negro could print
it. On several occasions Du Bois said he was a socialist.[102]

Nevertheless, prior to the 1930s Du Bois's socialism was luke-warm and idiosyncratic. He became a member of the American Socialist Party in 1910 but remained for only one year. He favored the Democrat Woodrow Wilson over the Socialist Eugene V. Debs in the presidential election of 1912. He refused to support the Socialist Party in its opposition to American intervention in the First World War, and he repeatedly affirmed that white racial prejudice made it impossible to achieve working-class solidarity in the United States. In one essay he wrote that "the lowest and most fatal degree of [black] suffering comes not from capitalists but from fellow white workers."[103]

During the Great Depression, however, Du Bois concluded that capitalism was not just down but finished. He thought free enterprise should give way to government direction of the economy. And he proposed that the *Crisis* should lead the way by encouraging black people to organize cooperatives that were at once socialistic and racial. "So long as I conduct it," Du Bois told one friend, "*The Crisis* . . . is going to be Socialist and Left Wing Socialist, and I am going to work out a philosophy on segregation that is going to take into account the realities of the situation in the South."[104]

Walter White, on the other hand, saw no need for the NAACP to break with its past. White was a "noneconomic liberal"—a person who was "convinced that the major problems confronting the world and the Negro were political and not economic in orientation."[105] His emphasis was on civil rights, lobbying, and lawsuits, not on agitation to restructure the American economy.

Like Walter White, J. E. Spingarn was also a noneconomic liberal. And during the Depression, Spingarn returned to play a key role in the NAACP, replacing Mary White Ovington as chairman of the board in 1932 (a reversal of the situation in 1917 when Ovington replaced Spingarn after Spingarn joined the army). Unlike White, however, Spingarn recognized that many influential African Americans thought that the NAACP's traditional insistence on political and civil liberties, although appropriate in the past, did not do enough for impoverished black workers. In the past, Spingarn wrote, "we had all the young colored intellectuals with us; now we have few or none with us. Our programme needs reconsidering, revamping."[106]

Shortly after returning as chairman of the board, Spingarn proposed to keep the NAACP informed about new currents of thought by hosting a second Amenia Conference. The first Amenia Conference of 1916 had sought to achieve a consensus among black leaders after the death of Booker T. Washington. When Spingarn proposed a second Amenia Conference, however, he was told that Walter White was "not particularly keen about the Amenia Conference of young people."[107] Although White did not oppose the conference openly, he neglected to send out invitations and generally dragged his feet.

Upon discovering that little was being done to prepare for the conference, Spingarn resigned as NAACP chairman in March 1933. Du Bois explained to his wife that Spingarn was "dissatisfied with Walter." "When I joined the Association we had . . . a thrilling programme," Spingarn wrote to Mary White Ovington and James Weldon Johnson. "Now we have only [legal] cases" and lobbying, and "every effort I have made . . . has been ignored or thwarted by [Walter White] or the Board."[108]

Eventually Spingarn withdrew his resignation, but only after White reassured Spingarn that his leadership was indispensable and after Du Bois took over the planning for the second Amenia Conference.[109] Because of White's obstruction, the conference had to be postponed from 1932 to 1933. Meanwhile Du Bois had compiled a list of some 300 young black leaders, of whom 43 were invited and 33 actually attended the conference. There were 22 men and 11 women. Their average age was thirty-two. Almost all were, as Du Bois put it, "independent thinking Negroes of strong, honest character . . . not men who have just finished school, but rather those who have been out a few years and yet are not fixed in their ideas."[110] Several of them later achieved considerable distinction: United Nations undersecretary and Nobel laureate Ralph Bunche, economist Abram Harris, sociologists E. Franklin Frazier and Ira DeA. Reid, attorneys Charles H. Houston and Louis Redding, and poet and literary critic Sterling Brown.

For Du Bois, planning the conference was a labor of love. He fondly recalled that the first Amenia Conference had established that there were no essential differences between the followers of Booker T. Washington, who had recently passed away, and many of the younger men who had vigorously criticized Washington's policies. He hoped that the second Amenia Conference would also establish a common ground between youth and age in the 1930s.[111] Like Spingarn, Du Bois relished the prospect of meeting with young black intellectuals and professional people "to discuss in a perfectly frank way

... the present situation of the American Negro and just what ought to be done."[112]

Although Spingarn and Du Bois hoped for a general consensus, they knew there were many different points of view. Du Bois recognized that outside the conference some blacks (a few, not many) endorsed a point that Marcus Garvey had made on some occasions, that "the American Negro is at present so palpably inferior to other American groups that he has no right to complain of his treatment by his fellows until he has made tremendous strides in advance." Others still believed, as Booker T. Washington had in his day, that the emphasis should be on vocational training so that blacks could be efficient skilled workers. Still others supported the NAACP's traditional program: higher education for a "Talented Tenth" combined with protest and unstinting demands for civil and political rights.[113]

Du Bois emphasized that the times were changing. The first Amenia Conference had faced the problem of how to secure rights for the Negro in an order that seemed to be permanent. The second Amenia Conference, on the other hand, presented the problem of adjusting to a changed order that seemed to be impending. Some countries were responding to the Depression by substituting socialism for capitalism. Others were abandoning democracy and embracing dictators. African Americans of the 1930s had to confront "a swiftly changing world scene in which monarchies and democracies have toppled and many doctrines thought revolutionary and impossible in 1916 are in vogue."[114]

When the Amenia delegates met for three days in August 1933, two themes came to the fore. The first, which Du Bois personally favored, called for black people, regardless of class differences within the race, to unite more closely in the interests of the group's economic welfare. E. Franklin Frazier expressed this point of view when he spoke in favor of a cooperative economy that would combine racialism and socialism. He explained that African Americans would have to identify positively with their own culture and heritage before they could attain either the disciplined bloc voting that politicians could not ignore or the group socialism that would assuage basic economic problems. J. E. Spingarn later wrote that some Amenia delegates considered "cultural nationalism for the American Negro as the most important thing for the Negro to aim at."[115]

Yet most of the Amenia delegates placed greater emphasis on the second theme. Instead of stressing racial unity, they called for working-class solidarity. They knew this would be difficult to achieve because most white unions had a history of discriminating against black workers. Nevertheless, most of the delegates thought there was an important distinction between a fundamentally sound principle (trade union organization) and an unsound policy (union discrimination), and they censured the older black leaders for having "conspicuously failed in facing a necessary alignment between black and white labor." The delegates insisted that enlightened black leaders should do more than protest against union discrimination; they should also take the initiative in fostering a new labor movement that would try to organize the great masses of workers, skilled and unskilled, black and white. They urged the NAACP and other black organizations to undertake a campaign to make the black worker "conscious of his relation to white labor and the white worker conscious that the purposes of labor, immediate or ultimate, cannot be achieved without full participation from the Negro worker."[116]

Du Bois was disappointed. Like the young Amenia delegates, he wanted the NAACP to develop a new program that placed more emphasis on economic problems. But unlike them, he thought there was no chance for achieving working-class solidarity in the midst of the Great Depression.

Du Bois never renounced his faith in the long-term value of working-class solidarity. But with the Depression and the increasing competition for jobs, he abandoned his tolerant attitude toward white unions. Everywhere he looked during the early 1930s, Du Bois saw black workers suffering "not from the capitalists but from fellow white laborers."[117] White workers seemed determined to keep Negroes down.[118] They excluded blacks from their unions, kept them out of their neighborhoods and, in general, made blacks "a lower proletariat as subservient to their interests as theirs are to the interests of capital."[119] Du Bois concluded that it was futile to continue making overtures for cooperation with white workers; these efforts had been rebuffed in the past, and he saw no prospect for success in an era of massive unemployment and intense competition for every available job. In the midst of the Depression Du Bois announced that, "until the trade union movement stands heartily and unequivocably at the side of Negro workers," he would have nothing to do with organized labor.[120]

His attitude toward labor was not surprising. Despite occasional statements favoring socialism, Du Bois as a young man had not sympathized with the white proletariat and had not questioned the established order except insofar as there was discrimination against colored people. "What was wrong," he wrote in *Dusk of Dawn*, "was that I and people like me and thousands of others who might have my ability and aspiration, were refused permission to be part of this world." "It was as though moving on a rushing express, my main thought was as to the relations I had to other passengers on the express, and not to its rate of speed and its destination."[121]

In his middle age, Du Bois had favored labor unions and welfare spending, and he was impressed by much of what he saw during a visit to the Soviet Union in 1926. Finally, during the Great Depression, he favored a reorganization and democratization of work and industry. Like Karl Marx, Du Bois thought the class struggle was a reality and he agreed with the labor theory of value. Nevertheless, throughout the 1930s Du Bois's relations with the American Socialist Party and with the Communist Party of the United States were strained. He thought both parties were trying to use African Americans for their own purposes and, more fundamentally, he thought the white proletariat was at least as racist as the capitalists and probably more so.[122]

Thus Du Bois believed that the NAACP's traditional emphasis on civil rights should be supplemented with a new plan to improve the economic status of the black masses, but his distrust of white workers precluded opting for working-class solidarity. Instead, he insisted that if blacks were to survive and prosper, they would have to help themselves. According to Du Bois, African Americans could best improve their position through self-reliance and racial solidarity.

This thinking led Du Bois to emphasize the need for a communatarian, cooperative form of socialism. "In fine, by cooperative effort in doing their own laundry, making their own bread, preparing most of their own food . . . printing their own papers and books and in hundreds of other ways, the colored people of the United States, . . . could . . . hir[e] themselves at decent wages to perform services which the Negro group needs."[123]

In the past the NAACP had challenged the customs, traditions, and laws that had relegated blacks to a separate and subordinate status in America. But Du Bois was convinced that segregation would continue for the foreseeable future. Consequently the practical problem that faced African Americans was "not a choice between segregation and no segregation. . . . The thing that faces us is given varying degrees of segregation, how shall we conduct ourselves so that in the end human differences will not be emphasized at the expense of human advance."[124] Du Bois urged the NAACP to continue its fight against discrimination, but he said that black leaders should also encourage racial self-help and self-organization "to supply those things and those opportunities we lack because of segregation."[125] Black leaders should do more than protest against segregation; they should also work toward developing the black community to the point where black people themselves could supply employment for black workers and protection for black consumers.

Du Bois continued to profess his faith "in the ultimate uniting of mankind and in a unified American nation."[126] He detested the fact that African Americans had been herded together beyond the pale in inferior neighborhoods. But it was necessary to face the fact that most white Americans did not regard blacks as equals. As Du Bois saw it, the time had come for African Americans to make the best of the fact that they were racially separated and would remain so for a long time. They should not simply "squat before segregation and bawl." In addition to protesting against segregation, they should also "use segregation. Use every bit that comes [their] way and transmute it into power, power that some day will smash all separation."[127]

"Power is now needed to reinforce appeal," Du Bois declared, "and this power must be economic power; that is, the nation must be shown that the Negro is a necessary part of the wealth-producing and wealth-consuming organization of the country, and that his withdrawal from these functions in any degree diminishes the wealth and efficiency of the country."[128] Du Bois estimated that the 2,800,000 black families spent about $166 million each month on consumer purchases. This would be a tremendous power if intelligently directed. Du Bois considered it "nothing less than idiotic" for a group with this leverage "to sit down and await the salvation of a white God."[129] Blacks should buy at black stores, patronize black professional people, and amuse themselves at their own resorts and theaters. Food grown on black farms, transported by black shippers, and processed by black factories ultimately would find its way to intelligent and loyal black customers who patronized black grocery stores and restaurants. Black people could help themselves during the Great Depression if only they would develop their own institutions. Du Bois called upon African Americans to build "A Negro Nation within the Nation."[130]

To build a cooperative black economy, Du Bois urged African Americans to submerge their individual selfish interests and to join together for the common good. This would be difficult, Du Bois conceded, because many elite blacks were ashamed of rank-and-file blacks, whose behavior led many whites to reject all Negroes. At the same time, many lower-class blacks refused to look to members of their own race for leadership and instead cultivated powerful whites. For these and other reasons there were strong centrifugal forces of class repulsion within the black community, forces that atomized black society and weakened the sense of racial loyalty.[131]

Du Bois nevertheless proposed to use the *Crisis* to educate his fellow blacks to the need for group loyalty, sacrifice, and devotion to the cause. He said the NAACP should "fight for *economic equality*" by "advocating . . . co-operation and socialization of wealth" and by encouraging the Talented Tenth to "think of themselves as the servants to do the work for the great mass of the uneducated and inexperienced."[132] In September 1933, he published an essay on the importance of racial pride, and he planned to devote each issue of the *Crisis* in 1934 to a discussion of the importance of solidarity and self-reliance.

This was nothing new. As a young man Du Bois had also called for self-improvement. ("We are developing criminal tendencies, and an alarmingly large percentage of our men and women are sexually impure," he had written in 1897. *"Unless we conquer our present vices they will conquer us."*)[133] After the Atlanta Riot of 1906, Du Bois had placed less emphasis on the need for moral reform—perhaps for fear that such emphasis would reinforce white racism. But he knew that the "Negro problem" was twofold—on the one hand, white discrimination; on the other, black weakness. In the midst of the Depression, Du Bois proposed to focus again on what blacks could do to help themselves. His own position was clear: "It is the race-conscious black man cooperating together in his own institutions and movements who will eventually emancipate the colored race, and the great step ahead today is for the American Negro to accomplish his economic emancipation through voluntary determined cooperative effort."[134]

Back to Atlanta

Du Bois's campaign was probably doomed from the start. For one thing, his calls for sacrifice and devotion to the cause asked more of African Americans than any but a handful of people could ever give. For another, the constellation of forces within the NAACP was not auspicious. As noted earlier, during the Depression the *Crisis* was on the rocks financially, and the NAACP was depending more and more on Walter White's skills as a fund-raiser.

Given the NAACP's need for money, White tried to take advantage of Du Bois's celebrity. At White's instigation, a NAACP committee, after saying that Du Bois's "duties on *The Crisis* [left] him a great deal of free time," stated that "if the Association gives Dr. Du Bois aid for *The Crisis,* he ought to do regular work for the Association." Du Bois refused to acknowledge that editing the *Crisis* was a part-time job, but he nevertheless promised to do more for the NAACP, adding only that "a basis of cooperation should be worked out by which the Association could get most from [me]."[135] White had fund-raising in mind, but Du Bois knew that "raising money was not a job for which I was fitted. It called for a friendliness of approach and . . . an adaptability which I did not have." Du Bois recognized that his forte was analysis; he had "knowledge of the Negro problem, an ability to express my thoughts clearly, and a logical method of thought."[136] He was willing to write more and lecture more. To placate White, however, Du Bois promised to spend four weeks cultivating donors. But White was never able to arrange a schedule which met with Du Bois's approval, and the work was not done—a situation that led White to complain that "during the incumbency of the present Secretary the Editor of the *Crisis* has never made one offer to help the NAACP."[137]

Finally, Du Bois decided on another, more congenial way for him to help out the financially strapped NAACP. In 1932 his closest friend, Atlanta University president John Hope, had broached the possibility of Du Bois's returning to Atlanta as a professor. "I wish you could work with me here," Hope had written. "We could do so much together. . . . What I need with me from now on is not simply good minds (and God knows there is a dearth of them) but understanding and sympathetic comradeship."[138]

After arranging to continue as editor-in-chief of the *Crisis* at one-fourth his regular salary, Du Bois accepted Hope's offer and moved to Atlanta in 1933. Although Nina stayed in New York with Yolande and a baby granddaughter,[139] Du Bois was pleased with his situation. Shorn of the usual family obligations, he had extra time for what would become his most important scholarly book, *Black Reconstruction.* He was "spending every spare minute" on it, taking no vacation, and working "practically every day, including Saturdays and Sundays."[140] He found the research fascinating and sensed that the writing was going well. This opinion was confirmed when his publisher, Alfred Harcourt, pronounced that an early draft of the book was "a really brilliant performance."[141]

Du Bois also enjoyed teaching at Atlanta University. To one friend he exclaimed, "It's inspiring to be in a school again and among intelligent and enthusiastic young folk." To another, he reported that he had two classes and a seminar. One class dealt with Reconstruction, another with the Fourteenth and Fifteenth Amendments, and the seminar with Marxism. It was all "very interesting," Du Bois wrote, "and if [the students] are learning as much as I, very successful."[142]

In addition, Du Bois appreciated the beauty of the campus, and he was especially pleased with his own accommodations in a corner suite of a dormitory at Spelman College (the undergraduate women's division of Atlanta University). "I have very beautiful living quarters," Du Bois wrote to Nina: "a parlor nearly as large as our living room, with a fireplace, couch, desk [and] table, . . . a bedroom [that] is nearly twice as large as my bedroom," and a view "down through the grove toward the old Atlanta University." His nearby campus offices—one for Du Bois and one for his secretary—were "nicely fitted up" with good furniture and a private bathroom.[143]

From his letters to Nina and others, one gets an impression of Du Bois's daily routine. He did not like the fact that breakfast was served at an "impossible time, 6:45," when Du Bois was about to begin a one-mile morning walk. So he had "bread and butter and cream and two eggs sent over and these I cook in my [office] at 8." There were occasional lunches at John Hope's home, which had fourteen rooms and was "a sort of hotel for people who pass through." And the evening meal was usually at the Spelman dining room, where Du Bois was "the only man on the job—a rather fearsome thing with fifty spinsters." In addition, there were "two home-cooking restaurants," and for recreation there was a movie theater nearby.[144]

Du Bois also traveled a good deal to give talks to various groups throughout the country. Most of the travel was in his Willis sedan. He bought his first car in 1920 chiefly for travel in the South and largely because he could not abide the conditions on segregated railroad cars. "In addition to the fact that they are always dirty," he said, "any poor white—drunk, filthy and obnoxious—may ride in the Jim Crow car, while no Negro—no matter how respectable he or she may be—can ride anywhere else."[145]

It was dangerous for Du Bois to drive alone in the South, but he tried to avoid trouble by never asking for service at a garage or a restaurant. Before leaving Atlanta, his mechanic checked the car thoroughly; and Du Bois was careful to carry spare parts, a pair of overalls, and heavy gloves. More than once he slid under the car to make repairs. In addition, he kept off the roads at night and almost always managed to reach a friend's house in time for dinner. In the morning he packed a lunch so that he could pull off to the side of the road and eat.[146]

All things considered, Du Bois was pleased with his life at Atlanta University. He was away from Nina, Yolande, and Baby Du Bois, but there were compensations. According to David Levering Lewis, during the course of his travels Du Bois carried on several adulterous affairs, and in Atlanta during the 1930s there were still more assignations. Du Bois was "a priapic adulterer," Lewis has written. Indeed, according to Lewis, when Du Bois was in Atlanta in his sixties his "relationships with women, always vigorous and varied, became sexually ever more exuberant to such a degree that they resembled the compulsiveness of a Casanova."[147]

Lewis has conceded, however, that "personal letters from Du Bois were seldom very personal" and has admitted that "the biographer [can not] always know with sufficient certainty whether a friendship with a particular woman was anything more than that."[148] Letters in the Du Bois papers mention "petty gossip about 'amours' in Atlanta,"[149] but reading Du Bois's personal correspondence casts doubt on at least some of the alleged affairs.[150]

This is not to say there were no transgressions.[151] In his *Autobi-*

ography, Du Bois wrote that Nina's early "training as a virgin made it almost impossible for her ever to regard sexual intercourse as not fundamentally indecent"—an assertion that can be interpreted as an excuse for a husband's philandering. Du Bois further noted that his marriage suffered from "a difference in aim and function between its partners," with himself "out in the world and not at home" for long periods while Nina was busy with "cooking, marketing, sweeping and cleaning and the endless demands of children." When Nina died after fifty-four years of marriage, Du Bois expressed regret at having left her alone so often.[152]

Whatever personal transgressions there may have been, in public Du Bois did not stray from the path of propriety. He never retracted his statement that "lack of respect for the marriage bond" was "the great weakness of the Negro family."[153] Some of Du Bois's women friends may have dreamed of becoming the second Mrs. Du Bois, but Du Bois would not offend public morality. He thought race leaders had a responsibility to set a good example. After Nina died in 1950, he wrote that it never occurred to him "that we should ever be separated or the family tie broken." "Both of us had been brought up under the old-fashioned concept of marriage as permanent, 'until death do us part.'"[154] He did not rationalize infidelity as a new form of morality.

Reorganization, Segregation, Resignation

Since Du Bois was away in Atlanta while the NAACP supplied the money that kept the *Crisis* alive, Walter White had plausible arguments for increasing his own authority over the magazine. White told Du Bois's friends that he was doing Du Bois a favor, saying, "in order for [Du Bois] to do his Atlanta job," the editor should be "relieved . . . of the actual detail work of getting out *The Crisis.*"[155] In December 1933, the board put more of White's supporters on the *Crisis* editorial committee, after White had led them to believe that Du Bois himself wanted to give the national office more responsibility for the magazine.

White's deceptive maneuver infuriated Du Bois. Reconstituting the *Crisis* editorial committee was "simply an underhand trick," Du Bois wrote to one of his friends. Because Roy Wilkins and Walter White were both on the new committee, Du Bois complained, White had acquired "'sole and complete' control of *The Crisis.*"[156] Du Bois was angry and had "great difficulty . . . withholding my wrath."[157] He was "mad way through" and "awfully tired of [the NAACP]."[158] But in 1933 he was not ready to quit; instead, he decided to brandish a letter of resignation with the hope that the gesture would bring the organization to its senses.[159] He told one member of the board, "Either I edit *The Crisis* magazine with full power over it, or I get entirely out of the magazine and the Association. And there's no need in wasting time on any compromises."[160]

To White's chagrin, the board refused to accept Du Bois's resignation. Joel Spingarn and his brother Arthur said the resignation would "ruin the Association," and Joel threatened to resign as chairman of the board if Du Bois resigned as editor.[161] The board then passed a new resolution that Du Bois himself had drafted and one that guaranteed Du Bois's control over the *Crisis*.[162] For his part, Du Bois had made up his mind that there would be "no more bickering with the persons in the Association. So long as they leave *The Crisis* in my hands, I will conduct it my way. When they decide that they do not want to do that, I shall leave the Association."[163]

The board accepted Du Bois's terms, but the editor was still nursing a grudge against White. "I'm not going to be caught napping again," Du Bois told one board member, after saying that the controversy over editorial independence "all goes back to the fact that I have believed for two or three years that Walter White is not the proper person to head the Association. I have told the Board frankly this in his presence."[164] Believing as he did, Du Bois tried to oust White as surely as White worked against him. "With White and Wilkins in the NAACP, any intelligent action of any sort is impossible," Du Bois wrote. "I can work with stupidity . . . I can work with open and frank dishonesty. But the combination of that with charm, double-crossing, and insincerity, is something that I can't waste time on."[165]

Early in 1933 Du Bois had hoped that the second Amenia Conference would undermine White's position. Later that year he nominated ten new people for membership on the NAACP's board of directors—people whom he hoped would oppose White and begin to reorganize the NAACP. A few of Du Bois's nominees were appointed to the board (Abram Harris and Rachel Davis DuBois, in particular), but White balanced these appointments with people who, according to Du Bois, were "either absolutely reactionary in their social and economic outlook or basically ignorant."[166]

Rebuffed in his attempt to realign the board of directors, Du Bois developed a plan that would have changed the organizational structure of the NAACP. "The time has come," he wrote to a few influential board members, "for a radical and thorough-going reorganization of the NAACP, if we wish the Association, not simply to survive, but to function during the next quarter century as effectively as it has in the last."[167] Du Bois wanted to reduce the authority of the board of directors and the executive officers and to increase the power of the rank-and-file members. "We must increase the power of the branches and of the Annual Conference," he wrote. "In the future, the NAACP "must . . . recognize that the interests of the masses are the interests of this Association, and that the masses have got to voice themselves through it."[168]

Yet Du Bois again ran into a roadblock. Harry Davis, one of the board members who was most favorably disposed toward Du Bois, candidly answered: "I am not in accord with your proposals. There is no doubt that the NAACP is in a desperate situation, but I do not believe this condition is caused by our policies, or by acts of omission or commission on the part of our executive staff." Arthur and Joel Spingarn similarly told Du Bois: "We are both of the opinion that your proposals are neither feasible nor advisable, and that they would inevitably result in the disruption of the Association."[169]

To his friend Abram Harris, Du Bois confided that the problem with the NAACP was not simply the "opportunism of White" but also "the reactionary economic philosophy of the Spingarns."[170] The Spingarns recognized that the Depression had caused great distress, and they wanted to help African Americans. But they were capitalists, Du Bois later wrote, and Joel especially was "afraid that I was turning radical . . . and he proceeded to use his power and influence in order to curb my acts and forestall any change of program of the Association."[171]

Du Bois was also troubled to discover that most of the black members of the NAACP's board shared the Spingarns' economic philosophy. "The colored group did not wholly agree with me," he wrote; "the Association had attracted the higher income group of colored people, who regarded it as a weapon to attack the sort of social discrimination which especially irked them; rather than as an organization to improve the status and power of the whole Negro group."[172]

By 1934 Du Bois admitted defeat in his attempt to realign the NAACP's board of directors. Yet he still thought the organization needed "fundamental and complete reorganization from top to bottom," and to that end he tried to organize African Americans at the grass roots.[173] He obtained a list of "people throughout the country who do not like Walter White,"[174] and in the winter of 1933–1934 he went on tour to recruit "fifty to one hundred people" of "education, modern economic outlook, and character."[175] In addition to set speeches to about seven thousand people, Du Bois had "a good many personal and heart-to-heart talks with people" and discovered that his "attitude of criticism toward the NAACP, and a realization of the necessity of reorganization, is widespread."[176] "I think we are going to be able to carry out our plans concerning the NAACP," Du Bois told one friend.[177] "I am sure we can put our plan over," he wrote to another.[178] He was "ready to unite with any persons who think as I do in a determined effort to rescue [the NAACP] and to prepare it for a new and worthy future."[179]

Yet a new civil rights organization was not in the offing. Du Bois wanted to promote a cooperative black economy, but some critics noted that blacks would not have the capital needed to organize their own versions of major corporations like General Motors and U.S. Steel. Others feared that an emphasis on racial unity would widen the breach between black and white workers and militate against biracial industrial unions.[180] Du Bois could answer—and did answer—that although the cooperative economy would not solve all the economic problems of black people, at least it made a start. But at the age of sixty-six and comfortably situated at Atlanta University, he did not have the energy and drive that were needed to establish a Depression-era counterpart of the Niagara Movement.

Nevertheless, Du Bois would not give up easily. Although he had not realigned the board and organizing the grass roots was problematic, Du Bois thought he had to do something. He felt an obligation to his race. He thought the NAACP was the greatest civil rights organization that the United States had ever known, but he was convinced that it had to be revamped if it were to be as effective in the future as it had been in the past. Once again, the most powerful weapon at Du Bois's command was his pen.

In January 1934, Du Bois captured the attention of black readers throughout the United States when he provocatively asserted that

African Americans should "stop being stampeded by the word *segregation.*" What they should be concerned about was *discrimination;* discrimination as practiced, for example, when the South "refus[ed] . . . to spend the same amount of money on the black child as on the white child for its education." But Du Bois noted that segregation and discrimination did "not necessarily go together," and he insisted that there should "never be an opposition to segregation pure and simple unless that segregation does involve discrimination." Indeed, Du Bois wrote, there "should not be any distaste or unwillingness of colored people to work with each other, to cooperate with each other, to live with each other." "Never in the world should our fight be against association with ourselves because by that very token we give up the whole argument that we are worth associating with."[181]

It is hard to imagine a statement that could have done more to raise Walter White's hackles. Even before White's father had died after being transferred to an inferior, segregated ward of an Atlanta hospital, White had sworn eternal, uncompromising opposition to any and all forms of racial segregation. "If the Association's attitude is not one of opposition to segregation," White wrote to J. E. Spingarn, "then . . . I am not interested in the Association."[182] White was convinced that "numbers of white people, perhaps the majority of Americans, stand ready to take the most distinct advantage of voluntary segregation and cooperation among colored people. Just as soon as they get a group of black folk segregated they use it as a point of attack and discrimination."[183]

White's criticism did not dissuade Du Bois. In February 1934, the editor wrote that for years the NAACP had been "faced by a fact and not a theory."[184] When army authorities made it clear during the First World War that there would be no African American officers unless there was a separate training camp, both Du Bois and J. E. Spingarn had campaigned for a separate camp. And when some cities and states said there would be no schools or hospitals for black people unless those institutions were segregated, most blacks acquiesced. They did not create the Hobson's choice, they might have explained. White people did that. But given the choice between a segregated institution and nothing at all, most African Americans chose segregation rather than play into the hands of their enemies. "Give us the schools," they said. "Give us black teachers for black students." According to Du Bois:

The NAACP has never officially opposed separate Negro organizations. It has never denied the recurrent necessity of united separate
action on the part of Negroes for self-defense and self-development;
but it has insistently and continually pointed out that such action is
in any case a necessary evil involving often a recognition from within
of the very color line we are fighting without.[185]

Earlier in his life Du Bois had placed less emphasis on racial
pride, loyalty, and self-help. When he first became a professor, Du
Bois recalled, he thought the basic problem was racial ignorance and
lack of culture: "That once Negroes know civilization, and whites
know Negroes, then the problem is solved."[186] As a young man Du
Bois had expected the walls of segregation to fall before a determined
campaign of education, agitation, and social science research.

During the Great Depression, however, Du Bois concluded that
his earlier assumptions were wrong. His own study of psychology,
with William James at Harvard in the 1890s, had preceded the
Freudian era with its emphasis on the "unconscious." But during the
1920s and 1930s Du Bois came to believe that blacks were facing "not
simply the rational, conscious determination of white folk to oppress
us; we were facing age-long complexes sunk now largely to unconscious habit and irrational urge." White racism was largely "the result
of inherited customs and of those irrational and partly subconscious
actions of men which control so large a proportion of their deeds."
Attitudes and habits thus built up over the centuries could not be
changed by a program that simply called on whites to stop segregation and discrimination. Rather, blacks needed to prepare for "a long,
patient, well-planned and persistent campaign." They needed "not
only the patience to wait but the power to entrench ourselves for a
long siege against the strongholds of color caste."[187]

To wage such a campaign, Du Bois advised blacks to build on
racial pride, loyalty, and unity. They should continue to protest
against separation and discrimination, of course; Du Bois urged
blacks to "make the protest, and keep on making it, systematically
and thoughtfully; perhaps now and then even hysterically and the-
atrically." But at the same time Du Bois also urged African Americans
to "go to work to prepare methods and institutions which will supply those things and those opportunities which we lack because of
segregation."[188]

As Du Bois saw it, the segregationists' goal was to isolate African

Americans so that they would be spiritually demoralized and economically dependent. Against this, blacks should protest. But if the protest did not succeed, the African American had no choice but "to see to it that segregation does *not* undermine his health; does *not* leave him spiritually bankrupt; and does *not* make him an economic slave."

> If he cannot live in sanitary and decent sections of a city, he must build his own residential quarters, and raise and keep them on a plane fit for living. If he cannot educate his children in decent schools with other children, he must, nevertheless, educate his children in decent Negro schools and arrange and conduct and oversee such schools. If he cannot enter American industry at a living wage, or find work suited to his education and talent, . . . he must organize his own economic life so that as far as possible these discriminations will not reduce him to abject exploitation.[189]

Unfortunately, Du Bois wrote, some African Americans thought "the fight against segregation consists merely of one damned protest after another; that the technique is to protest and wail and protest again, and to keep this up until the . . . walls of segregation fall down."[190] Others mistakenly emphasized *integration* as the best solution to America's race problem. But Du Bois was convinced that "not for a century and more probably not for ten centuries, will any such consummation be reached." "No person born will ever live to see . . . racial distinctions altogether abolished."[191] Indeed, Du Bois dismissed integration as "the absurd Negro philosophy of Scatter . . . Escape." He insisted that "the problem of 12,000,000 Negro people, mostly poor, ignorant workers, is not going to be settled by having their more educated and wealthy classes gradually and continually escape from their race into the mass of the American people." To the extent that occurred, Du Bois wrote, the black masses would be left without leaders and would "sink, suffer and die."[192]

While campaigning for voluntary cooperation and self-help, Du Bois recalled the paper he had written for the American Negro Academy in 1897, "The Conservation of Races." There Du Bois had rejected integration and assimilation in favor of pluralism. He had posed basic questions: "Am I an American or am I a Negro?" "Can I be both?" "Is it my duty to cease to be a Negro as soon as possible and be an American?" "Have we in America a distinct mission as a race—a distinct sphere of action and an opportunity for race development, or is self-obliteration the highest end to which Negro blood dare aspire?"[193] And he answered that black people wished neither to make America colored nor to bleach their Negro blood, but rather to be both Negroes and Americans—African Americans. Blacks wanted to be "Americans, full-fledged Americans, with all the rights of other American citizens," Du Bois had insisted.[194] But they also had a "duty . . . to maintain their race identity," to work cooperatively, and to develop their special genius.[195]

Thirty-seven years later, Du Bois still felt the same. When he reread his paper of 1897 he was "rather pleased to find myself still so much in sympathy with myself."[196] Du Bois's synthesis of cultural pluralism and cooperative economics was consistent with the views he had been expounding for decades.

But one thing was different. In 1934 most informed readers recognized that when Du Bois touted pluralism and pointed to the problems with assimilation and integration, he had Walter White in mind. White, after all, personified the idea that blacks should disperse rather than develop internal solutions for their problems. To remove any possible uncertainty on this score, Du Bois wrote an especially stinging editorial for the April 1934 issue of the *Crisis*. According to Du Bois, White favored integration because he was basically white and wanted to associate with white people: "He has more white companions and friends than colored. He goes where he will in New York City and naturally meets no color line for the simple and sufficient reason that he isn't 'colored.'" For this reason, Du Bois wrote, White "naturally" became "an extreme opponent of any segregation." White assumed that America's race problem would eventually be solved by following his example—by dispersing and moving into the mainstream. Du Bois, however, insisted that White's approach would not work for most black people, and he implied that White knew so, too. "[White] once took a friend to dine with him at the celebrated cafe of the Lafayette Hotel, where he had often been welcomed. The management humiliated him by refusing to serve [his black companion, the famous singer] Roland Hayes."[197]

One of Du Bois's friends predicted that "the editorial on Walter is going to bring hell down."[198] In the past J. E. Spingarn had supported Du Bois before the board of directors. Although the two men remained good friends, after Spingarn read Du Bois's statement about White, he sent Du Bois a scolding letter, saying that the "reference to Walter White in the April *Crisis* seems to me hitting below the belt."[199] Spingarn particularly criticized Du Bois for making his statements in print. In private correspondence with White, Spingarn himself wrote that "hundreds of Negroes think you are really a white man whose natural desire is to associate with white men."[200]

White was furious with Du Bois, and he persuaded his friends in the press to take up the cudgels. Several anti–Du Bois editorials and columns were placed in black newspapers. William Hastie, a young friend of White's who later joined the NAACP's legal team and eventually became a federal judge, sounded the keynote: According to Hastie, Du Bois had become another of the "abject, boot-licking, knee-bending, favor-seeking Negroes [who] have been insulting our intelligence with a tale that goes like this: 'Segregation is not an evil. Negroes are better off by themselves. They can get equal treatment and be happier, too, if they live and move and have their being off by themselves.'"[201] Later, Du Bois recalled that "it was astonishing and disconcerting . . . that this change of my emphasis was crassly and stupidly misinterpreted by the Negroes. Appropriating as their own (and indeed now it was their own) my own long insistence on self-respect and self-assertion and the demand for every equality on the part of the Negro, they seemed determined to insist that my newer emphasis was a repudiation of the older; that now I wanted segregation; that now I did not want equality."[202]

White waited until Spingarn was out of town and unable to attend a board meeting and then prevailed upon friends to introduce and pass as official NAACP policy a declaration that "both principle and practice necessitate unyielding opposition to any and every form of enforced segregation."[203] When Du Bois continued to write that African Americans should make the best of segregation by cooperating together, White said the editor had challenged the board and that failure to meet this challenge would "properly, cause a loss of respect for the Board."[204] White then persuaded the board to pass another resolution declaring that "*The Crisis* is the organ of the Association and no salaried officer of the Association shall criticize the policy, work, or officers of the Association in the pages of *The Crisis;* that any such criticism should be brought directly to the Board of Directors and its publication approved or disapproved."[205]

Joel Spingarn had returned to New York for the meeting at which the second resolution was discussed, and he found himself among a minority who reportedly grumbled that a "political intrigue" was afoot to muzzle Du Bois. Roy Wilkins later recalled that "in office politics, blacks can be just as rough as whites."[206]

Because the board's resolution restricted his editorial freedom, Du Bois submitted a letter of resignation in May 1934. Du Bois did not question the board's right to take sides "whenever differences of opinion among its officers become so wide as to threaten the organization," but he personally could not comply with the May directive. "In thirty-five years of public service," Du Bois wrote, "my contribution to the settlement of the Negro problem has been mainly candid criticism based on a careful effort to know the facts." "I have not always been right, but I have been sincere, and I am unwilling at this late date to be limited in the expression of my honest opinions in the way which the Board proposes." To his friend John Hope, Du Bois confided that the board had "passed a gag resolution which makes any free expression of my opinion impossible."[207]

Yet Du Bois's letter of resignation did not end the controversy. J. E. Spingarn immediately rallied several members of the board to support Du Bois; and when the directors gathered for their June meeting, they refused to accept the resignation. Instead, a committee on reconciliation was appointed and instructed to intercede with the editor "in the hope that an understanding can be reached not incompatible with the Association's policy of unconditional opposition to segregation . . . nor with the right of Dr. Du Bois . . . to give full and free expression to his personal views through the columns of *The Crisis*." In the meantime, to prevent Walter White from publicizing the fact that Du Bois had submitted a written resignation, the board gave Spingarn exclusive power to make statements for the Association.[208]

Spingarn's role in the dispute remains mysterious. At one point in April 1934, Du Bois told Spingarn that he "had about given up hope of understanding you or your attitude toward me and the organization." Nor was Du Bois the only person who was confused about Spingarn. One of Du Bois's supporters on the board compared the monthly meetings to a "maze" and said it was difficult to understand what was going on because there was "so much underneath." Du Bois's chief assistant at the *Crisis*, George Streator, confessed, "I can not understand the Spingarns." "I simply cannot reconcile all the things I hear." Perhaps, Streator speculated, Spingarn was trying to maintain his own position as chairman "by talking against one faction to the other."[209]

Given the confusion among contemporaries, it is problematic for historians to offer explanations. It appears that Spingarn agreed (to an extent) with Du Bois on matters of substance but not on procedure. After White pushed through the resolution that committed the NAACP to "unyielding opposition to any and every form of enforced segregation," Spingarn met with Du Bois in Atlanta. There the two men talked frankly and, according to Du Bois, Spingarn said "he agreed with me that the NAACP should be reorganized," acknowledged that White "was not the man for the present job," and said that White should be dismissed as chief executive officer as soon as another job could be arranged for him.[210]

Du Bois was naturally elated. "Think all is well and valuable cooperation established," he telegraphed to George Streator. In a letter, Du Bois added: "Of course I realize [Spingarn's] temperament, and I am not depending on him absolutely, but if we can have his power and cooperation on our side to a reasonable degree, it will facilitate anything we may want to do."[211]

After returning to New York, Spingarn complained about the resolution that had been passed in his absence, the one that committed the NAACP to oppose "any and every form of enforced segregation." In the old days, Spingarn told White, the NAACP could say that segregation was evil, but now the association was committed to the policy of no longer cooperating with and supporting segregated black schools and colleges. To illustrate the foolishness of the new position, Spingarn ordered that "in obedience to the Resolution of the Board, no officer of the Association should speak officially at any Negro school or college in the South."[212]

Spingarn also told White that Du Bois understood all of White's arguments perfectly, that White had made no arguments that Du Bois "had not already stated thirty years ago, and that is where you and I first heard of them." Du Bois was simply "raising the question whether his old opinions are not old-fashioned and need revision or at least further discussion." Further, Spingarn insisted that Du Bois had the right to use the *Crisis* "to discuss any problem freely and frankly, so long as it is made clear that the opinions are personal and not official."[213] Spingarn said Du Bois was "doing a service in trying to make the real meaning of [voluntary cooperation] clearer than it has been, and certainly a hot controversy on the subject will help to keep interest in the NAACP more lively than ever."[214]

If Spingarn had limited himself to lectures, White probably would have gritted his teeth and endured the criticism. But it was too much for White when the board of directors, at Spingarn's request, refused to accept Du Bois's resignation. Instead, the board appointed a three-member committee of reconciliation to work out a compromise to ensure Du Bois's continuation as editor of the *Crisis*.

At this point, White indicated that the board would have to choose between him and Du Bois. White protested that Du Bois, by continuing to use the *Crisis* to discuss segregation and voluntary cooperation, had ignored the board's own resolutions. White said the editor thereby "show[ed] his utter contempt for the Board and put it on the defensive. Nevertheless, to White's "utter disgust," the board refused to accept Du Bois's resignation and instead opted for reconciliation, a decision that "thoroughly nauseated" White because it could "only be construed as nothing [other] than a moral victory for Dr. Du Bois."[215]

Writing to Spingarn, White candidly said, "When I left the Board meeting yesterday [June 11, 1934], I very definitely had the feeling that with the present constitution of the Board it is no longer possible for me to remain with the Association as its Secretary. Certainly the situation is at the point where my own self-respect will not permit me to do so."[216]

If Du Bois had known that White was on the verge of resigning, Du Bois might well have cooperated with the committee on reconciliation and worked out a compromise. He still felt, as he put it in one letter, "my obligation to my friends and the race."[217] That was why he had been working to oust Walter White and reorient the NAACP. Du Bois also knew that the issue of voluntary cooperation could have been adjusted. Whatever the board officially declared, the NAACP would continue its policy of protesting against segregation. Then, if the protest failed, it would do whatever it could to make black institutions as good as possible. Thus, "the only thing . . . that remains for us is to decide whether we are openly to recognize this procedure as inevitable or be silent about it and still pursue it." The argument was "more or less academic," and there was "no essential reason that those who see different sides of this same shield should not be able to agree to live together in the same house."[218]

Even without knowing that White had threatened to resign, Du Bois seriously considered the possibility of a compromise. At one point he personally drafted a proposal and sent it to the chairman of the recently established committee on reconciliation.[219] If Du Bois had known of the possibility of White's resignation, he probably would have worked out an arrangement with the board of directors.

But Du Bois was away in Atlanta, out of touch with the NAACP's national office, and did not know that White had threatened to quit if Du Bois stayed on. Consequently, Du Bois did not pursue the compromise. Instead, a few days after submitting his proposal, Du Bois changed his mind and told the NAACP's leaders that compromise was impossible. The board of directors had "openly . . . curb[ed] my right of speech," he wrote, and therefore he decided to "stand by my resignation no matter what the board does or refrains from doing."[220]

Accounting for Du Bois's resignation necessarily involves speculation. On the one hand, he was tired of office politics and pleased with his life at Atlanta University. On the other, he had the defeatist belief that his efforts to oust White had come to naught. In one letter Du Bois wrote, "There's no use of hanging around when you're beaten in any particular line of endeavor. I have tried by my influence and written word to reform and re-organize the NAACP . . . and have been entirely unsuccessful."[221] Du Bois told George Streator, "It's a wise man who knows when he is beaten. There's simply nothing to be done so long as Walter White and Roy Wilkins are running the Association, and so long as the Spingarns and others are willing to allow them to run it." "I'm going to insist on my resignation," Du Bois wrote to his wife. "There's simply no use fooling along with those people [at the NAACP]."[222]

One other consideration should be mentioned. Du Bois did not know that White had threatened to resign, but he knew that some members of the board supported White. Thus the most Du Bois could hope for was a protracted struggle for control of the NAACP. At the age of sixty-six, Du Bois did not propose to get into anything of that sort. Moreover, he so distrusted White that he may have feared that White, if defeated in a factional fight, would leave the association in a rage and consciously attempt to disrupt the organization.

Confusion about the Spingarn brothers also contributed to Du Bois's resignation. On one occasion Du Bois wrote that he was "quite unable to understand what is in their minds . . . and that is the reason that I had to get out." The confusion derived from the Spingarns' ambivalence. They supported Du Bois's right to write as he pleased in the *Crisis*, but they also recognized that Du Bois's editorials raised "a rather delicate question: Can the 'organ' of an Association attack its policies and work and remain an 'organ'?" In one letter Joel Spingarn told Du Bois that Spingarn's support was "based on the assumption . . . that [Du Bois] would 'play the game' loyally from the inside." When Du Bois instead criticized White in the *Crisis* and also wrote that the NAACP should be reorganized, Spingarn said, Du Bois was forcing Spingarn to adopt a course that was "not the one I should prefer to follow, and that can only result in strengthening the forces you disapprove of." For Spingarn this was "a bitter blow," because "all my plans for reorganization have been based on having the advantage of your intellectual stimulation."[223]

Yet there may never have been a possibility for compromise. Spingarn could not envision Du Bois criticizing the association openly while remaining as a salaried executive of the NAACP. In Spingarn's mind, a compromise would have required Du Bois to become a full-time professor at Atlanta University and to resign as editor of the *Crisis*. The NAACP in return, in recognition of Du Bois's long service as a founder and executive of the organization, would give Du Bois a page in the *Crisis* where he would be completely free to express his personal opinions.[224] Du Bois's tentative compromise, on the other hand, envisioned Du Bois remaining as editor, the board rescinding the resolution that said the *Crisis* could not publish criticisms of the NAACP without approval of the board, and all members of the *Crisis* editorial committee being nominated by Du Bois.[225]

In the end, Du Bois rejected the possibility of reconciliation. "I have come to a final decision," he wrote to Spingarn; no compromise was possible.[226] Of course it was not easy to resign; Du Bois was cutting himself off "from old and good friends." But he sensed that there was no alternative: "*Gott helpe miche, ich kann nicht anders!*"[227] "To give up *The Crisis* was like giving up a child," he acknowledged; "to leave the Association was leaving the friends of a quarter of a century." On the other hand, staying apparently "meant silence, a repudiation of what I was thinking and planning," and a continuation of the factional strife.[228] Thus Du Bois decided that it was best to leave "in order to see if without my sometimes irritating personality, other and younger men could not accomplish what I failed to do."[229]

The board of directors rose to the occasion. Instead of carping, they praised Du Bois for his many years of pioneer work as a champion of civil rights, founder of the NAACP, and editor of its journal:

> He founded *The Crisis* without a cent of capital, and for many years made it completely self-supporting, reaching a maximum monthly circulation at the end of the World War of 100,000. This is an unprecedented achievement in American journalism, and in itself worthy of a distinguished tribute. But the ideas which he propounded in it and in his books and essays transformed the Negro world, so that the whole program of the relation of black and white races has ever since had a completely new orientation. He created what never existed before, a Negro intelligentsia, and many who have never read a word of his writings are his spiritual disciples and descendants. Without him the Association could never have been what it was and is. The Board has not always seen eye to eye with him in regard to various matters, and cannot subscribe to some of his criticism of the Association and its officials. But such differences in the past have in no way interfered with his usefulness, but rather on the contrary. For he had been selected because of his independence of judgment, his fearlessness in expressing his convictions, and his acute and wide-reaching intelligence. A mere yes-man could not have attracted the attention of the world, could not even have stimulated the Board itself to further study of various important problems. We shall be the poorer for his loss, in intellectual stimulus, and in searching analysis of the vital problems of the American Negro; no one in the Association can fill his place with the same intellectual grasp. We therefore offer him our sincere thanks for the services he has rendered, and we wish him all happiness in all that he may now undertake.[230]

Yet the board's tribute did not touch on the larger significance of the controversy within the NAACP. Walter White had promoted assimilation and dispersion as the best way to achieve progress for blacks. Du Bois, on the other hand, had rejected assimilation and proposed instead that African Americans should celebrate their distinctive culture, build up the institutions of the black community, and develop a cooperative economy. In the 1930s, Du Bois rejected Walter White's integrationism as surely as he had rejected Marcus Garvey's separatism in the 1920s.

Du Bois remained a pluralist. But White won the struggle for the soul of the NAACP.[231] Prior to 1934 the organization was dominated by Du Bois and his black and white allies. After 1934, the NAACP was ruled by Walter White and his faithful followers. Under White's leadership the NAACP continued to emphasize lobbying and legal cases, but the formal continuity in program cloaked significant changes in ideology and personnel. With White in charge, the NAACP turned away from pluralism and embraced integration as a panacea. As Du Bois saw it, the organization had been great for a quarter of a century but now found itself "without a program . . . [and] without executive officers who have either the ability or disposition to guide the NAACP in the right direction."[232]

Seven
The Final Years

Back to Atlanta

Du Bois's resignation from the NAACP in 1934 was a major turning point in his life. He lived for another twenty-nine years; but without his association with the NAACP, he was no longer a civil rights leader. He was, instead, a scholar and a sage who was widely respected for his experience, judgment, and wisdom.

From 1933 to 1944 Du Bois was involved in a series of academic projects that would have sapped the energy of most scholars who were only half his age. In addition to teaching classes at Atlanta University, he wrote three major books, a monograph, several articles, and a regular column for the *Pittsburgh Courier.* He also appeared on programs of the American Historical Association and the Southern Sociological Society, and he founded and edited a new scholarly journal on race relations, *Phylon.*

Black Reconstruction (1935) was an especially important book. It not only challenged the conventional wisdom of its time but also pointed toward new ideas that became popular during and after the civil rights movement of the 1960s.[1] In 1935 the regnant interpretation of post–Civil War history held that many of the northern whites who went South after the war did so for unscrupulous reasons—to hold office, to advance the political interests of the Republican Party, to wreak revenge on the South, and to enrich themselves at the expense of southern taxpayers. This interpretation also held that the recently emancipated former slaves were not prepared to vote and hold office, and that uneducated black freedmen had joined with northern "carpetbaggers" to subject the South to an era of bad government. The conventional wisdom suggested that political power was dangerous in the hands of inferior beings, that civilization had been damaged during an era when blacks had exercised significant political influence.

Because he did not do extensive research in primary sources, Du Bois could not challenge the evidence that other historians had presented. Instead, he quoted long passages from the speeches and proclamations of black and white Republicans. These statements were sufficient to establish that many of the white Republicans were motivated, at least in part, by a sincere desire to promote racial justice; and many of the blacks were far from the ignorant and venal political novices of conventional lore. In addition, Du Bois emphasized the two great achievements of the Reconstruction governments: establishing public schools for both races, and preparing new state constitutions that remained serviceable long after Reconstruction ended.

Black Reconstruction also included some arresting but questionable interpretations. The slaves' tendency to flee when the Union army drew near doubtless disrupted the Confederacy and contributed to the Northern victory in the Civil War. But to describe this phenomenon as a Marxian "general strike," as Du Bois did, provoked heated discussion and even some ridicule.[2] Du Bois was also wide of the mark when he described Reconstruction as "one of the most extraordinary experiments in Marxism that the world, before the Russian revolution, had seen."[3] In fact, most of those who supported Reconstruction, blacks as well as whites, believed in private ownership of the means of production.

Despite its problems, *Black Reconstruction* was a landmark in historiography. It took three years for the publisher to sell the first printing of 2,150 copies,[4] but in time the book enjoyed immense influence. In 1988 the historian Eric Foner acknowledged that "in many ways, *Black Reconstruction* anticipated the findings of modern scholarship."[5] In Du Bois's telling, the heroes and villains of the era were reversed.

Du Bois's next book in the decade following his resignation from the NAACP was *Black Folk: Then and Now* (1939), a summary of the history of black people from the dawn of civilization to the present.[6] In less than four hundred pages, Du Bois discussed the origin of the Negro race, the civilizations of the Nile and the Niger, the histories of Congo and Guinea, the transatlantic slave trade, and the experience of black people in the New World. The discussions were brief, and one could take exception to various points, but the book was a pioneering contribution to the field of world history.

Du Bois's 1940 autobiography, *Dusk of Dawn,* was more than an engrossing account of his life. It also pointed to the direction Du Bois would move in the future. In telling his story, he acknowledged that for most of his life, had it not been for the race problem, he would have been "an unquestioning worshiper . . . of the social order and economic development into which I was born." He had not doubted the wisdom of that order except as it discriminated against people of color. During the Great Depression, however, Du Bois saw "the collapse of capitalism." As noted in the previous chapter, his first response was to call for a form of black communitarianism. By 1937 he was endorsing "public control of private capital for the general welfare." And in *Dusk of Dawn* he espoused "the ultimate triumph of some form of Socialism."[7]

In addition to teaching and writing, Du Bois sought foundation support for a proposed *Encyclopedia of the Negro*. This time-consuming effort eventually came to naught. But in 1942 he persuaded the presidents of several black land-grant colleges to underwrite a cooperative program of research on economic and social conditions in black America, with Du Bois designated as the official coordinator of the studies. This involved a return to the sort of research that Du Bois had done with the Atlanta University Studies during the first decade of the twentieth century, only this time Du Bois, who by then was seventy-four years old, would have proper funding for the work.[8]

Yet in 1944, only two years after the research was supposedly funded, Du Bois was forced to retire from his professorship at Atlanta University. In Du Bois's account, "This was not merely a personal disaster. It was removing from leadership the one person who because of age and long experience, because of works published and a wide acquaintanceship . . . , happened to be the person to whom the presidents of Negro land-grant colleges and other Negroes of influence were willing to entrust this cooperative venture."[9] Without Du Bois, the new research program fizzled.

The retirement age at Atlanta University was sixty-five, although the university had chosen not to apply the rule to its most distinguished professor. Yet after the death in 1936 of Du Bois's best friend, President John Hope, Du Bois's relations with administrators on the campus were strained. Du Bois thought that Hope's successor, the "new young unknown president" Rufus Clement, was jealous of Du Bois's reputation.[10] And Du Bois clashed repeatedly with Florence Read, the president of Atlanta's sister institution, Spelman College. The accumulation of hard feelings reached a climax in the spring of 1944, when the trustees of Atlanta University, on motion of President Read seconded by President Clement, voted to retire Du Bois.

As Du Bois saw it, his forced retirement was "disastrous, not merely to me but to the American Negro. Up until this time the Negro himself had led in the study and interpretation of the condition of his race in the United States. Beginning with 1944, with accelerated speed the study of the Negro passed into the hands of whites." In addition, Du Bois found himself on the verge of financial ruin at age seventy-six. Initially the trustees made no mention of a pension, although eventually they gave Du Bois a year's full salary ($4,500) because he had not been given advance notice of the impending retirement. They also gave him a pension of $1,800 a year for five years and $1,200 a year thereafter.[11]

Retirement was financially difficult for Du Bois because throughout his life he had neglected saving. At the NAACP his annual salary had been $5,000—the equivalent of a six-figure income today—and he earned almost as much from Atlanta University. There was, in addition, supplemental income from lectures and writings. Nevertheless, almost every cent went for current expenses. At one time, he owned an apartment building in Harlem; but that investment went bad in 1928 and cost Du Bois all his savings. "In money matters," he wrote, "I was surely negligent and ignorant; but that was not because I was gambling, drinking or carousing; it was because I spent my income in making myself and my family comfortable instead of 'saving for a rainy day.'"[12]

After 1933 there had also been the additional expense of maintaining two households, one for himself in Atlanta and another for his wife, daughter, and granddaughter. At first Du Bois's daughter, Yolande, and her baby, Du Bois Williams (born in 1932), lived in Harlem in a double apartment that Du Bois and his wife had shared before Du Bois took the professorship at Atlanta. Yolande did so because her second husband, Arnett Williams, was still a student at Lincoln University (Pennsylvania), with Du Bois paying his bills. After Williams graduated from Lincoln, he and Yolande lived for a while in Baltimore while baby Du Bois remained with grandmother Du Bois. But Yolande's marriage quickly ended in an uncontested divorce amidst charges that Arnett Williams drank excessively and on occasion physically assaulted Yolande. Yolande, however, was far from a paragon. She found a job as a teacher in Baltimore but put on a great deal of weight, took up with a male lover who was ten years her junior, and led a life that both her parents considered appalling. In the circumstances, Nina Du Bois took responsibility for rearing Du Bois

Williams, a precocious little girl whose IQ measured 144 on a Stanford-Binet test. Years later, after she was fully grown and had been a college professor herself, Du Bois Williams recalled her upbringing: "Granma [Nina] made the whole thing work. Mama [Yolande] was the child, which I wasn't."[13]

For a few years Du Bois saw his family only when he was in New York, but in 1938–1939 his wife and granddaughter moved into family quarters with Du Bois on the Atlanta University campus. This reunion did not last, however, for Du Bois Williams despised her school in Atlanta, and the Du Boises decided to send her to the Modern School, a prestigious private academy in Harlem. Yet this did not solve the family's problems, for Yolande's dissolute lifestyle in Baltimore continued to cause concern. Therefore, although Du Bois continued to live and work at Atlanta University, he bought a four-bedroom brick house for his wife, daughter, and granddaughter near Morgan State College in Baltimore. Du Bois Williams had to be enrolled in a public school, but the arrangement allowed Nina to keep a watchful eye on both her charges. The situation was not ideal. It depleted Du Bois's finances. But it was the best that could be done in the circumstances.

The NAACP, Again

Du Bois's friends at the NAACP soon became aware of his financial plight. As a friendly gesture, they invited him to return to the association in 1944 as director of special research at his former salary of five thousand dollars a year. His job was to organize another Pan-African Congress and to prepare reports that would support the case for independence for the black colonies in Africa. Yet, as Du Bois himself recognized, the leaders of the NAACP did not want him to rock any boats. "They assumed . . . that at 75 my life work was done; that what I wanted was leisure and comfort and for that I would willingly act as window dressing, say a proper word now and then and give the Association and its secretary moral support."[14]

This was something that Du Bois did not do. As always, he expressed his views "even when there was no call for the telling and when silence would have been golden."[15] Before long he was on another collision course with Walter White—only this time the controversy revolved around the NAACP's approach to American foreign policy and to European imperialism.

For some years the NAACP had spoken out against white domination of black Africa, and in the mid-1940s the organization began to issue even stronger anti-imperialist statements, many of which were written by Du Bois. Yet in 1948 Walter White changed the NAACP's course for two reasons. First, with the United States involved in the Cold War against the Soviet Union, he thought it prudent to tone down the criticism of America's imperialist allies. Second, with the Truman administration supporting civil rights legislation and moving toward desegregation of the armed forces, White wanted blacks to become a key component in the coalition of the Democratic Party.[16]

This placed Du Bois in a difficult situation. In addition, the personal relations between him and White were just as strained in the 1940s as they had been a decade earlier. Du Bois thought White "wanted me visibly at his elbow so that at no point could my subordination to him be doubted." He complained that White had not given him enough office space. And he took exception to White's policy of having the office secretaries open all incoming mail, even personal correspondence, before delivering it to the officers of the NAACP. Du Bois fumed that the organization had become "a rigid dictatorship, virtually under the control of one man."[17]

For his part, White feared that Du Bois's increasing radicalism would compromise the reputation of the NAACP. Du Bois's drift toward socialism had begun with his communitarian plan for combatting the Great Depression and had accelerated during several months of travel through Europe and Asia in 1936 and 1937. In Germany, Du Bois had observed the Third Reich's official policy of discriminating against Jews. In one of his columns for the *Pittsburgh Courier*, he wrote about Adolf Hitler's "campaign of race prejudice carried on, openly, continuously and determinedly against all non-Nordic peoples, but specifically against the Jews, which surpasses in vindictive cruelty and public insult anything I have ever seen; and I have seen much." But Du Bois also regarded Hitler as a socialist who had established government control over the economy, built houses for the poor, and provided jobs for unemployed German workers. Indeed, according to Du Bois, economic conditions in Germany had been so desperate before Hitler that there simply had to be "a dictatorship—that was absolutely necessary to put the state in order." Hitler was admittedly a bigot, but he had provided "national health, a living wage,

. . . [and] a planned economy." The whole nation was "dotted with new homes for the common people, new roads, new public housing projects and new public works of all kinds."[18]

Du Bois also excused (or at least tried to explain) the excesses of Soviet Russia. Because of Soviet censorship, he was whisked through Russia in 1937. But he did not criticize the purge trials that were occurring then or the previous repression of the Russian peasantry. Instead he wrote that the Soviet Union had "made a brave start at scientific planning"; that it had set for itself the "enormous task" of controlling the private greed that had "frustrated democracy in the past"; that it was "investing the ownership of all land and materials in the public and then using natural wealth and resources for the ultimate good of the mass of inhabitants."[19]

While Du Bois made excuses for the excesses of Nazi Germany and Soviet Russia, he celebrated the rise of Imperial Japan. By the time of Du Bois's visit to China in 1937, Japan had already bombed Shanghai savagely and had established the puppet state of Manchkuo (Manchuria) in the northern three provinces of China. Shortly afterwards, "the Rape of Nanking" occurred, in which the Japanese murdered at least 260,000 Chinese noncombatants.[20] Nevertheless, Du Bois regarded the expansion of Japan as a necessary antidote to western, white imperialism. On one occasion he asked a group of Chinese journalists and businessmen, "Why is it that you hate Japan more than Europe when [historically] you have suffered more from England, France, and Germany than from Japan?" Du Bois acknowledged that Japan had problems with militarism and conformity, but he enthused that it was "above all a country of colored people run by colored people for colored people." The Japanese were "standing over against the white world," he wrote. As Du Bois saw it, "The basis of the trouble between China and Japan" was "China's submission to white aggression and Japan's resistance."[21]

Du Bois continued to promote socialism and to oppose white colonialism after he returned to the NAACP in 1944. As the decade progressed he increasingly praised the Soviet Union while criticizing American foreign policy. At a United Nations conference in San Francisco, for example, he described the Soviet foreign minister, V. I. Molotov, as "the one statesman . . . who stood up for human rights and the emancipation of colonies."[22] At the same time, he opposed American efforts to contain communism. He said that the Marshall

Plan was an instrument of capitalist imperialism and described the Truman Doctrine as "the most stupid and dangerous proposal ever made by the leader of a great modern nation."[23] When Walter White worked for the election of Harry Truman in 1948, Du Bois campaigned for Henry Wallace, who had been very sympathetic to the Soviet Union and who was the candidate of the left-wing Progressive Party.

This was too much for the NAACP. Its leaders had hoped that when Du Bois returned, he would sit back, take it easy, and give the organization additional prestige. Instead, Du Bois outspokenly censured American foreign policy and criticized the association's alliance with the Democratic Party. Finally, in September 1948, Du Bois was dismissed from the NAACP with a pension of twelve hundred dollars per year. The surprise was that Du Bois's second term with the NAACP lasted as long as it did.

He Married a Communist

In the 1940s Du Bois also experienced setbacks at home. Early in 1945 Nina Du Bois was injured in a bad fall and had to undergo several weeks of painful physical therapy. Later that year she suffered a stroke that paralyzed her left side. Death finally came in July 1950. After fifty-four years of marriage, Du Bois was single again.

He did not remain unwed for long. When he returned to the NAACP in 1944, he had renewed an acquaintance with Shirley Graham, and in February 1951, seven months after Nina's death, Du Bois and Graham were married.

Nina Du Bois and Shirley Graham Du Bois were archetypes of different ideals of femininity. Nina followed the Victorian ideal that a woman was most womanly when she was of service to others, while Shirley Graham abandoned her own children to achieve her individual ambitions. Nina had been avid for Du Bois's causes and proud of his accomplishments, but she focused on making a comfortable home for him and on rearing their two children and one grandchild. Shirley Graham, on the other hand, ended an early marriage in the 1920s and left the two children born to that union with her parents (and later with a series of boarding schools) while she pursued careers as a musical composer and as a writer. At various times she studied at Oberlin, Vassar, Yale, and the Sorbonne. She also worked at black colleges as well as for the Federal Theater Project, the YWCA, and the NAACP. Her Afrocentric opera *Tom-Tom* had been a success with critics in the 1930s, as had her plays *It's Morning, Elijah's Ravens,* and *Coal Dust.* Yet she remained financially strapped until the 1940s when she finally made money with a new genre of popular biography—"biographical novels" that combined fiction with fact. Some scholars disapproved when her biographies of George Washington Carver, Frederick Douglass, and Paul Robeson, among others, included invented dialogue and scenes. But the reading public bought the books. After years of struggle, Shirley Graham purchased a large house in New York and asked Arthur Spingarn to handle her business affairs. "Her stature was confirmed in 1947 when . . . she was awarded a prestigious fellowship from the Guggenheim Foundation. It seemed as if she were marching from triumph to triumph."[24]

She also moved steadily to the left. As a girl Graham had shared the politics of her father, an A.M.E. clergyman who was active in the NAACP and who "out of deference to Abraham Lincoln . . . always voted the Republican ticket."[25] During the Depression she became a New Deal liberal. Paradoxically, as Graham's royalties were increasing, she joined the Communist Party in 1943.[26] In 1945 she informed Earl Browder, the American Communist leader, that she was in a position to recruit Du Bois into membership in the party.[27] The party's national secretariat was intrigued and gave James Jackson, a young black party member, the specific assignment of cultivating Du Bois and assisting Graham in bringing Du Bois into the Communist fold.[28]

Du Bois was twenty-eight years older than Shirley Graham. He first met her in her youth when he had spent a night at her father's parsonage in Colorado. Their acquaintance had been renewed in the 1930s with a lively correspondence and occasional visits. When Du Bois returned to the NAACP in 1944, Shirley Graham helped him find an apartment with a view of the Hudson River and of the entire span of the new George Washington Bridge.

Graham also introduced Du Bois to a new circle of friends. In the past, Du Bois's life had been centered in the black community, although he dealt with whites in business and professional matters. Graham was reminded of this when Du Bois upbraided her for suggesting that he hire a white woman as a secretary in his office. "You should know I don't want a white woman," he huffed. Graham then made a definite effort to expose Du Bois to a group of white radicals.

Her son recalled that she "gradually drew Dr. Du Bois into contact with leading figures of [the] new progressive movement. . . . In his presence, they behaved like disciples at the feet of the prophet. Slowly Dr. Du Bois found these white Americans to be of a different breed from those who early in his career had discouraged him from seeking out or desiring white company."[29]

One instance of this occurred at a 1947 Christmas party at Shirley Graham's house, where Du Bois found himself side by side with several white radicals. They were singing songs like "Union Train," "Joe Hill," and "Ain't Gonna Study War No Mo'." During the course of the evening, Du Bois gave voice to "John Brown's Body Lies A-molding in the Grave, but His Soul Goes Marching On." The others then followed his lead. "Bravo!" they cried. "Sing Something else! . . . And he did. First a soft African lullaby . . . ; then the old spiritual, 'Many Thousands Gone.' They were very still as they listened to the lullaby, but when he began the spiritual they accompanied him with a hum."[30]

The Christmas party was symbolic of what was to come. Within a year Du Bois would be fired from the NAACP. Not long after that, several liberal magazines refused to publish his articles while radical journals filled the breach. Thereafter, many of Du Bois's essays and speeches would be featured in the Communist newspaper, the *Daily Worker,* and in the left-wing journal *Masses and Mainstream.* Du Bois also became a frequent contributor to a new "progressive" magazine, the *National Guardian,* which eventually published some 120 of Du Bois's articles (at fifty dollars per article). In 1949, the *Guardian's* principal backer also gave Du Bois an additional bonus in the amount of five thousand dollars.[31]

In addition to his new left-wing support network, Du Bois also had found comfort in the arms of Shirley Graham. By 1945 he was writing to Graham that they had been "blessed beyond most folk to have so free and happy a love." In 1946 he asked his "sweetheart" to "come to me Saturday at 4 p.m. and stay until Sunday night." Other notes were punctuated with phrases like, "I love and long to see you!" and "with love and kisses."[32] At this time Nina was already paralyzed and would live for only four more years. For her part, Graham addressed Du Bois as "Darling" and "Beloved," and confided, "I ache for you."[33] By the late 1940s, if not earlier, Du Bois and Graham were involved in an adulterous affair.[34]

Some observers have portrayed Graham as an "ideological se-
ductress, a courtesan with a radical mission," a woman who was significantly influential in moving Du Bois to the Left. The black scholar Harold Cruse said he "knew [Graham] pretty well" and thought
"she helped bring [Du Bois] closer and closer until, you know, he actually joined the [Communist] party." The writer John Henrik Clarke
also gave it as his "considered opinion" that Graham's liaison with Du
Bois was a "Communist arranged marriage."[35] Whatever the truth of
the "seduction theory," there is no doubt that Du Bois married a Communist when he married Shirley Graham.

To the Far Left

Du Bois and Graham were married in February 1951 during the
Korean War. One of the principal points of Communist propaganda
then called for all nations to renounce the use of nuclear weapons.
Such a renunciation would have benefited the Communists in Korea,
since they had deployed a much larger conventional army there. At
this time, Du Bois was also serving as the chairman of a group called
the Peace Information Center, which was circulating the "Stockholm
Peace Appeal"—an appeal in which Du Bois asked American citizens
to demand that "the Government of the United States will never be
the first to use the atom bomb, whether in Korea or in any other part
of the earth."[36] Ultimately, about two million Americans signed this
appeal.

Dean Acheson, the U.S. secretary of state, described the Stockholm appeal as "a propaganda trick in the spurious 'peace offensive'
of the Soviet Union," and in August 1950 Du Bois was informed that
he was required by law to register "as an agent of a foreign principal
within the United States."[37] When Du Bois refused to do so, he was
indicted, fingerprinted, arraigned, briefly handcuffed, and bound
over for trial. He faced a possible sentence of five years in prison and
a fine of ten thousand dollars.[38]

The trial of Du Bois and other officials of the Peace Information
Center did not achieve the result that the U.S. government had anticipated. One official from the center, O. John Rogge, testified for the
government and said that the center was supported by Soviet money and was "an agency for the foreign policy of the Soviet Union."[39]
But there was no evidence that Du Bois knew this. Nor was there any
evidence to support Rogge's testimony. There were no cancelled

checks, no records of telegraphs or telephone calls, nothing to show that Moscow was in communication with the Peace Information Center. The government's case was essentially one of "parallelism": that because Du Bois and the Soviet Union both wanted to ban the bomb, Du Bois must be acting at the behest of the Soviet Union.

Judge Matthew F. McGuire would not accept this logic. The government had to do more, he insisted. "You have got to show a tie-up between the principal so-called and the so-called agent. If you don't do that, you are out of court."[40] Judge McGuire would not permit the jury of eight Negroes and four whites to render a verdict. Instead, he directed a verdict of acquittal for Du Bois.

Du Bois emerged from his trial a free man, but one who was more alienated from his country and more isolated from black America than ever before. During the trial the NAACP had officially reaffirmed that Du Bois was "one of the great champions of civil rights," but it did so "without passing on the merits of the recent indictment." In addition, many individual Negroes were puzzled. Du Bois acknowledged that "They did not understand the indictment and assumed that I had let myself be drawn into some treasonable acts or movements."[41] Black institutions were also wary of Du Bois's radicalism. In 1949 the president of Morgan State College was so concerned about Du Bois's being "linked . . . in the public mind with the Communist movement," that he cancelled an earlier invitation for Du Bois to speak at the spring commencement.[42] The principal of the left-wing Elisabeth Irwin High School in Greenwich Village felt similarly, and vetoed the class of 1955's choice of Du Bois as their commencement speaker.[43]

Du Bois was undaunted. As the 1950s progressed, he became an unabashed apologist for Communism and an exponent of left-wing anti-Americanism. In 1953 he wrote that Harry Truman "ranks with Adolf Hitler as one of the greatest killers of our day." On the other hand, he described Josef Stalin as "a great man; few other men of the 20th century approach his stature."[44] Six years later, as some ten million Chinese perished in the famine of the Great Leap Forward, Du Bois lavished praise on the regime of Mao Tse-tung: "Fifteen times I have crossed the Atlantic and once the Pacific. I have seen the world. But never so vast and glorious a miracle as China."[45] Meanwhile, at a time when the civil rights movement was gaining momentum in the United States, Du Bois expressed scorn for the land of his birth. "Today the United States is fighting world progress," Du Bois told the faculty and students of Howard University in 1958, "progress which must be toward socialism and against colonialism."[46] According to Du Bois, the United States had "revers[ed] its traditional stand of centuries" and was "now siding with every reactionary movement in the world."[47] Capitalists "who profit from war, especially in the United States," had gained control of the American government and were trying "to make Europe and the world a quasi-colony of United States business."[48]

When Du Bois visited the Communist world in 1958 and 1959, he became even more set in his opinions. In part this was because the Communists were especially outspoken in condemning racism, segregation, and the colonization of Africa. But there were personal considerations as well. In East Berlin at age ninety-one, Du Bois was finally awarded the doctorate in economics that he had worked for in the 1890s. In Prague he was given an honorary doctorate in history. In Moscow he met with Prime Minister Nikita Khrushchev and was given a place of honor during a celebration in Red Square. In China he spent four hours with Mao Tse-tung and dined twice with Prime Minister Chou-En-lai.[49] In 1958 he wrote of Paul Robeson a passage that applies equally to himself:

> He did praise the Soviet Union; and he did that because . . . he was honored like a great man. The children of Russia clung to him, the women kissed him; workers greeted him. . . . He loved their homage. His eyes were filled with tears and his heart with thanks. Never before had he received such treatment. In America he was a "nigger."[50]

Robeson and many other men and women of the left were devastated psychologically when they eventually learned of the catastrophes that Stalin and Mao had inflicted on their people. But Du Bois and Shirley Graham accepted the excesses of Communism with equanimity. They regarded the brutality as a price that had to be paid for progress toward socialism.

In October 1961, five years after Khrushchev had exposed Stalin's crimes, Du Bois applied for membership in the Communist Party of the United States. "I have been long and slow in coming to this conclusion," he wrote, "but at last my mind is settled." He had reached "the firm conclusion [that] capitalism cannot reform itself; it is doomed to self-destruction. No universal selfishness can bring social good to all."[51] He and Graham then departed immediately for exile in Africa. There Du Bois renounced his American citizenship, became a citizen of Ghana, and thanked Prime Minister Kwame Nkrumah for making it possible for him to finish his life in the land of his black ancestors. Du Bois died two years later, at age ninety-five.

Du Bois's final decades present a problem. Had he died at age fifty, he once wrote, he "would have been hailed with approval. At 75 my death was practically requested."[52] This biography has focused on Du Bois's career as a civil rights leader and has provided only a brief sketch of his later years as a radical ideologue. With the Soviet Union and Communist China now exposed as two of the most brutal tyrannies in human history, and with socialism increasingly regarded as an inherently flawed system, the pronouncements of Du Bois's last decades seem not only wrong but foolish. Yet these statements can be ascribed to his old age, to his rejection by former allies, and to a sympathetic approval from a new support network. The vagaries in Du Bois's thinking cast a cloud over but should not obscure one of the great lives of the twentieth century.

Du Bois was a remarkable man. As a youth he recognized that black people were repressed by the racist notion that Negroes were inherently deficient and therefore doomed to servitude. As a young man he dedicated himself to demolishing the idea of racial inferiority. There could scarcely have been a more suitable person for the task. He was a Negro who was endowed with a first-rate intellect and an indomitable fighting spirit. His writings will endure as eloquent appeals for racial justice.

Du Bois also recognized that power was needed to reinforce scholarship and appeals for justice. With this in mind, he joined with others to found and foster the greatest of all American civil rights organizations, the National Association for the Advancement of Colored People. And the NAACP, during the years when Du Bois was influential, steered a pluralist course between the Scylla of separatism and the Charybdis of integration. Until 1934, the organization, like Du Bois, evinced a sense of double-consciousness. It insisted, as Du Bois did, that American blacks, while condemning unfair discrimination and demanding equal rights, also wanted to preserve and develop their own black distinctiveness so that they could foster and maintain a sense of racial identity, racial community, and racial pride.

Notes

Preface

1. Richard Hofstadter, *The American Political Tradition* (New York: Alfred A. Knopf, 1948; reprint, New York: Vintage Books, 1954).

2. Raymond Wolters, *Negroes and the Great Depression: The Problem of Economic Recovery* (Westport, Conn.: Greenwood Publishing Corporation, 1970); Raymond Wolters, *The New Negro on Campus: Black College Rebellions of the 1920s* (Princeton: Princeton University Press, 1975).

3. Raymond Wolters, *The Burden of Brown: Thirty Years of School Desegregation* (Knoxville: University of Tennessee Press, 1984); and *Right Turn: William Bradford Reynolds, the Reagan Administration, and Black Civil Rights* (New Brunswick: Transaction Publishers, 1996).

Introduction

1. Roy Wilkins, *Standing Fast: The Autobiography of Roy Wilkins* (New York: Viking Press, 1982), 293; W. E. B. Du Bois, *The Souls of Black Folk* (1903; reprint, Millwood, N.Y.: Kraus-Thomson Organization, 1973), 13.

2. W. E. B. Du Bois, "The Conservation of Races" (1897), reprinted in Herbert Aptheker, ed., *Pamphlets and Leaflets by W. E. B. Du Bois* (White Plains, N.Y.: Kraus-Thomson Organization, 1986, 5, 4) (hereafter cited as "Conservation of Races").

3. Du Bois, *Souls of Black Folk*, 3.

4. Du Bois, "Conservation of Races," 7.

5. Francis L. Broderick, *W. E. B. Du Bois: Negro Leader in a Time of Crisis* (Stanford: Stanford University Press, 1959); Elliott M. Rudwick, *W. E. B. Du Bois: A Study in Minority Group Leadership* (Philadelphia: University of Pennsylvania Press, 1960); Manning Marable, *W. E. B. Du Bois: Black Radical Democrat* (Boston: Twayne, 1986); Julius Lester, *The Seventh Son: The Thought and Writings of W. E. B. Du Bois* (2 vols. New York: Vintage Books, 1971); Arnold Rampersad, *The Art and Imagination of W. E. B. Du Bois* (Cambridge: Harvard University Press, 1976); Jack B. Moore, *W. E. B. Du Bois* (Boston: Twayne Publishers, 1981); Herbert Aptheker, ed., *The Correspondence of W. E. B. Du Bois* (Amherst: University of Massachusetts Press, 1973–1978); David Levering Lewis, *W. E. B. Du Bois: Biography of a Race, 1868–1919* (New York: Henry Holt, 1993) (hereafter cited as *W. E. B. Du Bois*, vol. 1); David Levering Lewis, *W. E. B. Du Bois: The Fight for Equality and the American Century, 1919–1963* (New York: Henry Holt, 2000) (hereafter cited as *W. E. B. Du Bois*, vol. 2).

6. W. E. B. Du Bois, "Strivings of the Negro People," *Atlantic Monthly* 80 (August 1897): 195.

7. W. E. B. Du Bois, "Criteria of Negro Art," *Crisis* 32 (October 1926): 290.

8. Du Bois, "Conservation of Races," 4.

9. Ibid., 7.

10. W. E. B. Du Bois, "The Conservation of Races," *Crisis* 41 (June 1934): 183.

11. W. E. B. Du Bois, *The Philadelphia Negro* (1899; reprint, Millwood, N.Y.: Kraus-Thomson Organization, 1973), 72.

12. Kevin K. Gaines, *Uplifting the Race: Black Leadership, Politics, and Culture in the Twentieth Century* (Chapel Hill: University of North Carolina Press, 1996); Robin D. G. Kelley, *Yo' Mama's DisFunktional: Fighting the Culture Wars in Urban America* (Boston: Beacon Press, 1997); Dinesh D'Souza, *The End of Racism* (New York: Free Press, 1995).

1. Du Bois

1. Du Bois to Rutherford B. Hayes, April 19, 1891, in Louis D. Rubin Jr., *Teach the Freeman: The Correspondence of Rutherford B. Hayes and the Slater Fund for Negro Education, 1888–1893* (Baton Rouge: Louisiana State University Press, 1959), 2:195. Like most other people of his era, Du Bois was conscious of color. In one letter he referred to his mother as "a mulatto," his father as "a quadroon," and his grandfather Du Bois as "an octoroon" (Du Bois to the Trustees of Harvard University, 1892, The Papers of W. E. B. Du Bois, University of Massachusetts Library [cited hereafter as Du Bois Papers], microfilm reel 2, frame 0070).

2. W. E. B. Du Bois, *Darkwater* (1921; reprint, Millwood, N.Y.: Kraus-Thomson Organization, 1975), 5–6; W. E. B. Du Bois, *The Autobiography of W. E. B. Du Bois* (New York: International Publishers, 1968), 62.

3. W. E. B. Du Bois, *Dusk of Dawn* (1940; reprint, Millwood, N.Y.: Kraus-Thomson Organization, 1975), 11.

4. Du Bois, *Autobiography,* 72.

5. Lewis, *W. E. B. Du Bois,* 1:11; Broderick, *W. E. B. Du Bois,* 1.

6. Du Bois, *Autobiography,* 71.

7. Du Bois, *Dusk of Dawn,* 108–9.

8. Lewis, *W. E. B. Du Bois,* 1:21–22.

9. William T. Ingersoll, interview with W. E. B. Du Bois, Columbia University Oral History Project, 1960, p. 4 (cited hereafter as Ingersoll Interview); Du Bois, *Autobiography,* 72; Shirley Graham Du Bois, *His Day Is Marching On: A Memoir of W. E. B. Du Bois* (Philadelphia: J. B. Lippincott, 1971), 199.

10. Du Bois, *Autobiography,* 72.

11. John Brown to Du Bois, January 25, 1942, Du Bois Papers, reel 53, frame 00836.

12. Ingersoll Interview, 6.

13. Du Bois, *Dusk of Dawn,* 19, 108.

14. Graham Du Bois, *His Day Is Marching On,* 199.

15. Du Bois, *Autobiography,* 71; Rampersad, *Art and Imagination,* 9.

16. Du Bois, *Autobiography,* 98.

17. Ingersoll Interview, 10.

18. Du Bois, *Autobiography,* 73, 79, 78. However, in a letter applying for a fellowship, Du Bois said that he and his mother were "often near pauperism." See Du Bois to the Board of Trustees of the John F. Slater Fund, 1892, in Aptheker, *Correspondence of Du Bois,* 1:15.

19. Du Bois, *Autobiography*, 93–94.

20. Du Bois, *Darkwater*, 11.

21. Du Bois, *Souls of Black Folk*, 2.

22. Du Bois, *Autobiography*, 94.

23. Ibid., 94.

24. Ibid., 83–88; Lewis, *W. E. B. Du Bois*, 1:33, 36, 37.

25. Du Bois, *Darkwater*, 5; Du Bois, *Autobiography*, 74.

26. *New York Globe*, September 29, 1883, May 26, 1883, February 23, 1884, and June 30, 1983, in Herbert Aptheker, ed., *Newspaper Columns by W. E. B. Du Bois* (White Plains, N.Y.: Kraus-Thomson Organization, 1986), 1:7, 3, 12, 5.

For a different view of Du Bois's youth in Great Barrington, see Allison Davis, *Leadership, Love, and Aggression* (New York: Harcourt Brace Jovanovich, 1983), 105–52. Davis maintains that Du Bois contrived "romanticized" versions of his ancestors and youth as "defensive fantasies" to protect against "deep-seated fears" that he himself was unworthy—fears that stemmed from his family's poverty, his mother's compromised position, the abandonment by his father, and incidents of color discrimination. However, Davis's account is mostly speculative and contains several factual errors. Davis says, for example, that Du Bois "had no genealogical records on either side" of his family history, when in fact many such records are available in the Du Bois Papers, especially in reel 89. Davis further says that there is no evidence with respect to Tom Burghardt's service in the American Revolution. However, in 1907 and 1908, with the assistance of a genealogist from Massachusetts, Du Bois collected records pertaining to Tom Burghardt—muster rolls and other records that enabled Du Bois to become "'Compatriot Number 2728' of the Massachusetts Society of the Sons of the American Revolution and Compatriot Number 19,728 of the National Society" (Du Bois to Miss Lewis, March 24, 1908, Du Bois Papers, reel 2, frame 0376). When there were objections from some members of the Sons of the American Revolution, Du Bois was drummed out of the organization—not because there was any question about the Revolutionary War service of his ancestor but because, owing to a fire at the local court house, Du Bois could not establish lineage by documenting the *marriage* of his great-great grandfather. See Du Bois to Herbert Wood Kimball, January 16, 1908; and Kimball to Du Bois, May 15, 1908, Du Bois Papers, reel 3, frames 0152 and 0161. The drumming-out tells more about the racial prejudice of some members than about Du Bois's lineage.

27. Du Bois, *Autobiography*, 101.

28. Ibid., 103; Lewis, *W. E. B. Du Bois*, 1:54–55.

29. Du Bois, *Dusk of Dawn*, 23.

30. Du Bois, *Autobiography*, 106, 105.

31. Du Bois, *Darkwater*, 13.

32. Moore, *W. E. B. Du Bois*, 22; Du Bois, *Autobiography*, 121.

33. Du Bois, *Autobiography*, 109.

34. W. E. B. Du Bois, "Diuturni Silenti," in Herbert Aptheker, ed., *The Education of Black People: Ten Critiques, 1906–1960* (Amherst: University of Massachusetts Press, 1973), 42.

35. Du Bois, *Autobiography*, 113.

36. Du Bois, "Diuturni Silenti," 42.

37. Ibid., 45, 38; Lewis, *W. E. B. Du Bois*, 1:73.

38. Du Bois, *Autobiography*, 114.

39. Du Bois, *Souls of Black Folk*, 68.

40. Broderick, *W. E. B. Du Bois*, 8; Marable, *W. E. B. Du Bois*, 11.

41. Du Bois, *Autobiography*, 126.

42. Ingersoll Interview, 22.

43. Du Bois, *Autobiography*, 134.

44. Ibid., 134–35.

45. Du Bois, *Dusk of Dawn*, 36.

46. W. E. B. Du Bois, "A Negro Student at Harvard at the End of the Nineteenth Century," *Massachusetts Review* (spring 1960): 444.

47. Du Bois, *Autobiography*, 141.

48. Ingersoll Interview, 90.

49. Ibid., 71.

50. Du Bois, *Autobiography*, 144.

51. Du Bois, *Autobiography*, 144. For Du Bois's other grades at Harvard, see Herbert Aptheker, ed., *Against Racism: Unpublished Essays, Papers, Addresses [of W. E. B. Du Bois], 1887–1961* (Amherst: University of Massachusetts Press, 1985), 23–24.

52. Aptheker, *Against Racism*, 20 n. 1, 17.

53. Du Bois, *Autobiography*, 145.

54. *Boston Herald*, November 2, 1890, as quoted in Du Bois to Rutherford B. Hayes, November 4, 1890, in Rubin, *Teach the Freeman*, 2:158–61.

55. Du Bois, *Dusk of Dawn*, 44; Du Bois to Rutherford B. Hayes, May 25, 1891, in Aptheker, *Correspondence of Du Bois*, 1:13–14. The letter is reprinted in Du Bois, *Autobiography*, 151–52.

56. Du Bois to the Trustees of the John F. Slater Fund, March 1893; and Du Bois to Rutherford B. Hayes, April 3, 1892, in Aptheker, *Correspondence of Du Bois*, 1:2, 17.

57. Du Bois, *Autobiography*, 159.

58. Ibid., 161; Lewis, *W. E. B. Du Bois*, 1:129. Also see W. E. B. Du Bois, "The Problem of Amusement," in Herbert Aptheker, ed., *Writings by W. E. B. Du Bois in Periodicals Edited by Others* (Millwood, N.Y.: Kraus-Thomson Organization, 1982), 1:39.

59. Du Bois, *Autobiography*, 161.

60. Graham Du Bois, *His Day Is Marching On*, 100–101.

61. Aptheker, *Against Racism*, 29.

62. Du Bois to D. C. Gilman, 1892 or 1893, Du Bois Papers, reel 3, frame 0132.

63. Du Bois, *Autobiography*, 160.

64. Francis L. Broderick, "German Influence on the Scholarship of W. E. B. Du Bois," *Phylon* 19 (winter 1958): 370; Rampersad, *Art and Imagination*, 44.

65. Du Bois to D. C. Gilman, March 29, 1894, with enclosed letters from Gustav Schmoller (March 5, 1894) and Adolph Wagner (March 28, 1894), in Aptheker, *Correspondence of Du Bois*, 1:26–28. After reexamining the situation, the University of Berlin belatedly awarded a doctorate to Du Bois in 1959.

66. Du Bois, *Autobiography*, 164.

67. Ibid., 168, 169. For another view of the way the experience in Germany

affected Du Bois, see Arthur Herman, *The Idea of Decline in Western History* (New York: Free Press, 1997).

68. Du Bois, *Autobiography*, 170–71; Lewis, *W. E. B. Du Bois*, 1:134–35. The complete diary entry is reprinted in Aptheker, *Against Racism*, 26–29.

69. Du Bois to the Trustees of the John F. Slater Fund, March 10, 1893, in Aptheker, *Correspondence of Du Bois*, 1:25.

70. Du Bois to D. C. Gilman, 1892 or 1893, Du Bois Papers, reel 3, frame 0132; Du Bois, *Autobiography*, 185.

71. Du Bois Diary, February 23, 1896, Du Bois Papers, reel 87, frame 00536; Broderick, *W. E. B. Du Bois*, 33; Rudwick, *W. E. B. Du Bois*, 28.

72. Du Bois, *Autobiography*, 186.

73. Ibid., 89, 110–11.

74. Lewis, *W. E. B. Du Bois*, 1:65; Ingersoll Interview, 129, 58; Du Bois, *Autobiography*, 285; Du Bois to Congregational Sunday School, September 29, 1892, in Aptheker, *Correspondence of Du Bois*, 1:19–20; Du Bois Diary, February 23, 1896, Du Bois Papers, reel 87, frame 00536; W. E. B. Du Bois, "Credo" in Du Bois, *Darkwater*, 3; Herbert Aptheker, "W. E. B. Du Bois and Religion: A Brief Reassessment," *Journal of Religious Thought* 39 (spring–summer, 1982): 5–11. David Levering Lewis maintains that even in the "Credo" Du Bois only "appeared to profess a belief in God." Lewis says that "White readers of a sanctimonious or myopic bent were profoundly gratified by the expression of religious sentiments, as were the overwhelming majority of his own people." But Lewis concluded that Du Bois's allusions to religion were not heartfelt (*W. E. B. Du Bois*, 1:312).

75. Ingersoll Interview, 138; Statement of Horace Bumstead, quoted in Du Bois, *Autobiography*, 210. Several of Du Bois's prayers were published in Herbert Aptheker, ed., *Prayers for Dark People* (Amherst: University of Massachusetts Press, 1980).

76. Du Bois, *Autobiography*, 190; Du Bois to Booker T. Washington, January 3, 1896, in Louis R. Harlan, ed., *The Booker T. Washington Papers* (14 vols. Urbana: University of Illinois Press, 1972–1989), 4:98–99.

77. Du Bois, *Autobiography*, 187; Lewis, *W. E. B. Du Bois*, 1:178.

78. W. E. B. Du Bois, "I Bury My Wife," *Negro Digest* 8 (October 1950): 37.

79. Du Bois, *Autobiography*, 280.

80. Du Bois, "I Bury My Wife," 38; Graham Du Bois, *His Day Is Marching On*, 125.

81. W. E. B. Du Bois, *The Suppression of the African Slave Trade to the United States of America, 1638–1870* (1896; reprint, Millwood, N.Y.: Kraus-Thomson Organization, 1973).

82. W. E. B. Du Bois, "The Enforcement of the Slave Trade Laws" (a paper for the American Historical Association, 1891), in Aptheker, *Writings by Du Bois in Periodicals*, 1:27.

83. Philip Curtin, *The African Slave Trade: A Census* (Madison: University of Wisconsin Press, 1969), 85.

84. Peter Kolchin, *American Slavery* (New York: Hill and Wang, 1993), 93, 242.

85. On this point, see Robert William Fogel and Stanley L. Engerman, *Time on the Cross* (Boston: Little, Brown, 1974).

86. Du Bois, *The Suppression of the African Slave Trade,* passim; Ronald T. Takaki, *A Pro-Slavery Crusade: The Agitation to Reopen the African Slave Trade* (New York: Free Press, 1971). Du Bois was probably off the mark, however, in suggesting that the slave trade was abolished not for moral reasons but because large-scale plantations were no longer profitable. On the profitability of slavery, see Alfred H. Conrad and John R. Meyer, *The Economics of Slavery and Other Studies in Econometric History* (Chicago: Aldine Publishing, 1964), and Fogel and Engerman, *Time on the Cross.*

87. Du Bois, *Suppression of the African Slave Trade,* 327–29.

88. Although David Levering Lewis does bestow this praise in *W. E. B. Du Bois,* 1:108.

89. Du Bois, *Autobiography,* 195.

90. Ibid., 196.

91. Du Bois, *Dusk of Dawn,* 58; Du Bois, *Autobiography,* 198.

92. Du Bois, *Philadelphia Negro,* 381, 373, 368.

93. C. C. Harrison to Whom It May Concern, August 15, 1896, in Aptheker, *Correspondence of Du Bois,* 1:40.

94. Du Bois, *Philadelphia Negro,* 97–146, 380–81.

95. Ibid., 384.

96. Ibid., 50, 249. Also see Roger Lane, *Roots of Violence in Black Philadelphia, 1860–1900* (Cambridge: Harvard University Press, 1986).

97. Du Bois, *Philadelphia Negro,* 67, 192, 68, 72.

98. Ibid., 394, 395.

99. Ibid., 389, 390.

100. Ibid., 391, 390.

101. Ibid., 392, 393.

102. Lewis, *W. E. B. Du Bois,* 1:210; *American Historical Review* 6 (October 1900): 163.

103. Rampersad, *Art and Imagination,* 53; Davis, *Leadership, Love, and Aggression,* 115; Lewis, *W. E. B. Du Bois,* 1:190.

104. Lewis, *W. E. B. Du Bois,* 1:189.

105. Du Bois, "Conservation of Races," 8, 7, 6 (italics in original).

106. Ibid., 2, 4, 7. Some scholars maintain that there is no scientific basis for believing that there are separate races of humanity. Thus Anthony Appiah has criticized Du Bois for believing in the biological reality of race. And Thomas C. Holt has defended Du Bois by noting that when he wrote "The Conservation of Races," Du Bois recognized that race was constructed historically and socially as well as based, in part, on biology. Holt also maintains that by 1940 Du Bois had come to believe that "race" was entirely a social and historical phenomenon and not at all based on biology. See Anthony Appiah, "The Uncompleted Argument: Du Bois and the Illusion of Race," in *"Race," Writing, and Difference,* Henry Louis Gates, ed. (Chicago: University of Chicago Press, 1986), 21–37; Anthony Appiah, "Illusions of Race," in *In My Father's House: Africa in the Philosophy of Culture* (New York: Oxford University Press, 1992), 28–46; and Thomas C. Holt, "W. E. B. Du Bois's Archeology of Race: Re-Reading 'The Conservation of Races,'" in Michael B. Katz and Thomas J. Sugrue, eds., *W. E. B. Du Bois, Race, and the City: The Philadelphia Negro and Its Legacy* (Philadelphia: University of Pennsylvania Press, 1998), 61–76.

107. W. E. B. Du Bois, "The Future and Function of the Private Negro College," *Crisis* 53 (August 1946): 235.

108. Du Bois, "Conservation of Races," 5, 4.

109. August Meier, *Negro Thought in America, 1880–1915: Racial Ideologies in the Age of Booker T. Washington* (Ann Arbor: University of Michigan Press, 1963), 43; Marable, *W. E. B. Du Bois,* 38.

110. Du Bois, "Conservation of Races," 5.

111. W. E. B. Du Bois, "Strivings of the Negro People," *Atlantic Monthly* 80 (August 1897): 194–95.

112. Du Bois, "Conservation of Races," 7.

113. W. E. B. Du Bois, "Miscegenation," in Aptheker, *Against Racism,* 100.

114. Sarah L. Delany and A. Elizabeth Delany with Amy Hill Hearth, *Having Our Say* (New York: Delta Trade Paperbacks, 1993), 76.

115. Alfred H. Stone, quoted by Lewis, *W. E. B. Du Bois,* 1:373.

116. Charles W. Eliot to Oswald Garrison Villard, November 4, 1915, Villard Papers, Harvard University.

117. Du Bois, *Philadelphia Negro,* 388, 394.

118. There are a number of books on white racial attitudes of this era. See William Stanton, *The Leopard's Spots: Scientific Attitudes toward Race in America, 1815–1859* (Chicago: University of Chicago Press, 1960); John S. Haller Jr., *Outcasts from Evolution: Scientific Attitudes of Racial Inferiority, 1859–1900* (Urbana: University of Illinois Press, 1971); I. A. Newby, *Jim Crow's Defense: Anti-Negro Thought in America, 1900–1930* (Baton Rouge: Louisiana State University Press, 1965); George M. Fredrickson, *The Black Image in the White Mind: The Debate on Afro-American Character and Destiny, 1817–1914* (New York: Harper and Row, 1971).

119. Sander L. Gilman, *On Blackness without Blacks: Essays on the Image of the Black in Germany* (Boston: G. K. Hall, 1982), 94.

120. Du Bois, *Autobiography,* 165.

121. Lewis, *W. E. B. Du Bois,* 1:99, 276–77.

122. Albert Bushnell Hart, *The Southern South* (New York: D. Appleton, 1910), 99.

123. Du Bois, *Souls of Black Folk,* 89, 221–22. In the last of these quotations, Du Bois was referring to Alexander Crummell; but I think it is not too much to suggest that he was also projecting his own concern.

124. Ingersoll Interview, 139.

125. James Weldon Johnson, *Along This Way* (New York: Viking Press, 1933), 203.

126. Horace Bumstead, quoted in Du Bois, *Autobiography,* 211.

127. Bessie Taylor Page to Du Bois, February 21, 1918, Du Bois Papers, reel 6, frame 1081. For more on Du Bois at Atlanta University, see Clarence A. Bacote, *The Story of Atlanta University* (Atlanta: Atlanta University, 1969), passim; and Dorothy Cowser Yancy, "William Edward Burghardt Du Bois' Atlanta Years: The Human Side—A Study upon Oral Sources," *Journal of Negro History* 63 (January 1978): 59–67.

128. Bessie Taylor Page to Du Bois, February 21, 1918, Du Bois Papers, reel 6, frame 1081.

129. Dorothy Cowser Yancy, "Du Bois' Atlanta Years," 61.

130. Du Bois to Mrs. Hazel, February 19, 1910, Du Bois Papers, reel 2, frame 0087.

131. University president Horace Bumstead said that he and trustee George Bradford "wanted a professor of sociology with special reference to investigating conditions concerning the Negro." See Du Bois, *Autobiography*, 210.

132. Twelve of the Atlanta monographs have been republished in a single volume, *The Atlanta University Publications* (New York: Arno Press and the New York Times, 1968).

133. Du Bois, *Dusk of Dawn*, 65.

134. *Atlanta University Publications, No. 13,* 39, 37, 41; Gaines, *Uplifting the Race*, introduction, chapter 6, and passim; Kelley, *Yo' Mama's DisFunktional,* passim.

135. Du Bois, "Strivings of the Negro People," 194–95.

136. Du Bois, *Dusk of Dawn*, 80; Lewis, *W. E. B. Du Bois,* 1:278.

137. Johnson, *Along This Way,* 203.

2. Du Bois and Booker T. Washington

1. Booker T. Washington, *Up from Slavery* (1901; reprint, New York: Oxford University Press, 1995), 2, 1, 7; Louis R. Harlan, *Booker T. Washington: The Making of a Black Leader, 1856–1901* (New York: Oxford University Press, 1972), 14 (cited hereafter as *Booker T. Washington,* vol. 1).

2. Washington, *Up from Slavery,* 4.

3. Ibid., 21, 1, 16; Harlan, *Booker T. Washington,* 1:9.

4. Washington, *Up from Slavery,* 2.

5. Ibid., 9, 10.

6. Ibid., 15–16. "Some of our neighbors were coloured people, and some were the poorest and most ignorant and degraded white people. It was a motley mixture."

7. Ibid., 26, 36.

8. Ibid., 26.

9. Harlan, *Booker T. Washington,* 1:44.

10. Washington, *Up from Slavery,* 29.

11. Henry Allen Bullock, *A History of Negro Education in the South* (New York: Praeger, 1967), 76.

12. Allen Johnson, ed., *Dictionary of American Biography* (New York: Charles Scribner's Sons, 1955), 1:359–60.

13. For a forceful statement of this view, see James D. Anderson, *The Education of Blacks in the South, 1860–1935* (Chapel Hill: University of North Carolina Press, 1988), chapters 2 and 3. When General Armstrong founded Hampton, the tradition of discipline and piety was in force at most schools. In the nineteenth century black and white students alike were closely chaperoned, were required to attend chapel, and were subject to inspection in their rooms at any time. Yet this tradition remained at black schools long after the leading white schools had deemphasized duty and had begun to emphasize the importance of secular scholarship. This eventually led some blacks to suspect that the strict disciplinary policies that were still in force in their schools in the early twentieth century were prompted by a racist belief that Negroes were particularly sensuous people who could not discipline themselves.

14. Harlan, *Booker T. Washington,* 1:61; Bullock, *History of Negro Education,* 89.

15. Edward K. Graham, "A Tender Violence: The Biography of a College" (unpublished manuscript); Louis R. Harlan, *Separate and Unequal: Public School Campaigns and Racism in the Southern Seaboard States, 1901–1915* (1958; reprint, New York: Atheneum, 1969), 75–76, 268–69, and passim; Lester, *Seventh Son,* 1:42; James M. McPherson, *The Abolitionist Legacy: From Reconstruction to the NAACP* (Princeton: Princeton University Press, 1975), 210–12; Wolters, *New Negro on Campus,* 139, 230; Robert F. Engs, *Educating the Disfranchised and Disinherited: Samuel Chapman Armstrong and Hampton Institute, 1839–1893* (Knoxville: University of Tennessee Press, 1999).

16. Washington, *Up from Slavery,* 32.

17. Edith Armstrong Talbot, *Samuel Chapman Armstrong: A Biographical Study* (1904; reprint, New York: Negro Universities Press, 1969), 208, 207.

18. Washington, *Up from Slavery,* 54, 53, 51, 52. For more on upper-class blacks, see Willard D. Gatewood, *Aristocrats of Color: The Black Elite, 1880–1920* (Bloomington: Indiana University Press, 1990); and Lawrence Otis Graham, *Our Kind of People: Inside America's Black Upper Class* (New York: Harper Collins, 1999).

19. Washington, *Up from Slavery,* 52.

20. Harlan, *Booker T. Washington,* 1:110.

21. Washington, *Up from Slavery,* 70; Booker T. Washington, Speech to the National Educational Association, July 16, 1884, in Harlan, *Washington Papers,* 2:255.

22. Washington, *Up from Slavery,* 70, 69, 74.

23. Harlan, *Booker T. Washington,* 1:124; Washington, *Up from Slavery,* 64.

24. Harlan, *Booker T. Washington,* 1:190.

25. Ibid.; Booker T. Washington, Speech before the Alabama State Teachers Association, April 11, 1888, in Harlan, *Washington Papers,* 2:432.

26. Booker T. Washington, *The Future of the American Negro,* in Harlan, *Washington Papers,* 5:328.

27. Washington, *Up from Slavery,* 90, 118–19.

28. Ibid., 165.

29. Louis R. Harlan, "Booker T. Washington and the National Negro Business League," in Raymond Smock, ed., *Booker T. Washington in Perspective: Essays of Louis R. Harlan* (Jackson: University Press of Mississippi, 1988), 105.

30. Washington, *Up from Slavery,* 90, 131.

31. Washington, *Future of the American Negro,* 351.

32. Washington, *Up from Slavery,* 49.

33. Washington, *Future of the American Negro,* 357.

34. Washington, *Up from Slavery,* 49.

35. Ibid., 117–18.

36. Booker T. Washington, *The Story of My Life and Work* (1900; reprint, New York: Negro Universities Press, 1969), 166–68; Roy Beck, *The Case against Immigration* (New York: W. W. Norton, 1996), 169–70.

37. Washington, *Story of My Life,* 168.

38. Ibid., 168, 171.

39. *New York World,* September 18, 1895, in Harlan, *Washington Papers,* 4:9.

40. Booker T. Washington to the *New York World,* September 19, 1895, in Harlan, *Washington Papers,* 4:16; Washington, *Up from Slavery,* 142.

41. Washington, *Up from Slavery,* 134. Julius Lester has written: "The black press was initially angered, . . . and it was only after the white press rewarded Washington with support and praise that blacks began to accept him. Washington also brought many blacks to his side by private meetings in which his tone differed from that of the Atlanta speech, and by giving financial support to a number of black newspapers" (*Seventh Son,* 1:43).

42. Edward Wilmot Blyden to Booker T. Washington, September 24, 1895, in Harlan, *Washington Papers,* 4:26–28; Du Bois to Booker T. Washington, September 24, 1895, in Aptheker, *Correspondence of Du Bois,* 1:39; Ingersoll Interview, 157; Du Bois, *Dusk of Dawn,* 55.

43. Meier, *Negro Thought in America,* 100–118.

44. Louis R. Harlan, *Booker T. Washington: The Wizard of Tuskegee, 1901–1915* (Urbana: University of Illinois Press, 1983), 135 (cited hereafter as *Booker T. Washington,* vol. 2).

45. Dewey W. Grantham Jr., "Dinner at the White House: Theodore Roosevelt, Booker T. Washington, and the South," *Tennessee Historical Quarterly* 17 (June 1958): 112–30.

46. Oswald Garrison Villard to Booker T. Washington, May 26, 1909, in Harlan, *Washington Papers,* 10:116–18.

47. Du Bois, *Dusk of Dawn,* 70.

48. Ibid., 76–77. Du Bois thought Washington controlled the black press by steering advertisements and through outright bribes. On this point there was an interesting correspondence between Du Bois and Oswald Garrison Villard, especially the following letters in the Villard Papers: Du Bois to Villard, March 24, 1905; Villard to Francis J. Garrison, April 6, 1905; Garrison to Villard, April 7, 1905, and April 9, 1905; Villard to Du Bois, April 18, 1905; Du Bois to Villard, April 20, 1905; Garrison to Villard, April 27, 1905; and Villard to Booker T. Washington, May 20, 1905.

49. William James to Du Bois, June 23, 1907, reel 2, frame 0273; Frank W. Tausig to Du Bois, May 10, 1907, reel 3, frame 0292; and Du Bois, Memorandum for J. H. Dillard, April 19, 1912, reel 4, frame 0397, Du Bois Papers. For a lower estimate—only five hundred dollars—see W. E. B. Du Bois, "The Laboratory in Sociology at Atlanta University," *Annals of the American Academy of Political and Social Science* 21 (1903): 504.

50. Du Bois, review of *Up from Slavery,* by Booker T. Washington, *Dial,* July 16, 1901, 53–55, reprinted in Herbert Aptheker, ed., *Book Reviews by W. E. B. Du Bois* (Millwood, N.Y.: Kraus-Thomson Organization, 1977), 3–5.

51. W. E. B. Du Bois, "The Suffrage Fight in Georgia," *Independent* 51 (November 30, 1899): 3226–28, reprinted in Aptheker, *Writings by Du Bois in Periodicals,* 1:64–66; Lewis, *W. E. B. Du Bois,* 1:231–32; Harlan, *Booker T. Washington,* 1:291–92; Du Bois to Booker T. Washington, November 1902, reel 3, frame 0619; Washington to Du Bois, November 28, 1902, reel 3, frame 0620; Du Bois to Washington, December 1902, reel 3, frame 0621; Washington to Du Bois, December 13, 1902, reel 3, frame 0642, Du Bois Papers; Meier, *Negro Thought in America,* 110–14; Louis R. Harlan, "The Secret Life of Booker T. Washington," *Journal of Southern History* 37 (August 1971): 393–416.

52. Washington, *Up from Slavery*, 118; Booker T. Washington to Charles W. Chesnutt, July 7, 1903 in Harlan, *Washington Papers*, 7:198.

53. Emma Lou Thornbrough, *T. Thomas Fortune: Militant Journalist* (Chicago: University of Chicago Press, 1972), 191; Emmett J. Scott to Booker T. Washington, August 23, 1899, in Harlan, *Washington Papers*, 5:181.

54. Emma Lou Thornbrough, "The National Afro-American League, 1887–1908," *Journal of Southern History* 27 (November 1961): 503–4.

55. Albert Bushnell Hart to Booker T. Washington, June 14, 1897, and August 10, 1897; and Washington to Du Bois, October 26, 1899, in Harlan, *Washington Papers*, 4:299, 320; 5:245.

56. Ingersoll Interview, 158.

57. Ingersoll Interview, 158, 157; Du Bois to Booker T. Washington, February 1, 1900, in Harlan, *Washington Papers*, 5:443–44.

58. Mary White Ovington, *Portraits in Color* (New York: Viking Press, 1927), 82–83.

59. Lewis, *W. E. B. Du Bois*, 1:212.

60. Du Bois, *Souls of Black Folk*, 208; Du Bois, "I Bury My Wife," 39.

61. Bessie Taylor Page to Du Bois, February 21, 1918, Du Bois Papers, reel 6, frame 1081

62. Du Bois, *Autobiography*, 243; Ingersoll Interview, 158.

63. Du Bois to Booker T. Washington, February 17, 1900; and Du Bois to Washington, April 10, 1900, in Harlan, *Washington Papers*, 5:443–44, 480.

64. Du Bois to Booker T. Washington, April 10, 1900; and Du Bois to Washington, February 26, 1900, in Harlan, *Washington Papers*, 5:480, 450.

65. Booker T. Washington to Du Bois, March 11, 1900; William A. Pledger to Washington, March 16, 1900; and Washington to T. Thomas Fortune, March 18, 1900, in Harlan, *Washington Papers*, 5:458–59, 466, 466.

66. Du Bois, *Autobiography*, 243.

67. Du Bois to Booker T. Washington, July 3, 1901, in Harlan, *Washington Papers*, 6:165. At the last minute, however, Du Bois was unable to go on this trip.

68. William Monroe Trotter to John Fairlie, June 15, 1902, Trotter Papers, Boston University Library.

69. Undated typescript, Trotter Papers; Stephen R. Fox, *The Guardian of Boston: William Monroe Trotter* (New York: Atheneum, 1970), 27.

70. Booker T. Washington to Archibald H. Grimke, June 5, 1899, in Harlan, *Washington Papers*, 5:126.

71. Fox, *Guardian of Boston*, 36.

72. Ibid., 38. Also see the *Boston Guardian*, April 9, 1904, quoted ibid., 33; and Edward Henry Clement to Booker T. Washington, January 2, 1898 [1899], in Harlan, *Washington Papers*, 5:5.

73. Fox, *Guardian of Boston*, 39; *Boston Guardian*, October 4, 1902, Trotter Papers; W. E. B. Du Bois, "William Monroe Trotter," *Crisis* 41 (May 1934): 134.

74. Charles W. Chesnutt to William Monroe Trotter, December 28, 1901, Trotter Papers.

75. Fox, *Guardian of Boston*, 40; Du Bois to George Foster Peabody, December 28, 1903, Du Bois Papers, reel 2, frame 1162.

76. Fox, *Guardian of Boston*, 50.

77. *Boston Globe*, July 31, 1903, 1; *New York Times*, August 1, 1903, 6.

78. Booker T. Washington to Whitefeld McKinlay, August 3, 1903, in Harlan, *Washington Papers*, 7:252.

79. *Washington Bee*, August 8, 1903, and *Chicago Broad-Ax*, August 8, 1903, quoted in Fox, *Guardian of Boston*, 53–54. However, the reaction of the black press was mixed, with the *Indianapolis Freeman*, the *New York Age*, and the *Washington Colored American* supporting Washington.

80. Fox, *Guardian of Boston*, 57.

81. Du Bois, *Souls of Black Folk*, 43, 59, 44, 53, 54.

82. Du Bois to George Foster Peabody, December 28, 1903, Du Bois Papers, reel 2, frame 1162.

83. Du Bois to Clement Morgan, October 19, 1903, Du Bois Papers, reel 2, frame 0668; Fox, *Guardian of Boston*, 62; Kelly Miller to Du Bois, November 4, 1903, reel 2, frame 0625.

84. Booker T. Washington to Robert Curtis Ogden, October 20, 1903, in Harlan, *Washington Papers*, 7:298.

85. Du Bois, *Autobiography*, 252.

86. Booker T. Washington to Clark Howell, November 23, 1910, in Harlan, *Washington Papers*, 10:483–84.

87. Fox, *Guardian of Boston*, 70–73, 68–69, 64–66; Harlan, *Booker T. Washington*, 2:54–56; Sheldon Avery, *Up from Washington: William Pickens and the Negro Struggle for Equality* (Newark: University of Delaware Press, 1989), 16–18; Horace Bumstead to Booker T. Washington, December 5, 1902, in Harlan, *Washington Papers*, 7:36. By threatening George W. Forbes's civil service job at the Boston library, Washington's supporters also succeeded in getting Forbes to quit the *Guardian*.

88. Kelly Miller, *Radicals and Conservatives and Other Essays on the Negro in America* (New York: Schocken Books, 1968; originally published in 1908 under the title, *Race Adjustment: Essays on the Negro in America*), 28.

89. Du Bois to George Foster Peabody, December 28, 1903, Du Bois Papers, reel 2, frame 1162; Du Bois, *Dusk of Dawn*, 87.

90. In 1904 Du Bois and Washington tried to reconcile their differences, but by then the gulf between the two men was too great. For more on the efforts at reconciliation, see Herbert Aptheker, "The Washington–Du Bois Conference of 1904," *Science and Society* 13 (fall 1949): 344–51; Rudwick, *W. E. B. Du Bois*, 77–93; Harlan, *Booker T. Washington*, 2:63–83; Lewis, *W. E. B. Du Bois*, 1:297–313.

91. The call is reprinted and the signatories and attendees are listed in Aptheker, *Pamphlets and Leaflets by Du Bois*, 53–54. This information is also available in the Du Bois Papers, reel 2, frame 0844 ff.

92. Aptheker, *Pamphlets and Leaflets by Du Bois*, 53–54, 55.

93. Leroy Davis, *A Clashing of the Soul: John Hope and the Dilemma of African American Leadership and Black Education in the Early Twentieth Century* (Athens: University of Georgia Press, 1998), 152–53. On the other hand, some members favored complete assimilation into the American mainstream. Manning Marable has noted that there was a "cultural distance" between these "integrationists" and Du Bois (*W. E. B. Du Bois*, 67–68).

94. W. E. B. Du Bois, "The Growth of the Niagara Movement," *Voice of the Negro* 3 (January 1906), 43–45, reprinted in Aptheker, *Writings by Du Bois in Periodicals*, 1:274; Du Bois to Archibald Grimke and Kelly Miller, March 21, 1905, Grimke Papers, Howard University; Albert Bushnell Hart to Du Bois, April 24, 1905, Du Bois Papers, reel 2, frame 0047.

95. Du Bois, *Autobiography*, 240.

96. "Niagara Address of 1906," in Herbert Aptheker, ed., *A Documentary History of the Negro People in the United States* (New York: Citadel Press, 1964), 2:909.

97. Aptheker, *Education of Black People*, 11, 9.

98. Du Bois to George Foster Peabody, December 28, 1903, Du Bois Papers, reel 2, frame 1162.

99. Du Bois's annotation of Albert Bushnell Hart to Du Bois, April 24, 1905, Du Bois Papers, reel 2, frame 0047; Du Bois, *Dusk of Dawn*, 73–74.

100. Johnson, *Along This Way*, 313; Kelly Miller to Du Bois, April 23, 1904, Du Bois Papers, reel 2, frame 0627.

101. T. Thomas Fortune to Emmett J. Scott, July 13, 1903, Booker T. Washington Papers, container 275, Library of Congress; Charles W. Anderson to Booker T. Washington, January 26, 1904, in Harlan, *Washington Papers*, 7:413–14; Wilford H. Smith to Booker T. Washington, July 31, 1903, in Harlan, *Washington Papers*, 7:246–47; Emmett J. Scott to T. Thomas Fortune, November 23, 1903, Booker T. Washington Papers, container 258.

102. Booker T. Washington to Theodore Roosevelt, September 15, 1903, in Harlan, *Washington Papers*, 7:284–85.

103. Booker T. Washington to Emmett J. Scott, August 7, 1905, Booker T. Washington Papers, container 24.

104. Booker T. Washington to Theodore Roosevelt, September 15, 1903, in Harlan, *Washington Papers*, 7:284–85.

105. "Trotter and Trotterism," unsigned typescript, corrected and annotated by Emmett J. Scott, Booker T. Washington Papers, container 308.

106. Harlan, *Booker T. Washington*, 2:57–58, 90–94, 86; Booker T. Washington to J. R. Cox, July 10, 1905, Booker T. Washington Papers, container 556; Clifford Plummer to Washington, July 16, 1905, in Harlan, *Washington Papers*, 8:328–29.

107. Lewis, *W. E. B. Du Bois*, 1:300; Harlan, *Booker T. Washington*, 2:18–19.

108. Charles W. Anderson to Booker T. Washington, July 14, 1905, Booker T. Washington Papers, container 27.

109. Lewis, *W. E. B. Du Bois*, 1:319.

110. David Wallace to Du Bois, October 16, 1905, Du Bois Papers, reel 3, frame 0581.

111. Lewis, *W. E. B. Du Bois*, 1:329; Du Bois, "Growth of the Niagara Movement," 43–45.

112. Jacob Schiff to Du Bois, April 9, 1905, reel 3, frame 0049; Du Bois to Schiff, reel 3, frame 0047; and Charles W. Chesnutt to Du Bois, reel 1, frame 0590, Du Bois Papers.

113. For example, see Du Bois to Jean Seligman, 1906, Du Bois Papers, reel 3, frame 0077.

114. Lewis, *W. E. B. Du Bois,* 1:246; Du Bois to Jean Seligman, 1906, reel 3, frame 0077; and Ed L. Simon to Du Bois, December 22, 1906, reel 3, frame 0102, Du Bois Papers; Du Bois, *Autobiography,* 252–53; Booker T. Washington to Wilbur Patterson Thirkeld, August 15, 1909; Washington to John R. Francis, September 4, 1909; James A. Cobb to Emmett J. Scott, December 21, 1909; and Cobb to Scott, September 3, 1906, in Harlan, *Washington Papers,* 10:156–57, 160–61, 248–49; 9:68 ("[Du Bois] seems determined to land in Washington if he can possibly do it." "Du Bois is turning heaven and earth to be appointed assistant superintendent.")

115. J. Douglas Wetmore to Booker T. Washington, October 13, 1905, Booker T. Washington Papers, container 5; Johnson, *Along This Way,* 203; William Monroe Trotter to Du Bois, April 1, 1905, Du Bois Papers, reel 3, frame 0357; Du Bois, *Autobiography,* 283; Du Bois, *Dusk of Dawn,* 94.

116. Mary White Ovington to Du Bois, October 8, 1907, reel 2, frame 1108; Du Bois to Executive Committee, 1907, reel 2, frame 0952; and "A Brief Resume of the Massachusetts Trouble in the Niagara Movement," 1907 typescript, reel 2, frame 0955, Du Bois Papers.

117. Charles W. Anderson to Booker T. Washington, July 14, 1905, in Harlan, *Washington Papers,* 8:327; Marable, *W. E. B. Du Bois,* 68; J. Milton Waldron to Fellowmember, 1907, Du Bois Papers, reel 2, frame 0953.

118. Fred R. More to Booker T. Washington, September 28, 1905, in Harlan, *Washington Papers,* 8:378–79; Booker T. Washington to Charles W. Anderson, September 29, 1905, in Harlan, *Washington Papers,* 8:380–81.

119. Booker T. Washington to the Editor of the *New York Age,* September 7, 1908, in Harlan, *Washington Papers,* 9:619.

120. Davis, *Clashing of the Soul,* 87, 91.

121. John Hope to Du Bois, January 17, 1910, Du Bois Papers, reel 2, frame 0154.

122. Ibid.

123. Ibid.

124. Du Bois to John Hope, January 22, 1910, Du Bois Papers, reel 2, frame 0161.

125. Frank Shay, *Judge Lynch* (Montclair, New Jersey: Patterson Smith, 1969), 109; Du Bois, *Dusk of Dawn,* 67–68; Du Bois, *Autobiography,* 222.

126. Joel Williamson, *The Crucible of Race: Black/White Relations in the American South since Emancipation* (New York: Oxford University Press, 1984), 128, 124, 129; for accounts of the Atlanta Riot, see 209–23, and W. E. B. Du Bois, "The Tragedy at Atlanta," *World Today* 11 (November 1906): 1173–75; Ray Stannard Baker, *Following the Color Line* (1908; reprint, New York: Harper Torchbooks, 1964), 3–25; John Dittmer, *Black Georgia in the Progressive Era* (Urbana: University of Illinois Press, 1977), 123–40; and Charles Crowe, "Racial Violence and Social Reform—Origins of the Atlanta Riot of 1906," *Journal of Negro History* 53 (July 1968): 234–56; and Crowe, "Racial Massacre in Atlanta, September 22, 1906," *Journal of Negro History* 54 (April 1969): 150–73.

127. Baker, *Following the Color Line,* 5.

128. Crowe, "Racial Violence and Social Reform," 249.

129. Du Bois, "Tragedy at Atlanta," 1175, 1173.

130. Timothy B. Tyson, "Robert F. Williams, 'Black Power,' and the Roots of the African American Freedom Struggle," *Journal of American History* 85 (September 1998): 545.

131. Lewis, *W. E. B. Du Bois*, 1:388; James L. Crouthamel, "The Springfield Race Riot of 1908," *Journal of Negro History* 45 (July 1960): 164–81.

132. Charles Flint Kellogg, *NAACP: A History of the National Association for the Advancement of Colored People* (Baltimore: Johns Hopkins Press, 1967), 11 and passim; Mary White Ovington, *The Walls Came Tumbling Down* (1947; reprint, New York: Schocken Books, 1970), 103 and passim.

133. Booker T. Washington to T. Thomas Fortune, February 21, 1906, in Harlan, *Washington Papers,* 8:531.

134. Du Bois, *Autobiography,* 253.

3. Du Bois and the National Association for the Advancement of Colored People

1. Annual Report of the NAACP, 1911, NAACP Papers, Library of Congress; Du Bois, *Crisis* 41 (February 1934): 52.

2. Johnson, *Along This Way,* 309–10; Kellogg, *NAACP,* 41.

3. Johnson, *Along This Way,* 314–15.

4. Lewis, *W. E. B. Du Bois*, 1:416, 544; Du Bois, *Autobiography,* 260.

5. The *National Review* currently has a circulation of about 150,000; the *New Republic,* 85,000; and the *Weekly Standard,* 55,000.

6. Albert E. Pillsbury to Du Bois, July 26, 1910, Du Bois Papers, reel 2, frame 0794.

7. Du Bois, *Autobiography,* 261.

8. Anthony M. Platt, *E. Franklin Frazier Reconsidered* (New Brunswick: Rutgers University Press, 1991), 60; J. Saunders Redding, "W. E. Burghardt Du Bois," *American Scholar* 18 (1949): 93.

9. Kellogg, *NAACP,* 48.

10. *Grunspan v. Walling,* 121 New York 270; *New York Age,* August 5, 1909, 4; *New York Tribune,* February 24, 1911, 9; Lewis, *W. E. B. Du Bois*, 1:429; Kellogg, *NAACP,* 32–33; Editor's note, Booker T. Washington to Charles W. Anderson, March 3, 1911, in Harlan, *Washington Papers,* 10:614. "Yes," Oswald Garrison Villard wrote to his uncle, "Walling's retirement as Executive Chairman . . . was in part due to his domestic trouble. . . . It is most unfortunate from every point of view, and I think it has about ruined his usefulness for a long time to come. How any man could have put such foolish things on paper as he has set down is beyond me, and the lawyers' defense . . . that she is a bad woman does not help his situation in any way" (Villard to Francis J. Garrison, February 27, 1911, Villard Papers).

11. Oswald Garrison Villard to Booker T. Washington, December 13, 1910, in Harlan, *Washington Papers,* 10:505–6.

12. Oswald Garrison Villard to Du Bois, February 7, 1905, reel 2, frame 0771; Du Bois to Villard, March 24, 1905, reel 2, frame 0774; Du Bois to William Monroe Trotter, March 15, 1905, reel 3, frame 0352; and Trotter to Du Bois, February 22, 1905, reel 3, frame 0353, Du Bois Papers.

13. Herbert Aptheker, introduction to W. E. B. Du Bois, *John Brown* (1909; reprint, Millwood, N.Y.: Kraus-Thomson Organization, 1973), 9, 18. It seems odd that Du Bois, after having had an education that particularly emphasized the importance of primary source material, would have conceived of a project that relied heavily on secondary sources. This is hard to explain, but it does show that even before he left Atlanta University for the NAACP, Du Bois was turning toward popular writing.

14. *Nation* 89 (October 28, 1909): 405.

15. Du Bois to Paul E. Moore, November 15, 1909, Du Bois Papers, reel 2, frame 0722. Villard's biography was published under the title, *John Brown, 1800–1859: A Biography Fifty Years After* (Boston: Houghton Mifflin, 1911).

16. Du Bois, *Autobiography,* 256.

17. Ibid., 260; Oswald Garrison Villard to J. E. Spingarn, April 16, 1914, J. E. Spingarn Papers, Howard University. In particular, Villard thought the *Crisis* was not receiving as much advertising revenue as it could have if it were operated more efficiently. See Mr. Scholz to Oswald Garrison Villard, December 16, 1914, Du Bois Papers, reel 4, frame 1104.

18. Statement of W. E. B. Du Bois, December 1915, Du Bois Papers, reel 5, frame 0134.

19. *American Historical Review* 15 (July 1915): 781–99; *Sociological Review* 4 (October 1911): 303–13; *Annals of the American Academy of Political and Social Science* 49 (September 1913): 233–37; *Atlantic Monthly* 115 (May 1915): 707–17; Du Bois, Memorandum to the NAACP Board, November 1914, Du Bois Papers, reel 4, frame 1099.

20. Oswald Garrison Villard to Francis J. Garrison, February 7, 1913, Villard Papers.

21. Statement of W. E. B. Du Bois, December 1915, Du Bois Papers, reel 5, frame 0134.

22. Du Bois, *Autobiography,* 257–58.

23. Oswald Garrison Villard to J. E. Spingarn, March 20, 1913, Spingarn Papers, Howard University; Du Bois to Oswald Garrison Villard, March 18, 1913, Du Bois Papers, reel 4, frame 0512; Oswald Garrison Villard to Du Bois, April 2, 1913, Du Bois Papers, reel 4, frame 0557; Oswald Garrison Villard to Archibald H. Grimke, December 22, 1915, Grimke Papers.

24. Mary White Ovington to J. E. Spingarn, November 7, 1914, Spingarn Papers, Howard University; May Childs Nerney to Archibald H. Grimke, December 4, 1914, Grimke Papers.

25. Kelly Miller to Edward Ware, November 17, 1911, reel 4, frame 0357; and Du Bois to Kelly Miller, June 11, 1912, reel 4, frame 0359, Du Bois Papers. Du Bois's assessment appeared not in the *Crisis* but in *The College-Bred Negro American* (Atlanta University Publication 15, 1910; reprint, New York: Arno Press and the New York Times, 1968), 22.

26. *Crisis* 8 (August 1914): 191–94; W. S. Scarborough to Oswald Garrison Villard, September 10, 1914; and Scarborough to J. E. Spingarn, September 18, 1914, Spingarn Papers, Howard University.

27. Fox, *Guardian of Boston,* 177–78; *Crisis* 7 (February 1914): 171.

28. Albert E. Pillsbury to Archibald Grimke, May 17, 1915, June 7, 1915; and J. E. Spingarn to Grimke, December 14, 1915, Grimke Papers.

29. *Crisis* 7 (March 1914): 240.

30. *Crisis* 4 (May 1912): 24.

31. Roy Nash to Archibald Grimke, May 25, 1916, Grimke Papers.

32. Unnamed observer, quoted in John Hope to Du Bois, June 5, 1915, reel 5, frame 0022; and John Hope to Du Bois, June 5, 1915, reel 5, frame 0022, Du Bois Papers.

33. Oswald Garrison Villard to Francis Garrison, April 28, 1916, and May 10, 1916; and Garrison to Villard, April 27, 1916, Villard Papers.

34. *Crisis* 11 (April 1916).

35. Oswald Garrison Villard to Francis Garrison, April 28, and May 10, 1916; and Garrison to Villard, April 27, 1916, Villard Papers. In his biography of Du Bois, Elliott M. Rudwick subscribes to Villard's view. According to Rudwick, "Du Bois's sharp tongue and editorial autonomy created . . . problems for the NAACP." Although the association needed the support of the black press and the black clergy, Du Bois's criticisms alienated both groups. Moreover, Rudwick maintains, Villard was justified in taking exception when Du Bois procrastinated about doing non-*Crisis* work for the NAACP. Like Villard, Rudwick thinks Du Bois was "too self-absorbed" and "was forwarding his own designs instead of pursuing activities directly related to the immediate needs of the NAACP." See Rudwick, *W. E. B. Du Bois,* 156, 165–69.

36. Du Bois to Board of Directors, December 13, 1915, reel 5, frame 0129; and Du Bois, Statement for Files, December 1915, reel 5, frame 0134, Du Bois Papers; William English Walling to J. E. Spingarn, November 14, 1914, J. E. Spingarn Papers, New York Public Library; Mary White Ovington to J. E. Spingarn, November 7, 1914, Spingarn Papers, Howard University; Mary White Ovington to Oswald Garrison Villard, August 10, 1915, Villard Papers.

37. Walter White, Memorandum for the Files, May 18, 1934, NAACP Papers.

38. Oswald Garrison Villard to Archibald Grimke, December 17, 1915, Grimke Papers. The dispute between Du Bois and Villard extended over several years but was especially heated between 1913 and 1915. During this period each man wrote more than one letter of resignation—although some of the letters were never handed in. In the interest of narrative and clarity, I have compressed the story. Villard resigned as chairman in 1913 and as treasurer in 1915, but he remained on the board of directors and later served other terms as treasurer.

39. Oswald Garrison Villard to J. E. Spingarn, November 3, 1915, Spingarn Papers, Howard University; Mary White Ovington to Oswald Garrison Villard, November 23, 1913, Villard Papers.

40. B. Joyce Ross, *J. E. Spingarn and the Rise of the NAACP* (New York: Atheneum, 1972); Lewis, *W. E. B. Du Bois,* 1:486–90; Kellogg, *NAACP,* 106–7.

41. J. E. Spingarn to Du Bois, January 11, 1914, Du Bois Papers, reel 4, frame 0955. The official was Roger Baldwin, a future leader of the American Civil Liberties Union.

42. Ross, *J. E. Spingarn,* 43, 33.

43. George C. Bradford to J. E. Spingarn, December 2, 1914, Spingarn Papers,

Howard University; J. E. Spingarn to Du Bois, October 24, 1914, Du Bois Papers, reel 4, frame 0175.

44. Du Bois to Mary White Ovington, January 5, 1913, Du Bois Papers, reel 4, frame 0570.

45. Du Bois to J. E. Spingarn, October 28, 1914, Du Bois Papers, reel 4, frame 1080.

46. J. E. Spingarn to Du Bois, October 24, 1914, Du Bois Papers, reel 4, frame 1075.

47. Du Bois to J. E. Spingarn, October 28, 1914, Du Bois Papers, reel 4, frame 1080.

48. Ingersoll Interview, 164; Lewis, *W. E. B. Du Bois,* 1:469.

49. Lewis, *W. E. B. Du Bois,* 1:469; J. E. Spingarn to Du Bois, October 24, 1914, Du Bois Papers, reel 4, frame 1075.

50. *New York Age,* December 8, 1910 (reprinting an article that appeared originally in the *Atlanta Independent*); Du Bois to Charles Young, January 21, 1916, Du Bois Papers, reel 5, frame 0621.

51. Du Bois to J. E. Spingarn, October 28, 1914, Du Bois Papers, reel 4, frame 1080; Du Bois to Mary White Ovington, April 9, 1914, in Aptheker, *Correspondence of Du Bois,* 1:188–91.

52. Du Bois to J. E. Spingarn, October 28, 1914, Du Bois Papers, reel 4, frame 1080. However, in a handwritten note to Spingarn—a note that was written in an entirely different context—Nerney stated that she considered Du Bois's ability "infinitely superior to my own" (Nerney to J. E. Spingarn, n.d., Spingarn Papers, Howard University).

53. Du Bois to J. E. Spingarn, October 28, 1914, Du Bois Papers, reel 4, frame 1080.

54. Du Bois to Mary White Ovington, April 9, 1914, in Aptheker, *Correspondence of Du Bois,* 1:188–91.

55. Du Bois to J. E. Spingarn, October 28, 1914, Du Bois Papers, reel 4, frame 1080.

56. Du Bois, Memorandum to J. E. Spingarn and Oswald Garrison Villard, November 10, 1914, reel 4, frame 1084; and Moorfield Storey to Villard, reel 4, frame 1086, Du Bois Papers; "The Crisis and the NAACP," *Crisis* 11 (November 1915): 25–28.

57. Ross, *J. E. Spingarn,* 71; J. E. Spingarn, Memorandum to Dr. Du Bois, 1914, Du Bois Papers, reel 4, frame 1087.

58. Ovington, *Walls Came Tumbling Down,* 108.

59. Lewis, *W. E. B. Du Bois,* 1:475, 483, 499; Du Bois, *Autobiography,* 257; Du Bois to Butler Wilson, December 12, 1916, quoted in Lewis, *W. E. B. Du Bois,* 1:468.

60. *Twenty-first Annual Report of the NAACP,* 1930, 68, NAACP Papers. However, there is some evidence that points toward a different conclusion. In late 1914 or early 1915, Du Bois made three proposals: 1) that the *Crisis* become autonomous (the course that Du Bois favored); 2) that if the *Crisis* remained under the NAACP, Mary White Ovington should "become Chairman of the Board [and] a young colored man be selected as secretary and organizer"; and 3) that if neither of these proposals proved feasible Du Bois said he was "willing to combine the offices of Director of Publications and Research and Secretary, and thus become Executive Secretary

of the organization." Du Bois said he liked the third proposal "least of any but in emergency I will accept it" (Du Bois to J. E. Spingarn, A. B. Spingarn, and Mary White Ovington, n.d., J. E. Spingarn Papers, Yale University).

61. Lewis, *W. E. B. Du Bois*, 1:425.

62. *Crisis* 9 (April 1915): 312.

63. Charles Flint Kellogg, introduction to Ovington, *Walls Came Tumbling Down*, xvii; Carolyn Wedin, *Inheritors of the Spirit: Mary White Ovington and the Founding of the NAACP* (New York: John Wiley, 1998); Ralph Luker, *Black and White Sit Down Together: The Reminiscences of an NAACP Founder* (New York: City University of New York Press, 1995).

64. Ovington, *Walls Came Tumbling Down*, 54.

65. Mary White Ovington to Oswald Garrison Villard, June 2, 1909, Villard Papers.

66. Ibid.

67. Rudwick, *W. E. B. Du Bois*, 115; Kellogg, *NAACP*, 23 n. 71.

68. Lewis, *W. E. B. Du Bois*, 1:349–50.

69. Mary White Ovington to J. E. Spingarn, November 7, 1914, Spingarn Papers, Howard University.

70. May Childs Nerney to Archibald Grimke, January 1915, Grimke Papers.

71. Ovington, *Walls Came Tumbling Down*, 152.

72. Mary White Ovington to Du Bois, April 11, 1914, in Aptheker, *Correspondence of Du Bois*, 1:191–93; *Crisis* 9 (September 1913): 238.

73. Du Bois, "Conservation of Races," 6.

74. *Crisis* 7 (November 1913): 337.

75. J. Saunders Redding, *To Make a Poet Black* (Chapel Hill: University of North Carolina Press, 1939), 83.

76. Du Bois, *Darkwater*, 54.

77. *Crisis* 5 (March 1913): 239.

78. Du Bois, *Autobiography*, 257; Kellogg, *NAACP*, 94.

79. Ray Stannard Baker to Du Bois, May 10, 1907, Du Bois Papers, reel 1, frame 00307

80. Du Bois to Ray Stannard Baker, 1907, Du Bois Papers, reel 1, frame 00306.

81. W. E. B. Du Bois, "The Value of Agitation," in Philip S. Foner, ed., *W. E. B. Du Bois Speaks: Speeches and Address, 1890–1919* (New York: Pathfinder Press, 1970), 176.

82. For the pathbreaking article on this subject, see August Meier, "Booker T. Washington and the Rise of the NAACP," *Crisis* 61 (February 1954): 69–76, 117–23.

83. Booker T. Washington to Oswald Garrison Villard, May 28, 1909, in Harlan, *Washington Papers*, 10:119.

84. Booker T. Washington to Ray Stannard Baker, May 24, 1910, in Harlan, *Washington Papers*, 10:333–34. Washington also told Baker that "a majority of the colored people in [the NAACP] are not sincere. I know the individuals. I have tried to work with them. I have found them in most cases either without sincerity or without stability." And Du Bois said: "Oh, Washington was a politician. He was a man who believed we should get what we could get. It wasn't a matter of ideals or anything of that sort. He had no faith in white people, not the slightest, and he was most popular among them, because if he was talking with a white man he sat there

and found out what the white man wanted him to say, and then as soon as possible he said it" (Ingersoll Interview, 150).

85. Harlan, *Booker T. Washington,* 2:375.

86. Booker T. Washington to Fred Moore, July 15, 1911; Emmett J. Scott to H. T. Kealing, May 16, 1910; Kealing to Scott, May 27, 1910; and Washington to Robert H. Terrell, April 17, 1910, in Harlan, *Washington Papers,* 11:268–69; 10:331, 334–35, 323; Oswald Garrison Villard to Francis J. Grimke, June 7, 1909; and Garrison to Villard, June 8, 1909, Villard Papers; Rudwick, *W. E. B. Du Bois,* 139; Scott to Ralph W. Tyler, March 3, 1910, Booker T. Washington Papers, container 413.

87. Du Bois to Charles Young, January 21, 1916, Du Bois Papers, reel 5, frame 0621.

88. Charles W. Anderson to Booker T. Washington, July 12, 1910, Washington Papers, container 413.

89. Du Bois to Charles Young, January 21, 1916, Du Bois Papers, reel 5, frame 0621.

90. Booker T. Washington to Charles W. Anderson, March 3, 1911, in Harlan, *Washington Papers,* 10:614; *New York Age,* March 23, 1911.

91. Emmett J. Scott to Charles W. Anderson, January 28, 1911, in Harlan, *Washington Papers,* 10:564; Harlan, *Booker T. Washington,* 2:376–78.

92. *New York Press,* January 25, 1911, in Harlan, *Washington Papers,* 10:560–63.

93. Kellogg, *NAACP,* 72.

94. Mary White Ovington to Oswald Garrison Villard, May 6, 1908, Villard Papers; Kellogg, *NAACP,* 72.

95. Booker T. Washington to T. Thomas Fortune, January 20, 1911, in Harlan, *Washington Papers,* 10:555–56.

96. H. A. Rucker to Booker T. Washington, October 2, 1908, Washington Papers, container 380.

97. Booker T. Washington to Ray Stannard Baker, May 3, 1919, in Harlan, *Washington Papers,* 10:323–24.

98. Du Bois, *Autobiography,* 223.

99. *Boston Transcript,* March 19, 1910, quoted in Harlan, *Booker T. Washington,* 2:363.

100. "An Appeal to England and Europe," in Aptheker, *Pamphlets and Leaflets by Du Bois,* 95–98.

101. Harlan, *Booker T. Washington,* 2:379; W. E. B. Du Bois, interview with Charles H. Thompson, Thompson Papers, Howard University; Lewis, *W. E. B. Du Bois,* 1:430.

102. Harlan, *Booker T. Washington,* 2:380; Willard B. Gatewood, "Booker T. Washington and the Ulrich Affair," *Phylon* 30 (fall 1969): 286–302.

103. Oswald Garrison Villard to Francis J. Garrison, March 20, 1911, Villard Papers.

104. *Crisis* 1 (April 1911): 11; *Crisis* 1 (May 1911): 7. "I have warned Du Bois on this point," Villard wrote to his uncle, "and he told me that . . . to attack Washington would be to injure the whole race" (Oswald Garrison Villard to Francis J. Garrison, March 20, 1911, Villard Papers).

105. Lewis, *W. E. B. Du Bois,* 1:432.

106. Oswald Garrison Villard to Booker T. Washington, March 31, 1911, in Harlan, *Washington Papers,* 11:69. The resolution expressed "profound regret at the recent assault on Dr. Booker T. Washington in New York City in which the Association finds renewed evidence of race discrimination and increased necessity for the awakening of the public conscience."

107. Booker T. Washington to Charles W. Anderson, March 28, 1911, in Harlan, *Washington Papers,* 11:46.

108. Booker T. Washington to Oswald Garrison Villard, March 30, 1911, in Harlan, *Washington Papers,* 11:54–55.

109. Washington remained wary, as well. Two months after the assault, Washington was using his influence to deny Du Bois an honor that Du Bois coveted—that of serving as a member of a U.S. commission to Haiti. On this point, see Booker T. Washington to Charles W. Anderson, May 24, 1911, in Harlan, *Washington Papers,* 11:169–70.

110. W. E. B. Du Bois, interview with Charles H. Thompson, Thompson Papers, Howard University. In his conversation with Thompson, in the 1940s, Du Bois expressed the opinion that on a previous occasion Washington's friend Charles W. Anderson had probably taken Washington to a brothel, but when Washington "went back by himself and tried to find the place he got into difficulty."

111. *Crisis* 2 (June 1911): 62–64.

112. *Crisis* 11 (December 1915): 82.

113. Du Bois to Robert Russa Moton, November 21, 1910, in Harlan, *Washington Papers,* 10:480–81.

114. Robert Russa Moton to Booker T. Washington, March 29, 1911, in Harlan, *Washington Papers,* 1:53.

115. Du Bois to the Chairman of the Board, the Treasurer, and the Secretary, December 14, 1915, Spingarn Papers, Yale University.

116. Roy Nash to J. E. Spingarn, August 15, 1916, Spingarn Papers, Howard University.

117. Roy Nash to J. E. Spingarn, with enclosure, August 16, 1916, Spingarn Papers, Howard University.

118. W. E. B. Du Bois, "The Amenia Conference" (pamphlet, 1925; reprinted in David Levering Lewis, ed., *W. E. B. Du Bois: A Reader* [New York: Henry Holt, 1995]), 383; Circular in the J. E. Spingarn Papers, Howard University.

119. "Purpose of the Conference," handwritten notes by J. E. Spingarn, Spingarn Papers, Howard University.

120. Du Bois, "Amenia Conference," 385.

121. Ibid., 384.

122. Ibid., 385–86.

123. Emmett J. Scott to J. E. Spingarn, September 6, 1916, Spingarn Papers, Howard University; Fred R. Moore to Robert Russa Moton, September 1, 1916, Robert R. Moton Papers, Tuskegee Institute; *New York Age,* September 14, 1916; Mary Church Terrell, statement in Amenia Autograph Album, J. E. Spingarn Papers, Howard University.

124. Mrs. W. Scott Brown Jr. to J. E. Spingarn, September 10, 1916, Spingarn Papers, Howard University.

125. Du Bois, "Amenia Conference," 383. For an informative and detailed ac-

count of the conference see Allen B. Clark, "The Amenia Conference," unpublished seminar paper, 1973, University of Delaware.

126. Eugene D. Levy, *James Weldon Johnson: Black Leader, Black Voice* (Chicago: University of Chicago Press, 1973).

127. Roy Nash to Kathryn M. Johnson, August 15, 1916, Du Bois Papers, reel 5, frame 0525; Johnson to Arthur B. Spingarn, late July or early August 1916, NAACP Papers; Johnson to Roy Nash, July 31, 1916, NAACP Papers; Johnson to Nash, August 17, 1916, NAACP Papers; Nash to Johnson, August 30, 1916, NAACP Papers; Arthur B. Spingarn to Johnson, September 30, 1916, NAACP Papers.

128. John Hope to J. E. Spingarn, October 21, 1916, Spingarn Papers, Howard University; Du Bois to John Hope, January 26, 1916, Du Bois Papers, reel 5, frame 0426; Hope to Du Bois, February 2, 1916, Du Bois Papers, reel 5, frame 0427; Davis, *Clashing of the Soul*, 212–13; Ridgely Torrence, *The Story of John Hope* (New York: Macmillan, 1948), 198–99.

129. J. E. Spingarn to NAACP Officers, on John Hope to J. E. Spingarn, October 21, 1916, Spingarn Papers, Howard University.

130. Roy Nash to J. E. Spingarn, October 27, 1916, Spingarn Papers, Howard University.

131. Ibid.

132. Levy, *James Weldon Johnson*, 179; Johnson, *Along This Way*, 203.

133. James Weldon Johnson to Du Bois, February 4, 1915, Du Bois Papers, reel 4, frame 0550.

134. J. E. Spingarn to James Weldon Johnson, October 28, 1916; and Johnson to Spingarn, November 5, 1916, James Weldon Johnson Papers, Yale University; Levy, *James Weldon Johnson*, 169–70.

135. Du Bois to James Weldon Johnson, November 1, 1916, in Aptheker, *Correspondence of Du Bois*, 1:219–20.

136. Ibid.

137. Levy, *James Weldon Johnson*, 186.

138. Ibid., 195; Lewis, *W. E. B. Du Bois*, 1:481.

139. J. E. Spingarn to James Weldon Johnson, October 28, 1916, Johnson Papers.

140. August Meier and Elliott M. Rudwick, *From Plantation to Ghetto* (New York: Hill and Wang, 1966), 190.

141. Carl Matthews, "After Booker T. Washington: The Search for a New Negro Leadership, 1915–1925," Ph.D. diss., University of Virginia, 1971, chapter 1 and passim.

142. Glenn Porter, *The Rise of Big Business, 1860–1910* (Arlington Heights, Ill.: AHM Publishing Corporation, 1973), 19.

143. Johnson, *Along This Way*, 203.

144. Du Bois, *Dusk of Dawn*, 290, 255, v.

145. J. E. Spingarn to Du Bois, October 24, 1914, Du Bois Papers, reel 4, frame 1075.

146. Mary White Ovington to J. E. Spingarn, November 7, 1914, Spingarn Papers, Howard University.

147. Levy, *James Weldon Johnson*, 295.

148. Ross, *J. E. Spingarn*, 28–29.

149. Levy, *James Weldon Johnson*, 70, 67–70, 111, 320.

150. For a different assessment of the matters discussed in this chapter, see Rudwick, *W. E. B. Du Bois*, and Broderick, *W. E. B. Du Bois*. Rudwick basically sided with Villard in the dispute over editorial independence at the *Crisis* and with Washington on the need to conciliate the white South (although not on the value of concentrating so much power and influence at Tuskegee). Rudwick also says Du Bois was "self-absorbed" and "pontificated monthly" in his editorials for the *Crisis*. See Rudwick, chapters 6 and 7 and pp. 166 and 153. Both Broderick and Rudwick are quite critical—hypercritical, I think—in assessing Du Bois's personality. Rudwick emphasizes Du Bois's "serious personality defect[s]": his "snobbery," his "habitual little 'digs' at antagonists," his "obvious weakness as an organizational leader," and his "conspicuous fondness for grand conferences." And Broderick mentions Du Bois's "stubbornness, arrogance, and irresponsibility," saying that Du Bois "magnified every personal difference into a question of principle" and that "his failure to work in harness with his colleagues threatened to destroy" the NAACP. See Rudwick, 133, 132, 143; and Broderick, 100, 99. Rudwick and Broderick's assessment of Du Bois's cultural pluralism also differs from my judgment, with Broderick characterizing Du Bois's pluralism as "Negro racism" (p. 101) and Rudwick calling it racial chauvinism (p. 149).

4. Du Bois and the First World War

1. Du Bois, *Dusk of Dawn*, 245.

2. Ibid., 255; Du Bois, *Autobiography*, 274.

3. W. H. Crogman to Du Bois, January 29, 1917, reel 5, frame 0865; John Haynes Holmes to Du Bois, January 24, 1917, reel 5, frame 0949; J. E. Spingarn to Du Bois, December 12, 1916, reel 5, frame 0573; and Mary Church Terrell to Du Bois, January 29, 1917, reel 5, frame 1174, Du Bois Papers.

4. Du Bois to Carrie W. Clifford, January 29, 1917, Du Bois Papers, reel 5, frame 0853.

5. Du Bois to George W. Cook, February 5, 1917, Du Bois Papers, reel 5, frame 0862.

6. Frank Hosmer to Du Bois, February 8, 1918, Du Bois Papers, reel 6, frame 0561. In appreciation, Du Bois told Hosmer: "I owe more to you, more than to any single person, the fact that I got started toward the higher training in my youth" (Du Bois to Hosmer, February 16, 1918, Du Bois Papers, reel 6, frame 0564).

7. G. H. McClellan to Du Bois, February 21, 1918, Du Bois Papers, reel 6, frame 0782.

8. Maud Cuney Hare to Du Bois, February 28, 1918, Du Bois Papers, reel 6, frame 0448.

9. George A. Towns to Du Bois, February 20, 1918, reel 7, frame 0057; Du Bois to Towns, March 2, 1918, reel 7, frame 0059; Bessie Taylor Page to Du Bois, February 21, 1918, reel 6, frame 1081; and Sadie Conyers to Du Bois, February 4, 1917, reel 5, frame 0856, Du Bois Papers.

10. J. Max Barber to Du Bois, February 23, 1918, reel 6, frame 0025; and Mrs. N. J. Burroughs to Du Bois, February 1918, reel 6, frame 0147, Du Bois Papers.

11. Francis J. Grimke to Du Bois, February 8, 1918, Du Bois Papers, reel 6, frame 0434.

12. J. Max Barber to Du Bois, February 23, 1918, Du Bois Papers, reel 6, frame 0025.

13. L. M. Hershaw to Du Bois, February 24, 1918, Du Bois Papers, reel 6, frame 0497.

14. H. A. Hurst to Du Bois, February 21, 1918, Du Bois Papers, reel 6, frame 0573.

15. Moorfield Storey to John R. Shillady, February 23, 1918, Du Bois Papers, reel 6, frame 1269.

16. A. W. Ricks to Du Bois, February 16, 1918, Du Bois Papers, reel 6, frame 1146.

17. Hallie S. Brow to Du Bois, February 22, 1918, reel 6, frame 1145; Lewis Caldwell to Du Bois, reel 6, frame 0161; and Laura Killingsworth to Du Bois, February 20, 1918, reel 6, frame 0696, Du Bois Papers.

18. Estelle Matthews to Du Bois, January 28, 1918, Du Bois Papers, reel 6, frame 0814.

19. Hofstadter, *American Political Tradition,* 276.

20. W. E. B. Du Bois, "The African Roots of War," *Atlantic Monthly* 115 (May 1915): 709, 710.

21. W. E. B. Du Bois, "The World War and the Color Line," *Crisis* 9 (November 1914): 28–30.

22. Broderick, *W. E. B. Du Bois,* 107.

23. Du Bois, "African Roots of War," 711.

24. *Crisis* 14 (June 1916): 59.

25. Du Bois, "World War and the Color Line," 29.

26. Ibid.

27. *Crisis* 14 (June 1917): 59.

28. *Crisis* 16 (June 1918): 60.

29. *Crisis* 16 (September 1918): 217.

30. Du Bois to M. O. Zimmerman, March 31, 1908, Du Bois Papers, reel 3, frame 0784; Du Bois, *Dusk of Dawn,* 233.

31. Du Bois to M. O. Zimmerman, March 31, 1908, Du Bois Papers, reel 3, frame 0784.

32. John Hope Franklin, *From Slavery to Freedom* (New York: Alfred A. Knopf, 1974), 334.

33. Du Bois, *Dusk of Dawn,* 235.

34. Nancy Weiss, "The Negro and the New Freedom: Fighting Wilsonian Segregation," *Political Science Quarterly* 84 (May 1969): 61–79; George S. Osborn, "The Problem of the Negro in Government, 1913," *The Historian* 23 (May 1961): 330–48; Kathleen L. Wogelmuth, "Woodrow Wilson and Federal Segregation," *Journal of Negro History* 44 (April 1959): 158–73; and Wogelmuth, "Woodrow Wilson's Appointment Policy and the Negro," *Journal of Southern History* 24 (November 1958): 457–71.

35. *Crisis* 9 (February 1915): 181.

36. *New York Age,* September 28, 1916.

37. Du Bois, *Dusk of Dawn,* 248.

38. W. E. B. Du Bois, "A History of the Black Man in the Great War," *Crisis* 18 (June 1919): 64–65.

39. *Crisis* 13 (April 1917): 270.

40. *Crisis* 14 (June 1917): 60.

41. *Cleveland Gazette,* March 24, 1917, and March 10, 1917.

42. Ross, *J. E. Spingarn,* 84–97.

43. Kwame Anthony Appiah and Henry Lewis Gates, eds., *Africana: The Encyclopedia of the African and African American Experience* (New York: Basic Civitas Books, 1999), 2028.

44. Charles Young to Du Bois, June 20, 1917 (enclosed with Du Bois to Walter Lippmann, June 29, 1917), reel 5, frame 0984; and Ada Young to Du Bois, August 2, 1917, reel 5, frame 1240, Du Bois Papers.

45. Du Bois to Walter Lippmann, June 29, 1917, Du Bois Papers, reel 5, frame 0984; *Crisis* 16 (May 1918): 7–8.

46. *New York Age,* December 17, 1917, November 22, 1917, July 6, 1918, March 1, 1919, December 8, 1919.

47. *Crisis* 16 (May 1918): 114. However, General C. C. Ballou did see to it that charges were pressed against the theater manager, who was convicted and fined ten dollars.

48. *Crisis* 15 (January 1918): 114.

49. "Let us raise our hats to Newton Diehl Baker, Secretary of War. He has not done everything we could wish, but he accomplished so much more than President Wilson or any other member of this administration that he deserves all praise. He has carried out the draft with absolute fairness. . . . He has put black troops in nearly every cantonment. He has commissioned nearly 700 Negro officers. . . . He has sent black troops to the front. He has made no discrimination in pay. . . . And he has crowned his well-doing by appointing an official advisor who belongs to the Negro race" (*Crisis* 15 [December 1917]: 61–62).

50. *Crisis* 14 (May 1917): 23.

51. *Crisis* 15 (December 1917): 77.

52. *Crisis* 14 (June 1917): 62.

53. Du Bois, *Dusk of Dawn,* 255, 253.

54. Ibid., 255, 256.

55. *Crisis* 16 (July 1918): 111.

56. Petition of thirty-one black editors, written by Du Bois and published in *Crisis* 16 (August 1918): 163–64.

57. Byron Gunner to Du Bois, July 25, 1918, in Aptheker, *Correspondence of Du Bois,* 1:228; *Boston Guardian,* quoted in the *Cleveland Gazette,* July 27, 1918.

58. Lewis, *W. E. B. Du Bois,* 1:556.

59. *Cleveland Gazette,* August 24, 1918.

60. *Cleveland Gazette,* December 7, 1918, September 14, 1918, December 7, 1918.

61. *Cleveland Gazette,* July 27, 1918.

62. L. M. Hershaw to Du Bois, July 30, 1918, Du Bois Papers, reel 6, frame 0501. For the official resolution of the Washington Branch, asserting that "Close Ranks" was "inconsistent with the work and spirit of the Association," see *Crisis* 16 (September 1918): 218.

63. F. E. Young to Du Bois, August 5, 1918, Du Bois Papers, reel 6, frame 1039.

64. Charles Studin to Du Bois, May 1, 1918, Du Bois Papers, reel 6, frame 0925.

65. John Price Jones and Merrick Hollister, *The German Secret Service in America* (Boston: Small, Maynard, 1918), frontispiece. For more on the effort to combat "German subversion," see Mark Ellis, *Race, War, and Surveillance: African Americans and the United States Government during World War I* (Bloomington: Indiana University Press, 2001).

66. Mark Ellis, "'Closing Ranks' and 'Seeking Honors': W. E. B. Du Bois in World War I," *Journal of American History* 79 (June 1992): 102–5.

67. J. E. Spingarn to Amy Spingarn, n.d., Spingarn Papers, Howard University; Lewis, *W. E. B. Du Bois*, 1:553.

68. J. E. Spingarn to Du Bois, July 16, 1918, Du Bois Papers, reel 6, frame 0977.

69. Du Bois to John Hope, July 12, 1918, Du Bois Papers, reel 6, frame 0534.

70. William A. Byrd, "Who Is Our Leader?" *Cleveland Gazette,* September 14, 1918.

71. *Cleveland Gazette,* July 27, 1918.

72. Lewis, *W. E. B. Du Bois,* 1:555.

73. Du Bois to L. M. Hershaw, August 5, 1918, reel 6, frame 0502; and Du Bois to F. E. Young, reel 6, frame 1040, Du Bois Papers.

74. Archibald S. Pinkett to Du Bois, July 11, 1919, Du Bois Papers, reel 6, frame 1127.

75. Broderick, *W. E. B. Du Bois,* 121; Rudwick, *W. E. B. Du Bois,* 203–4.

76. Ellis, "'Closing Ranks' and 'Seeking Honors,'" 98 and passim; Lewis, *W. E. B. Du Bois,* 1:555; William Jordan, "'The Damnable Dilemma': African-American Accommodation and Protest During World War I," *Journal of American History* 81 (1995): 1580. In his biography of John Hope, Leroy Davis sided with Jordan; see *Clashing of the Soul,* 389 n. 59.

77. Du Bois, *Dusk of Dawn,* 290.

78. Du Bois to NAACP Board of Directors, July 2, 1918, reel 6, frame 0952; Du Bois to L. M. Hershaw, August 5, 1918, reel 6, frame 0502; and Du Bois to F. E. Young, August 8, 1918, reel 6, frame 1040, Du Bois Papers. This sort of financial arrangement was not unusual at the time.

79. Minutes of the Meeting of the NAACP Board of Directors, July 8, 1918, Du Bois Papers, reel 6, frame 0964; Lewis, *W. E. B. Du Bois,* 1:558.

80. Du Bois to John Hope, July 12, 1918, Du Bois Papers, reel 6, frame 0534.

81. Du Bois to J. E. Spingarn, July 12, 1918, Du Bois Papers, reel 6, frame 0976.

82. Du Bois to J. E. Spingarn, July 9, 1918, Du Bois Papers, reel 6, frame 0970.

83. J. E. Spingarn to Du Bois, July 16, 1918, Du Bois Papers, reel 6, frame 0977.

84. Du Bois to J. E. Spingarn, July 12, 1918, Du Bois Papers, reel 6, frame 0976.

85. Mary White Ovington to Du Bois, July 10, 1918, reel 6, frame 0972; and Du Bois to Mary White Ovington, July 11, 1918, reel 6, frame 00975, Du Bois Papers.

86. Du Bois to John Shillady and Charles Studin, July 10, 1918, Du Bois Papers, reel 6, frame 0400.

87. Lewis, W. E. B. Du Bois, 1:559–60; Ellis, "'Closing Ranks' and 'Seeking Honors,'" 113–18; Ross, J. E. Spingarn, 101–2. As noted, shortly before the army made its decision, Du Bois told Mary White Ovington that he had "decided not to go to Washington." After the army made its decision, however, Du Bois modified his statement. "In case the commission had been offered," he wrote to F. M. Young, "it would have been necessary for me . . . to take the commission, as the call of the country at this time is paramount upon each citizen." Du Bois made the same point in another letter to L. M. Hershaw: "I should probably have accepted the commission . . . but the General Staff finally decided not to establish the bureau. The offer, had, as you may be sure, absolutely nothing to do with the editorial utterances in The Crisis" (Du Bois to Ovington, July 10, 1918, reel 6, frame 00975; Du Bois to Hershaw, August 5, 1918, reel 6, frame 0502, Du Bois Papers).

88. Crisis 16 (August 1918): 164–65.

89. Crisis 18 (May 1919): 7.

90. Fox, Guardian of Boston, 224–26.

91. New York Age, December 7, 1918.

92. Crisis 17 (January 1919): 112.

93. W. E. B. Du Bois, "The Pan-African Congress," Crisis 17 (April 1919): 271–74.

94. Chandler Owen to Mary White Ovington, April 11, 1919, NAACP Papers.

95. Du Bois to New York Age, 1919, Du Bois Papers, reel 7, frame 1160.

96. Wilkins, Standing Fast, 52; Cleveland Gazette, February 8, 1919.

97. Crisis 17 (February 1919): 173 (italics added).

98. Du Bois, Memorandum in re African Colonies, 1918, Du Bois Papers, reel 7, frame 0225.

99. Du Bois, "The Pan-African Congress," 273.

100. Crisis 17 (February 1919): 165.

101. Du Bois, fragmentary draft of a resolution for the Pan-African Congress, 1919, Du Bois Papers, reel 8, frame 0071.

102. Du Bois, Memorandum in re African Colonies, 1918, Du Bois Papers, reel 7, frame 0225.

103. Du Bois to New York Age, 1919, Du Bois Papers, reel 7, frame 1160.

104. Crisis 18 (May 1919): 8.

105. Du Bois, Dusk of Dawn, 262. There were three additional Pan-African Congresses during the 1920s and another after World War II.

106. Crisis 17 (November 1918): 10.

107. Crisis 18 (July 1919): 128.

108. W. E. B. Du Bois, "The Black Man in the Revolution of 1914–1918," Crisis 17 (March 1919): 219; Du Bois, "History of the Black Man in the Great War," 64–65.

109. Du Bois, "History of the Black Man in the Great War," 65. For more on these "laborers in uniform," see Arthur E. Barbeau and Florette Henri, The Unknown Soldiers: Black American Troops in World War I (Philadelphia: Temple University Press, 1974), chapter 6.

110. Du Bois, "Black Man in the Revolution of 1914–1918," 220.

111. Du Bois, "History of the Black Man in the Great War," 73; Barbeau and Henri, *Unknown Soldiers,* chapter 7.

112. Newton D. Baker, Press Release Statement with Regard to the 368th Infantry Regiment, n.d.; Baker to Moton, November 1, 1919; and Moton to Baker, December 3, 1919, Moton Papers; *New York Age,* June 21, 1919, and November 15, 1919; Barbeau and Henri, *Unknown Soldiers,* chapter 8.

113. Du Bois, "History of the Black Man in the Great War," 70.

114. Allen J. Greer to Senator Kenneth D. McKellar, December 6, 1918, Du Bois Papers, reel 6, frame 0430.

115. Allen J. Greer, Memorandum, August 21, 1918, Moton Papers; Barbeau and Henri, *Unknown Soldiers,* 141–42.

116. Barbeau and Henri, *Unknown Soldiers,* 100, 106, 108.

117. French Military Mission, "Secret Information Concerning Black American Troops," August 7, 1918, in W. E. B. Du Bois, ed., "Documents of the War," *Crisis* 18 (May 1919): 16–17.

118. Barbeau and Henri, *Unknown Soldiers,* 52–55; F. P. Boas, "The Relative Prevalence of Syphilis among Negroes and Whites," *Social Hygiene* 1 (1914–1915): 616; George Walker, *Venereal Disease in the American Expeditionary Forces* (Baltimore: Medical Standard Book Company, 1922), 1, 101, 122–23, and passim.

119. Robert R. Moton, "Principal Tells of His Investigations Overseas," *New York Age,* April 19, 1919.

120. Charles H. Williams, "The Matter of 'Rape' in the 92nd Division, AEF," April 5, 1919, manuscript in Moton Papers.

121. *New York Age,* April 19, 1919; Barbeau and Henri, *Unknown Soldiers,* 144.

122. Matthews, "After Booker T. Washington," 142.

123. *Crisis* 18 (May 1919): 13.

124. *Crisis* 18 (July 1919): 128.

125. Ibid., 129.

126. *Crisis* 18 (May 1919): 14.

127. *Crisis* 18 (August 1919): 179.

128. Ovington, *Portraits in Color,* 64.

129. W. E. B. Du Bois, "Moton of Hampton and Tuskegee," *Phylon* 1 (1940): 351.

130. *Crisis* 9 (April 1915): 310.

131. Du Bois, "Moton of Hampton and Tuskegee," 351.

132. Robert Russa Moton, *Finding a Way Out: An Autobiography* (Garden City: Doubleday, Page, 1920), 12, 3–5, 8–11.

133. Ibid., 32–33.

134. Ibid., 61–62.

135. *New York Age,* December 23, 1915, and December 9, 1915.

136. *New York Age,* December 23, 1915, and December 2, 1915.

137. Matthews, "After Booker T. Washington," 204, 194–95. For a different emphasis, see Claude A. Barnet, "A Southern Statesman," in William Hardin Hughes and Frederick D. Patterson, *Robert Russa Moton of Hampton and Tuskegee* (Chapel Hill: University of North Carolina Press, 1956).

138. Principal's Annual Report, 1922–1923, Moton Papers.

139. *Baltimore Afro-American,* quoted in *Crisis* 12 (August 1916): 187; *Crisis* 12 (July 1916): 136.

140. For excerpts from the press coverage, see *Crisis* 12 (August 1916): 185–87.

141. *Crisis* 12 (July 1916): 136, 137.

142. Davis, *Clashing of the Soul,* 242–46.

143. Robert R. Moton, Report to Newton D. Baker, n.d.; Baker to Moton, December 3, 1919; Baker, Press Release Statement with Regard to the 368th Infantry Regiment, n.d.; and Moton to Robert S. Abbott, February 10, 1919, Moton Papers; Moton, *Finding a Way Out,* 261.

144. Moton, *Finding a Way Out,* 255–56; Memorandum of Lt. Col. R. H. Leavitt, August 22, 1919, Moton Papers; Williams, "Matter of 'Rape' in the 92nd Division." For Moton's own report on his activities in France, see the *New York Age,* April 19, 1919.

145. Robert R. Moton to Woodrow Wilson, June 15, 1918, and August 8, 1919, Moton Papers.

146. *Crisis* 18 (May 1919): 9; *Crisis* 18 (July 1919): 128–29.

147. Moton, *Finding a Way Out,* 262, 263; *New York Age,* April 12, 1919.

148. *New York Age,* April 12, 1919, and August 25, 1919.

149. *Crisis* 18 (May 1919): 9.

150. *New York Age,* 17 May 1919.

151. *Crisis* 18 (May 1919): 10.

152. Thomas Jesse Jones to Robert R. Moton, June 10, 1919; and Lester A. Walton to Albon Holsey, May 31, 1919, Moton Papers; *Indianapolis Freeman,* February 15, 1919; *New York Age,* May 17, 1919.

153. Robert R. Moton to Du Bois, July 5, 1919, Moton Papers.

154. Matthews, "After Booker T. Washington," 194.

155. Robert R. Moton to Du Bois, January 19, 1919, Moton Papers.

156. Robert R. Moton to Robert S. Abbott, February 10, 1919, Moton Papers.

157. Robert R. Moton to Fred R. Moore, July 22, 1918; and Lester A. Walton to Robert S. Abbott, May 10, 1919, Moton Papers.

158. *Crisis* 18 (May 1919): 10.

159. *Crisis* 18 (July 1919): 185.

160. Albon Holsey, Biographical Sketch of Emmett J. Scott, 1917, Emmett J. Scott Papers, Morgan State College.

161. Louis R. Harlan, "Emmett Jay Scott," in Rayford W. Logan and Michael R. Winston, eds., *Dictionary of American Negro Biography* (New York: W. W. Norton, 1982), 550.

162. Emmett J. Scott to Roscoe Conkling Bruce, January 5, 1916, Scott Papers; Robert R. Moton to Seth Low, August 14, 1916, Moton Papers.

163. Emmett J. Scott to Charles W. Anderson, September 15, 1916, Scott Papers.

164. Emmett J. Scott to Roscoe Conkling Bruce, January 5, 1916, Scott Papers; Matthews, "After Booker T. Washington," 47–50.

165. *New York Age,* July 26, 1919.

166. *New York Age,* May 24, 1919, and July 26, 1919.

167. Emmett J. Scott to Fred R. Moore, *New York Age,* July 26, 1919.

168. Emmett J. Scott to Robert E. Jones, May 3, 1919, Scott Papers.

169. Emmett J. Scott to E. W. D. Jones, May 23, 1919, Scott Papers.

170. Emmett J. Scott to John Mitchell Jr., May 23, 1919, Scott Papers.

171. Neval H. Thomas to Emmett J. Scott, May 3, 1919, Scott Papers.

172. Annotation on copy of Neval H. Thomas to Emmett J. Scott, May 3, 1919, which was enclosed in Du Bois to J. E. Spingarn, June 18, 1919, Spingarn Papers, Howard University.

173. Du Bois, "Moton of Hampton and Tuskegee," 351.

174. Emmett J. Scott to Charles M. Thomas, February 24, 1923, Scott Papers. In another letter, Scott mentioned "how appreciative Howard is in counterdistinction to the deal I received down there [Tuskegee]" (Scott to J. B. Ramsey, December 31, 1923, Scott Papers).

175. Author's conversation with Walter Fischer, July 10, 1974.

5. Du Bois and Marcus Garvey

1. Franklin, *From Slavery to Freedom,* 357–59; Robert L. Zangrando, *The NAACP Crusade against Lynching, 1909–1950* (Philadelphia: Temple University Press, 1980), 6; Arthur I. Waskow, *From Race Riot to Sit-In: 1919 and the 1960s* (New York: Anchor Books, 1967); William M. Tuttle, *Race Riot: Chicago in the Red Summer of 1919* (New York: Atheneum, 1970).

2. *Messenger* 2 (October 1919): 12.

3. Claude McKay, *A Long Way from Home* (1937; reprint, New York: Arno Press, 1969), 31; McKay, *Harlem Shadows: The Poems of Claude McKay* (New York: Harcourt, Brace, 1922), 53.

4. Judith Stein, *The World of Marcus Garvey: Race and Class in Modern Society* (Baton Rouge: Louisiana State University Press, 1986), 24–25.

5. Marcus Garvey, "The Negro's Greatest Enemy," *Current History* 18 (September 1923): 952; Lawrence W. Levine, "Marcus Garvey and the Politics of Revitalization," in John Hope Franklin and August Meier, eds., *Black Leaders of the Twentieth Century* (Urbana: University of Illinois Press, 1982), 106–7.

6. Amy Jacques Garvey, *Garvey and Garveyism* (1970; reprint, New York: Octagon Books, 1986), 7.

7. E. David Cronon, *Black Moses: The Story of Marcus Garvey and the Universal Negro Improvement Association* (Madison: University of Wisconsin Press, 1962), 15.

8. Stein, *World of Marcus Garvey,* 31–32.

9. Marcus Garvey to Robert R. Moton, February 29, 1916, in Robert A. Hill et al., eds., *The Marcus Garvey and UNIA Papers* (9 vols. Berkeley and Los Angeles: University of California Press, 1983–1996), 1:178.

10. Hill, *Garvey Papers,* 6:216–17.

11. See W. E. B. Du Bois, "Back to Africa," *Century Magazine* 105 (February 1923): 540–41; Jacques Garvey, *Garvey and Garveyism,* 12–13; and Carl N. Degler, *Neither Black nor White* (New York: Macmillan, 1971), 105 and passim.

12. Amy Jacques Garvey, ed., *The Philosophy and Opinions of Marcus Garvey* (Dover, Mass.: Majority Press, 1986; reprint of a book first published in two volumes in 1923 and 1925), 127.

13. Booker T. Washington to Marcus Garvey, April 27, 1915, April 12, 1915, and September 27, 1915, in Harlan, *Washington Papers*, 13:284, 261, 372–73; Garvey to Washington, September 8, 1914, and September 11, 1915, in Hill, *Garvey Papers*, 1:66–67, 141.

14. Tony Martin, *Race First: The Ideological and Organizational Struggles of Marcus Garvey and the Universal Negro Improvement Association* (Westport, Conn.: Greenwood Press, 1976), 37.

15. Ibid., 69.

16. Levine, "Marcus Garvey and the Politics of Revitalization," 124.

17. Jacques Garvey, *Philosophy and Opinions of Marcus Garvey*, 83.

18. Hill, *Garvey Papers*, 4:59–60.

19. Although Garvey emphasized the achievements of the blacks of antiquity, he also celebrated the Zulu warriors who had fought against British rule, the Haitian rebellion against French colonialism, and the achievements of the Moorish and Ethiopian empires.

20. Jacques Garvey, *Philosophy and Opinions of Marcus Garvey*, 82–83.

21. Mary Lefkowitz, *Not Out of Africa* (New York: Basic Books, 1996), 132; Jacques Garvey, *Philosophy and Opinions of Marcus Garvey*, 82.

22. *New York Times*, August 3, 1920, 7.

23. John Henrik Clarke, ed., *Marcus Garvey and the Vision of Africa* (New York: Random House, 1974), 220–21; Cronon, *Black Moses*, 66.

24. Roi Ottley, *New World A-Coming* (Boston: Houghton Mifflin, 1943), 76.

25. Martin, *Race First*, 44.

26. *New York Times*, August 3, 1920, 7.

27. Cronon, *Black Moses*, 129.

28. Levine, "Marcus Garvey and the Politics of Revitalization," 127.

29. Cronon, *Black Moses*, 56; Ovington, *Portraits in Color*, 22.

30. In 1923 Du Bois reckoned that Garvey "had some 80,000 members in his organization, and perhaps 20,000 or 30,000 were paying regularly thirty-five cents a month into his chest" (Du Bois, "Back to Africa," 543).

31. Du Bois, interview with Charles Mowbray White, August 22, 1920, in Hill, *Garvey Papers*, 2:620–21; Lewis, *W. E. B. Du Bois*, 2:2, 55, 62, 73.

32. Levine, "Marcus Garvey and the Politics of Revitalization," 107; Du Bois, "Back to Africa," 541; James Weldon Johnson, *Black Manhattan* (1930; reprint, New York: Atheneum, 1968), 253.

33. Cronon, *Black Moses*, 81–84.

34. Martin, *Race First*, 160, 157–60; Cronon, *Black Moses*, 104; W. E. B. Du Bois, "The Black Star Line," *Crisis* 22 (September 1922): 212.

35. Du Bois to Marcus Garvey, July 22, 1920, in Aptheker, *Correspondence of Du Bois*, 1:245–46.

36. James Burghardt to Du Bois, August 21, 1919, reel 7, frame 686; and Du Bois to James Burghardt, August 27, 1919, reel 7, frame 687, Du Bois Papers.

37. Hill, *Garvey Papers*, 4:381n.

38. W. E. B. Du Bois, "Marcus Garvey," *Crisis* 21 (December 1920): 60.

39. W. E. B. Du Bois, "Marcus Garvey," *Crisis* 21 (January 1921): 112, 113, 115.

40. Report by Special Agent P-138, January 4, 1921, in Hill, *Garvey Papers*, 3:125. Special Agent P-138 was Herbert Boulin, a friend of Garvey's and the own-

er of a company that manufactured Negro dolls. For more on the government's surveillance of Garvey, see Martin, *Race First*, 174–214; and Theodore Kornweibel, *Seeing Red: Federal Campaigns against Black Militancy, 1919–1925* (Bloomington: Indiana University Press, 1998).

41. See Hill, *Garvey Papers*, 4:753–54 and 3:xxxvii; and correspondence in the Du Bois Papers, reel 8, frames 115, 1231, 1284, and 1168; and reel 9, frame 160. Also see Du Bois to Department of State, August 3, 1922, and Du Bois to Wilbur J. Carr, September 6, 1922, National Archives, RG 59, 195.7 (Kanawha).

42. See Garvey's "Address Denouncing W. E. B. Du Bois," published in the *Negro World* on April 5, 1920, in Hill, *Garvey Papers*, 1:394–400. Garvey's criticism forced the Pan-African Congress to modify its stance. In 1921, Du Bois told a reporter for *La Depeche Coloniale et Maritime* that the congress wanted "autonomous governments to be established everywhere in Africa, where blacks will govern themselves; they will, initially, require guidance, but this guidance must favor the natives and not the interests of the administrative authorities" (Hill, *Garvey Papers*, 9:178).

43. Hill, *Garvey Papers*, 3:544.

44. Ibid., 5:438.

45. Rudwick, *W. E. B. Du Bois*, 228.

46. Hill, *Garvey Papers*, 5:438, 439.

47. Hill, *Garvey Papers*, 6:217, 4:79, 7:631, 4:79.

48. Ibid., 7:285, 5:205, 6:167.

49. W. E. B. Du Bois, "The Social Equality of Whites and Blacks," *Crisis* 21 (November 1920): 18; W. E. B. Du Bois, "Social Equality and the Intermarriage of Races," typescript in Du Bois Papers, reel 82, frame 0017.

50. Du Bois, "Social Equality of Whites and Blacks," 18.

51. Du Bois, "Conservation of Races," 4, 7; Du Bois, "Social Equality of Whites and Blacks," 18.

52. Elliott M. Rudwick, "Du Bois versus Garvey: Race Propagandists at War," *Journal of Negro Education* 28 (fall 1959): 423, 427; Hill, *Garvey Papers*, 6:167, 97; 5:216.

53. *Negro World*, January 1, 1921, reprinted in the *Baltimore Afro-American*, January 7, 1921.

54. Charles S. Johnson, "After Garvey—What?" *Opportunity* 5 (August 1923): 233.

55. Hill, *Garvey Papers*, 9:101–2, 6:351–52.

56. *Messenger* 4 (August 1922): 470.

57. Theodore Kornweibel, *No Crystal Stair: Black Life and the* Messenger, *1917–1923* (Westport, Conn.: Greenwood Press, 1975), 169.

58. *Messenger* 5 (March 1923): 638, 648.

59. Anonymous to Department of State, August 11, 1919, National Archives, RG 60, 198940. The secretary was Amy Ashwood, whom Garvey would later marry. When Ashwood and Garvey were divorced after a short marriage, other correspondents recommended that Garvey be prosecuted for traveling across state lines with Amy Jacques, who would become the second Mrs. Marcus Garvey. See William Smith to Charles Evans Hughes, July 1, 1921, and Charles Latham to Hughes, August 24, 1921, National Archives, RG 59, 811.108 G 191/24; and Martin, *Race First*, 189.

60. Chandler Owen et al. to Harry M. Daugherty, January 15, 1923, National Archives, RG 60, 198940.

61. Chandler Owen, Robert S. Abbott, and George W. Harris were the editors of the *Messenger,* the *Chicago Defender,* and the *New York News,* respectively. Dr. Julia P. Coleman was the president of a cosmetics company. Harry H. Pace and John E. Nail were with the Urban League, and Robert W. Bagnall and William Pickens with the NAACP.

62. Du Bois to Charles Evans Hughes, January 5, 1923; and Du Bois to W. A. Domingo, January 18, 1923, in Aptheker, *Correspondence of Du Bois,* 1:260–61, 263–64.

63. *New York Age,* August 14, 1920.

64. Jacques Garvey, *Philosophy and Opinions of Marcus Garvey,* 308, 305, 303.

65. Kornweibel, *No Crystal Stair,* 147–48.

66. Hill, *Garvey Papers,* 2:609–12.

67. This was a matter of emphasis. In its official Declaration of Rights, the UNIA protested against "the wrongs and injustices [that Negroes] are suffering at the hands of their white brethren" and "demand[ed] and insist[ed] upon" equal rights. See Theodore G. Vincent, *Black Power and the Garvey Movement* (Berkeley: Ramparts Press, 1971), 257–63. However, Theodore Kornweibel has noted that, although "the rhetoric of Declaration of Rights was noble enough, . . . it was not backed up by the enthusiasm of top leadership in actively developing strategies to deal with lynching, forced segregation, and similar indignities" (*No Crystal Stair,* 154).

68. *New York Age,* August 14, 1920.

69. Chandler Owen et al. to Harry M. Daugherty, January 15, 1923, National Archives, RG 60, 198940. The package was supposedly sent by the Ku Klux Klan but an accompanying note said, "If you are not in favor with your own race movement you can't be with ours." E. David Cronon has noted that "Randolph and other UNIA opponents were inclined to believe that the threat had come from a Negro Garveyite rather than from a white Klansman" (*Black Moses,* 108–9).

70. Martin, *Race First,* 317–19; Stein, *World of Marcus Garvey,* 171–85.

71. Hill, *Garvey Papers,* 1:lxxxii; Cronon, *Black Moses,* 194.

72. Hill, *Garvey Papers,* 5:205, 9:188.

73. Cronon, *Black Moses,* 189.

74. Jacques Garvey, *Philosophy and Opinions of Marcus Garvey,* 71.

75. Ibid., 37–43.

76. Martin, *Race First,* 348–52; Vincent, *Black Power and the Garvey Movement,* 228–29.

77. Martin, *Race First,* 32.

78. *Messenger* 4 (July 1922): 437.

79. Hill, *Garvey Papers,* 5:537–38.

80. Vincent, *Black Power and the Garvey Movement,* 257–63.

81. *Messenger* 4 (July 1922): 437; *Crisis* (May 1924): 9.

82. Cronon, *Black Moses,* 106.

83. Ibid., 190, 189.

84. Du Bois, "Back to Africa," 547.

85. Jacques Garvey, *Garvey and Garveyism,* 100.

86. Cronon, *Black Moses,* 100.

87. Du Bois, "Black Star Line," 210–14; Cronon, *Black Moses,* chapters 4, 5, and passim; Martin, *Race First,* chapter 8 and passim; Marcus Garvey, "Why the Black Star Line Failed," in Clarke, *Marcus Garvey and the Vision of Africa,* 139–49.

88. Johnson, "After Garvey—What?" 232. For excerpts from the trial transcript and discussion of the case, see Jacques Garvey, *Philosophy and Opinions of Marcus Garvey,* 145–216.

89. Cronon, *Black Moses,* 115.

90. Ibid., 117.

91. Ibid., 115.

92. *Garvey v. U.S.,* 4 F. 2d (1925): 975; Jacques Garvey, *Philosophy and Opinions of Marcus Garvey,* 175.

93. Garvey, "Negro's Greatest Enemy," 954, 956, 957. For another statement of this view, see Garvey, "An Answer to His Many Critics," in Clarke, *Marcus Garvey and the Vision of Africa,* 247–52.

94. The demise of the UNIA suggests that, despite Garvey's large personal following, the organization never sank deep roots in the black community. As noted in the text, there were fewer than one hundred thousand dues-paying members of the UNIA, and many of the branch chapters were not active in their locales. Unlike the papers of the NAACP branches, which document an involvement in their communities, the records of the UNIA's branches focus on the speeches and activities of Garvey himself. For the extensive activities of the local branches of the NAACP, see Mark Robert Schneider, *We Return Fighting: The Civil Rights Movement in the Jazz Age* (Boston: Northeastern University Press, 2001), chapter 8. Also see Stein, *World of Marcus Garvey,* 223–47.

95. Du Bois, "Black Star Line," 210, 212.

96. *Crisis* 22 (June 1921): 53; Lewis, *W. E. B. Du Bois,* 2:76–77.

97. *Crisis* 28 (May 1924): 8–9.

98. *Cincinnati Gazette,* June 7, 1924, in Hill, *Garvey Papers,* 5:598–99.

99. Du Bois, *Dusk of Dawn,* 277, 278.

100. Du Bois, *Autobiography,* 273–74.

101. Martin, *Race First;* John White, *Black Leadership in America: From Booker T. Washington to Jesse Jackson* (2d. ed., London: Longman, 1990), 102–3.

102. Lewis, *W. E. B. Du Bois,* 2:152.

103. For a similar view, see George M. Frederickson's review of Lewis, *W. E. B. Du Bois,* vol. 2, *New York Review of Books,* February 8, 2001, 35.

104. Du Bois, "Back to Africa," 546.

105. Ibid., 547.

106. Hill, *Garvey Papers,* 7:628–31.

6. Du Bois and Walter White

1. W. E. B. Du Bois, "The Talented Tenth," in Booker T. Washington, ed., *The Negro Problem* (New York: James Pott, 1903), 33, 75. There are several good books on the Harlem Renaissance. See especially David Levering Lewis, *When Harlem Was in Vogue* (New York: Penguin Books, 1997); Jervis Anderson, *This Was Harlem* (New

York: Farrar, Straus and Giroux, 1982); Nathan Irvin Huggins, *Harlem Renaissance* (New York: Oxford University Press, 1971); and Carole Marks and Diana Edkins, *The Power of Pride* (New York: Crown Publishers, 1999). For a fuller account of Du Bois's ambivalent attitudes toward the Renaissance, see Lewis, *W. E. B. Du Bois,* vol. 2, chapter 5.

2. *Crisis* 1 (April 1911): 21. Du Bois probably was thinking of William Stanley Braithwaite as the poet, Charles W. Chesnutt as the novelist, and himself and Booker T. Washington as two of the essayists.

3. Du Bois, *Dusk of Dawn,* 270; Langston Hughes, *The Big Sea* (1940; reprint, New York: Hill and Wang, 1963), 223; Rampersad, *Art and Imagination,* 189.

4. Lewis, *When Harlem Was in Vogue,* 149.

5. Rampersad, *Art and Imagination,* 198; *Crisis* 38 (July 1931): 230. Du Bois shifted between celebrating art for its own sake and demanding art for uplift. In March 1926 he said "an attitude completely inimical to art" was sometimes behind efforts to suppress "fiction which attempts to picture the lower strata of the race." The key point, Du Bois implied, was whether the depiction was honest, the characters true to life. But seven months later he wrote that "all Art is propaganda and ever must be, despite the wailing of the purists. I stand in utter shamelessness and say that whatever art I have for writing has been used always for propaganda for gaining the right of black folk to love and enjoy. I do not care a damn for any art that is not used for propaganda." See W. E. B. Du Bois, "The Negro in Art," *Crisis* 31 (March 1926): 219; and Du Bois, "Criteria of Negro Art," *Crisis* 33 (October 1926): 290–97.

6. *Crisis* 33 (December 1926): 81–82. Van Vechten was a white writer who was friendly with many blacks.

7. *Crisis* 36 (July 1929): 234.

8. Lewis, *When Harlem Was In Vogue,* 225.

9. On these points, see Du Bois, "Negro in Art," 219; and Broderick, *W. E. B. Du Bois,* 157–60; and Lewis, *W. E. B. Du Bois,* 2:181.

10. Du Bois to Hughes Allison, September 15, 1932, the Du Bois Papers, reel 36, frame 0732.

11. *Crisis* 38 (September 1931): 304; Rampersad, *Art and Imagination,* 197.

12. Arna Bontemps, *100 Years of Negro Freedom* (New York: Dodd, Mead, 1961), 221; Rampersad, *Art and Imagination,* 188.

13. Broderick, *W. E. B. Du Bois,* 159n.

14. *Crisis* 34 (October 1927): 276.

15. For an account of the black college rebellions of the 1920s, see Wolters, *New Negro on Campus.*

16. *New Orleans Times-Democrat,* quoted in "A Blow at Negro Education," *Current Literature* 36 (January–June 1904): 491–92; Senator James K. Vardaman, quoted in Baker, *Following the Color Line,* 247.

17. W. E. B. Du Bois, "Hampton," *Crisis* 15 (November 1917): 10–12; W. E. B. Du Bois, "Hampton Institute," *Crisis* 26 (August 1929): 277–78.

18. "Enrollment in Negro Universities and Colleges," *School and Society* 28 (September 29, 1928): 401–2.

19. "The Strike at Hampton," *Southern Workman* 56 (1927): 569–72; Wolters, *New Negro on Campus,* 259.

20. Robert A. Coles, quoted in the *Baltimore Afro-American,* November 19, 1927.

21. George Foster Peabody to Francis Greenwood Peabody, December 1, 1927, Moton Papers.

22. Wolters, *New Negro on Campus,* chapter 2.

23. W. E. B. Du Bois, "Dilemma of the Negro," *American Mercury* 3 (October 1924): 183.

24. Du Bois, "Diuturni Silenti," 43, 44.

25. W. E. B. Du Bois, "Fisk," *Crisis* 28 (October 1924): 251–52.

26. Wolters, *New Negro on Campus,* 40, 39.

27. Robert McMurdy to Paul Cravath, April 16, 1925, Fayette Avery McKenzie Papers, Tennessee State Archives.

28. Dora Scriber to Alumni, February 14, 1925, Du Bois Papers, reel 15, frame 0447; Wolters, *New Negro on Campus,* 48.

29. Wolters, *New Negro on Campus,* 48–69.

30. Ibid., 39.

31. Du Bois, *Autobiography,* 241.

32. *Crisis* 29 (April 1925): 250.

33. Du Bois to Mrs. M. V. Boutte, December 27, 1927, in Aptheker, *Correspondence of Du Bois,* 1:369–70.

34. Ibid.

35. *Time,* 65 (April 4, 1955), 18.

36. Walter White, *A Man Called White* (1948; reprint, Bloomington: Indiana University Press, 1970), 3–27; Walter White, "Why I Remain a Negro," *Saturday Review* 30 (October 11, 1947): 13–14, 49.

37. White, *Man Called White,* 10–11.

38. Ibid., 11; White, "Why I Remain a Negro," 13.

39. White, *Man Called White,* 27.

40. Ibid., 34.

41. Levy, *James Weldon Johnson,* 224.

42. Arthur B. Spingarn, quoted in White, *Man Called White,* 29.

43. "The White House," *Ebony,* April 1946, 4.

44. Poppy Cannon, *A Gentle Knight: My Husband, Walter White* (New York: Rinehart, 1952), 17.

45. E. J. Kahn, "Profile II," *New Yorker* 24 (September 11, 1948): 38.

46. Ibid., 39. The incident was humorous, but the general situation in Tulsa was grim. A scholarly study concluded that 75 people lost their lives in the rioting, and White estimated that 50 whites and perhaps 150–200 black people were killed. See Scott Ellsworth, *Death in a Small Town: The Tulsa Race Riot of 1921* (Baton Rouge: Louisiana State University Press, 1982); and Walter White, "The Eruption in Tulsa," *Nation* 112 (June 29, 1921): 909–10.

47. White, *Man Called White,* 45–46.

48. There are various estimates of the casualties. See White, *Man Called White,* chapter 6; Walter White, "'Massacring Whites' in Arkansas," *Nation* 109 (December 6, 1919): 715–16; Waskow, *From Race Riot to Sit-In;* and Richard C. Cordner, *A Mob Intent on Death: The NAACP and the Arkansas Riot Cases* (Middletown: Wesleyan University Press, 1988).

49. White, *Man Called White*, 49, 50.

50. Ibid., 50.

51. Ibid., 51.

52. For statistics on lynching, by year and by race, 1882–1968, see Zangrando, *NAACP Crusade against Lynching*, 6–7.

53. See William Hixson, "Moorfield Storey and the Defense of the Dyer Anti-Lynching Bill," *New England Quarterly* 42 (1969): 65–81; Hixson, *Moorfield Storey* (New York: Oxford University Press, 1972); and Levy, *James Weldon Johnson*, chapter 11.

54. See Levy, *James Weldon Johnson*, passim; and Zangrando, *NAACP Crusade against Lynching*, passim.

55. Zangrando, *NAACP Crusade against Lynching*, 6.

56. Cannon, *Gentle Knight*, 17; Kahn, "Profile II," 49.

57. Johnson, *Along This Way*, 379.

58. Anderson, *This Was Harlem*, 343.

59. *Ebony*, April 1946, 7; E. J. Kahn, "Profile I," *New Yorker* 24 (September 4, 1948): 32.

60. The novel was *Fire in the Flint* (New York: Alfred A. Knopf, 1924); the non-fiction book was *Rope and Faggot: A Biography of Judge Lynch* (New York: Alfred A. Knopf, 1929).

61. Wolters, *Negroes and the Great Depression*, 339.

62. Kahn, "Profile II," 40.

63. Richard L. Watson Jr., "The Defeat of Judge Parker: A Study in Pressure Groups and Politics," *Mississippi Valley Historical Review* 50 (September 1963): 213–34.

64. Zangrando, *NAACP Crusade against Lynching*, 105.

65. White, *Man Called White*, 134–38; Cannon, *Gentle Knight*, 5–9.

66. Kahn, "Profile I," 30.

67. There are many books on both topics. With respect to the military, see Richard M. Dalfiume, *Desegregation of the U.S. Armed Forces* (Columbia: University of Missouri Press, 1969). On school desegregation, see Richard Kluger, *Simple Justice* (New York: Alfred A. Knopf, 1976); Mark Tushnet, *The NAACP's Legal Strategy against Segregated Education, 1925–1950* (Chapel Hill: University of North Carolina Press, 1987); and two books that take account of the problems that followed: Lino A. Graglia, *Disaster By Decree* (Ithaca: Cornell University Press, 1976), and Wolters, *Burden of Brown*.

68. Du Bois, *Autobiography*, 293.

69. Levy, *James Weldon Johnson*, 295; Du Bois, *Autobiography*, 294; Wilkins, *Standing Fast*, 116.

70. Mary White Ovington to J. E. Spingarn, December 15, 1931, Spingarn Papers, New York Public Library; Ross, *J. E. Spingarn*, 134.

71. Mary White Ovington to Walter White, December 15, 16, and 21, 1936, NAACP Papers.

72. Report of the Budget Committee, December 1931, NAACP Papers, copy in the Du Bois Papers, reel 35, frame 0452.

73. Ibid.; Report on Branch Appointment Record for 1930, November 25, 1930, NAACP Papers; Walter White to Charles Edward Russell, November 30, 1931, NAACP Papers; Wolters, *Negroes and the Great Depression*, 268–70.

74. Du Bois, *Autobiography,* 294. For a different version, see Wilkins, *Standing Fast,* 116–17. According to Wilkins, it was not the other executives who appealed to Du Bois to lead the protest, but Du Bois himself who instigated an effort to topple White.

75. William Pickens to Du Bois, January 22, 1932, reel 37, frame 0299; and Robert Bagnall to Du Bois, December 1931, reel 35, frame 0468, Du Bois Papers.

76. Du Bois, Herbert Seligmann, William Pickens, Robert Bagnall, and Roy Wilkins to Board of Directors, December 1931, Du Bois Papers, reel 35, frame 0458.

77. Herbert Seligmann to Walter White, December 22, 1931, reel 35, frame 0463; William Pickens to Du Bois, December 23, 1931, reel 35, frame 0464; and Robert Bagnall to Du Bois, December 1931, reel 35, frame 0468, Du Bois Papers.

78. J. E. Spingarn to Du Bois, December 29, 1931, reel 35, frame 0466; and Du Bois to J. E. Spingarn, December 31, 1931, reel 35, frame 0467, Du Bois Papers.

79. Du Bois, *Autobiography,* 294.

80. Herbert Seligmann to Walter White, 1932, Du Bois Papers, reel 37, frame 0437; Minutes of the Meeting of the Board of Directors, January 9, 1933, NAACP Papers.

81. Report of the Committee on Budget for the Fiscal Year, 1933, NAACP Papers.

82. Avery, *Up from Washington,* 178.

83. James Weldon Johnson to Du Bois, August 30, 1931, reel 36, frame 0169; Mary White Ovington to Du Bois, March 20, 1933, reel 40, frame 00637; and Memorandum on Circulation, reel 38, frame 00880, Du Bois Papers; Wolters, *Negroes and the Great Depression,* 266; Lewis, *W. E. B. Du Bois,* 2:302.

84. Reports of the Budget Committee, 1930, 1933, and 1934; Report of the Budget Committee for the Fiscal Year 1933; and Memorandum from the Budget Committee, June 13, 1932, NAACP Papers.

85. Mary White Ovington to Charles Edward Russell, December 9, 1921, NAACP Papers.

86. Mary White Ovington to Du Bois, December 20, 1930, in Aptheker, *Correspondence of Du Bois,* 1:430–31.

87. Du Bois to Mary White Ovington, December 24, 1930, in Aptheker, *Correspondence of Du Bois,* 1:431; Lewis, *W. E. B. Du Bois,* 2:282.

88. Minutes of the Meeting of the Board of Directors, December 12, 1932, NAACP Papers.

89. Minutes of the Meetings of the Board of Directors, July 14, 1930, and September 8, 1930, NAACP Papers.

90. Minutes of the Meeting of the Board of Directors, May 13, 1929, NAACP Papers.

91. Minutes of the Meeting of the Board of Directors, February 9, 1931, NAACP Papers; Du Bois to James Weldon Johnson, February 26, 1931, Johnson Papers.

92. Du Bois to J. E. Spingarn, December 18, 1930, Spingarn Papers, Yale University.

93. Du Bois, Memorandum to J. E. Spingarn, December 13, 1933, Spingarn Papers, Yale University.

94. Du Bois to J. E. Spingarn, December 14, 1933, Spingarn Papers, Yale University.

95. Du Bois to Lillian Alexander, December 15, 1933, Du Bois Papers, reel 39, frame 00535.

96. Du Bois to Daisy Lampkin, December 15, 1933, Du Bois Papers, reel 40, Fame 00824.

97. Du Bois to George Streator, January 2, 1934, Du Bois Papers, reel 43, frame 00369.

98. Du Bois to Nina Du Bois, March 17, 1933, Du Bois Papers, reel 39, frame 00959.

99. Du Bois, *Autobiography,* 292.

100. Du Bois to the Board of Directors, June 26, 1934, Du Bois Papers, reel 42, frame 00930.

101. Du Bois speech to 23rd Annual Conference of NAACP, NAACP Papers.

102. Graham Du Bois, *His Day Is Marching On,* 65; *Crisis* 37 (May 1930): 160; Lewis, *W. E. B. Du Bois,* 1:338, 540.

103. Lewis, *W. E. B. Du Bois,* 2:309.

104. Du Bois to George Streator, January 10, 1934, Du Bois Papers, reel 43, frame 00379.

105. Ross, *J. E. Spingarn,* 163. Ross was speaking of J. E. Spingarn, but the same could be said of White.

106. J. E. Spingarn, Statement for the Committee on Administration, February 1932, Spingarn Papers, New York Public Library; Ross, *J. E. Spingarn,* 168.

107. Walter White to James Weldon Johnson, April 3, 1933, Johnson Papers.

108. J. E. Spingarn to NAACP Board of Directors, March 6, 1933, Johnson Papers; Ross, *J. E. Spingarn,* 171, 173–75; Du Bois to Nina Du Bois, March 17, 1933, Du Bois Papers, reel 39, frame 00959; J. E. Spingarn to Mary White Ovington, March 28, 1933, Spingarn Papers, New York Public Library; Spingarn to James Weldon Johnson, April 4, 1933, Johnson Papers.

109. Walter White to J. E. Spingarn, March 14, 1933, Spingarn Papers, New York Public Library.

110. Du Bois to Sadie Tanner Alexander, March 14, 1933, Du Bois Papers, reel 39, frame 00540.

111. W. E. B. Du Bois, "Youth and Age at Amenia," *Crisis* 40 (October 1933): 226–27.

112. Du Bois to Sadie Tanner Alexander, March 14, 1933, Du Bois Papers, reel 39, frame 00540.

113. Du Bois, Notes on Second Amenia Conference, Du Bois Papers, reel 39, frame 00592.

114. Press Release in Du Bois Papers, reel 39, frame 00561.

115. Ibid.; Wilkins, *Standing Fast,* 151; Wolters, *Negroes and the Great Depression,* 224–25; J. E. Spingarn to Walter White, January 10, 1934, NAACP Papers.

116. Findings of the Second Amenia Conference, August 1933, NAACP Papers. Also see the press release in the Du Bois Papers, reel 39, frame 00561; Wolters, *Negroes and the Great Depression,* 225–26; and Ross, *J. E. Spingarn,* 181–82.

117. W. E. B. Du Bois, "Marxism and the Negro Problem," *Crisis* 40 (May 1933): 104.

118. W. E. B. Du Bois, "White Labor," *Crisis* 38 (September 1931): 315.

119. Du Bois, "Marxism and the Negro Problem," 104.

120. *Crisis* 37 (May 1930): 160.

121. Du Bois, *Dusk of Dawn*, 27, 27–28.

122. See W. E. B. Du Bois, "Postscript," *Crisis* 38 (September 1931): 313–15, 318, 320; Du Bois, "Marxism and the Negro Problem," 103–4, 118; Marable, *W. E. B. Du Bois*, 108–13; Lewis, *W. E. B. Du Bois*, 1:420–21, 540; and Lewis, *W. E. B. Du Bois*, 2:196–97, 207–8, 308.

123. W. E. B. Du Bois, "The Negro and Social Reconstruction" (1936), in Aptheker, *Against Racism*, 146, 148–49.

124. *Crisis* 41 (April 1934): 117.

125. *Crisis* 41 (June 1934): 183.

126. W. E. B. Du Bois, "A Negro Nation within the Nation," *Current History* 42 (June 1935): 268.

127. *Crisis* 41 (June 1934): 183, 183–84.

128. W. E. B. Du Bois, Memorandum, The Economic Condition of the American Negro in the Depression, November 20, 1934, National Archives, RG 96, and Du Bois Papers, reel 42, frame 01104.

129. *Crisis* 41 (March 1934): 85; Du Bois, "Negro Nation within the Nation," 269.

130. Du Bois, "Negro Nation within the Nation," 265–70.

131. Du Bois, *Dusk of Dawn*, chapter 7; W. E. B. Du Bois, "On Being Ashamed of Oneself: An Essay on Race Pride," *Crisis* 40 (September 1933): 199–200.

132. *Crisis* 37 (May 1930): 174; Marable, *W. E. B. Du Bois*, 147.

133. Du Bois, "Conservation of Races," 7.

134. *Crisis* 41 (January 1934): 20.

135. Minutes of the Meeting of the Board of Directors, April 11, 1932, NAACP Papers; Du Bois, undated memorandum, 1932, Du Bois Papers, reel 39, frame 00819.

136. Du Bois, *Autobiography*, 257–58, 258.

137. Walter White, Memorandum re the NAACP and *Crisis*, March 12, 1934, NAACP Papers.

138. John Hope to Du Bois, April 24, 1932, Du Bois Papers, reel 36, frame 0779. David Levering Lewis has noted that Joel Spingarn instigated this move by writing to Hope in 1932 and pleading that Du Bois "be afforded a distinguished exit from a sinking enterprise [the *Crisis*]." Spingarn said it was "of the greatest importance to [Du Bois] to have it go out to the world that he is leaving New York to accept an important post rather than because the paper [the *Crisis*] is forced to suspend" (*W. E. B. Du Bois*, 2:303, 301).

139. After a divorce from Countee Cullen, Yolande married Arnett Williams in 1931. Williams later become a teacher, but in 1933 he was living on the campus of Lincoln University in Pennsylvania, where he was a student. The granddaughter was named Du Bois Williams.

140. Du Bois to J. E. Spingarn, June 5, 1933, reel 40, frame 00694; and Du Bois to John Hope, September 14, 1933, reel 39, frame 00669, Du Bois Papers.

141. Alfred Harcourt to Du Bois, reel 39, frame 00696; Du Bois to Rachel Davis DuBois, March 27, 1933, reel 39, frame 010322; and Du Bois to J. E. Spingarn, October 16, 1933, reel 40, frame 00788, Du Bois Papers.

142. Du Bois to Matthew Boutte, March 13, 1933, reel 39, frame 00787; and Du Bois to Rachel Davis DuBois, March 27, 1933, reel 39, frame 01032, Du Bois Papers.

143. Du Bois to Nina Du Bois, October 4, 1933, reel 39, frame 00987; Du Bois to Nina Du Bois, January 2, 1933, reel 39, frame 00940; and Du Bois to J. E. Spingarn, October 16, 1933, reel 40, frame 00788, Du Bois Papers.

144. Du Bois to Nina Du Bois, January 2, 1933, reel 39, frame 00940; and Du Bois to Rachel Davis DuBois, March 27, 1933, reel 39, frame 01032, Du Bois Papers.

145. Graham Du Bois, *His Day Is Marching On,* 45.

146. Ibid., 46.

147. Lewis, *W. E. B. Du Bois,* 2:267.

148. Ibid., 269, 267.

149. George Streator to Du Bois, May 16, 1934, reel 43, frame 00488; and Streator to Du Bois, May 11, 1934, reel 43, frame 00487, Du Bois Papers.

150. For more on this, see Lewis, *W. E. B. Du Bois,* vols. 1 and 2, sections on Virginia Margaret Alexander, Ellen Irene Diggs, Rachel Davis DuBois, Jessie Fauset, Shirley Graham, Mildred Bryant Jones, Elizabeth Prophet, and Louie Davis Shivery. Also see Gerald Horne, *Race Woman: The Lives of Shirley Graham Du Bois* (New York: New York University Press, 2000), chapter 5. Of course, it is difficult to keep such transgressions secret; the problem is that there are two parties that must never tell. The fact that none of Du Bois's alleged lovers ever admitted to such liaisons casts further doubt upon the supposed trysts.

151. For the most convincing evidence of an adulterous affair (in the 1940s, after Nina Du Bois was partially paralyzed) see Horne, *Race Woman,* 131.

152. Du Bois, *Autobiography,* 281; Horne, *Race Woman,* 132.

153. Du Bois, *Philadelphia Negro,* 72.

154. W. E. B. Du Bois, "I Bury My Wife," 39.

155. Walter White to Martha Gruening, January 10, 1934, NAACP Papers.

156. Du Bois to Harry E. Davis, February 1, 1934, reel 42, frame 00019; and Du Bois to Harry E. Davis, January 16, 1934, reel 42, frame 00014, Du Bois Papers.

157. Du Bois to Lillian Alexander, December 15, 1933, Du Bois Papers, reel 39, frame 00535.

158. Du Bois to Harry E. Davis, February 1, 1934, reel 42, frame 00019; and Du Bois to Daisy Lampkin, December 15, 1933, reel 40, frame 00824, Du Bois Papers.

159. Du Bois to Daisy Lampkin, December 15, 1933, Du Bois Papers, reel 40, frame 00824.

160. Du Bois to Lillian Alexander, December 15, 1933, Du Bois Papers, reel 39, frame 00535.

161. Du Bois to Lillian Alexander, January 2, 1934, Du Bois Papers, reel 42, frame 00863.

162. Arthur B. Spingarn to Du Bois, January 4, 1934, Du Bois Papers, reel 42, frame 00867; Du Bois to J. E. Spingarn, December 13, 1933, and December 14, 1933, Johnson Papers.

163. Du Bois to Lillian Alexander, January 2, 1934, Du Bois Papers, reel 42, frame 00863.

164. Du Bois to Harry E. Davis, February 1, 1934, reel 41, frame 00019; and Du Bois to Davis, January 16, 1934, reel 42, frame 00014, Du Bois Papers.

165. Du Bois to Harry E. Davis, July 18, 1934, Du Bois Papers, reel 42, frame 00026.

166. Du Bois, *Dusk of Dawn,* 312; Du Bois to J. E. Spingarn, October 16, 1933, Johnson Papers; Walter White to Lillian Alexander, November 9, 1933, NAACP Papers. Rachel Davis DuBois was not related to W. E. B. Du Bois.

There is some question as to what Du Bois meant by "reorganization." B. Joyce Ross has written that Du Bois wanted the NAACP to "completely revise its administrative structure so as to afford the rank-and-file membership a major, if not the controlling, voice in the organization's administration." However, although Du Bois mentioned "democratization" and "increasing the power of the local branches" in some of his letters, my impression is that he thought of reorganization primarily in terms of adding sympathetic people to the board of directors and, most of all, removing Walter White from his position as chief executive officer. See Ross, *J. E. Spingarn,* 199 and passim.

167. Du Bois to Lillian Alexander, George W. Crawford, Harry E. Davis, A. B. Spingarn, J. E. Spingarn, and Louis T. Wright, April 21, 1933, Du Bois Papers, reel 40, frame 00664.

168. *Crisis* 39 (July 1932): 218.

169. Harry E. Davis to Du Bois, April 25, 1933, reel 40, frame 00668; and J. E. Spingarn to Du Bois, April 26, 1933, reel 40, frame 00672, Du Bois.

170. Du Bois to Abram Harris, January 16, 1934, Du Bois Papers, reel 42, frame 00427.

171. Du Bois, *Dusk of Dawn,* 290–91.

172. Ibid., 297.

173. Du Bois to Harry E. Davis, February 1, 1934, Du Bois Papers, reel 42, frame 00019.

174. John S. Brown Jr. to Du Bois, April 22, 1934, Du Bois Papers, reel 41, frame 01093.

175. Du Bois to George Streator, February 1, 1934, Du Bois Papers, reel 43, frame 00402.

176. Du Bois to George Streator, March 21, 1934, reel 43, frame 00455; and Du Bois to John Hope, March 28, 1934, reel 41, frame 00879, Du Bois Papers.

177. Du Bois to Virginia Alexander, February 1, 1934, Du Bois Papers, reel 41, frame 00829.

178. Du Bois to George Streator, February 1, 1934, Du Bois Papers, reel 43, frame 00402.

179. Du Bois to Dear Friends, February 5, 1934, Du Bois Papers, Aptheker Briefcase.

180. For criticism of Du Bois's proposed program, see Benjamin Stolberg, "Black Chauvinism," *Nation* 140 (May 15, 1935): 570–71; Eleanor Ryan, "Toward a National Negro Congress, *New Masses,* June 4, 1935, 14–15; Abram Harris, *The Negro as Capitalist* (Philadelphia: American Academy of Political and Social Science, 1936), 184 and passim; Wolters, *Negroes and the Great Depression,* 250–58; Marable, *W. E. B. Du Bois,* 147–49.

181. *Crisis* 41 (January 1934): 20, italics added.

182. Walter White to J. E. Spingarn, January 15, 1934, NAACP Papers.

183. *Crisis* 41 (March 1934): 80. White was quoting a statement of Du Bois's. But Du Bois had written these sentences as a dependent introduction to his larger point: that blacks should oppose discrimination, but not allow concern over segregation (unless it was accompanied by discrimination) to impede voluntary cooperation. White turned Du Bois's dependent introduction into his own thesis: that blacks should oppose every sort of segregation.

184. *Crisis* 41 (February 1934): 53.

185. *Crisis* 41 (March 1934): 85.

186. *Crisis* 41 (June 1934): 182.

187. Du Bois, *Dusk of Dawn,* 296, 194.

188. *Crisis* 41 (June 1934): 183.

189. *Crisis* 41 (April 1934): 116.

190. *Crisis* 41 (June 1934): 183.

191. *Crisis* 41 (April 1934): 117.

192. Du Bois, "Negro Nation within the Nation," 269.

193. Du Bois, "Conservation of Races," 5.

194. W. E. B. Du Bois, "Strivings of the Negro People," *Atlantic Monthly* 80 (August 1897): 195.

195. Du Bois, "Conservation of Races," 7.

196. *Crisis* 41 (June 1934): 183.

197. *Crisis* 41 (April 1934): 115.

198. George Streator to Du Bois, March 16, 1934, Du Bois Papers, reel 43, frame 00452.

199. J. E. Spingarn to Du Bois, March 27, 1934, Du Bois Papers, reel 42, frame 00887. According to George Streator, Spingarn also said that "every mulatto, J[ohn] Hope included, is incensed over [Du Bois's] calling W. W. 'white'" (Streator to Du Bois, May 16, 1934, Du Bois Papers, reel 43, frame 00488).

200. J. E. Spingarn to Walter White, January 10, 1934, NAACP Papers.

201. Wilkins, *Standing Fast,* 152–53.

202. Du Bois, *Dusk of Dawn,* 307.

203. Minutes of the Meeting of the Board of Directors, April 9, 1934, NAACP Papers; *Crisis* 41 (May 1934): 149.

204. Walter White to Arthur B. Spingarn, May 3, 1934, NAACP Papers.

205. Minutes of the Meeting of the Board of Directors, May 14, 1934, NAACP Papers.

206. Walter White to J. E. Spingarn, June 12, 1934, NAACP Papers; Wilkins, *Standing Fast,* 155.

207. Du Bois to Board of Directors, May 21, 1934, reel 42, frame 00903; and Du Bois to John Hope, May 21, 1934, reel 41, frame 00896, Du Bois Papers.

208. Minutes of the Meeting of the Board of Directors, June 11, 1934, NAACP Papers; George Streator to Du Bois, June 12, 1934, Du Bois Papers, reel 43, frame 00503. Nevertheless, the news of Du Bois's written resignation was leaked to the press.

209. Du Bois to J. E. Spingarn, April 21, 1934, reel 42, frame 00895; Rachel

Davis DuBois to Du Bois, May 23, 1934, reel 42, frame 00179; George Streator to Du Bois, June 28, 1934, reel 43, frame 00520; George Streator to Du Bois, dated Monday [June 4, 1934], reel 43, frame 00499; and George Streator to Du Bois, March 2, 1934, reel 43, frame 00446, Du Bois Papers.

210. Du Bois to George Streator, May 2, 1934, Du Bois Papers, reel 43, frame 00481.

211. Du Bois to George Streator, April 26, 1934, reel 43, frame 00477; and Du Bois to George Streator, May 2, 1934, reel 43, frame 00481, Du Bois Papers.

212. J. E. Spingarn to Walter White, April 25, 1934; and Spingarn to White, May 9, 1934, NAACP Papers.

213. J. E. Spingarn to Walter White, January 10, 1934, NAACP Papers.

214. J. E. Spingarn to Walter White, January 12, 1934, NAACP Papers.

215. Walter White to J. E. Spingarn, June 12, 1934, NAACP Papers.

216. Ibid.

217. Du Bois to John S. Brown Jr., January 16, 1934, Du Bois Papers, Aptheker Briefcase.

218. Du Bois to Board of Directors, June 26, 1934, Du Bois Papers, reel 43, frame 00513.

219. Du Bois, Memorandum to J. E. Spingarn, June 16, 1934, reel 43, frame 00509; and Du Bois to Spingarn, June 16, 1934, reel 43, frame 00511, Du Bois Papers.

220. Du Bois to Louis T. Wright, June 25, 1934, NAACP Papers.

221. Du Bois to Mrs. E. R. Alexander, June 11, 1934, Du Bois Papers, reel 41, frame 00824. Du Bois added: "Sooner or later the divergence from my thought and that of the executive officers was bound to become so manifest that some change should be made. Of course there was nothing in the talk about segregation that necessitated any radical action, but the vote of the Board was an excellent excuse. . . . Never before has the Board of Directors openly and defiantly sought to gag my expression. I, therefore, resigned."

222. Du Bois to George Streator, June 26, 1934, reel 43, frame 00517; and Du Bois to Nina Du Bois, June 25, 1934, reel 42, frame 00106, Du Bois Papers.

223. Du Bois to George Streator, July 17, 1934, reel 42, frame 01250; J. E. Spingarn to Du Bois, May 1, 1934, reel 43, frame 00480; and J. E. Spingarn to Du Bois, March 27, 1934, reel 42, frame 00887, Du Bois Papers.

224. J. E. Spingarn to Du Bois, June 14, 1934, Du Bois Papers, reel 43, frame 00505.

225. Du Bois to J. E. Spingarn, June 16, 1934, reel 43, frame 00509; and Du Bois to Spingarn, June 16, 1934 (second letter), reel 43, frame 00511, Du Bois Papers.

226. Du Bois to J. E. Spingarn, June 25, 1934, Du Bois Papers, reel 42, frame 00928.

227. Du Bois to J. E. Spingarn, May 31, 1934, Johnson Papers.

228. Du Bois, *Dusk of Dawn*, 311–12.

229. Du Bois to George Foster Peabody, June 26, 1934, Du Bois Papers, reel 42, frame 01024. For Du Bois's formal letter of resignation, see Du Bois to Board of Directors, June 26, 1934, reel 43, frame 00515.

230. *Crisis* 41 (August 1934): 246; Du Bois, *Autobiography,* 299.

231. Thomas C. Holt, "The Political Uses of Alienation: W. E. B. Du Bois on Politics, Race, and Culture, 1903–1940," *American Quarterly* 42 (June 1990): 323 n. 46.

232. Du Bois to Board of Directors, June 26, 1934, Du Bois Papers, reel 43, frame 00513. For different assessments, see Broderick, *W. E. B. Du Bois,* 164–79; Rudwick, *W. E. B. Du Bois,* chapter 11; and Elliott Rudwick and August Meier, "The Rise of the Black Secretariat in the NAACP, 1909–1935," in Meier and Rudwick, *Along the Color Line: Explorations in the Black Experience* (Urbana: University of Illinois Press, 1976), 94–127.

7. The Final Years

1. W. E. B. Du Bois, *Black Reconstruction* (1935; reprint, Millwood, New York: Kraus-Thomson Organization, 1976).

2. However, some modern scholars have come close to embracing Du Bois's notion of a general strike. This is especially true in the "self-liberation" thesis put forth by historians Ira Berlin and Barbara Fields. See Ira Berlin et al., *Slaves No More: Three Essays on Emancipation and the Civil War* (Cambridge: Cambridge University Press, 1992), chapter 1; and Berlin, "Emancipation and Its Meaning in American Life," *Reconstruction* 2 (1994): 41–44. For a critical assessment of this view, see James M. McPherson, *Drawn with the Sword: Reflections on the American Civil War* (New York: Oxford University Press, 1996), 192–207.

3. Lewis, *W. E. B. Du Bois,* 2:373.

4. Herbert Aptheker, introduction to Du Bois, *Black Reconstruction,* 34.

5. Eric Foner, *Reconstruction: America's Unfinished Revolution, 1863–1877* (New York: Harper and Row, 1988), xxi.

6. W. E. B. Du Bois, *Black Folk: Then and Now* (1939; reprint, Millwood, N.Y.: Kraus-Thomson Organization, 1975).

7. Du Bois, *Dusk of Dawn,* 27, 198, 321; W. E. B. Du Bois, "Forum of Fact and Opinion," *Pittsburgh Courier,* February 13, 1937, in Aptheker, *Newspaper Columns by Du Bois,* 1:167.

8. Du Bois, *Autobiography,* chapter 18. For an account of the encyclopedia effort, see Lewis, *W. E. B. Du Bois,* vol. 2, chapter 12.

9. Du Bois, *Autobiography,* 321–22.

10. Ibid., 322.

11. Ibid., 323, 323–24.

12. Ibid., 279.

13. Lewis, *W. E. B. Du Bois,* 2:459.

14. Du Bois, *Autobiography,* 327.

15. Ibid., 277.

16. See Gerald Horne, *Black and Red: W. E. B. Du Bois and the Afro-American Response to the Cold War, 1944–1963* (Albany: State University of New York Press, 1986), chapters 7–9 and passim.

17. Du Bois, *Autobiography,* 329, 337.

18. Du Bois, "Forum of Fact and Opinion," *Pittsburgh Courier,* December 5,

1936, and December 12, 1936, in Aptheker, *Newspaper Columns by Du Bois,* 1:143, 146. For more on Du Bois's impressions of Nazi Germany, see Werner Sollars, "W. E. B. Du Bois in Nazi Germany," *Chronicle of Higher Education,* November 12, 1999, B4–5; and Lewis, *W. E. B. Du Bois,* vol. 2, chapter 11.

19. Du Bois, "Forum of Fact and Opinion," *Pittsburgh Courier,* January 23, 1937, and February 6, 1937, in Aptheker, *Newspaper Columns by Du Bois,* 1:164, 161, 163. Although Du Bois's views on Nazi Germany and Communist Russia seem extraordinary today, during the 1930s thousands of Americans had similar views.

20. Iris Chang, *The Rape of Nanking: The Forgotten Holocaust of World War II* (New York: Basic Books, 1997).

21. Du Bois, "Forum of Fact and Opinion," *Pittsburgh Courier,* February 27, 1937, and March 20, 1937, in Aptheker, *Newspaper Columns by Du Bois,* 1:174, 182.

22. Lewis, *W. E. B. Du Bois,* 2:508.

23. W. E. B. Du Bois, "The Winds of Time," *Chicago Defender,* April 19, 1947, in Aptheker, *Newspaper Columns by Du Bois,* 2:711.

24. Horne, *Race Woman,* 107 and passim.

25. Graham Du Bois, *His Day Is Marching On,* 33.

26. Horne, *Race Woman,* 30.

27. Shirley Graham to Earl Browder, April 27, 1945, quoted in Horne, *Race Woman,* 31–32.

28. Lewis, *W. E. B. Du Bois,* 2:523–24.

29. Graham Du Bois, *His Day Is Marching On,* 101; David G. Du Bois, "W. E. B. Du Bois: The Last Years," *Race and Class* 24 (autumn 1982): 180.

30. Graham Du Bois, *His Day Is Marching On,* 103.

31. Lewis, *W. E. B. Du Bois,* 2:541 and passim.

32. Du Bois to Shirley Graham, November 9, 1945, August 13, 1946, November 3, 1946, and April 27, 1947, in Horne, *Race Woman,* 131.

33. Shirley Graham to Du Bois, June 1, 1949, reel 63, frame 1104; and Graham to Du Bois, May 21, 1949, reel 63, frame 1102, Du Bois Papers.

34. David Levering Lewis believes that Du Bois and Graham began their sexual intimacy several years earlier, "on the second night in January 1936." Gerald Horne is less certain about this date, although he concedes the possibility. See Lewis, *W. E. B. Du Bois,* 2:387 and passim; and Horne, *Race Woman,* 125, 309 n. 44, and passim.

35. Horne, *Race Woman,* 31.

36. Horne, *Black and Red,* 132.

37. *New York Times,* July 13, 1950, 1; Du Bois, *Autobiography,* 358; Lewis, *W. E. B. Du Bois,* 2:547.

38. W. E. B. Du Bois, *In Battle for Peace* (1952; reprint, Millwood, N.Y.: Kraus-Thomson Organization, 1976), 71 and passim.

39. Du Bois, *Autobiography,* 381.

40. Ibid., 382.

41. Du Bois, *In Battle for Peace,* 90, 74.

42. Martin D. Jenkins to Du Bois, March 23, 1949, April 23, 1949, and April 29, 1949, in Aptheker, *Correspondence of Du Bois,* 3:257–59.

43. Ronald Radosh, *Commies: A Journey through the Old Left, the New Left, and the Leftover Left* (San Francisco: Encounter Books, 2001), 27.

44. W. E. B. Du Bois, "The Hard-Bit Man in the Loud Shirts," *National Guardian,* January 22, 1953; and W. E. B. Du Bois, "On Stalin," *National Guardian,* March 16, 1953, both in Aptheker, *Newspaper Columns by Du Bois,* 2:905, 910.

45. W. E. B. Du Bois, "The Vast Miracle of China Today," *National Guardian,* June 8, 1959, in Aptheker, *Newspaper Columns by Du Bois,* 2:1015.

46. Lewis, *W. E. B. Du Bois,* 2:558.

47. W. E. B. Du Bois, Opposition to Military Assistance Act of 1949, U.S. Congress, Committee on Foreign Affairs, Hearings on H.R. 5748 and 5895, 81st Congress, 1st Session, 1949, in Lewis, *W. E. B. Du Bois: A Reader,* 762.

48. W. E. B. Du Bois, "Russophobia," *National Guardian,* October 4, 1950; and Du Bois, "The Marshall Plan," *Chicago Globe,* June 10, 1950, both in Lewis, *W. E. B. Du Bois: A Reader,* 769, 773.

49. Du Bois, *Autobiography,* 23, 25, 48; Lewis, *W. E. B. Du Bois,* 2:560.

50. W. E. B. Du Bois, "The Real Reason behind Paul Robeson's Persecution," *National Guardian,* April 7, 1958, in Aptheker, *Newspaper Columns by Du Bois,* 2:1008–9.

51. "Application for Membership in the Communist Party," *Worker,* November 26, 1961, in Lewis, *W. E. B. Du Bois: A Reader,* 631–33.

52. Du Bois, *Autobiography,* 414.

Index